AF413360

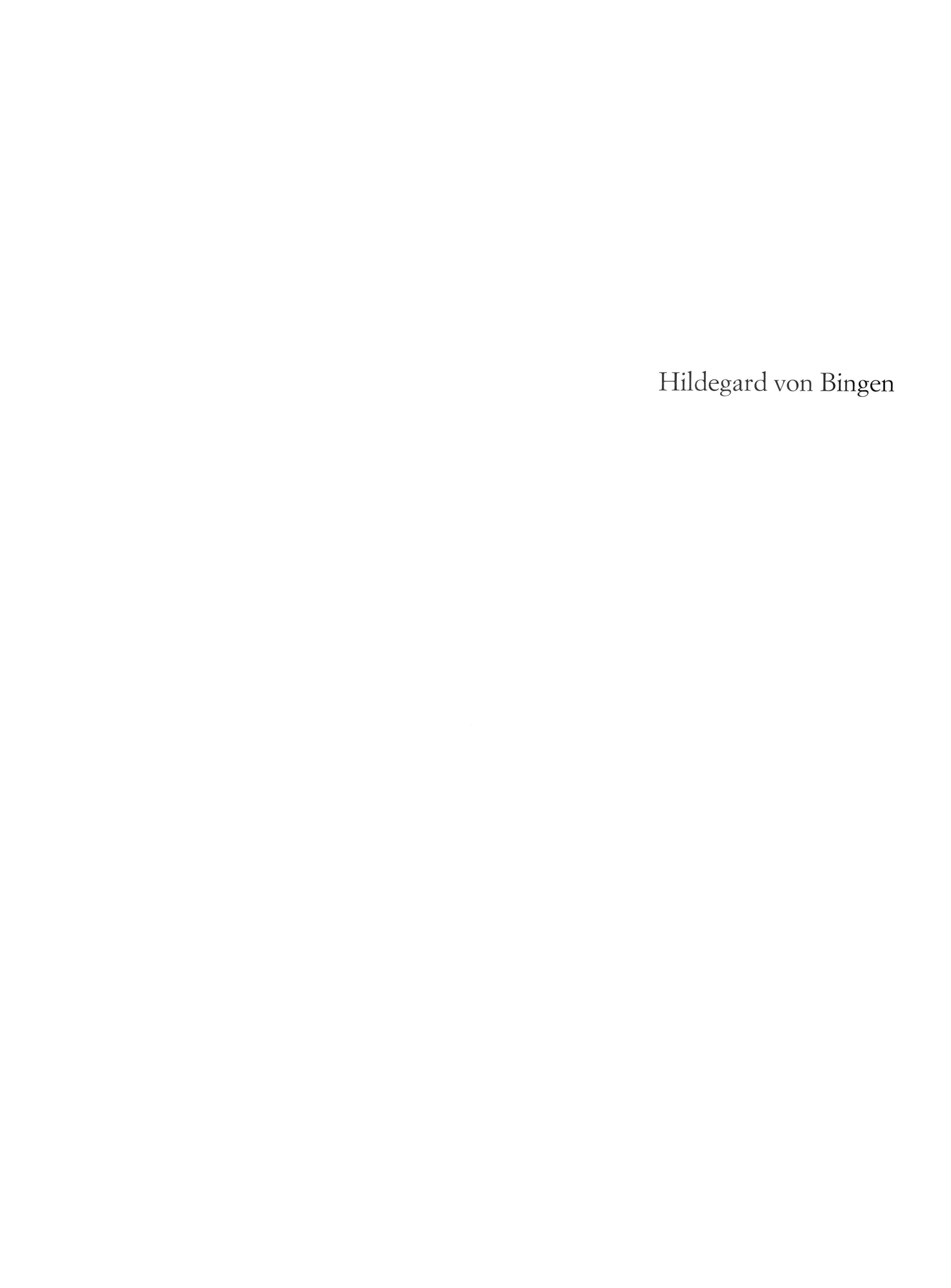

Hildegard von Bingen

Sara Salvadori

Hildegard von Bingen

In the Heart of God

Liber Divinorum Operum
The Lucca Miniatures

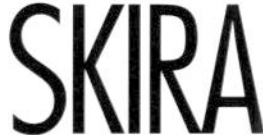

This book was produced thanks to the contribution of

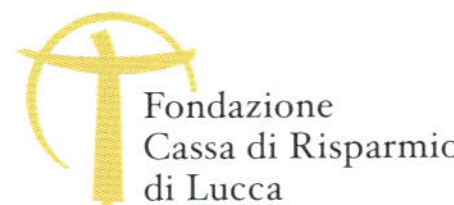

Fondazione
Cassa di Risparmio
di Lucca

Cover
Plate I.2

Art Director
Marcello Francone

Design
Luigi Fiore

Editorial Coordination
Emma Cavazzini

*Copy Editing and
Translations Revision*
Maria Conconi

Layout
Barbara Galotta

Translations
Oona Smyth and Susan Ann White
for *Scriptum*, Rome

First published in Italy in 2021 by
Skira editore S.p.A.
Palazzo Casati Stampa
via Torino 61
20123 Milano
Italy
www.skira.net

© 2021 Abtei St. Hildegard –
Eibingen for the images
© 2021 Biblioteca Statale di Lucca
for the images
© 2021 The authors for their texts
© 2021 Skira editore, Milano

Printed and bound in Italy.
First edition

ISBN: 978-88-572-4659-8

Distributed in USA, Canada,
Central & South America
by ARTBOOK | D.A.P.
75, Broad Street Suite 630,
New York, NY 10004, USA.
Distributed elsewhere in the world
by Thames and Hudson Ltd.,
181A High Holborn, London
WC1V 7QX, United Kingdom.

The reproduction of the miniatures of the
Liber Divinorum Operum was authorized
by Monica Maria Angeli, director of the
Biblioteca Statale di Lucca where codex
1942 with the illuminated manuscript
of the *Liber Divinorum Operum* is kept

The reproduction of the miniatures of
Scivias was authorized by Sister Philippa
Rath of the Abtei St. Hildegard – Eibingen,
where the copy/facsimile of the Rupertsberg
Codex Hs 1 is kept

The translations of the Latin of the *Liber
Divinorum Operum* are by Nathaniel
M. Campbell, in *St. Hildegard of Bingen,
The Book of Divine Works*, The Catholic
University of America Press, Washington
D.C. 2018

The extracts of *Scivias* have been translated
into English from the Italian translations of
Michela Pereira

Processing of the images of the
Liber Divinorum Operum
Sara Salvadori

Graphic design of the images of the
Liber Divinorum Operum
Lorenzo Bejarano Libreros

Processing of the images of
Scivias
Patrizia Elena Bertini

Graphic design of the images of
Scivias
Oihane Fabbrini

Construction of the model of the Building
Sofia Basilissi
Plastici SB

Photographs of the model of the Building
Enos Mantoani

Much of the extraordinarily rich literary and documentary heritage conserved in the libraries and archives of Lucca is little-known to the wider public. Safeguarding these hidden treasures is complicated by the difficulties involved both in their conservation and in raising awareness about them. They include manuscripts with an inestimable historic and documentary value as well as illuminated masterpieces of great artistic worth, which passed from hand to hand, city to city, spreading styles and innovations in a continuous exchange of techniques and culture. When the historic publisher Skira approached us with a proposal for an initiative for a book dedicated to Hildegard von Bingen's Divinorum, *which is housed in the Biblioteca Statale di Lucca, the Foundation did not hesitate to offer its support. The figure of Hildegard, a woman peerless in her time, continues to fascinate us today and it was clear that the time had come for this manuscript, unique for its extreme rarity, its bewitching beauty, and technical particularities, to "emerge" from the inner recesses of the Library where the codex is carefully stored and safeguarded.*

This publication represents the occasion for the wider public to become acquainted with the Divinorum, *and for it to tell its story and reveal the glowing images of its illustrations, giving the whole world a small glimpse of the vast heritage of culture and history stored on the shelves in Lucca.*

Marcello Bertocchini
President of the Fondazione
Cassa di Risparmio di Lucca

Contents

O quam mirabilis est
prescientia divini pectoris,
que prescivit omnem creaturam.
Nam cum Deus inspexit
faciem hominis quem formavit,
omnia opera sua
in eadem forma hominis
integra aspexit.
O quam mirabilis est inspiratio,
que hominem sic suscitavit.

How wondrous is the prescience
of the heart of God,
which foretold every creature.
For when God looked on the face
of man whom he formed,
he saw all his works complete
in that same human form.
Oh, how wondrous is the holy breath
that brought man to life.

Michela Pereira

The Fullness of Creation. Incarnation and Humanity in the *Liber Divinorum Operum*

The generative nucleus of the entire *Liber Divinorum Operum* (hereafter *LDO*), *Book of Divine Works*, which concludes Hildegard von Bingen's prophetic trilogy with a broad and original treatment of the creation and history, is located centrally in the work. In fact, it is condensed in the last chapter of the fourth vision in part one—a concise commentary on the prologue to the Gospel of John—in which the original and foundational nexus between creation and incarnation is established and articulated with a radically renewed understanding of the meaning of the human being as *imago Dei*.

For God created the world, which he wished to prepare as a tabernacle for man; and because it was his will that he should be clothed in humankind, he made man in his own image and likeness (256). The Word is at the origin of the creation (*In principio erat Verbum*), but is also its completion, as is evident from the citation *I determined my every activity in my Son, the seventh day* (345). Thus Hildegard records the words spoken to her by the voice of God in a passage from the other biblical commentary, on Genesis 1:1–28, which forms the main part of the next vision (II.1, chaps. 17–49). In the incarnation, which *blossomed in the primal bud* (345), is manifest the joyous fullness of the ordinance established by the Creator; hence the human form, the tunic in which the divinity itself would also be clothed, was foreseen before the beginning of time in the ancient council, by virtue of which *my Son, who is my seventh work, proceeding from the Virgin's womb through humanity, accomplished all these things with me in the Holy Spirit* (346).

The existence of a primordial link between creation and incarnation is far more credible than the latter's stemming from the original sin, as was maintained by the majority of theologians in Hildegard's time, and the following centuries. On this theme, central to the life of the Church, she did not adopt a wholly unprecedented stance; indeed, as with various other aspects of her thought, she took the same line as the leading exponents of coeval monastic speculation. This showed how deeply her ideas were rooted in the Benedictine tradition, which had reached the pinnacles of spirituality and thought but seemed to have stopped there during the period of profound cultural change at the beginning of the 12th century, which radically modified the approach to theological and philosophical specula-

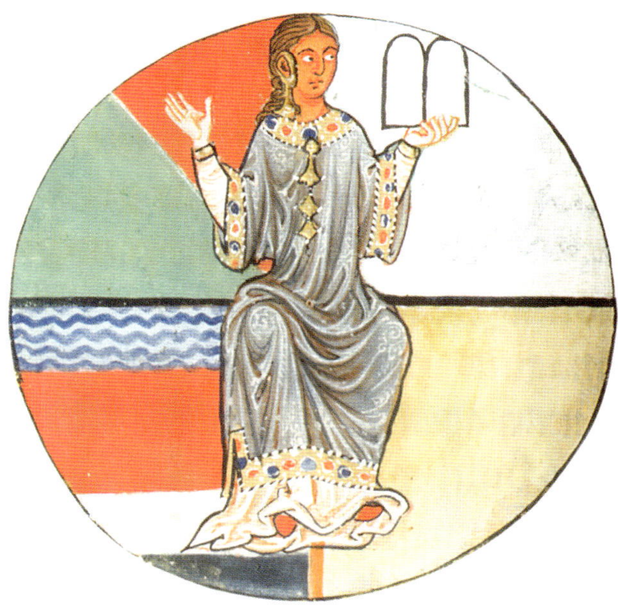

tion, and its developments. Thus, an important part of monastic theology, of which Hildegard's work is certainly one of the most significant products, remained on the sidelines or, at most, was interpreted as "opposing" the culture of the various schools, for example in the judgment of Bernard of Clairvaux.

Like the two previous works of the trilogy, *Scivias* and *Liber Vite Meritorum*, the structure of the *LDO* is based on a series of visions, that is to say on the development of an initial vision in a sequence of images, whose prophetic value was acknowledged precisely by St. Bernard. As was the case with the two earlier texts, the visions in the *LDO* appeared to her inner eye while she remained awake and conscious, as Hildegard herself specifies in various autobiographical passages. Outstanding among these is the Protestificatio (introduction) to *Scivias*, in which she writes that the visions *I saw did not come to me in dreams, neither while I was sleeping nor in a frenzy; nor with bodily eyes nor with the ears of the outer person nor in hidden places. But I received them while waking and attentive, in a clear mind, with the eyes and ears of the inner person, in open places, according to God's will* (*Scivias*, 4); and *Epistola* 103R, the letter written in the 1170s: *Since I was a child, in truth, and until this very day, when I am in more than my seventieth year, I continue to see this radiance* (lumen), *which I do not perceive with my external eyes nor in the thoughts of my heart nor with all my external senses, indeed the external*

*eyes remain open and all the other senses awake as usual
[…]. Moreover, I preserve the memory of what I see and
apprehend in the vision for a long time, and at the same
time I see, I listen and I know, and almost immediately
understand what I know* (Hildegardis Bingensis Epistolarium, II, 261–262).

Thus, Hildegard was always able to grasp and
transmit the content and meaning of the visual phenomena revealed to her by the *vox de caelo*, which she then
elaborated through detailed reflection in dialogue with
her spiritual confidant and secretary-cum-editor Volmar,
who transcribed her description of what she saw and
heard. They worked together with one of the nuns, who
assisted in writing the text—though at the time of the
LDO it was no longer the beloved *filia* Richardis von
Stade, who had left after collaborating on *Scivias*, and
had died some years earlier. The continuing presence of
a nun assistant and of the secretaries who after Volmar's
death in 1173 helped Hildegard to prepare the definitive version of the book, attests to a consistent working
method and shows that the religious community collab-
orated willingly and conscientiously with the charismatic
figure of the prophetess. At Rupertsberg, the first of the
two convents founded by Hildegard, there was in fact a
flourishing *scriptorium*, which produced the miniatures
of *Scivias* and possibly those of the *LDO* decades later, as well as preparing other important manuscripts of
works by the *magistra*. This aspect, which certainly had
to do with the enhancement of Hildegard's prophetic
charisma, was also in keeping with the organizational
criteria of Benedictine monasticism, as was Hildegard's
medicinal work for which she was equally renowned.

In 1163, the year she began to write the *LDO*
but some time before she had the vision with which it
opens, Hildegard had an experience of a completely
different nature to those described in the passages quoted above: *At last in the time that followed I saw a mystic
and wondrous vision, so that my whole being was shaken
and the sensation of my body was extinguished, for my
knowledge had been transformed into another mode, as
if I no longer knew myself. And from God's inspiration
as it were drops of gentle rain splashed into the knowledge of my soul, even as the Holy Spirit imbued John
the Evangelist, when he absorbed the deepest revelation
from Jesus' breast. At this his sense-perception was so
touched by holy divinity that he laid open hidden mysteries and works, saying "In the beginning was the Word,"
and all that follows. Indeed the Word, which was without beginning before the creatures and will be without
end after them, commanded all the creatures to manifest
themselves and did his work in a manner similar to the
smith when he labors and makes sparks fly, since what
was predestined before the beginning of time became visible at that moment. Thus the human being and all of creation is the work of God. But he is also the worker of the
divinity and the shadow of his mysteries and in all things
he must reveal the Holy Trinity, because God has made
him in his own image and likeness. And just as Lucifer in
all his impiety cannot harm God, neither will he be able
to destroy the human condition, no matter how much
he sought to do this with regard to the first man. This
vision gave me the doctrine and the capacity to explain all*

*that he had written in his Gospel about the beginning of
God's work. Thus I understood that this explanation had
to be the beginning of another book that had not yet been
revealed, in which the creatures of the divine mystery
were to be thoroughly investigated* (multe scrutaciones
creaturarum diuini mysterii querende essent).

This autographical passage, which occupies a
whole chapter in the *Vita Sanctae Hildegardis* (II, XVI,
43–44), differs from Hildegard's other accounts of the
visions she experienced in one important respect. Here,
she loses consciousness, falling into a state of ecstasy
in which her knowledge (*scientia*) is mysteriously transformed, and she is thus able to understand the profound
meaning of John's Prologue—one of the most elevated
texts in the New Testament—and to flank the Evangelist
with a new *scriptura* which, like the Johannine text, is
immersed in the revealed mystery of the divine works.
Although Hildegard normally uses the term *scriptura*
in the singular in reference to her own works, reserving
the plural for the Scriptures themselves, the entire context of the above account stresses the affinity she now
clearly senses between her own inspiration and that of
the prophet of the Apocalypse (in the Middle Ages the
author of the only prophetic text in the New Testament
was not distinguished from the Evangelist), which enables her not only to interpret but also to thoroughly
investigate the mysteries of the creation. She recognizes
that it centers on the mystery of the human being, who
is *imago Dei*, since he has been given the divine spark of
reason, and has *similitudo* with the Word, because of his
divine and human nature: soul and flesh, *a single work in
two natures* (242), man and woman, since *man signifies
the divinity, while woman the humanity of the Son of God*
(238). Created to be the garment of God incarnate, humanity in its complex doubly dual and relational constitution is therefore modeled on the fullness of the Word,
and present from the origins in the plan of the Creator
as the completion of the creation: the seventh day.

Hildegard's exegesis of the Johannine prologue
fully expresses the anthropological concept that was
always the cornerstone of her thought. In fact, the scope
of her entire multifaceted work is to show humanity
the ways of salvation (virtues, health, harmony of song)
by reintegrating into the concord of the origin all the
areas of spiritual and bodily experience into which the
original sin introduced separation and discord.

The *Anthropos*, namely the divine and human ar-
chetype that in the *LDO* is born of the Lamb in the
heart of God, manifesting as the fulcrum of the entire
created world, is the visual symbol of this concept that
underpins the development of the whole work, in which
the human being, *miraculum Dei*, is called to *give witness to God's wonders* (253). The last of the creatures,
which in its bodily form reconnects all of them with
their Creator, it is then defined by Hildegard as *ple-
num opus Dei*, fullness of God's work, even though,
compared with the great work that is the world, it is
a *parvum opus*, small work: a microcosm in which the
creator *signified all creatures in humankind, just as every
creature came forth through his Word* (139).

Hence, in writing the *LDO* Hildegard developed
her fundamental intuition stemming from the *mystic and*

The Fullness of Creation. Incarnation and Humanity in the Liber Divinorum Operum

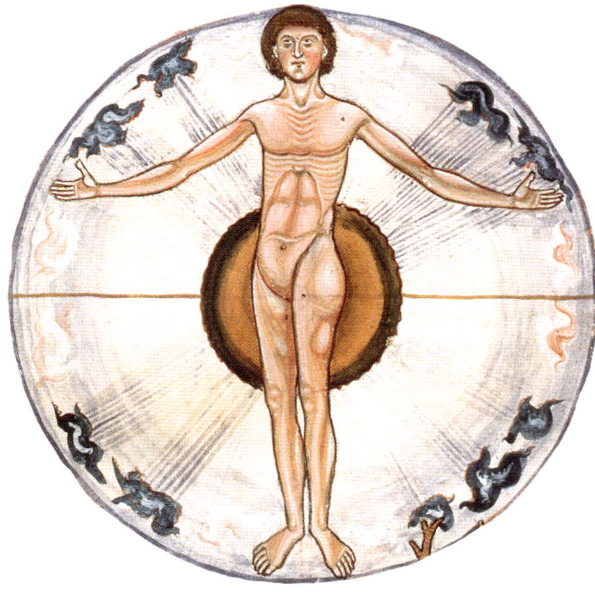

wondrous vision. This origin is confirmed by the inclusion in the work of two exegetic texts: the commentary on the Prologue of the Gospel of John, in fact, and the one on the work of the six days, in Genesis I:1–28, both of which aim to clarify in philosophical as well as spiritual terms the meaning of what lies *in the beginning.* And in both, as Peter Dronke observes in his enlightening introduction to the critical edition of the *Liber*, the fullness of the microcosmic reading is particularly striking (LIX). The style of the two commentaries is similar to that of works linked to Hildegard's teaching and preaching activities, rather than to her prophecy (*Expositiones Evangeliorum, Explanatio Symboli Sancti Athanasii*). However, the fact that these commentaries were given a prominent position in the visionary text—immediately before and after the central vision that (as Sara Salvadori shows in her analysis) summarizes the entire trajectory of the *Liber*—confirms the inspirational nature of the Johannine text and highlights the exemplary function of the commentary on Genesis, in which the three levels of interpretation (literal, allegorical, and tropological-moral) offer a well-ordered example of the multiplicity of meaning conveyed on every page of Hildegard's work, which is echoed in the various levels on which the miniatures can also be read.

The backbone of the *LDO* consists in the sequence of visions, where the centrality, both in terms of structure and meaning, of the fifth vision—in which the destiny of human beings comes to pass on earth and in the places of *purgatorial punishments* (274)—not only corresponds to that of the microcosmic *Anthropos*, but is pivotal to the transition from the theo-cosmic development of the first part to the historical-prophetic evolution of the third. If, as maintained by some, Hildegard was to some extent able to "prompt" her visions—a possibility that seems to emerge from some letters—we must recognize that the Trinitarian representation in the first vision, which initiates the *multe scrutaciones* into the divine mysteries that her ecstatic experience had tasked her with, is manifest *quasi hominis forma* (*like a human in form*, 33), as was the explosive nucleus of the event that had revealed to her the meaning of the creation, *in principio.*

The anthropomorphic figure of *Charitas* (Divine Love)-Trinity as creator initiates the subsequent development of the visions, starting from the movement *upon the breast of the aforementioned image [...][where] there appeared a wheel, wonderful to see* (167). [...] *In the beginning of the very beginning, when God's will disclosed that it was now ready to make creation—which existed without beginning within him, though it had not yet unfolded* (246–247). The divinity creates a space within itself and thus generates the world, which Hildegard depicts by foregrounding those aspects—the spherical shape, internal dynamism, and size—that enable a comparison with the representation she had offered in *Scivias*, which is explicitly referenced here; and also with the cosmological thought of the philosophers of her time, first and foremost the Platonists of Chartres, who had attempted to explain the *in principio* by reconciling the Genesian narrative with the myth of *Timaeus*, an authoritative philosophical text central to the renewal of the various schools. Some of them had initially believed that the third person of the Trinity could be identified with the *Anima mundi*, to which Plato attributed the fundamental function of linking eternal immutable ideas with the world of multiplicity and becoming, but their approach was harshly accused of being pantheistic. The schools sought to defend themselves against such accusation by engaging in further reflection, which led them to separate the immanent plane from the transcendence of the third person of the Trinity, and ultimately to develop the idea of nature as a universal intramundane reality, which was life-giving and autonomous (though at the service of the divine will) and the object of physical knowledge. The latter was boosted by the translations from Arabic of philosophical texts (including all of Aristotle's works) and scientific and medical writings. In the *Liber Subtilitatum Diversarum Naturarum Creaturarum* or *Physica* the *magistra* shows that she had some knowledge of the last two in particular.

Hildegard devoted some particularly valid speculative passages to the life of the world and its relation to divine life, including the immanent reality in the transcendence of the Spirit from which life originates. Not the Spirit in the world, therefore, but the world of the Spirit, thus eliminating the problem of pantheism at the root, and overshadowing the Hildegardian conception with a form of panentheism. Hence, we find no trace of the universal and abstract notion of nature—a term she always uses in its traditional sense of "nature of" (of the human being, of the spirit, of the soul, and so forth)—in her writings. For her, the world is *creature* and place of incarnation of the Word, since it is as if the human being, planned from the beginning as the garment of the Word, existed in the cosmic structure, *in its middle, as it were* (62), *circumscribed by the powers of the soul as they stretch themselves throughout the whole circle of the earth* (63). Hildegardian thought is not oriented toward theoretical speculation on the physical reality of creation, despite the fact that the entire first part of the *LDO* abounds with references to the physical and naturalistic and medicinal knowledge of the period. Instead, as we find also in the *Liber Subtilitatum*, she investigates the world as the seat of humanity, the place where, after

  The Fullness of Creation. Incarnation and Humanity in the Liber Divinorum Operum

being expelled from the Garden of Eden, the *operarius Dei* finds the means to complete the work for which he is destined, and to follow the way of salvation that will lead him back, along with all the creatures of which he is the sum (microcosm), to the harmony of the origins.

This path, which culminates in the *Way of virginitas*, i.e. complete human integrity, is the leitmotif of the *LDO*, and its unfolding is clearly and consistently readable in the visions and the explanations of them provided by the *vox de caelo*, as shown by the study of the images conducted by Sara Salvadori. However, the chapters of the commentary on the visions do not simply perform the basic function of clarifying the meaning of each one in detail and their significance as a whole, on a literal and allegorical and tropological level. Indeed, Hildegard introduces in these chapters a series of theological and philosophical themes which, rather than being addressed in a specific order, seem to rhapsodically reveal the profound structure of her thinking, by starting from the commentary and then elaborating on it. Yet another series of chapters, interposed somewhat at random with the main narrative, references and interprets passages from the Old and New Testaments, to confirm events or themes treated therein, as if to renew its typological reading (the two commentaries on Revelation 6 and 13, in chaps. 8 and 16 respectively, are noteworthy). Thus, despite its being asystematic and a little disordered, her third prophetic work can be considered a veritable *summa* of Hildegardian thought, nourished by reflection and by the knowledge acquired throughout her life.

The comprehensive "outline" that precedes the text in some manuscripts, which philological analysis has shown to have been added after the work was completed, provides an overview of the text. This already gives us an idea of how the *magistra* of Bingen's thought covers the entire range of speculative themes in her time: God, the world, the human being, history. This is not the place for a detailed analysis of the overall work, but it is worth describing it briefly to give readers an idea of its extraordinary richness.

At the origin of all reality, God Trinity Creator manifested as winged Wisdom, *Charitas*, energy of fire (*ignea vis*), whole and perfect life from which every single life sprang, *racionalitas* in which the resounding Word flowered. *God is this life, self-moving and active, yet one life in three energies (*in tribus viribus*). Therefore, Eternity is called the Father, the Word is called the Son, and the breath connecting these two is called the Holy Spirit, just as God is signified in human beings, in whom are body, soul, and rationality* (35). Omnipotence and prescience are of God and have always resided *amid his power* (401).

The cosmos created by the one omnipotent God is the physical world, which is described in visions I.2–4 and developed far more extensively than the cosmological vision in *Scivias*, with an evident desire to offer a rational explanation of its being rooted in divine life, the *ignea vis* of the Spirit that is manifested in the *viriditas*, viridity, of all living things: *But I am also the fiery life of the essence of divinity; […] I quicken all things with some invisible life that sustains them all* (34). At

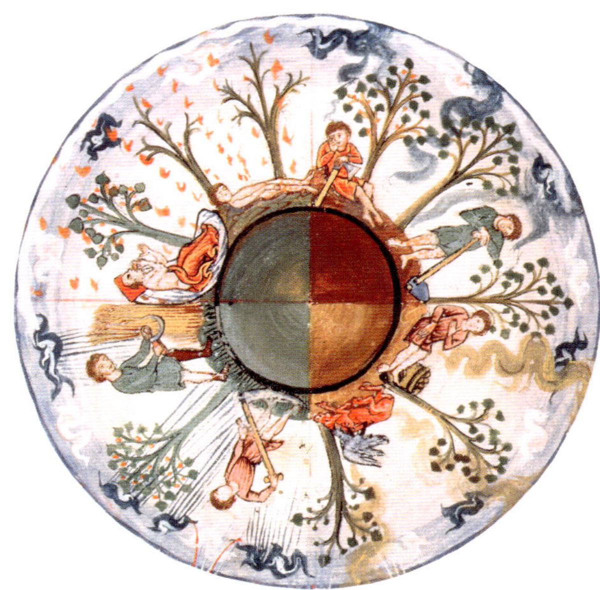

a physical level, life is transmitted by a force known as the winds, which are addressed broadly in the *LDO*; a force that not only explains the dynamics of the cosmic forces, but also their strict relationship to the corporeal life of human beings. The third vision of the first book, which proceeds rather differently from all the others, is in fact a detailed description of the relationship between the winds and the humors deriving from the four elements (fire/choler [yellow bile], air/blood, water/phlegm, earth/melancholy), which form the basis of human physiology in Hildegardian medicine, which is thus heir to the hippocratic-galenic tradition. In this way, the third vision is pivotal to the transition from the realistic description of the cosmos and all its parts (I.2: the firmament, stars and planets, clouds, and, in fact, the winds) to that of the human body with its proportionate limbs in precise relation to the macrocosm (I.4).

The microcosm/macrocosm relationship places the human being at the center of the world, giving him responsibility for that world, rather than dominion over it: *God made all parts of creation in both the upper and lower realms and directed them to be useful for humankind—but if humankind perverts them with corrupt actions, the judgment of God brings creation down upon them with vengeance* (112). This aspect renders concrete the moral significance of the structural relationship between the creatures and those parts of creation (the above-quoted passage continues: *Furthermore, though they aid humankind in the necessities of the body, they must be understood to attend no less to the health of the soul*), and clearly differentiates Hildegard's naturalism from that of the Platonists of her day, offering a diverse reading of the cornucopia of scientific knowledge that poured into the West during the 12th century. Hildegard interpreted the world and man in terms of shared and relational *creaturality*; a reading that was not developed in the scholarly culture of her day, but which in the not too distant future was to emerge by other means in the message of Francis of Assisi and in other late-medieval expressions of the value of creation, for example in the figurative arts and in the development of knowledge regarding corporeity (medicine, alchemy).

Hildegard had the extraordinary vision mentioned above and began to write the *LDO* in 1163, the same year she penned her letter concerning the Cathars (*Epistola* 169R), who professed dualist doctrines—condemned as heretical—affirming two originary principles: a good God creator of everything that is spiritual and an evil creator of matter and bodies. Hildegard's insistence on the oneness of God omnipotent creator and her argument that corporeity was present in the originary divine plan due to incarnation, may actually have been driven by her desire to combat radical dualism, which also fired the articulate and impassioned anthropological speculation of the *magistra* of Bingen concerning the originary soul-body duality and the possibility of reintegrating it by going beyond the conflictual dualism that humanity had experienced since the Fall. This had originated with the rebellion of the angels who, proud of their own splendor, *wished to vilify God* (39) and *wanted to be like him in a way that was impossible* (40). After the creation of man they continued to attack God through his creature, *clothed with a body* (ivi).

Human history begins with the original sin. Placed *in the unchangeable land of pleasure* (377), Adam led a harmonious life in the light of knowledge, which was then "clouded" by diabolical temptation, resulting in his expulsion. This was the beginning of historical events and man's arduous journey, on which he is constantly threatened by the enemy of God, but also guided by the light of the incarnation of Christ, who *possessed great wisdom* (379) and showed that *the devil's reckoning—he thought that humankind was totally lost—was misled, because he did not know that God had been clothed in human form* (ivi). The third part of the *LDO* traces the whole story from beginning to end, with the focus on the incarnation and the founding of the Church, in which human beings complete the way of salvation. *God [...] said to himself, "Now let us make humankind in our image and likeness, for the building of the Church. [...] So humankind is to build the Church with divine work and righteous human deeds"* (335). Thus God assigns the task of building the Church, that is the *Catholic* universal community made up of all human beings, to his *operarii*, who must carry it out through time according to the law of the Son incarnate, *who was born from my heart*. But this does not always happen.

In the Old Testament we read, *And so the Word was incarnate [...] and to this miracle the prophets' tongues swiftly crossed the world when they affirmed that to the lands he would come, fair beyond the sons of men* (369), but after the coming of Christ humanity's path was never consistent, nor has it ever been, since the *virtues' viridity withered, and all justice sank into decay* (428). Thus Hildegard was given a prophetic mission, to which she dedicated her whole life, and which in the concluding vision of the *LDO* leads her to put into the mouth of Christ himself a supplication that begins by describing the dire state of the world—which today we would call the ecosystem. *So too the Son speaks to his Father, saying: "In the beginning, all creation was verdant, flowers blossomed in its midst; only later did viridity fall away"* (429), because men's foolish, unjust behaviors, *through the creation that I made for human use, [...] are also often judged, so that by fire and water they are strangled, and by wind and air they lose the fruits of the earth. The sun and moon prove themselves out of sorts [...]. So too the earth is disturbed for a time like a chariot overturned by some bump* (431).

Christ's prayer to the Father had first rung out as the epilogue to *Ordo Virtutum* (*The Play of the Virtues*, ca. 1150), the musical play by Hildegard that depicts the virtues sent by God to succor the soul harassed by the Devil. In commenting and elaborating it, the *magistra* becomes an exegete of herself, treating her own work as she does passages from the Scriptures. The words of the invocation embody the theme of *viriditas*, the unifying thread running through all of Hildegard's production. Difficult to translate, due to its multiple meanings at all levels of reality from the divine to the earthly, the term means vital energy, spiritual and physical fecundity and vigor—visual artist Maurizio Osti, struck by its epiphanic splendor, defined it as "creative cosmic energy in a nascent state." The integrated reading of the creation and history, which has Christ as its focal point and finds its complete expression in the last of Hildegard's prophetic works, is thus rooted in an original notion conceived and upheld by the saint with a strength that is still palpable; namely, the reciprocal belonging of the world and the human being, expressions of the one divine *life/viriditas* in its multiple manifestations, and throne and garment of God *incarnate in the Virgin's womb* (430).

Note
The Hildegardian bibliography, though extensive, does not contain a monograph devoted to the *Liber Divinorum Operum* in its entirety. A synthetic picture of the book can be found in Peter Dronke's comprehensive presentation, with a study of the sources, that introduces the critical edition of the work (*Hildegardis Bingensis* 1996), and also in the shorter but dense introduction by Nathaniel M. Campbell to his recent English translation (*St. Hildegard of Bingen* 2018; see also Campbell 2017), from which the above citations are taken (with the page numbers in brackets). The notes to Campbell's translation constitute an analytical guide to the entire text and, when read in sequence, offer an interpretative, albeit not systematic, thread.

The recent monograph by Georgina Rabassó (2018) is an exemplary work on a methodological level, though limited to the philosophical-naturalistic content of the *Liber Divinorum Operum*. The intertwining of theology and anthropology in the theme of the incarnation is brought into sharp focus by Marco Rainini (2019), while Sara Ritchey (2009) is helpful in contextualizing it. Maura Zátony's (2012) study is devoted to Hildegard's biblical hermeneutics. For Maurizio Osti's creative work on *viriditas* see *Viriditas*, Viriditas logotype, Accademia di Belle Arti Bologna, Course in designed graphics, lecturer Maurizio Osti, academic year 2005/2006, FA&BA Press, November 2013.

The Fullness of Creation. Incarnation and Humanity in the Liber Divinorum Operum

Sara Salvadori

Introduction

From the outermost edge of the firmament Hildegard contemplates the wheel of creation in the heart of God. A revolving sphere, a cosmological *instrumentum*, inhabited by Man, whose measurements and proportions are described, along with the internal motions of his body and soul. This is the scenario presented in the *Liber Divinorum Operum* (hereafter *LDO*), *Book of Divine Works*. A long sequence composed of ten scenes that invites humanity to complete the journey from earth to heaven by following the *way* of *virginitas* (virginity), toward the reconstruction of the self, culminating in the mystic marriage in which male and female are reunited in Divine Love (*Caritas*), in God's heart.

Hildegard's visions are represented in the ten extremely refined miniatures of the Lucca Codex, which are reproduced in the central plates of the *Grammar* section. However, it is as if the language of these images were covered by an interpretative veil: although of extraordinary beauty, they were executed twenty years after Hildegard's death. This first impression, together with some incongruities between the text and images, led us to follow a research path marked by a series of steps: the figurative transcription of the visions according to the sapiential indications of measurement and proportions found in the text; the constant dialogue with the images her first work, *Scivias* (*Know the Ways*), executed under Hildegard's guidance, which enabled us to enliven the new drawings with forms and colors; the preparation of a model of the *building*; the use of three-dimensional drawings, and lastly the placement of the text alongside the drawings so that the reader might see the relationship between them.

Thus there emerged vibrant visions of a spherical cosmos, of a bright celestial vault, of the inner motions of Man and the liveliness of the way followed in the *civitas Dei*, described on the pages of *Rhetoric*. The reconstruction of the *wheel* has revealed within it the graphic representation, according to a sapiential layering, of the movements of the earth, the moon and the solstices, of a meridian and a windrose, in an intense contemplation of the supreme divine ordinance. It is the expression of an extremely topical and prophetic theology of the creation: *All who do not […] wish to observe the rising and setting of the sun, moon, and stars, which God has placed in the sky, nor the wind with the air, nor the earth with its waters and the rest of creation, all of which God created on account of humankind, to recognize in all of them how great an honor it is to be created; […] hold me, who am without beginning and without end,* *in contempt and destroy all of creation, not understanding correctly either it or themselves* (I.2,22, 71–72).

At the same time, the analysis of the constructive design of the miniatures and of the refined syllogism that emerges in the description of the visions, which is contained in the pages of the *Dialettica*, synthetically communicates the central message of the work, i.e., humanity has always and will always be held, *cor ad cor loquitur*, in the heart of God.

The volume is framed by two essays: in the first, by Michela Pereira, reflections and intuitions filtered through more than forty years of research on Hildegard converge, becoming the contemplation of the fullness of creation and anticipating the images of the starry firmament at whose center shines the bright star of Man incarnate, *imago Dei*; in the second, José C. Santos Paz explores the text of the *Berlin Fragment*, putting forward the theory that there may have existed a written outline that was used as a guide by the miniaturist.

These are the salient features of a volume born of stories and meetings that reveal a greater plan between the lines. Recounting it becomes a kind of testimony, and is the best way to thank those who have been "called" to participate in the various stages.

September 2011, pieve of Sant'Alessandro a Giogoli, in the countryside near Florence. Father Giorgio Mazzanti interrupts his meeting, leads me into the first room of his library, and takes a volume from a high shelf. A rare book, published in only a few copies.[1] The pages are of parchment paper and the gold of the miniatures floods our souls in the darkness of the room. I try to resist, but the invitation cannot be declined: "Begin! Hildegard is important for these times." After leafing timorously through the book, almost without daring to touch it, I return it after a few weeks. One year later, on October 7, 2012, Pope Benedict XVI proclaims Hildegard of Bingen the fourth woman Doctor of the Church, saying, "The teaching of the holy Benedictine nun stands as a beacon for *homo viator*. Her message appears extraordinarily timely in today's world."

Ten years have passed since then—it took me that long to accept the invitation—during which the heavens repeatedly sent signs to which, in the end, one had to respond. In fact, four episodes that occurred in the space of a few months convinced me to dedicate myself to the Lucca miniatures. The first was the invitation in June 2019 from Silvia Castelli, Head of the Gabinetto dei Disegni e delle Stampe of the Biblioteca Marucelliana in Florence, to

Father Giorgio Mazzanti, myself, and Michela Pereira, to go to the Biblioteca Statale di Lucca to see the codex, where we were given a warm and scholarly welcome by the director Monica Maria Angeli. This time I found myself in front of the manuscript for a longer, more dilated time and with an inner calm that was different from what I had felt on the visit with Father Bernardo Gianni six years previously, when I had been so struck by the vibrancy of the blood red and blue flowing through the human body at the center of the wheel that I was unable to take in other details. Now we slowly turned the pages and studied them next to the reproductions of the *Scivias* miniatures in the original size, which had just been published. There emerged the vision of a single cosmological and human reality seen from two perspectives that were different but in dialogue with each other. In August 2019 there was another invitation, this time from Gilbert Casaburi, who asked me to explain the images of *Scivias* at a conference in Lucca in November and to act as guide for a group of visitors who were coming to see the manuscript. In October of that year José C. Santos Paz, who was in Florence for his usual teaching engagements, asked me if I was thinking of extending my research on the images to other works by Hildegard; and some months later, when the research was already underway, if I was thinking of doing three-dimensional reconstructions also for the *LDO*—an idea that has led to our having a model of the *civitas Dei*, masterfully executed by Sofia Basilissi and painstakingly photographed by Enos Mantoani. A month after this meeting, during an intense morning at the Biblioteca Statale in Lucca, for the first time I found myself explaining Hildegard's visions to the public with the pages of the manuscript in front of me. This moment of hushed and attentive togetherness, convinced me of the importance of offering readers the whole cycle of the miniatures depicting the visions. Monica Maria Angeli encouraged me to pursue this path, by explaining that it would be an important tool for many visitors to the library. This aspect was welcomed with foresight by the President of the Fondazione Cassa di Risparmio di Lucca, Marcello Bertocchini, who, having been committed for years to enhancing the city's treasures, immediately understood the significance of the publishing project, enabling its realization. A perception shared—and amplified by the theological significance of the work—also by the bishop of the city Paolo Giulietti. Of fundamental importance during the research were the intense conversations with astrophysicist Franco Lisi, thanks to which it was possible to transcribe the cosmological description in images and to show that the apparent incongruities in the images were none other than creative expedients used by the miniaturist to represent the diverse perspectives. Equally invaluable was the collaboration with Antonella Barolini, thanks to which we were able to visually transcribe the humoral movements within the human body. This work produced the drawings and notes that the creative hand of Lorenzo Bejarano Libreros transformed into "beautiful form," while Elisabetta Benelli's unstinting generosity enabled us to clarify the text and make it readable. A text in which it is possible to read Hildegard's words in direct quote, thanks to the translations made available by Michela Pereira and Nathaniel M. Campbell. For the English text, thanks to Caitlin Swanson, who took my place as listener. And if all this finally took the form of a book, it was thanks to Ilaria Perticucci—otherwise Milan would not be home—and to the editorial team at Skira, especially Pietro Della Lucia, Emma Cavazzini, Luigi Fiore, Barbara Galotta, Cinzia Morisco, and Maria Conconi: without their invaluable work books would simply remain scattered words and images.

Lastly, heartfelt thanks go to Maria Stella Curti for sharing through sisterly communion, and my deep gratitude to Giuseppina Antognini for her friendship, and her being the only one to welcome all my stories and to remind me always that to realize your dreams you have to let yourself be helped where you are most vulnerable. Pina does this by supporting you during the lonely period of research, invisible to many, through the Fondazione Pasquinelli of which she is president. Thanks also to our bishop and cardinal Giuseppe Betori, who recognized the pure faith of this journey, and to Michela Pereira and Father Giorgio Mazzanti, who shared the emotion of each stage, with a vision that only true masters possess. I like to think that Father Giorgio is now looking at all this amidst the bright stars of the celestial spirits, arrayed on high in the golden sky of the firmament, where the Hildegard supernova shines resplendent.

---

[1] Calderoni Masetti and Dalli Regoli 1973. The volume, published by the Cassa di Risparmio di Lucca, is still the only reference text for the study and interpretation of the images of the *LDO*.

CHAPTER I

Prologue

*I*n the sixth year after the completion of her second work, *Liber Vite Meritorum* (*Book of the Rewards of Life*), on which she had labored for *five years*, Hildegard again began to experience visions. Like the previous ones, they did not come to her in a state of *ecstasy*, but were seen *with the inner eyes and perceived with the inner ears*, with her gaze and listening directed toward heaven and the *Living Light* that guided her. Yet again she was commanded to *commit to fixed writing* what she saw and heard and to be the witness of *life without beginning and end*, by recording *not things* she had imagined, but what had been *foreordained before the beginning of the world* by God himself.

And so in 1163, when she was *sixty-five years old*, she embarked once more on the process of listening/vision and writing, which would occupy her for around *seven years*, accompanied by a group of *three* as before, made up, with Hildegard, of a *deeply religious man, devout in his observance of the Rule of St. Benedict, and a girl* (Prologue and Epilogue). The number *seven* refers to the gifts of the Holy Spirit, and *three* to the Trinity. The *Liber Divinorum Operum* (*LDO*) with its ten visions completes the Trinitarian arc of the great triptych of her three theological works, consisting in a sequence of forty-two visions in all.

Synchronicity
The words of the Liber Divinorum Operum and the images of Scivias

Historians tell us that the decade between 1163 and 1174, when the elderly Hildegard wrote this last work, coincided with the period during which she founded her second convent, at Eibingen, near which the present Abtei St. Hildegard is located. It also coincided with some of her preaching journeys on which she followed the Rhine, Maine and Moselle, thus moving in the *four directions of the world* that spread out from the Rupertsberg convent on which her life centered. Lastly, that decade saw the execution of the thirty-five miniatures that make up the extraordinary mosaic of *Scivia*s, which were executed in the *scriptorium*/workshop of the Rupertsberg convent. Hence it was a period in which she opened up to the world and spread the message received through the visions that had always accompanied her.

These experiences led Hildegard to understand that she had to go beyond the spoken and written word and extend her means of communication to a different kind of writing that was analogical and syncretic: writing with images.

She chose to do this by returning to her first work, *Scivias*, the great compendium in which the *Lux vivens*, voice of God, showed her the *ways* to follow in order to know the Light. Thus the writing of the *LDO* text and of the *Scivias* images became synchronic.

These two works have come down to us in several manuscript copies, but the two codices to which we shall refer are both illuminated manuscripts: the *Scivias* manuscript known as the Rupertsberg Codex, and manuscript 1942 of the *LDO*, known as the Lucca Codex, held by the Biblioteca Statale in Lucca.

All the words and images, indeed every single part of the Rupertsberg Codex of *Scivias*, were executed under Hildegard's direct guidance. The original manuscript disappeared in Dresden in 1945, leaving us with the illuminated facsimile that the abbess of Eibingen, Regintrudis Sauter, fortunately was inspired to have made in the interwar years. We devoted the volume *Hildegard von Bingen. A Journey into the Images* (2019) to the miniatures in that manuscript.

The Lucca Codex of the *LDO* is a large manuscript, embellished with an illuminated illustration for each vision. It was made after Hildegard's death, in the 1320s or thereabouts, most likely by the *scriptorium* at Rupertsberg. The text—transcribed from another codex—is an original work by the saint, while the illustrations were created by one or more artists around the 1320s–1330s, the period to which the codex dates. The origin of this manuscript seems to be linked to the canonization process initiated a few years after Hildegard's death, and to indicate that the codex was destined to be viewed by Pope Gregory IX in Rome.

Three things should be emphasized at this point: one, that the prophetic text of the *LDO* is an original work by Hildegard while the images are not; two, that the *Scivias* illustrations are the only original images designed and created under Hildegard's guidance; three, that the *LDO* text and the *Scivias* miniatures were created in the same period. Thus we may conclude that the images of *Scivias* should be seen as the sole reference for understanding Hildegardian symbolic iconography, and that the contemporaneous execution of the two works resulted in their being closely linked at a structural level.

The dialogue between the two works, which shed light on each other, enables a reconstruction of the visions that totally adheres to the text of the *LDO*. This permits us to lift the veil of interpretive interference by authors and illuminators who were unable to benefit from Hildegard's personal guidance during the composition of the exquisite images of the Lucca Codex.

In dialogue
Scivias and Liber Divinorum Operum

So God created Man in his own image, in the image of God he created him [...]. And God blessed them, and God said unto them, Be fruitful, and multiply, and replenish the earth, and subdue it: and have dominion over the fish of the sea, and over the fowl of the air, and over every living thing that moveth upon the earth. [Et factum est…] And the evening and the morning were the sixth day (Gn 1.27–28, 31).

If we place *Scivias* and the *LDO* in dialogue, we note a structural correspondence between the overall architecture and the passages of the text. This evidences the affinity between the works, which, like two frescoes on the walls of the same church, occupy the same space within an identical frame and have a similar tripartite composition, while depicting two different scenes from the story of God's encounter with Man.

In the peaceful context of the metaphorical church, the reader is thus able to study each fresco individually, while also benefiting from the overall and synchronic vision of both, whose comparison brings out significant elements conducive to understanding the meaning and symbol preserved in the content of each. On the one hand, this further confirms that Hildegard deliberately chose to work on the two "frescoes" contemporaneously, accenting both similarities and individual passages. On the other hand, it makes it possible to follow the threads she knowingly traced, and to grasp the content and the most profound and unitary message of the entire story offered by the visions and captured by her. Lastly, the dialogue created between the two works and the Bible reveals an underlying third fresco: the divine plan that encapsulates the whole story.

The new life
Christ, door to Wisdom

Factum est in millesimo centesimo quadragesimo primo (*Scivias*, Protestificatio, cited in Pereira 2017, 3).

And it was in the year 1141 from the incarnation of the Son of God: these are the opening words of the second paragraph of the Protestificatio (introduction) to *Scivias*, in which Hildegard historically places her calling, which came through flames that rained down from heaven upon her *head*, her *heart* and her *limbs*. In the opening quote, *And it was* is a reference to the phrase (*Et factum est / And it was so*) that concludes the account of each

day of the week of the creation in Genesis, the book of origins; *1141* signifies the number seven, obtained by adding the individual digits together, which represents the seven gifts of the Holy Spirit who descends upon Hildegard; and *the Incarnation of the Son of God* attests to the fact that the Holy Spirit can only enter into every living creature on earth after Christ has become the door between heaven and earth, thus giving the new life.

The life
God creates Man in his image

Et factum est in sexto anno (*LDO*, Prologue, 130).

And it was in the sixth year: with these words Hildegard opens her last work, the *LDO,* twenty years later. Here, the reference to Genesis is more precise, not only due to the reprisal of *Et factum est / And it was so*, but also the addition of the specific temporal reference *in sexto* (*in the sixth*), indicating that her story takes place on the sixth day of the creation. The opening phrase thus shows that the theme of the *LDO* is the contemplation of the divine creation by Man, created by God *in his image*. This takes us back to a time before the narration of the incarnation of the Son of God, on which *Scivias* focused to indicate the *ways* of salvation. This leap backward invites us to contemplate the creation before time existed, and also the pure Love of God, who gives life and embraces it with timeless love and care. God shows man the only way to follow in accepting and abiding by the gifts so generously bestowed on him, and thus be able to achieve fullness and to fulfill his destiny.

Human wisdom
Scivias, know the ways

Say and write these things that you see and hear; […] and not according to yourself or any other person, but according to the will of He who knows, sees, and disposes all things in the hidden places of his mysteries (*Scivias*, Protestificatio, cited in Pereira 2017, 35).

These are the words with which the *Lux vivens*, living Light—the name with which God identifies himself at the beginning of the Protestificatio in *Scivias*—commands Hildegard to write. A God who presents himself to her as *the One who knows, sees, and disposes all things in the hidden places*. This aspect of mystery unfathomable to the human mind and of the revelation of secrets, is preserved and presented to us in *Scivias*. Through Hildegard, God invites man to follow the way that will lead him to know secrets heretofore inaccessible to him, by embracing the new life through the powerful agency of the Holy Spirit. Hildegard is the first to testify to the power of this way and its fruits, when she recounts that she *suddenly was able to understand the exposition of books, that is, of the Psalter, the Gospel, and of the other orthodox volumes of the Old and the New Testaments* (*Scivias*, Protestificatio, cited in Pereira 2017, 36). Thus the secrets are offered, in a mysterious manner, to those who accept the invitation to make the journey into the images and words of *Scivias*.

The prescience of God
The Book of Divine Works, way
of contemplation and adherence

*Write them indeed not according to your own
heart, but according to my testimony, I who am life
without beginning and end. You did not invent them,
nor did any other human consider them in advance;
rather, they were foreordained by me before the
beginning of the world. For as I foreknew humankind
before ever they were created, so too I foresaw those
things that would be necessary for their existence*
(*LDO*, Prologue, 30).

In the Prologue of the *LDO* God no longer presents
himself to Hildegard as he who knows the mysteries to
reveal, but as *life without beginning and end* that presents the Creation as being known and foreordained *before the beginning of the world*. The *LDO* is not the revelation of knowledge through the *ways* to be followed,
but the realization that everything is *without beginning
and end*, and was foreknown and foreseen. Eternity
outside time—everything in everything since the beginning—before any act of creation, is what man is called
on to worship and contemplate when in the visions he
is shown a depiction of the *wheel* that springs from the
breast of Love that embraces it. The *ways* brought together in the *LDO* are not those that man knew through
grace in *Scivias* and that enabled him to lift his eyes to
heaven. Instead, they are the *ways* for him to abandon
himself to contemplation beyond knowledge, in order to
complete the last stage of purification by trusting in the
Light, knowing that what is *necessary* to him was already
foreseen, seen before and provided for by God himself.
Before the beginning of time everything was already in
man, in whose soul is the temple/curtain/*tabernacle* in
which this timeless essence is preserved.

    Man is invited to follow the way in complete faith,
in the belief that everything, the life and the way, has
been given to him. In fact, the *LDO* no longer speaks
of ways of knowledge but of a single *way, virginitas*
(virginity), to be traveled by adhering to one's consti-
tutive essence. On passing through the door opened
by Christ, we are offered the new life, in which it is
possible to appreciate the mirror and to rediscover the
gift of life steeped in the pretemporal beginning illuminated by divine prescience.

Light (*Lux*)
God's acts in the creation

*Speak and write these things [...] as you see
and hear them among heavenly matters from above,
in the wonders of God* (*Scivias*, Protestificatio,
cited in Pereira 2017, 35).

In *Scivias*, the *Lux vivens* exhorts Hildegard to look
heavenward as she embarks on her journey and to accept what comes thence, so that she may perceive the
Light that reaches and does its work on earth. Although
it is still not possible to contemplate the Light directly,
it can be glimpsed in its acts in the creation.

Light (*Lumen*)
God as light for creation

I have looked up to (aspexi) *the true and living
light* (Lumen) (*LDO*, Prologue, 30).

At the beginning of the journey in the *LDO* the *Lux vivens*
becomes *Lumen vivens*, light that illuminates. Hildegard
is asked to lift her eyes to heaven once again, not so much
to see the light descending as to contemplate the radiance,
the light without beginning and without end. She is in-
structed to learn from this light. Here, she uses the word
aspexi to emphasize the looking toward, the immersing
oneself in the light. Hildegard also utilizes the same term
in one of her sequences, *Columba aspexi*, in which she
praises St. Maximinus who *like a dove looks toward, beyond the bars of a window*. The narrative of the *LDO* is es-
sentially an appeal to look beyond the bars of the confines
of existence toward the constantly turning *wheel* of love.

Prophecy

*Say and write these things that you see and hear
[...] just as also a listener, receiving the words of his
teacher, makes them known according to the tenor of
the teacher's speech, as he wishes, shows, and instructs*
(*Scivias*, Protestificatio, cited in Pereira 2017, 35).

Lastly, the *Lux vivens* in *Scivias* exhorts Hildegard to
make *known* the words she has heard, to announce the
message, to be a prophetess. She actually begins to do
this in the title of the introduction, Protestificatio, the
first word of the work, which has as its root *protestor*,
meaning to state publicly, to give public testimony. In
doing so she announces her acceptance of the call to
be a prophet, linking herself to Isiah and John, the two
great prophets who respectively symbolize the Old and
New Testaments. When the *Lux vivens* commands her
to *cry out and write*, it is asking her to follow in their
footsteps and bring a dramatic force to her work.

Worship

*Commit to fixed writing these things, [...] to be useful
for humankind; so that through them, humans might
understand their Creator and not flee from worshipping
him with worthy honor* (*LDO*, Prologue, 30).

The power of prophecy, which in *Scivias* is the driv-
ing force necessary to redirect humanity to the *ways* of
God—an explosive force on a level with the fearsome
flames that descended on Hildegard in her *forty-third
year*—takes on a different, more subdued tone in the
LDO. The Protestificatio is replaced by the quieter
Prologue, while *cry out and write* gives way to *commit
to fixed writing these things*. The power of prophecy
demanded by the *Lux vivens*, which calls for dynamic
action, vigorous movement and active appeal, is substi-
tuted by the *Lumen vivens*, which invites her to forego
powerful action and to adopt a calm attitude of contemplation and worship, in other words to lose herself
in the embrace of Divine Love.

General Map

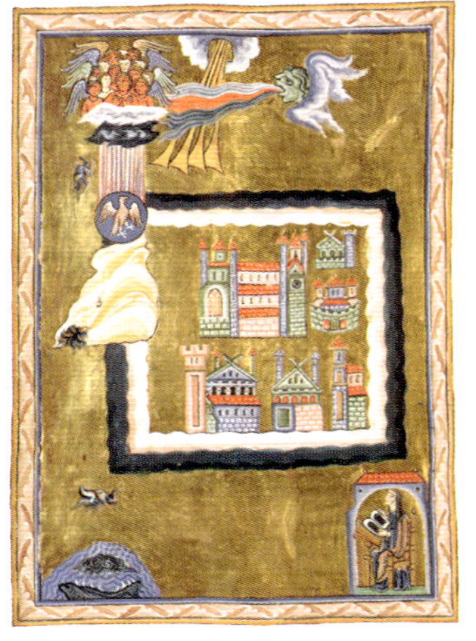

1

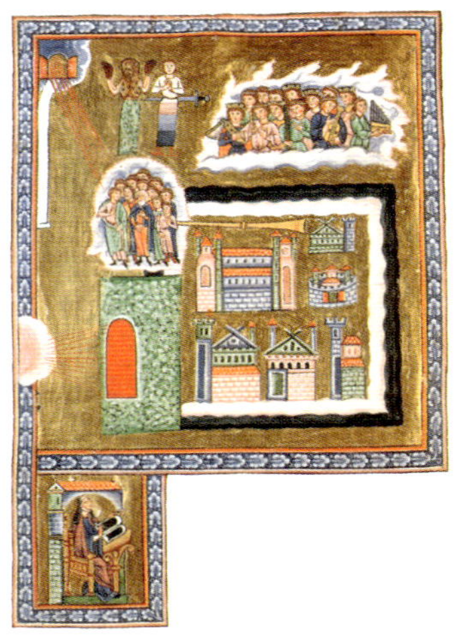

2

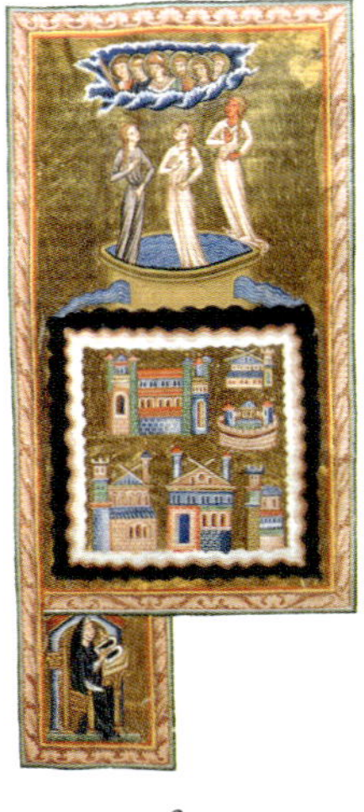

3

III

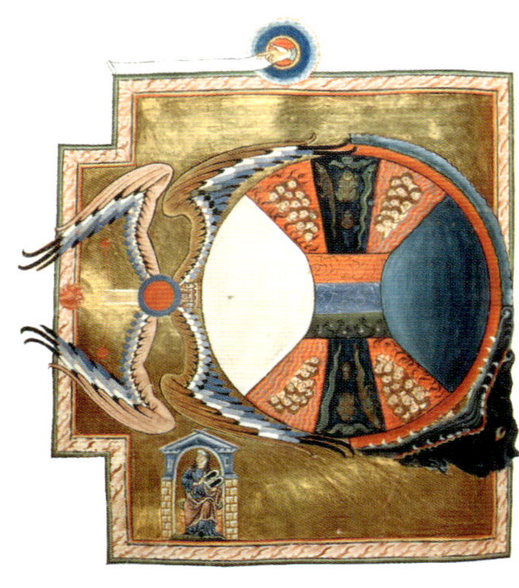

1

II

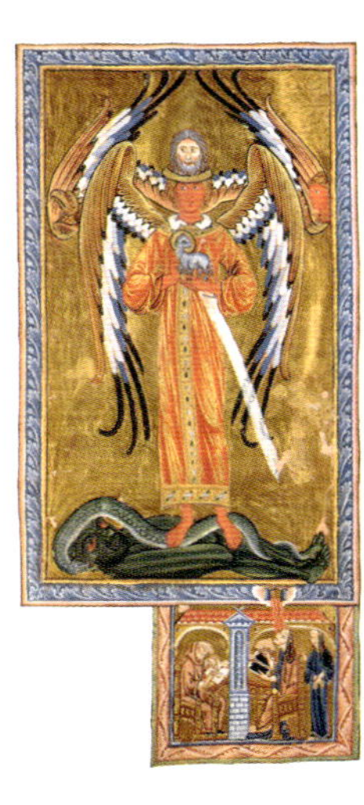

1

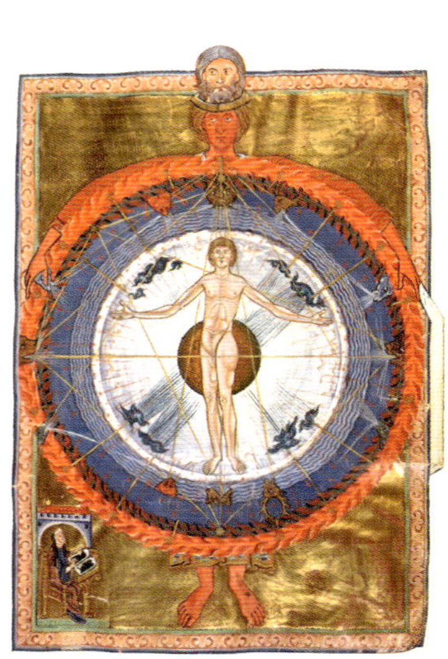

2

3

I

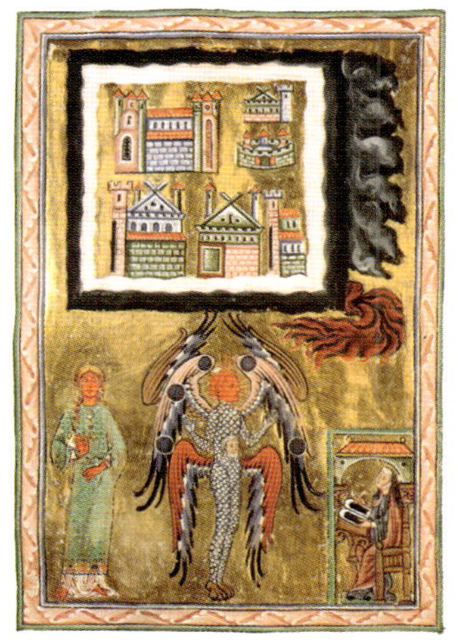

4

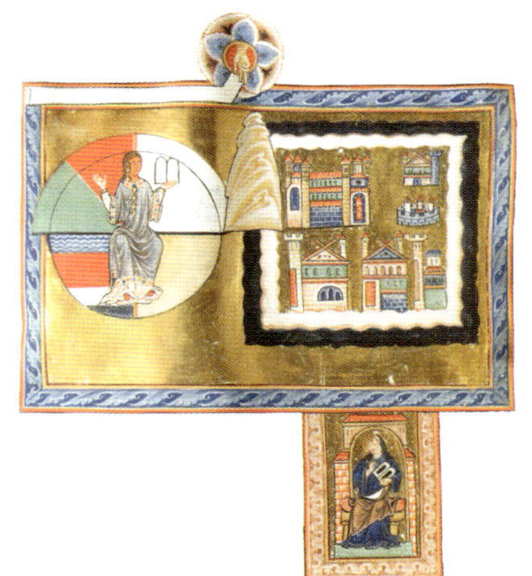

5

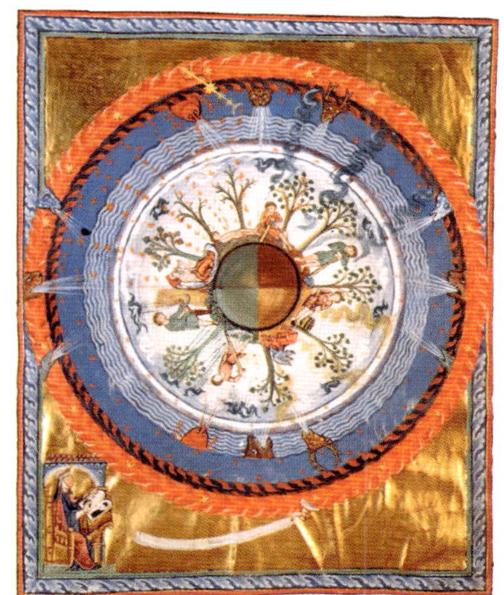

4

 Prologue

CHAPTER II

Liber Divinorum Operum

Itineraries

Scivias and the *LDO* have the same basic structure. Each book is divided into three parts, balanced so that the sum of the visions in the first and second part is equal to the number of those in the third part. In *Scivias* the first two parts contain thirteen visions, as does the third part; in the *LDO* there are five visions in the first and second part, and the same number in the third. This structure corresponds to that of a Greek cross, with the first two parts being equivalent to the vertical arm and the third part to the horizontal arm of the cross, on the center of which two miniatures are superimposed. While in *Scivias* the two visions united through the superimposition show the salvific incarnation of Christ (II.1 and III.7), in the *LDO* the vision with the description of man (I.3) is joined with the vision of the three virtues and of the clearest fountain (III.3), thus highlighting the fact that the creation of man in God's image and likeness was written by God in the visible shadow in the reflection of the water of the fountain. In fact, we read: *For I have composed humankind, who was rooted in me like a shadow, just as an object's reflection is seen in water. So too I am the living fountain, because all that was made existed in me like a shadow* (*LDO*, III.3,2, 388). Yet again it is emphasized that in *Scivias* the focus is on the way to salvation of man, created thanks to the gift of the Son of God, while the *LDO* pivots on the relationship between God and man and on the contemplative dialogue of love.

Another hallmark, both explicit and hidden, of the structure of the two works is the total number of visions, which highlights the essence of their message.

In *Scivias* the visions are twenty-six. A number that, according to the ancient Judeo-Christian tradition, indicates the name of God, YHWH, which must never be uttered aloud. Hence *Scivias* indicates the *ways* that can be known on the sapiential path that leads to the ultimate goal of knowing God himself in his mystery, YHWH, who is signified by the sum of the visions.

In the *LDO*, instead, the visions are ten, the number that indicates the completeness of the divine plan. Hildegard explains this meaning by saying that man has taken the place of the fallen angel and that when the times are fulfilled humanity, thanks to the Son of God, will ascend to heaven and thus recompose the ten celestial ranks (*LDO*, I.1,1, II.2,14 and 15). Thus there will be fulfillment, as a desired moment, in which humanity will finally be able to eternally contemplate life without beginning and without end. The story of the *LDO* is therefore that of the *way* of purification and adherence to the foreseen divine plan that will lead to fullness, to the end of time.

The visions in the *LDO* are introduced by the Prologue, which provides historical facts and an account of the mystical experience and the command received from God himself to write them down, in order to transform them into a message. The Prologue is positioned and structured in a similar way to the Protestificatio in *Scivias*. In the Epilogue to the *LDO*, Hildegard tells of the death of her helper and friend Volmar, which occurred just before the work was completed. After paying him a fond and heartrending tribute, she tells how other trusted collaborators came after him, and prays that the *Lux vivens* may grant them all *eternal radiance in the heavenly Jerusalem* for their services.

Following the scheme already adopted in the other works, each vision opens with a clear and precise description of what Hildegard sees, followed by the words of the *Lux vivens* that illuminate the vision, set down in ordered chapters.

To help the reader, on the previous pages there is an general map of the work in which the ten miniatures of the visions are placed in three rows, one above the other, corresponding to each of three parts (see pages 20–21).

			Epilogue		
III	Part	13	III	Part	5
II	Part	7	II	Part	1
I	Part	6	I	Part	4
Protestificatio			Prologue		
Scivias			*Liber Divinorum Operum*		

Divine Love and the story of the divine works

I am also the fiery life of the essence of divinity. I flame above the beauty of the fields, and I shine in the waters, and I burn in the sun, the moon, and the stars. With the airy wind I quicken all things with some invisible life that sustains them all (I.1,2, 34).

The three parts of the opus
This great story/vision opens with one of the most intense passages Hildegard ever wrote. It is a lengthy hymn to the Spirit/Love, a *fiery force* which, after quickening all of creation, remains in it eternally as *life, breath, resounding Word and ordering rationality*, which with *wings of wisdom* flies around the circlet of existence in which *man, created in God's image and likeness*, is placed. And it is precisely man who, through Hildegard, is given the possibility of seeing God as Love, showing *symbolically that through her, he is recognized in faith who is not seen visibly with the visible eyes* (I.1,3, 36). The vision indicates the way to purification that will lead man to become part of the *building* of living stones, thus reconstructing the plan that God had foreseen before the beginning of time. The imitation of Christ, on the way to integrity of the self—the *way to virginitas*—will enable man to return to heaven. The story unfolds in three parts (see pages 24–25).

Part one
First we see God as a human figure, fiery energy and Divine Love (*Caritas*) who crushes the *monster, eternal discord* (I.1). On his chest, between his outstretched arms, there is a *wheel* that reveals the essence of God (I.2). It is a wheel without beginning or end, whole and in continuous movement. In fact, just as *the wheel surrounds all things, God comprises and surrounds the body of the world*. The *imago of man* is placed within the *wheel*/firmament. They are composed of the same elements and linked by relationships between their forms and measurements. If we look inside the wheel we glimpse the movements of winds in the firmament and their effect on the humors of man; the properties of the firmament and their influence on the human body and soul; and, lastly, the parts of the human body in relation to the firmament (I.2–I.4).

Part two
In a vision that brings together and summarizes all ten visions of the *LDO*, the second part again shows God, who embraces the *wheel* with his wings—indicating divine protection. This time the *wheel* appears in greater closeup, enabling us to see its innermost part, the earth, which occupies the space that previously contained the firmament. The inside of the wheel is divided into five parts corresponding to the five senses and to the physical places in which men are accommodated according to their punishments, and the ways through which man can purify himself are described therein. The *two faces* with human features and the great *golden circlet* of the preceding vision are seen here as *two globes*—one red surrounded by a sapphire circle, and the other simply red—and there is a *star* in the space between them.

They represent God and are a manifestation respectively of the zeal and justice of Divine Love, the gift of the Son of God and the presence of the Holy Spirit. The last element visible from this closer point of view is the *city/building* on the circumference of the Earth, where the blessed souls who praise God are gathered. This symbolism evokes the celestial Jerusalem as the point of contact between creation and the Creator, which thus resembles the Building standing on a hill, firmly embedded in the rock of Godly fear, in the third part of *Scivias* (III.1 and III.2). The song of the blessed rings out from the building, from which the *way* of *virginitas* climbs upward toward the east, leading man from the wheel of the earth until he is reunited with God, thus imitating the Son of God, symbol of integrity/*virginitas* represented by the *star* shining on the golden *way*.

Part three
In a more extreme close-up, we enter the *building* in the previous vision. Hence the miniatures in the third part enable us to see the scenes taking place around the *building*, and the figures moving around. They are all manifestations of God: the *mirror* and the *city* that represent the *foreknowledge* and *predestination* with which he has ordered all things (III.1); the extremely solid *stone/mount* that symbolizes the power of God communicated in the various ages of history through prophecy (III.2); the *clearest fountain*, offered to man together with the example of the three virtues *Charity*, *Humility*, and *Peace* (III.3) and, in front of them, the angels and saints praising God; and *Wisdom* and the definitive *victory over darkness* (III.4). The work concludes with a synthetic vision that shows again the *city/building*, the *mount*, and the *wheel* containing the *image* of Divine Love (*Caritas*).

The one great vision and the three landscapes
As we have seen, the ten visions are nothing but one great vision (see pages 24–25), which can be compared to a film sequence. It starts with the *form of a winged man*/Divine Love, in whose chest the *wheel*/firmament appears. Then we enter the wheel and see the firmament in the center: the earth and the faces of the previous figure are transformed into globes while the wings in the first vision remain unchanged and encircle the earth. A *building* appears above the earth. We enter it and see all the details. Shifting our gaze eastward from the building, we see the figure of Divine Love from the opening image, now represented as a female in the miniature.

Thus the long sequence shows three scenes. Scene one: the *form of a winged man*/Divine Love; scene two: the *wheel*/firmament and man; scene three: the *building*/city of living stones. It concludes with the image of Divine Love and that of the *building*, which marks the point of arrival of the journey. The three landscapes are unified in the vision in the second part (II.1), which illustrates the complete journey of purification from earth to heaven. This vision is thus a synthesis, in which all the elements of the visions of both the first and the third part converge, in a single vision (see pages 26–27).

Three Parts and Three Landscapes

First landscape
HUMAN FORM/Divine Love

Second landscape
WHEEL/*firmament/man/movements*

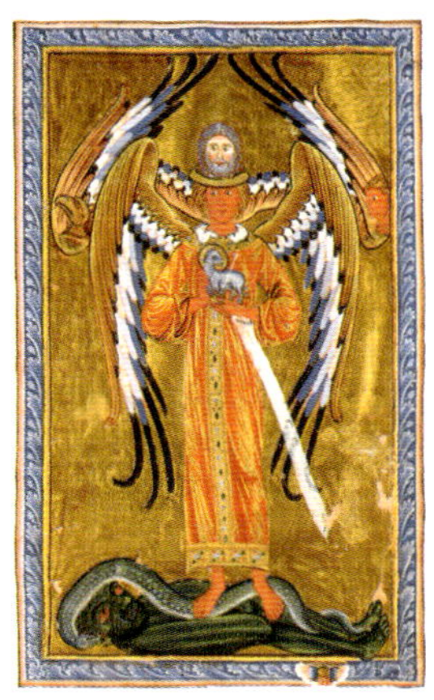

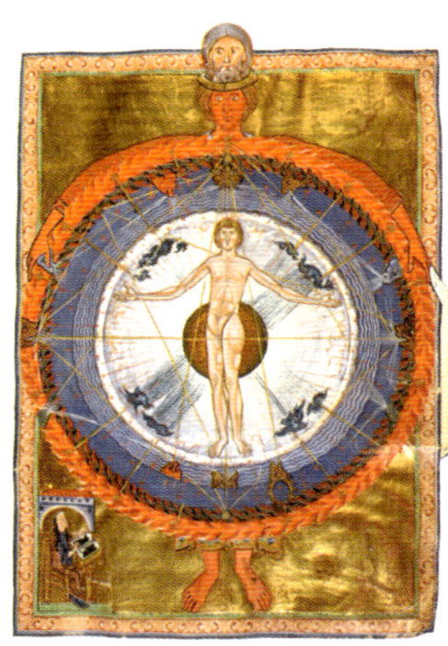

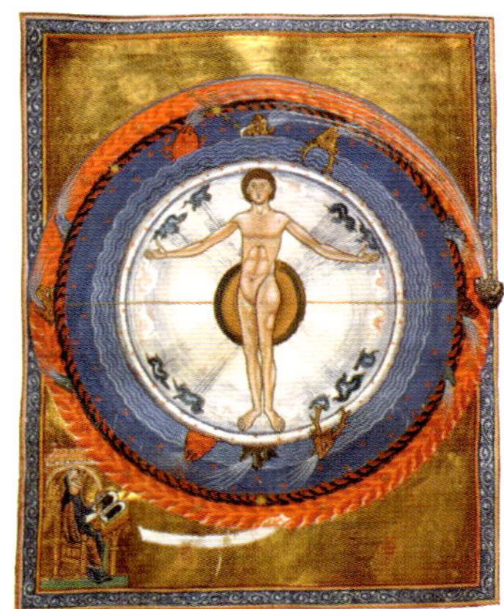

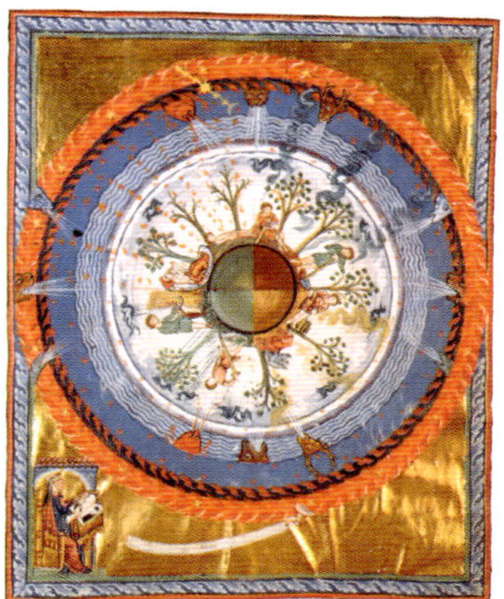

I.1
HUMAN FORM
God/Divine Love
WINGS
*Love of God
and neighbor*

I.2–I.3–I.4
WHEEL
instrument *(egg, wheel, globe)*
firmament, earth, human

The WHEEL on the breast of the HUMAN FORM
*The divinity is like a wheel, integrating,
comprising, and surrounding all things
firmament and human beings*

Third landscape
BUILDING/*divine predestination*

The three unified landscapes

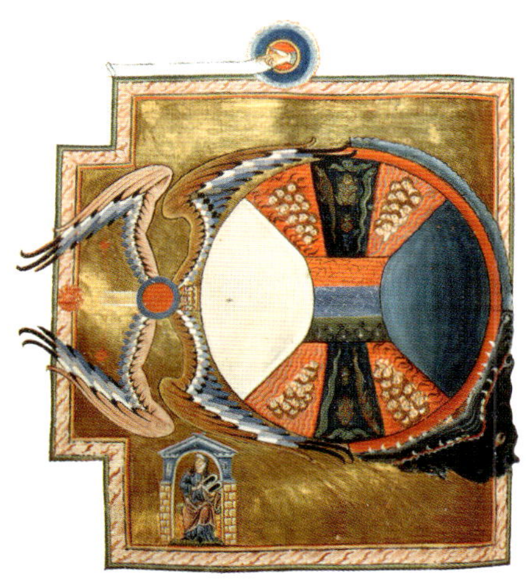

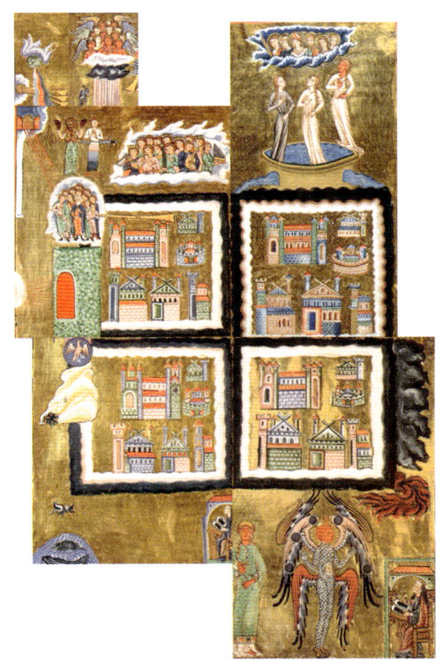

Divine Love and the building

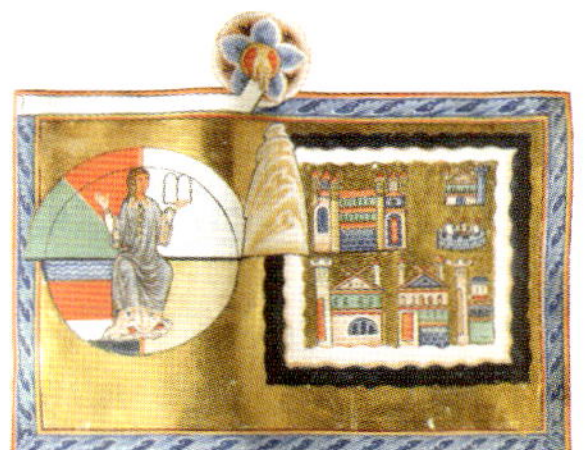

II.1
RED GLOBE
Holy Spirit
WAY
Virginity
STAR
Son of God
RED AND SAPPHIRE GLOBE
Divine Love and justice
WINGS
God's protection

BUILDING
God and the journey of humankind

ROUND EARTH
*The five human senses, the path of the soul,
the places of humans, the places of punishment*

III.1
MOUNTAIN and MIRROR
*God and divine foreknowledge
Order and justice
The angels*

III.2
DOOR
*God's will
The prophecy, the law, circumcision
The believers*

III.3
FOUNTAIN and THE THREE IMAGES
*The Spirit of God
Divine Love, Humility, and Peace
The saints*

III.4
TWO IMAGES
Wisdom and God and Victory over darkness

III.5
DIVINE LOVE, WHEEL, MIRROR,
MOUNTAIN, BUILDING

WHEEL
The power of God
LINE
The will of God
IMAGE
*Divine Love united with God
in peace gazes at the*
CRYSTAL TABLET
Divine foreknowledge

One Great Vision

WHEEL

DIVINE LOVE

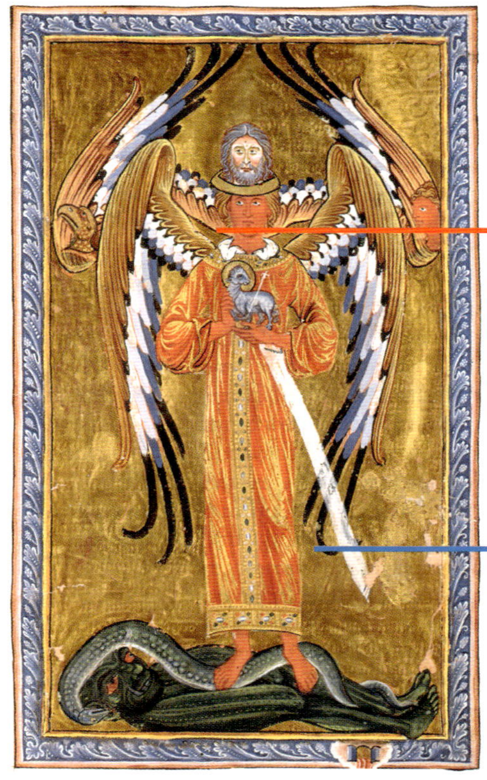

WINGS

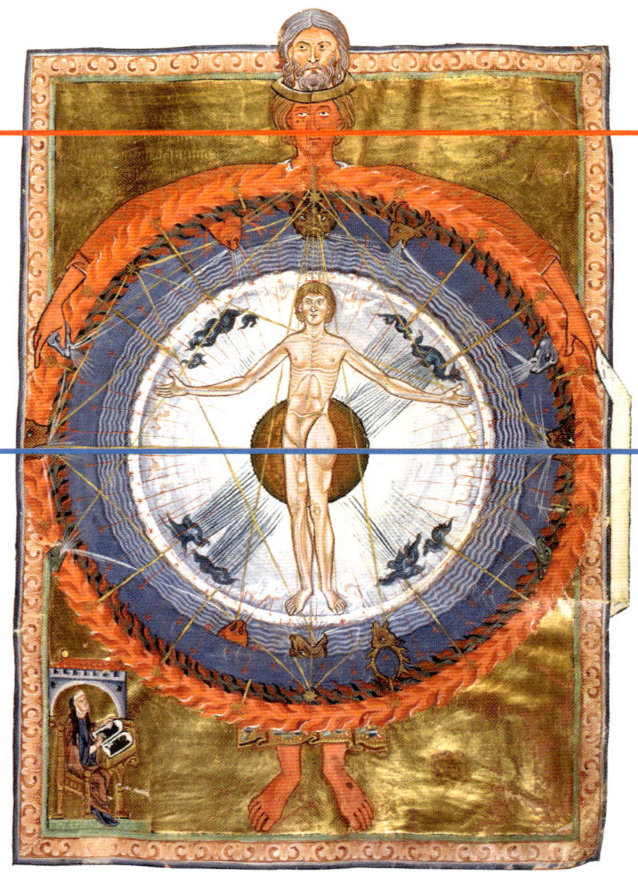

DIVINE LOVE

HUMAN FORM/*God/Divine Love*
The faces coincide with the elements
of vision II.1, in particular with the
RED GLOBE, the WAY, and the STAR

The RED GLOBE/*Divine Love/Justice*
coincides with the image of DIVINE LOVE
of the final vision in the third part, III.5

WINGS

WINGS/*the love of God and neighbor*
coincide with the vision in II.1
WINGS/*God's protection*

WHEEL

The WHEEL/God/*firmament and earth*
of the three visions in the first part, I.2, I.3, I.4,
coincides with the circumference of the earth in vision II.1
ROUND EARTH/*the form of the world*

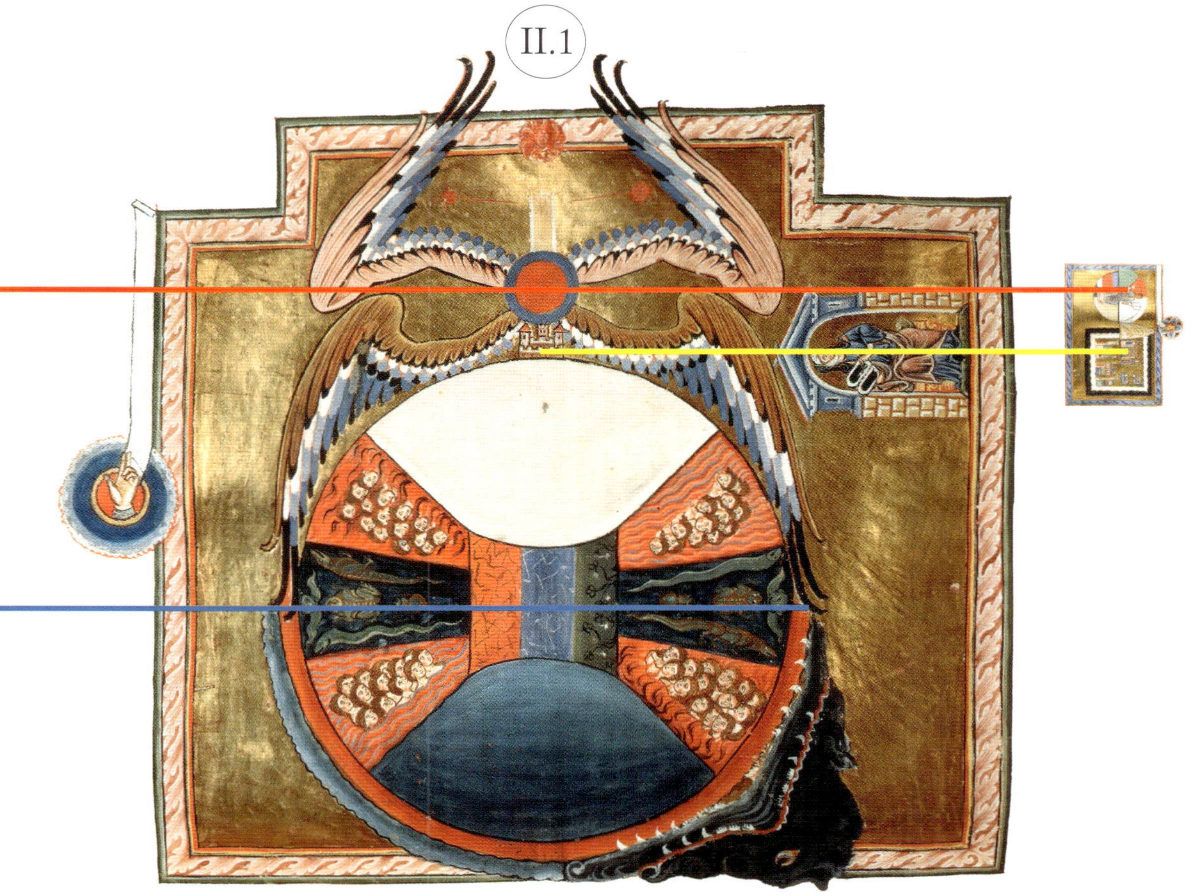

BUILDING

BUILDING

The BUILDING/*divine predestination*
of the five visions in part III
coincides with the vision in II.1
BUILDING/*living stones*

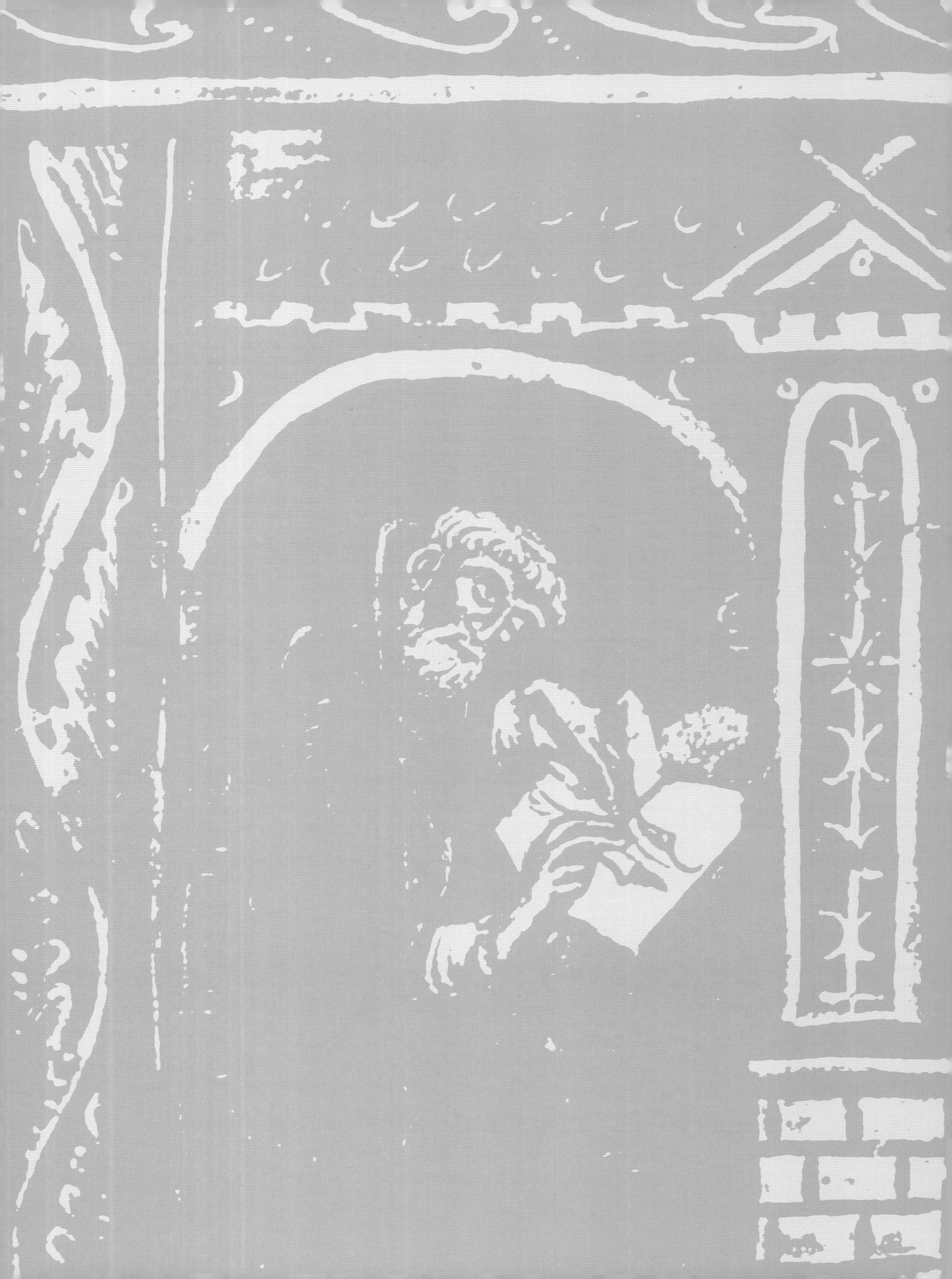

CHAPTER III

Grammar

Images and Words

Hildegard sensed that she had to become a *magistra* to reveal the message in her visions as she was commanded, since it was the only way she could lead the reader to see, listen to, and know the prophecy for which she was the mouthpiece.

From her very first work *Scivias*, she transmits the message in a clear and orderly style and form of writing that is maintained in all three prophetic works.[1]

In order to convey the unity of the vision also through form, her account is based on a solid narrative structure and a precise language of images and words. Thus we have:

• an architectural structure with a clear and orderly *organization of the work* and a balanced division of the parts;

• a format defined through the *description of each individual vision*: title, list of chapters, description of what Hildegard saw in the vision, explanation of the words spoken by the *Lux vivens* that sheds light on the meaning of the vision, and references to biblical passages that permit the introduction of relevant themes;

• the identification of *visual elements* that recur in the various visions;

• a reference *language* which, defined through a sapiential glossary,[2] precisely renders the recurrent visual elements.

This enables the traveler/reader to orient himself in the work and to gradually master the divine language through which the vision was communicated, whose grammar is imparted by Hildegard.

[1] The reader can appreciate the structural consistency of all three works and the language, but reflection on the images must temporarily stop here because, as we have seen, in the *LDO* we are not dealing with original miniatures (for this aspect, see following chapters).

[2] For a first analysis of the sapiential glossary used by Hildegard and a detailed description of the architecture of the visions, see *Hildegard von Bingen. A Journey into the Images*, Skira, Milan 2019, 36–38.

Plates

A Guide for the Reader

The plates that follow present the ten miniatures that illustrate the ten visions arranged in the same order followed in Manuscript 1942 in Lucca. A double page spread is devoted to each miniature.

The right-hand page bears a facsimile of the illuminated page, which, though reduced to 75 percent of the original size, respects the proportional balance between the ten miniatures.

The left-hand page is structured as follows (from the top down):

• the *numerical title* of the vision;

• a *descriptive title* added by us to facilitate identification, but which is not present in the manuscript;

• a *Bible quote* used by Hildegard or a significant passage from the Hildegardian text;

• a *brief summary of the vision* providing a synthetic, easily understandable image of it for the reader approaching the *LDO* for the first time. The words highlighted in small capitals are direct quotes from Hildegard's text.

Each corresponds to an element in the legend below, so that it can rapidly be identified in the miniature;

• the symbolic elements of the vision that are present in other miniatures, listed in the *notes*;

• a *reproduction* of the miniature in a smaller format;

• a *legend* referencing with a number all the elements described in the vision and present in the miniature. First comes the keyword contained in the description of the image, followed by its corresponding symbolic meaning; for example, LAMB and the meekness of faith (I.1).

At the bottom of the page a series of numbers indicates:

• the *position of the vision* (e.g. Part I.1);

• the *number of the vision* in a general count from 1 to 10 without taking into account the division of the visions into three parts (e.g. vision II.2 corresponds here to no. 5);

• the *number of chapters* of the vision;

• the *position on the pages* of the manuscript (e.g. Fol. c. 1v).

Prologue

And it happened in the sixth year after the wonderful and true visions, on which I had labored for five years, when a true vision of the unfailing light had shown to me, a human being, the diversity of various morals, of which I had been quite ignorant—that was the first year and the beginning of the present visions. When I was sixty-five years old, I saw a vision of such mystery and power that I trembled through and through and then fell ill because of the weakness of my body. […]
In the 1163d year of the Lord's Incarnation […].
There happened a voice from heaven, saying to me: "[…] Commit to fixed writing these things that you see with the inner eyes and perceive with the inner

ears of the soul, to be useful for humankind […]. Write them indeed not according to your own heart, but according to my testimony, I who am life without beginning and end. You did not invent them, nor did any other human consider them in advance; rather, they were foreordained by me before the beginning of the world. For as I foreknew humankind before ever they were created, so too I foresaw those things that would be necessary for their existence." Therefore, I, a POOR *and feeble* FORM[1] *[1] worn down by many infirmities, have at last turned my trembling hands to writing. This is witnessed by that person [*MAN, 2*] whom I had sought and found in secret, as I have related in my previous visions; it is also witnessed by*

that GIRL *[3] of whom I made mention in my most recent visions. As I have done this, I have looked up to the true and living light to see what I ought to write. For everything I have written from the beginning of my visions or come to know since while keeping watch upon the heavenly mysteries in body and mind, I saw with the inner eyes of my spirit and heard with the inner ears, and not in dreams or ecstasies, just as I affirmed in my previous visions. With truth as my witness, I have not offered anything of human sentiment, but only what I perceived in the heavenly mysteries* (Prologue, 29–31).

[1] Form: Divine Love (I.1); wings (I.1); God (III.4).

POOR FORM [1]
Hildegard

MAN [2]
(*Volmar*)

GIRL [3]

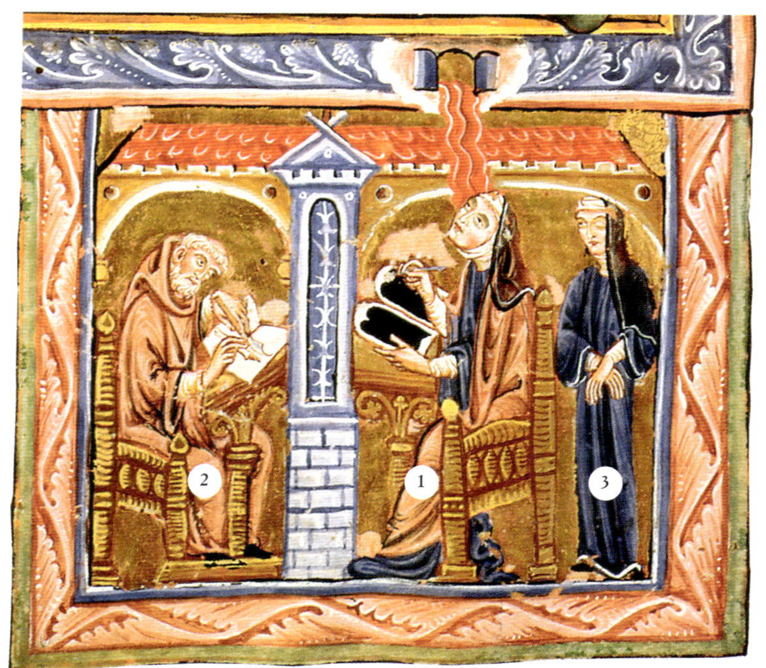

Miniature 1 (detail), Fol. c. 1v

     Grammar

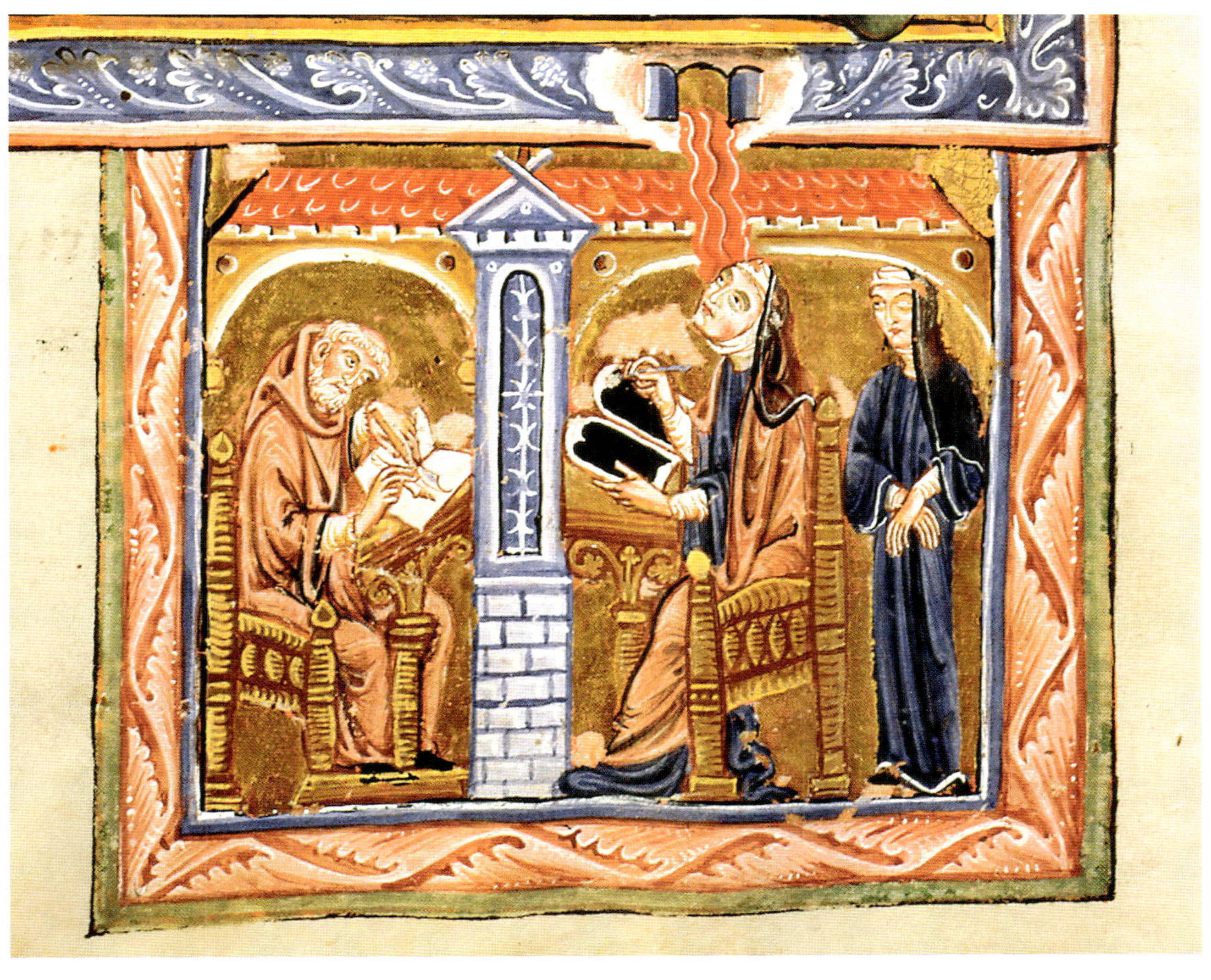

 Grammar

I.1

Divine Love

And so Love is in the wheel of eternity outside of time (I.1,13, 42).
And thus Divine Love reveals humankind. For when the Son of God put on flesh, he redeemed fallen humankind through the service of Love (I.1,3, 36).

In the middle of the *southern sky* appears an IMAGO[1] ALMOST LIKE A HUMAN FORM:[2] this is Divine Love *(Caritas)*. Its FACE [1] is of such *beauty and clarity that you could more easily look at the light of the sun*. One cannot understand its magnificence and gifts using intelligence, only through faith. *Its head* is surrounded by A GREAT CIRCLE OF GOLDEN COLOR [2]: this is the faith that rises in the dawn with exceptional brilliance. Above the circle appears another FACE AS AN OLD MAN [3]: this is the goodness of divinity bringing comfort to the faithful. His *chin and beard* touch the *crown* of the human's head: this is the zenith reached by Divine Love when the lost humans were led back to heaven through the incarnation of the Son of God. Rising up, from the sides of the image's *neck*, are two

WINGS[3] (FORM[2] OF) [4] that join together at their tips: they are the love of God and love of neighbor. In the right wing is the HEAD OF AN EAGLE [5] with *eyes of fire*: they are the spiritual humans who gaze at God with devotion, imitating the gaze of the angels. The *fulgor of the angels* is reflected in the eagle's *eyes* as if in a *mirror*. In the left wing is A HUMAN FACE [6]: it is humankind beginning to live in honesty according to human nature, not as a herd animal. With the protection of the creator and the help of humility, they will combat hostile earthly conditions. Their works will become righteous and good, following the intentions of their hearts, shining with a *splendor* like the *fulgor of the stars*. Two further WINGS [7] descend from each *shoulder* of the image to its knees: they are the righteous and the sinners, whom God bears on his shoulders and knees as humans do when carrying a burden. The image is clothed in a TUNIC[4] [8] emanating the *fulgor of the sun*, because God clad the body of his Son with Divine Love protecting him from sin. In its *hands* it holds a LAMB [9], shining like

the light of the day: it is the meekness of the faith revealed by Divine Love when the Son of God chose his martyrs, confessors, and penitents from among tax collectors and sinners, making the wicked righteous so that they might fly above the wings of the wind towards celestial harmony, as when he made Paul from Saul. The image crushes a MONSTER [10] beneath its *feet*: this is discord's injury. Horrible in its perversity, poisonous in its deception, and black in its perdition. The ancient SERPENT [11] puts its mouth to the right ear of the MONSTER [10], because it tempts the faithful through their hearing, as Satan did, and it will not cease doing so until the end of time as signified by his *tail*, which reaches the *feet*.

[1] *Imago*: human (I.2); virtue (III.1), before and after the flood (III.2); Divine Love, Humility, and Peace (III.3); Wisdom and God (III.4); Divine Love (III.5).
[2] Form: Hildegard (Prologue); God (III.4).
[3] Wings: Divine Love (II.1); dove (III.1); *imago* (III.4).
[4] Tunic: first *imago* (III.2); Wisdom and God (III.4); Divine Love (III.5).

IMAGO ALMOST LIKE A HUMAN FORM
Divine Love

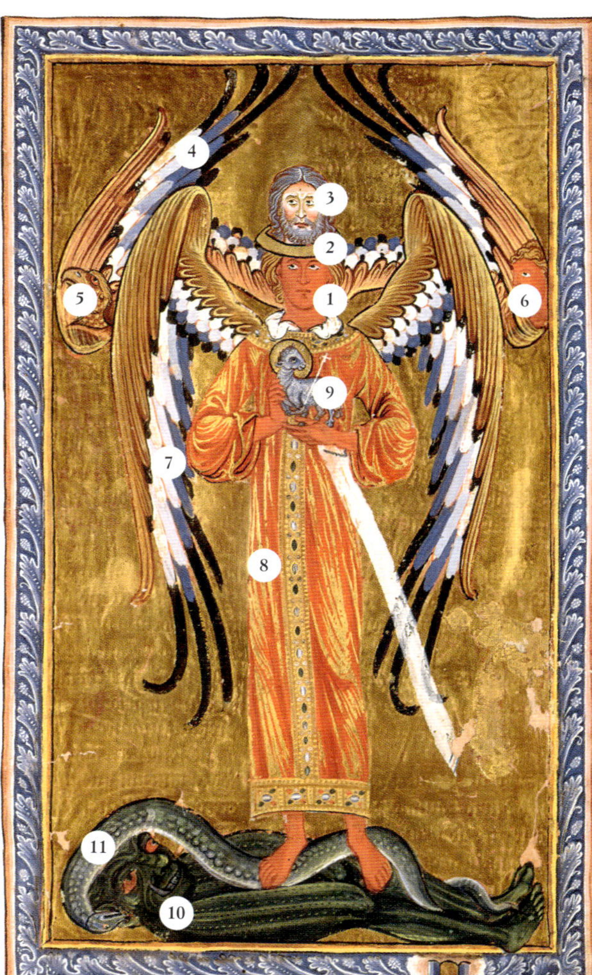

FACE [1]
the abundance of Divine Love with its gifts

A GREAT CIRCLE OF GOLDEN COLOR [2]
universal faith

FACE AS AN OLD MAN [3]
the goodness of divinity

WING (FORM OF) [4] and [5, 6]
the love of God and neighbor
   HEAD OF AN EAGLE [5]
   spiritual humans
   A HUMAN FACE [6]
   honest humans

WING (FORM OF) [7]
the righteous and the sinners

TUNIC [8]
*the Son of God clad in Divine Love
the human body*

LAMB [9]
gentleness of true faith

MONSTER [10]
discord's injury

SERPENT [11]
cunning and deceit

Part I.1 – Vision 1 – Chapters 17 – Fol. c. 1v

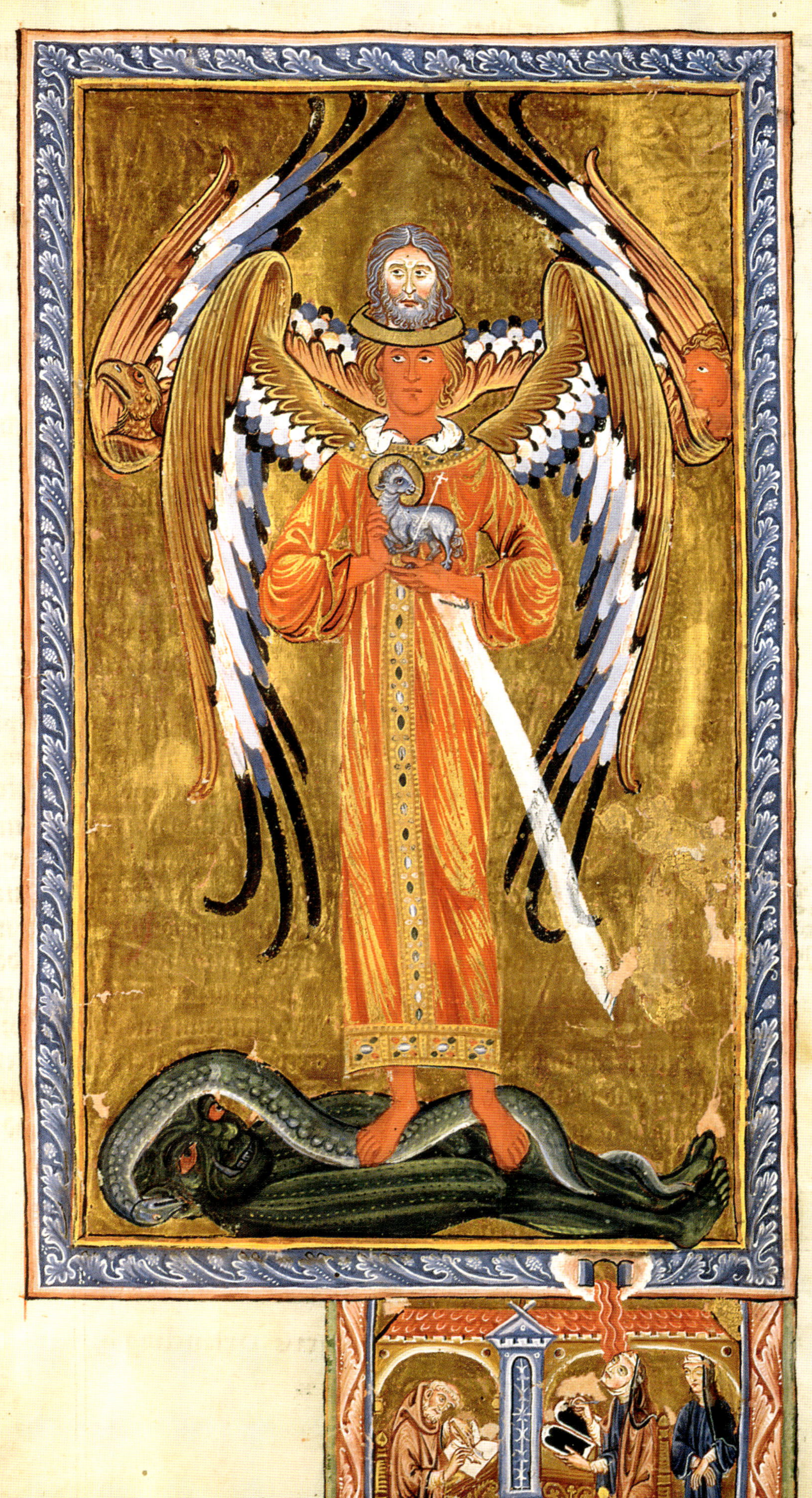

I.2

Wheel 1
A wheel appears upon the breast of God/Divine Love

Divinity is like a wheel, whole and utterly undivided, for it has neither beginning nor ending, nor can anything grasp or surround it, for it is outside of time (I.2,2, 54).

A WHEEL[1] appears upon the breast of the preceding image: it is God/Love, which contains and surrounds all things. The WHEEL has SIX CONCENTRIC CIRCLES [1–6]. The LUCID[2] FIRE [1] is the power of God, which illuminates the elements and diffuses joy among all creatures; the DARK FIRE [2] is the fire of judgement; anyone opposing God will fall into darkness. The PURE ETHER [3] is penitence for sins, enkindled in men by God's grace. The WATERY AIR [4] represents the works of the just; it is transparent and washes away unclean works. The STRONG, WHITE, LUCID[2] AIR [5] is Discretion, which prevents the waters from flooding the firmament, protecting it from the excesses of holy works. The THIN AIR [6] quickens and sustains all things that are in the world and supports the CLOUDS[3] [7–8]. Some are LOFTY AND BRIGHT [7], representing the humans who humbly follow the saints/stars and keep their minds pure; others are LOW-HANGING AND SHADOWY [8], representing the humans who yield to their bodily needs, clouding their minds and bringing rains, or tears. The LINE[4] [9] is the path of the sun, the faithful person opposing iniquity. The GLOBE[5] [10] in the centre is the earth, tempered by the elements just as an active life, in the midst of right desires, is kept steady by devotion, discernment, and discretion. The two LUMINARIES, the SUN [12], and the MOON [13], are the knowledge of good and evil, and make the firmament steady. Humans, imitating them, become stable and splendid. In the wheel, the *IMAGO*[6] OF A MAN [11] touches the elements at four points where there are four animal heads. They represent the principal winds blowing their breaths, the virtues. They have the characteristics of animals and derive their strength from the elements in which they are situated: the LEOPARD [14], in *pure ether*, is the fear of God; the WOLF [15], in *watery air*, stands for hellish punishments; the LION [16], in *lucid fire*, is God's judgment; the BEAR [17], in the *dark fire*, represents physical suffering and anguish. Beside them are the collateral winds: the CRAB [18], signifying Trust; the STAG [19], meaning Faith; the LAMB [20], Patience; and the SERPENT [21], Prudence. Above them are the SEVEN PLANETS [22], which represent the seven gifts of the Spirit. The LUCID FIRE [1] contains SIXTEEN FIXED STARS[7] [23], Doctors who show how the law and their rays instil the beatitudes. Other STARS[7] IN THE ETHER [24] and IN THE THIN AIR [25] are repentance and discernment. The two TONGUES [26–27] coming forth from the clouds on the RIGHT [27] and on the LEFT [26] represent the Old and the New Testaments. Lastly, the mouth of Divine Love brings forth a LIGHT BRIGHTER THAN THE DAY in the form of threads [28]: this is the supreme divine order that shines on all things and contains them all.

[1] Wheel: God/firmament (I.3–4); power of God (III.5).
[2] Lucid: splendor (III.2); divine foreknowledge (III.5).
[3] Clouds: blessed and damned (I.4 and III.1); prophets (III.2); saints (III.3).
[4] Line: fullness and perfection of God (III.5).
[5] Globe: zeal of God (II.1); Holy Spirit (II.1).
[6] *Imago*: Divine Love (I.1); virtue (III.1), before and after the flood (III.2); Divine Love, Humility, and Peace (III.3); Wisdom and God (III.4); Love (III.5).
[7] Stars: angels (II.1); prophets (III.2).

SIX CIRCLES [1–6]
  LUCID FIRE [1]
    The Power of God
  DARK FIRE [2]
    judgment and hellish fire
  PURE ETHER [3]
    the penitence of sinners
  WATERY AIR [4]
    works of the just
  STRONG, WHITE, LUCID AIR [5]
    Discretion
  THIN AIR [6]
    quickens and sustains all things that are in the world

CLOUDS [7–8]
  LOFTY AND BRIGHT [7]
    humble humans, pure minds
  LOW-HANGING AND SHADOWY [8]
    humans who follow their bodily needs, clouded minds

LINE [9]
the path of the sun

GLOBE [10]
earth

IMAGO OF A MAN [11]
human being

LUMINARIES, SUN [12], AND MOON [13]
knowledge of good and evil

WHEEL
the Divinity contains and exceeds all things

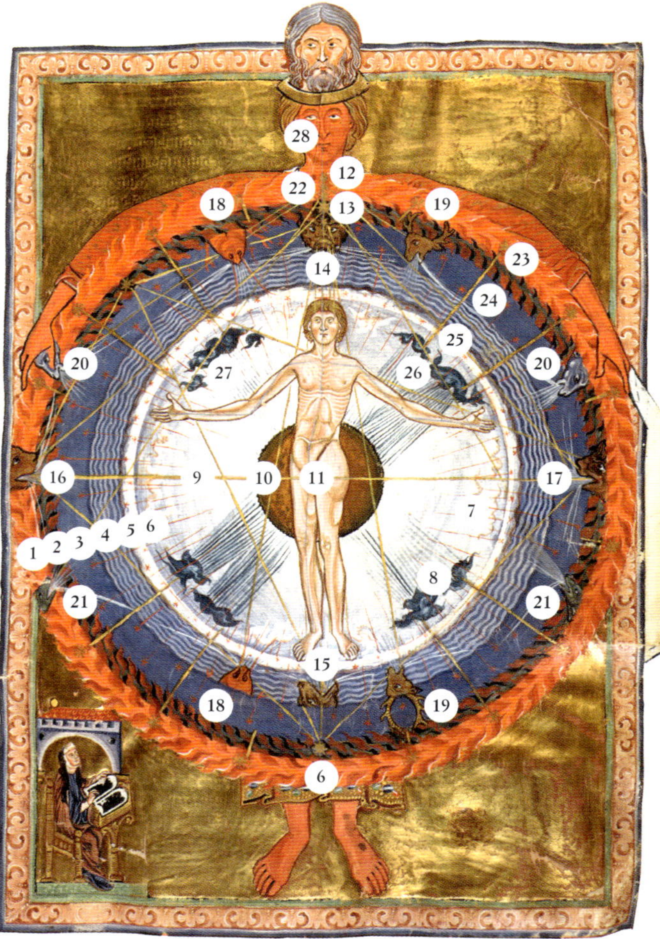

Part I.2 – Vision 2 – Chapters 47 – Fol. c. 9r

WINDS [14–17]
  LEOPARD [14]
    Fear of God
  WOLF [15]
    fear of hellish punishments
  LION [16]
    fear of God's judgment
  BEAR [17]
    fear of physical suffering
COLLATERAL WINDS [18–21]
  CRAB [18]
    Trust
  STAG [19]
    Faith
  LAMB [20]
    Patience
  SERPENT [21]
    Prudence

SEVEN PLANETS [22]
seven gifts of the Spirit

SIXTEEN FIXED STARS [23]
Doctors

STARS IN THE ETHER [24]
penitence

STARS IN THE THIN AIR [25]
discernment

TONGUES FROM THE CLOUDS [26–27]
  LEFT [26]
    body and spirit
  RIGHT [27]
    love of God and of neighbor

LIGHT BRIGHTER THAN THE DAY [28]
supreme divine order

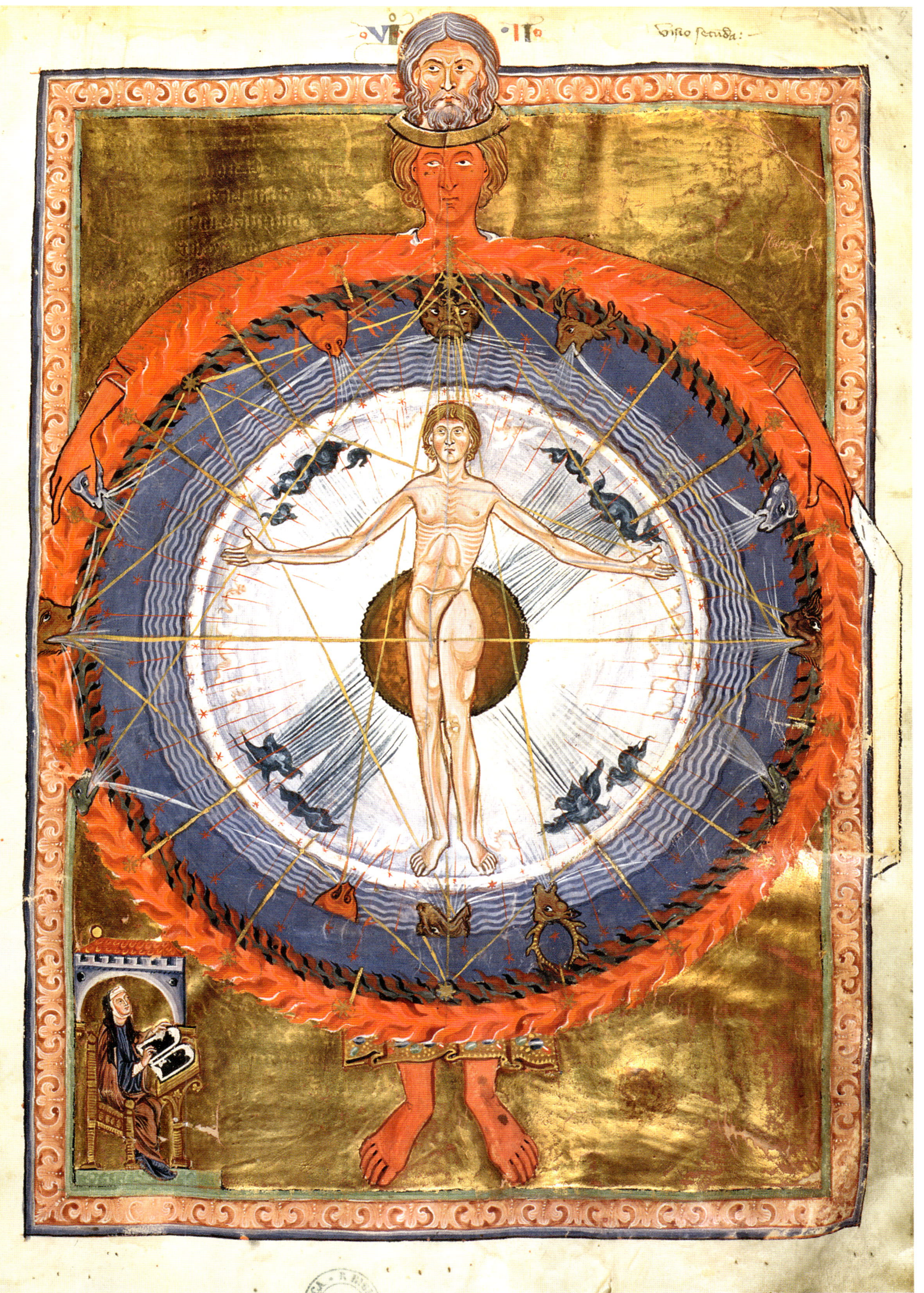

libro secundo

Wheel 2
The movements of the firmament and of humans

When a person whose natural quality coincides with that breeze, inhales and exhales that air, it is transformed within him so that he takes it up into his spirit and transmits it to the inner parts of his body. So the humors that are in him are also transformed and often introduce into him either infirmity or health (I.3,1, 119).

The WHEEL[1] is in endless movement, influencing the movement of the soul as well as the human body. The winds/virtues propel the wheel through five movements. The first movement is caused by the EAST WIND [1]—the Fear of God—by the SOUTH WIND [3]—the fear of God's judgment—and by their collateral winds. They make the firmament revolve FROM EAST TO WEST [A] and, with the power of their breath, they cause men to carry out good works (east), thereby overcoming the temptations of the flesh (west). The second movement is caused by the WEST WIND [2]—the fear of hellish punishments—and by the NORTH WIND [4]—the fear of physical suffering—and by their collateral winds. They support and drive humans, sending them from WEST TO EAST [B], terrorizing them with hellish punishments, with bodily tribulations, and shaking them with fear. In fact, when instilled with courage, humans failing to carry out good works because of weariness and fatigue (west) may find the strength to return to justice (east). The third movement is caused by the SOUTH WIND [3]—the fear of God's judgment—and by its collateral winds. It supports the firmament and raises the spirit of humans with faith, causing them to fight against temptation until they conquer lust. It pushes the firmament UPWARDS, FROM SOUTH TO NORTH [C] and lifts humans up in goodness and causes them to reach a good end. In the fourth movement, the NORTH WIND [4]—the fear of physical suffering—and its collateral winds cause humans who are overcome by tiredness and laziness to reach the depths of their spirit. It then pushes them DOWNWARDS, FROM NORTH TO SOUTH [D], suggesting that they place a limit on penitence, raising them up again and leading them back to the original strength of virtue. The fifth movement is preceded by the appearance of a CIRCLE [6], which indicates the fullness of the sanctity protecting humankind. It is then that the WIND PROCEEDING FROM THE WEST [5], and moving the SEVEN PLANETS [7]—the gifts of the Spirit—causes them to shake humans, whenever they slumber in weariness, giving them the courage to awake to justice and return to the beginning, proceeding FROM WEST TO EAST [E]. When the different qualities of the winds/virtues and of the air meet, the humors present in humans become agitated and transform, assuming their qualities and causing their bodies to either fall sick or return to health. The movements of the humors in their bodies and their influences upon their organs, described in the vision, are not present in the codex miniature (there is a proposed reconstruction on pages 90–91).

[1] Wheel: God/firmament (I.2, I.4); power of God (III.5).

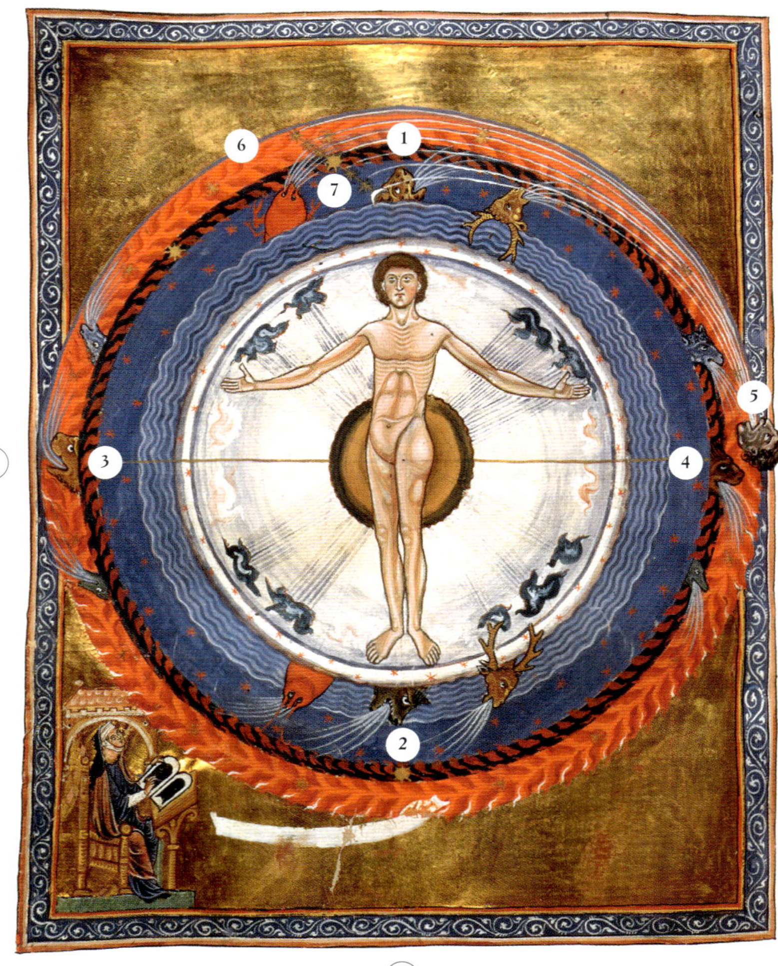

Part I.3 – Vision 3 – Chapters 19 – Fol. c. 28v

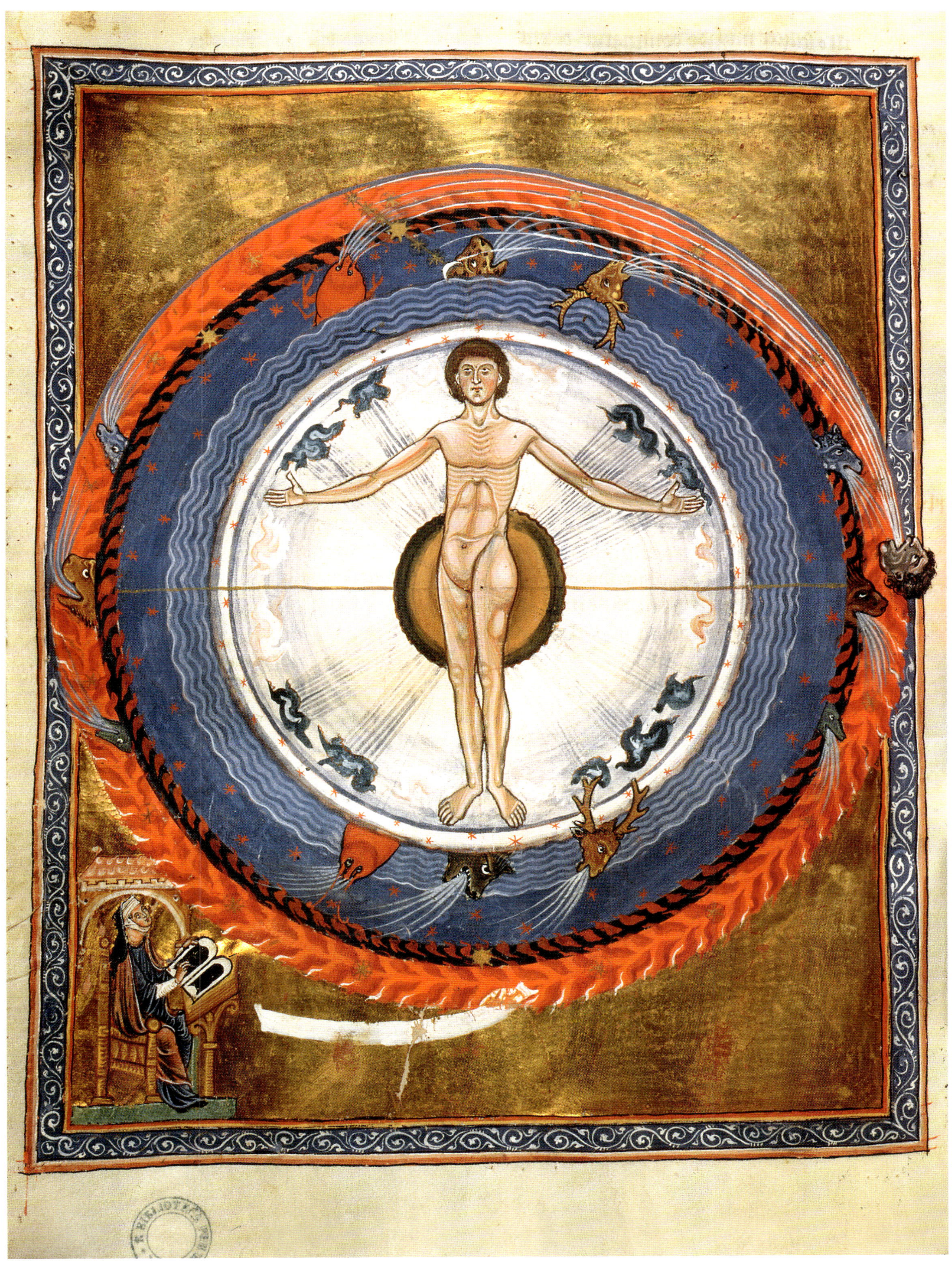

     Grammar

I.4

Wheel 3
The firmament and its influences upon the body and soul of humans
The measurements and similarities between firmament and humans

For God strengthened the firmament with fire lest it dissolve; he lightened it with the ether so that it could move; he flooded it with the waters lest it dry up; he illumined it with the stars so that it could shine; and he sustains it with the winds to keep up its course unceasingly (I.4,3, 132).
For when soul and body agree in rightness, they obtain with one joy the rewards of heaven (I.4,2, 132).

The fourth vision begins with the voice of the heavens explaining that each human being, the firmament, and the earth have the same density. The actions of God in the firmament therefore become the actions of God upon humans. Sometimes he agitates the elements of the *wheel*[1]/firmament to create sparks, fog, clouds, and rain that inflict wounds upon humans, upon the animals and fruits of the earth so that humankind might again head in the right direction. At the same time, the elements of the ether and of the watery air ensure that these actions are not excessive. God's protection is strong but also gentle. The LUCID FIRE causes SPARK-LIKE SCALES (*SQUA-MAS*) [1] to descend upon the earth: this is vengeance for the depraved actions of humankind. The DARK FIRE forms a FOG[2] [2] that descends upon the earth, withering its viridity and drying up the humidity of the fields: this is vengeance against sinners and carnal desires. Thanks to its purity, PURE ETHER [3] can resist both the scales and the mist, ensuring that they do not afflict creatures excessively: this is the pure penitence that softens the punishment and vengeance of God. The STRONG, WHITE, LUCID AIR forms a FOG[2] [4] that extends down towards the earth, causing plagues: this is God, using discretion to fight against works lacking discernment. The WATERY AIR [5] resists the FOG [4], ensuring that it does not inflict excessive damage, tempering its effects through the examples of the just and their works, revealing the importance of moderation. The THIN AIR produces HUMIDITY [6], causing viridity and making fruits grow. This air is like a shield protecting man from wounds, taking the form of SNOW [6.1] or DEW [6.2] purifying from filth and stench. To ensure that it does not have an excess of RAIN [7.1], the humidity of the thin air supports the CLOUDS [7] that anchor the CANDID[3] CLOUD[4] [8]. This cloud represents the humans who successfully accomplish both earthly and heavenly matters. The cloud curves up like a bow, revealing how humans sometimes perceive the frailty of the flesh. The vision concludes with the description of the physical body of humans, comparing its parts to the firmament and the movements of the soul (not depicted in the miniature, there is a proposed reconstruction on page 92 and ff.).

[1] Wheel: God/firmament (I.2 and I.4); power of God (III.5).
[2] Fog: wicked suggestions (III.1).
[3] Candid: the Son of God (II.1); blessed spirits (III.1); as far as the navel (III.2); fulgor and garment (III.3); mercy (III.5).
[4] Cloud: men (I.2); blessed and damned (III.1); prophets (III.2); saints (III.3).

SPARK-LIKE SCALES (*SQUAMAS*) [1]
God inflicts his vengeance upon the depraved actions of humans

FOG FROM THE DARK FIRE [2]
vengeance upon sinners and upon carnal desires (inundation)

PURE ETHER [3]
pure penitence that softens God's punishment and vengeance

FOG FROM THE STRONG, WHITE, AND LUCID AIR [4]
against works lacking discernment, through discretion (pestilence)

WATERY AIR [5]
vengeance proceeding from discernment wounds everything lacking in moderation

HUMIDITY FROM THE THIN AIR [6]
a shield defending a man from blows, purifying from filth and stench
    SNOW [1]
    DEW [2]

CLOUDS [7]
humans producing the fruits of good works with the right desire
    RAIN [1]

CANDID CLOUD [8]
humans who successfully accomplish both earthly and heavenly matters

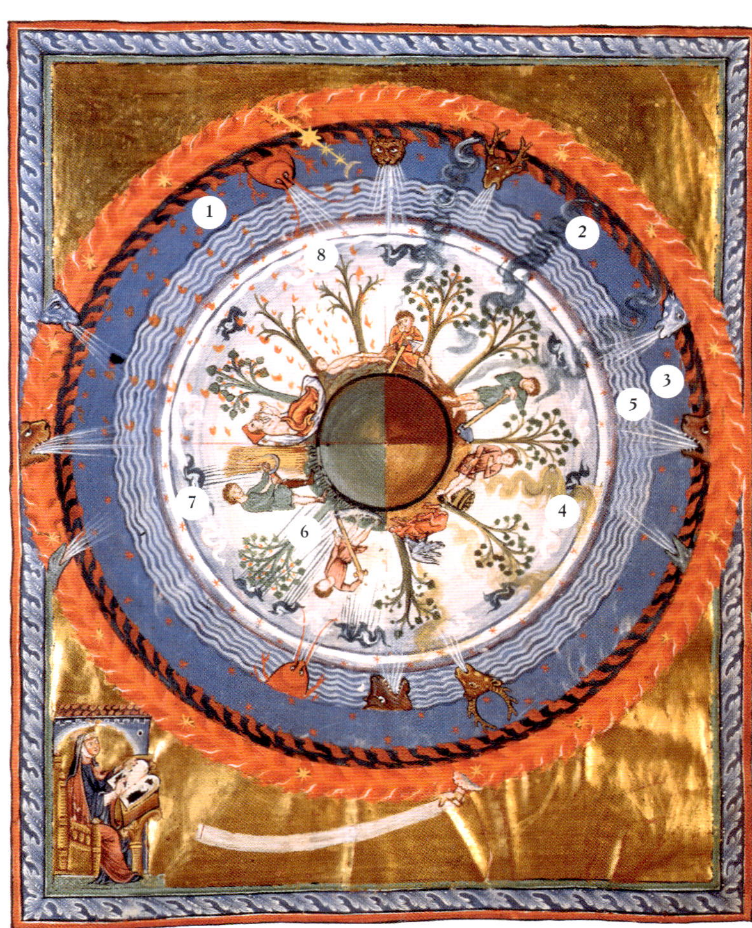

Part I.4 – Vision 4 – Chapters 105 – Fol. c. 38r

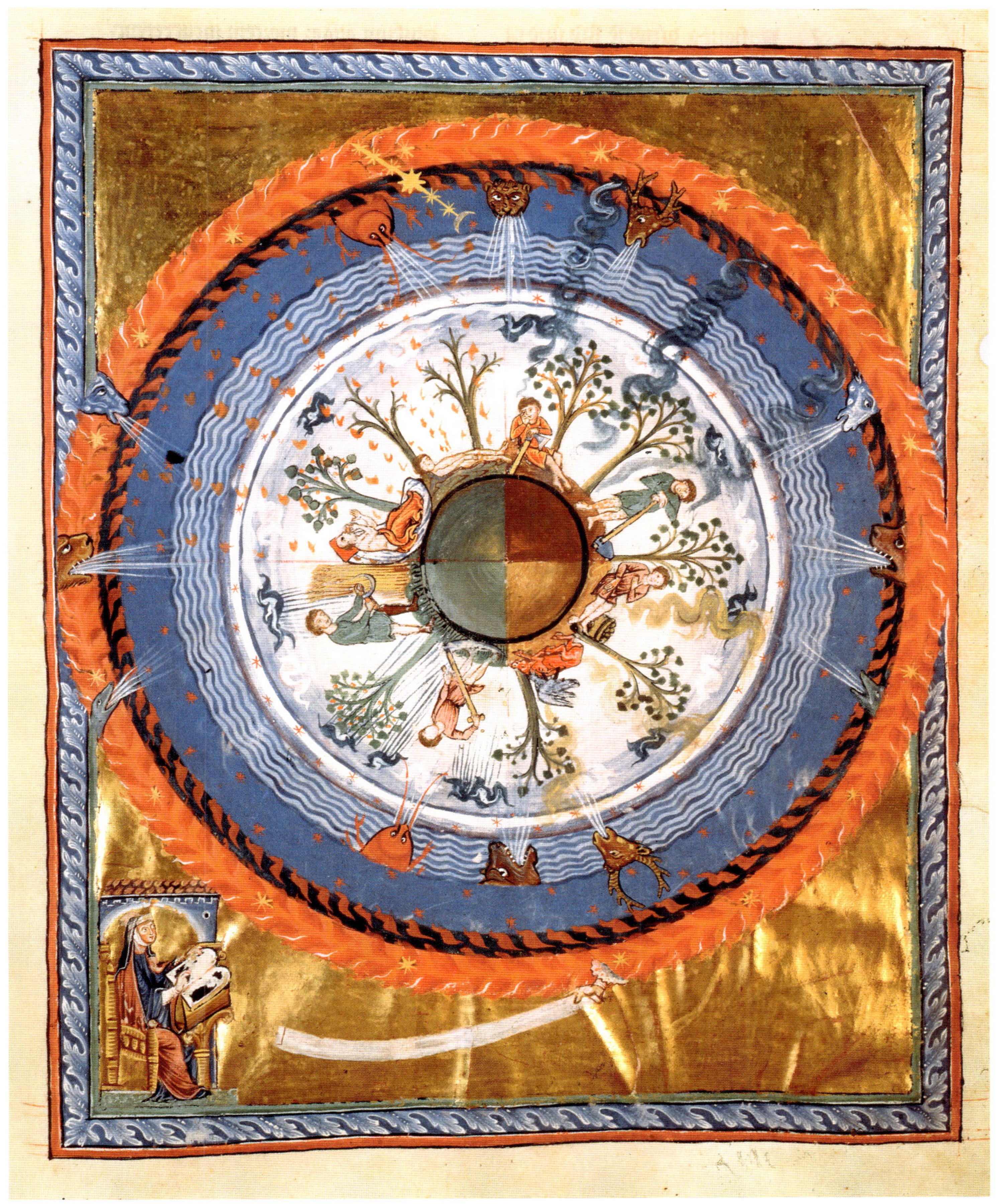

Grammar

The Round Earth, the Building, the Way, the Star, and the Globes
The five senses, the influence of the winds upon the earth and upon humankind, the places of punishment
The judgment, Divine Love, the protection of God, the path to salvation, and the gifts of the Holy Spirit

In my Father's house there are many dwellings (II.1,40, 325; Jn 14:2).

This complex vision reveals the *way* of purification which follows in the footsteps of Christ to lead humans from earth to heaven. The ROUND EARTH is divided into FIVE PARTS: they are the five human senses and the five places of punishment where the sinning souls are gathered together. The EASTERN PART [1], which is *light* in color, grants useful viridity. It is like human *sight* which ensures the health of their bodies and souls whenever they look at its origin. It welcomes the *blessed souls*. The WESTERN PART [2], which is *dark* in color, grants humidity. It is like human *hearing*, which can bring humans either the soul's salvation or its despair. It holds humans who commit *minor sins*. The SOUTHERN PART [3] grants heat tempered by the cool breeze of the winds. It represents *smell* and contains *serious sins*. The NORTHERN PART [4] brings the cold wind of the North and heat from the east. It is the *taste* that allows us to distinguish

cold and hot things. It contains the souls who have to purify themselves because they have preferred the concupiscence of the flesh, that is, *harsh sins*, to the taste for true life. IN THE MIDDLE [5] lies the part that is influenced by all of the others. This is *touch*. It holds the *unbelievers* in the two uninhabitable parts and the *faithful* in the temperate part. Towards the east, there is a RED GLOBE[1] [6] that is God's zeal, surrounded by a CIRCLE OF SAPPHIRE COLOR [7], the justice of Divine Love. Extending from the GLOBE [6] are two pairs of WINGS[2] [8 and 9]; they are the divine protection that guards humans, embraces all things that seek to rise out of love for it [8] and protects those who exist on the earth [9]. The wings curve downwards until they reach the midpoint of the earth where a RED CIRCLE [10] stretches out. This is the fire of the zeal of God, when he passes a just judgement and takes vengeance to the right extent. Rising from the surface of the earth is a BUILDING [11]; it is the *city*[3] constructed with living stones, which are the blessed souls praising God. Above the RED GLOBE [6] is

a WAY [12], where *virginity* flourishes; it is illuminated by a CANDID[4] STAR[5] [13], the Son of God, who is imitated by all those traveling along the path. At the highest point, a FIERY GLOBE [14], the Holy Spirit, grants its gifts to the elect and produces RAYS OF STARS [15], angels guarding *virginity*. Lying beyond the earth is DARKNESS[6] [16], where the ancient enemy inflicts torments upon the souls consigned to oblivion. Alongside lies more darkness, taking the form of a HORRIBLE MOUTH [17], the mouth of hell, with beside it yet another DEVOURING MOUTH [18]. They are places of punishment where there is no consolation. The darkness is infinite but cannot be seen by humans as long as they still live.

[1] Globe: earth (I.2).
[2] Wings: Divine Love (I.1); dove (III.1); *imago* (III.4).
[3] City: divine predestination (III.1–5).
[4] Candid: men (I.4); blessed spirits (III.1); as far as the navel (III.2); brilliance and garment (III.3); mercy (III.5).
[5] Star: Doctors and penitence and discernment (I.2); prophets (III.2).
[6] Darkness: places of punishment (III.4).

FIVE PARTS

EAST [1]
sight
fecund viridity
health of body and soul
blessed souls

WEST [2]
hearing
humidity
the soul's salvation or despair
minor sins

SOUTH [3]
smell
heat tempered by the cool breeze of the winds
the fragrance of heaven
grave sins
    murderers, rapists, thieves [1]
    purified souls [2]
    epidemics [3]

NORTH [4]
taste
the cold of the North and the heat of the East
the different flavors and the sweetness of heavenly things
harsh sins
    unbelievers repenting at the moment of death [1]
    foul adulterers, gluttons, drunkards [2]
    epidemics [3]

IN THE MIDDLE [5]
touch
    strengthened and supported by the other parts
    faithful [1]
    unbelievers against the word of God [2]
    unbelievers [3]

ROUND EARTH

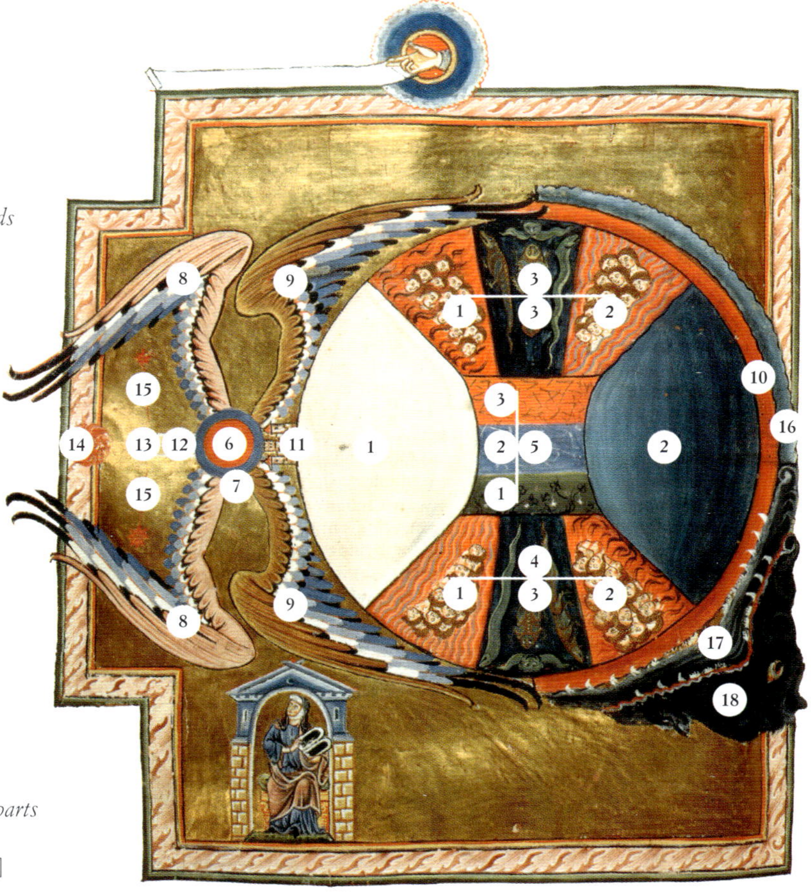

RED GLOBE [6]
zeal of God

CIRCLE OF SAPPHIRE COLOR [7]
justice of Divine Love

WINGS [8, 9]
divine protection
    the men and creatures who tend upwards [8]
    the things that exist on the earth [9]

RED CIRCLE [10]
fire of God's zeal

BUILDING [11]
city of living stones, the blessed souls praising God

WAY [12]
way where virginity flourishes

CANDID STAR [13]
Son of God

FIERY GLOBE [14]
Holy Spirit

RAYS OF STARS [15]
the ways of virginity are surrounded and defended by angels on all sides

DARKNESS [16]
space lying beyond the world where the ancient enemy dwells

HORRIBLE MOUTH [17]
mouth of hell

DEVOURING MOUTH [18]
infernal places

Part II.1 – Vision 5 – Chapters 49 – Fol. c. 88v

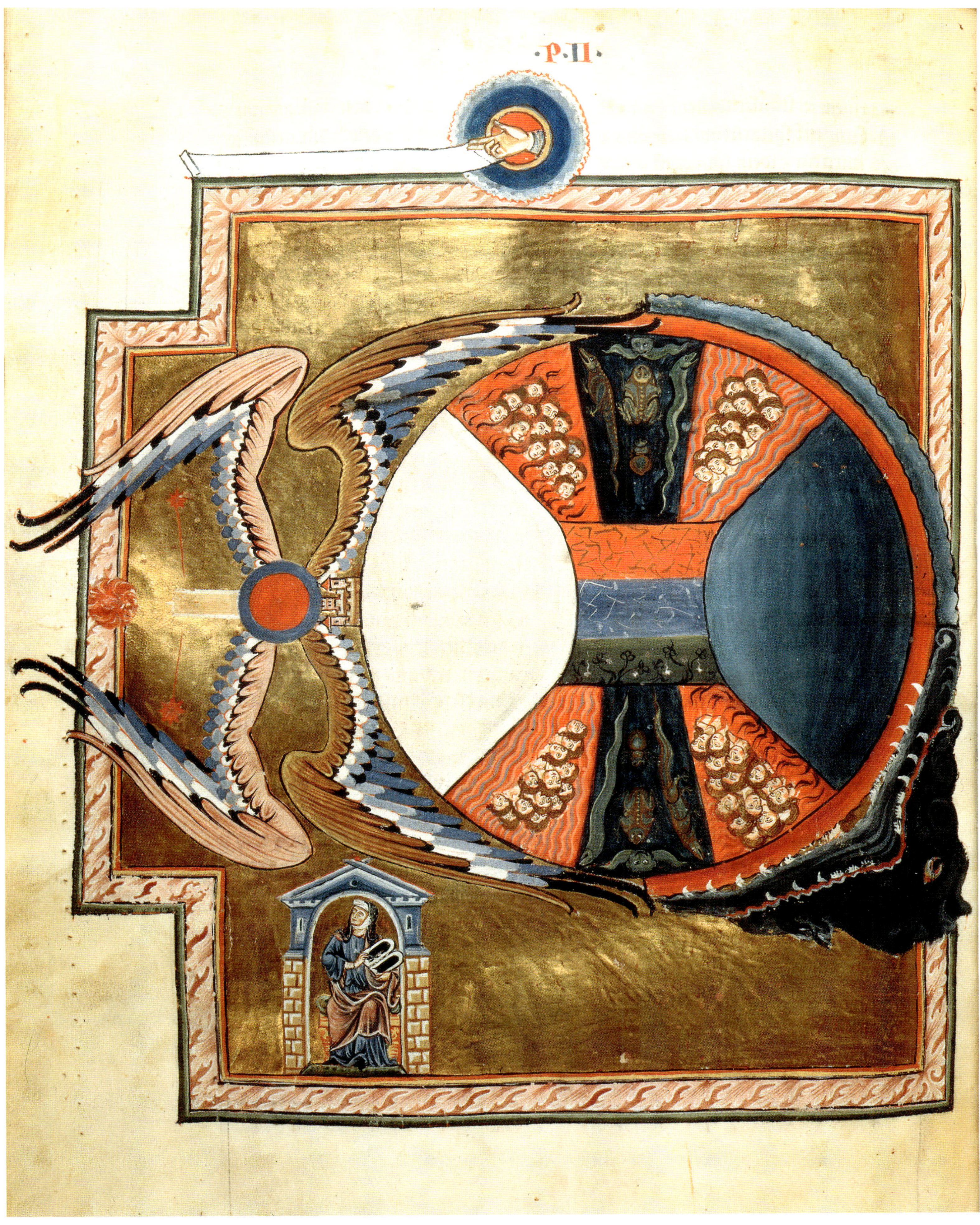

·P·II·

III.1

The City, the Mountain, and the Mirror
Divine foreknowledge, predestination, and the divine order

God knows all things in his foreknowledge, for before creation came into existence in its forms, he foreknew them; and from him nothing is hid that comes forth from the beginning of the world to its ending. (III.1,2, 350). *So too the soul remembers that it was created by God and looks to him in faith, as in a mirror one considers one's face and how it is formed* (III.1,5, 354–355).

Divine predestination takes the shape of a SQUARED IN-STRUMENT. It is a CITY[1]/BUILDING [1] surrounded by a WALL [2], the just judgment, formed by SPLENDOR[2] [2.1], the faithful, and by DARKNESS [2.2], the unfaithful. Inside, the city is adorned with MOUNTAINS AND IMAGES[3] [3], miracles and virtues by means of which God causes his works to be strong and stable. Halfway along the eastern side is a MOUNTAIN[4] [4]; it is the strength of God's justice, *great* in power, *lofty* in glory, made of *hard white stone*, harshness, and gentleness. The rock has a *form like that from which fire is belched* because it issues all his judgments in the ardor of fairness. On the summit of the mountain is the MIRROR[5] [5] of divine foreknowl-edge, whose brightness surpasses the gleam of all cre-ations. In the mirror is A DOVE WITH ITS WINGS[6]

SPREAD [6] meaning that the divine order opens out and begins to manifest itself in divine foreknowledge. It is God's will that causes every creature to come forth. The mirror emits a diffused SPLENDOR [7], God's knowl-edge, revealing marvels and miracles. In the splendor a CLOUD[7] [8] appears: above, it is CANDID[8] [8.1], the bless-ed spirits, while beneath, it is DARK [8.2], the damned spirits. Above the cloud shines a MULTITUDE OF ANGELS [9]: some, who appear *fiery*, remain still, contemplating the face of God; others, who are *luminously transparent*, move to aid human works, while, finally, those who seem like *stars* suffer for the nature that leads humans to carry out evil works. The WIND [10] is the living spirit of God whose zeal moves the angelic spirits against his enemies like *burning lamps*. It is full of *many voices* re-sounding like the roar of the sea, amplifying and trans-forming the words by means of which he judges the just into words of punishment for the damned. In the dark part of the cloud, it lights a FIRE [11], which burns *with-out a flame and without changing color*: it is the ven-geance of the blessed spirits against the betrayal of the lost angels. The wind blows, causing them to dissipate like SPIRALS OF SMOKE [12], casting them out into the

infinite darkness, causing them to sink in it, and annihi-lating the rebellion of the wicked. Sometimes a FOG[9] [13] rises from the darkness and spills out over the earth: it represents wicked suggestions. The vision con-cludes with Hildegard hearing HEAVENLY TRUM-PETS [14] and a voice recalling that St. Michael an-nounced the judgement of God with a blare of trum-pets. Lastly, the CANDID CLOUD emits rays more splendid than before because they realized that *never again would there be such a battle in heaven* (III.1,6, 355).

[1] City: divine predestination (II.1, III.2–5).
[2] Splendor: order (III.2); shines upon the prophets (III.2).
[3] *Imago:* Divine Love (I.1); virtue before and after the flood (III.2); Divine Love, Humility, and Peace (III.3); Knowledge and God (III.4); Divine Love (III.5).
[4] Mountain: God (III.2); mountain (III.5).
[5] Mirror: five luminaries (III.4).
[6] Wings: Divine Love (I.1 and II.1); *imago* (III.4).
[7] Cloud: men (I.2); blessed and damned (I.4); prophets (III.2); saints (III.3).
[8] Candid: men (I.4); the Son of God (II.1); as far as the navel (III.2); brilliance and garment (III.3); mercy (III.5).
[9] Fog: vengeance and discretion (I.4).

SQUARED INSTRUMENT ALMOST A *CIVITAS*
divine predestination

CITY [BUILDING] [1]
divine predestination

WALL [2]
just judgment
   SPLENDOR [1]
   faithful
   DARKNESS [2]
   unfaithful

MOUNTAINS AND IMAGES [3]
miracles and virtues

MOUNTAIN [4]
strength of the justice of God

MIRROR [5]
divine foreknowledge

A DOVE WITH ITS WINGS SPREAD [6]
divine order

SPLENDOR [7]
knowledge of God

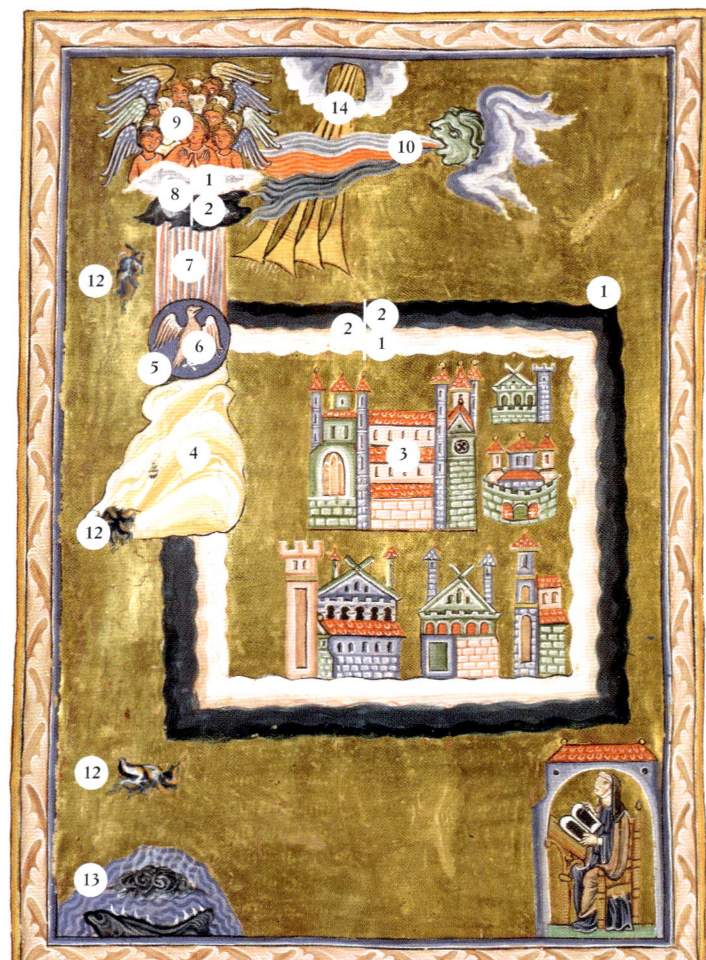

CLOUD [8]
   CANDID [1]
   blessed spirits
   DARK [2]
   damned spirits

MULTITUDE OF ANGELS [9]
angels

WIND [10]
living Spirit of God, God's zeal
   THREE MODULATIONS OF HIS VOICE [1]

FIRE [11] (INVISIBLE)
burning fire of vengenace against the lost angels

SPIRALS OF SMOKE [12]
wicked

FOG [13]
wicked suggestions

HEAVENLY TRUMPETS [14]

Part III.1 – Vision 6 – Chapters 6 – Fol. c. 118r

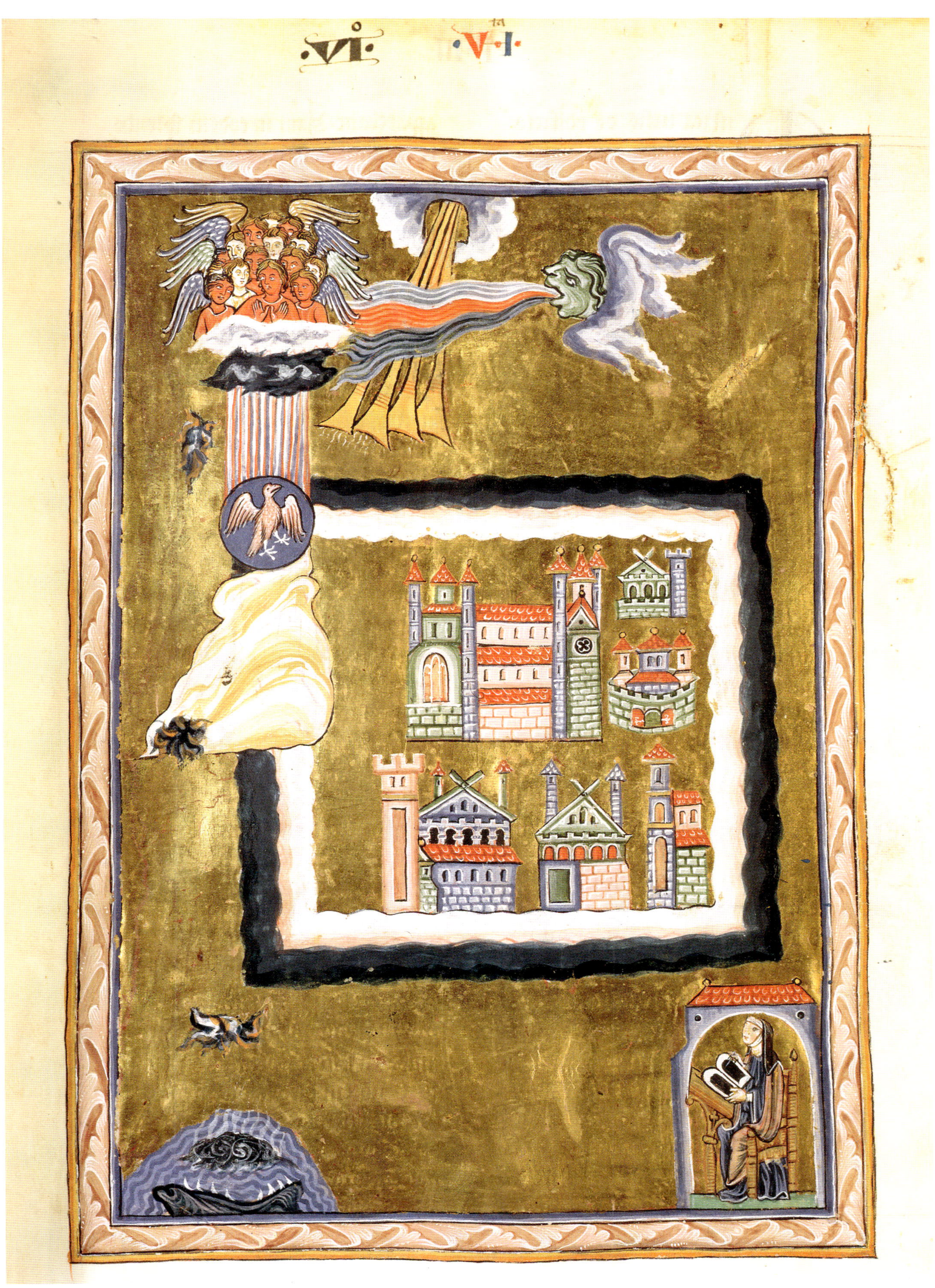

Grammar

III.2

The Mountain, Men, and two Images
God, the faithful, the time before and after the flood

Prophecy exists in humankind like the soul in the body (III.2,2, 360).

After casting out the lost angels, God ordered humankind to take their place and entrusted his message to the prophets. The vision opens with a MARBLE STONE[1] LIKE A MOUNTAIN[2] [1], *which is very great, high, and regular in form:* it is God, who is powerful, whole, stable, and unchanging. Set into the mountain is a DOOR [2] opening onto the CITY[3] [3]. It is God's will, which opens up onto everything that is good. The city is pervaded by a LUCID[4] SPLENDOR[5] [4], the order of the purest divinity. To the sides lie STARS[6] OBSCURED BY A CLOUD[7] [5], humans of all ages; they are the gift of prophecy that began with Adam. They make a SOUND [6], like the waves of the sea, and they are illuminated by a SPLENDOR[5] FROM ABOVE [7]. This is the prophecy that resounds and shines until the end of the world. Alongside are TWO IMAGES [8 and 9]: the FIRST IMAGO[8] [8] shows humans before the flood, when they were receptacles of all vices, *with the head and chest of a leopard but the arms of a man*; they imitated the nature of beasts, with *hands resembling the paws of a bear*;

they were clad in the hardness of sins, *a stone tunic*;[9] and they did not convert to good: *it moves neither here nor there, merely turning its gaze towards the north.* The OTHER IMAGO[8] [9] shows humans after the flood, when they gave themselves over to fleshly pleasures, *human face and hands, with hands folded together, and the feet of a sparrowhawk*; they followed the ancient law, neglecting the spiritual fruits, *a tunic seemingly made of wood.* The image, which is divided into four parts, each with a different color, represents four ages: the first, which extends *from the top down as far as the navel* and is *candid*,[10] represents the time from Noah to Abraham; the second, which *goes from the navel to the loins* and is *reddish*, is the time of the circumcision and prefiguration of the Son of God, from Abraham to Moses; the third, which goes *from the loins to the knees* and is *grayish*, is the time of the harsh law and vanity, from Moses to the exile in Babylon; the fourth, *from the knees to the feet*, and *dark*, is the time from the Babylonian exile to the coming of the Son of God. The sword *placed sideways across its loins,* symbol of circumcision, refers to God's judgment. *The immobile imago turns its gaze to the west.* It knows of the ancient

serpent's fall but does not advance towards spiritual intelligence. Lastly, there are many faithful represented as IMAGES OF MEN, AS A FLOATING CLOUD[7] [10], because the soul yearning for God's help is like a stream running to the sea without flooding. They raise their minds to the desires of the heart, *golden crowns*; they show victory over evil, *decorated palms*; they are rewarded for their love of learning, *flutes*, and receive the reward of the narrow path leading to life, *harps*; finally, with multiple virtues, they praise God, *organs*.

---

[1] Stone: fountain (III.3).
[2] Mountain: judgement (III.1); mountain (III.5).
[3] City: divine predestination (II.1, III.1, III.3–5).
[4] Lucid: fire and clouds, and air (I.2); divine foreknowledge (III.5).
[5] Splendor: wall/faithful and Knowledge of God (III.1).
[6] Stars: Doctors and penitence and discernment (I.2); angels (II.1).
[7] Cloud: men (I.2); blessed and damned (I.4 and III.1); saints (III.3).
[8] *Imago*: Divine Love (I.1); virtues (III.1); Divine Love, Humility, and Peace (III.3); Wisdom and God (III.4); Divine Love (III.5).
[9] Tunic: Divine Love (I.1); Wisdom and God (III.4); Divine Love (III.5).
[10] Candid: men (I.4); the Son of God (II.1); blessed spirits (III.1); brilliance and garment (III.3); mercy (III.5).

MARBLE STONE LIKE A MOUNTAIN [1]
God

DOOR [2]
God's will

CITY [3]
all that is good

LUCID SPLENDOR [4]
order of the most pure divinity

STARS OBSCURED BY A CLOUD [5]
prophets

SOUND [6]
words inspired by the Holy Spirit

SPLENDOR FROM ABOVE [7]

TWO IMAGES [8, 9]
  FIRST *IMAGO* [8]
  before the flood without law
  OTHER *IMAGO* [9]
  after the flood under the law

IMAGE OF MEN, AS A FLOATING CLOUD [10]
believers from all times

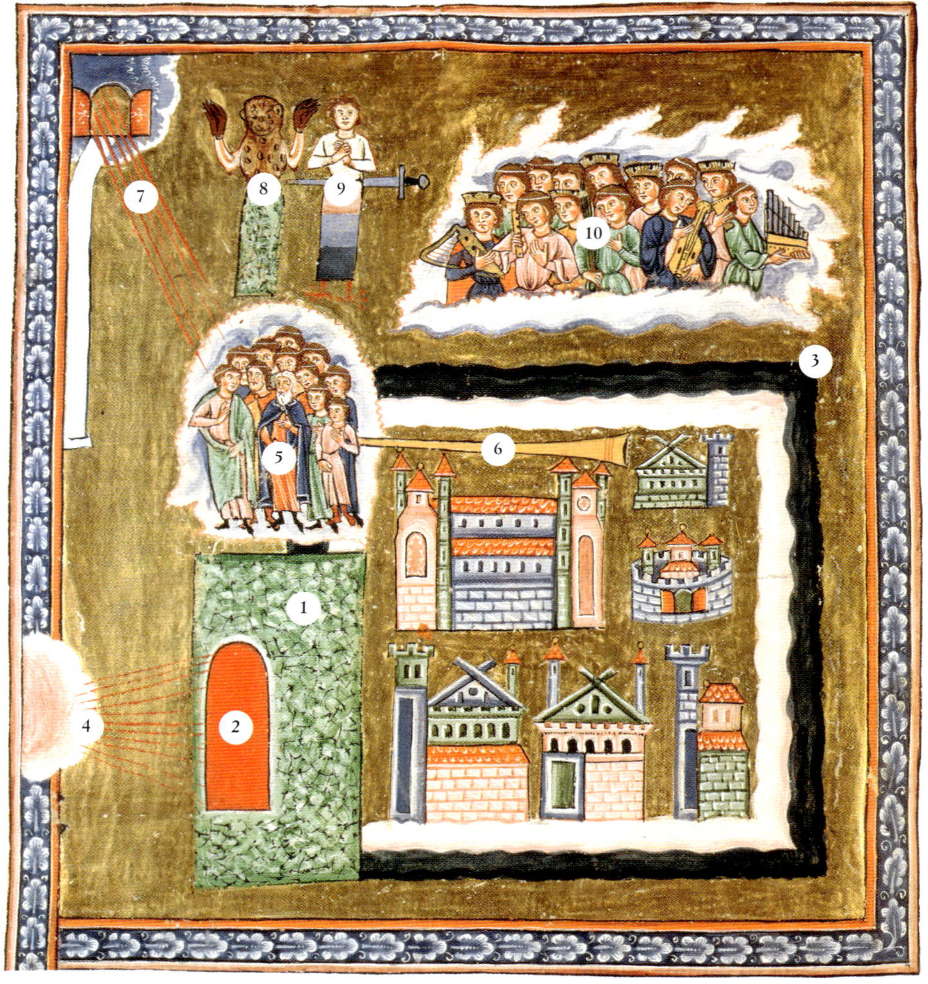

Part III.2 – Vision 7 – Chapters 17 – Fol. c. 121v

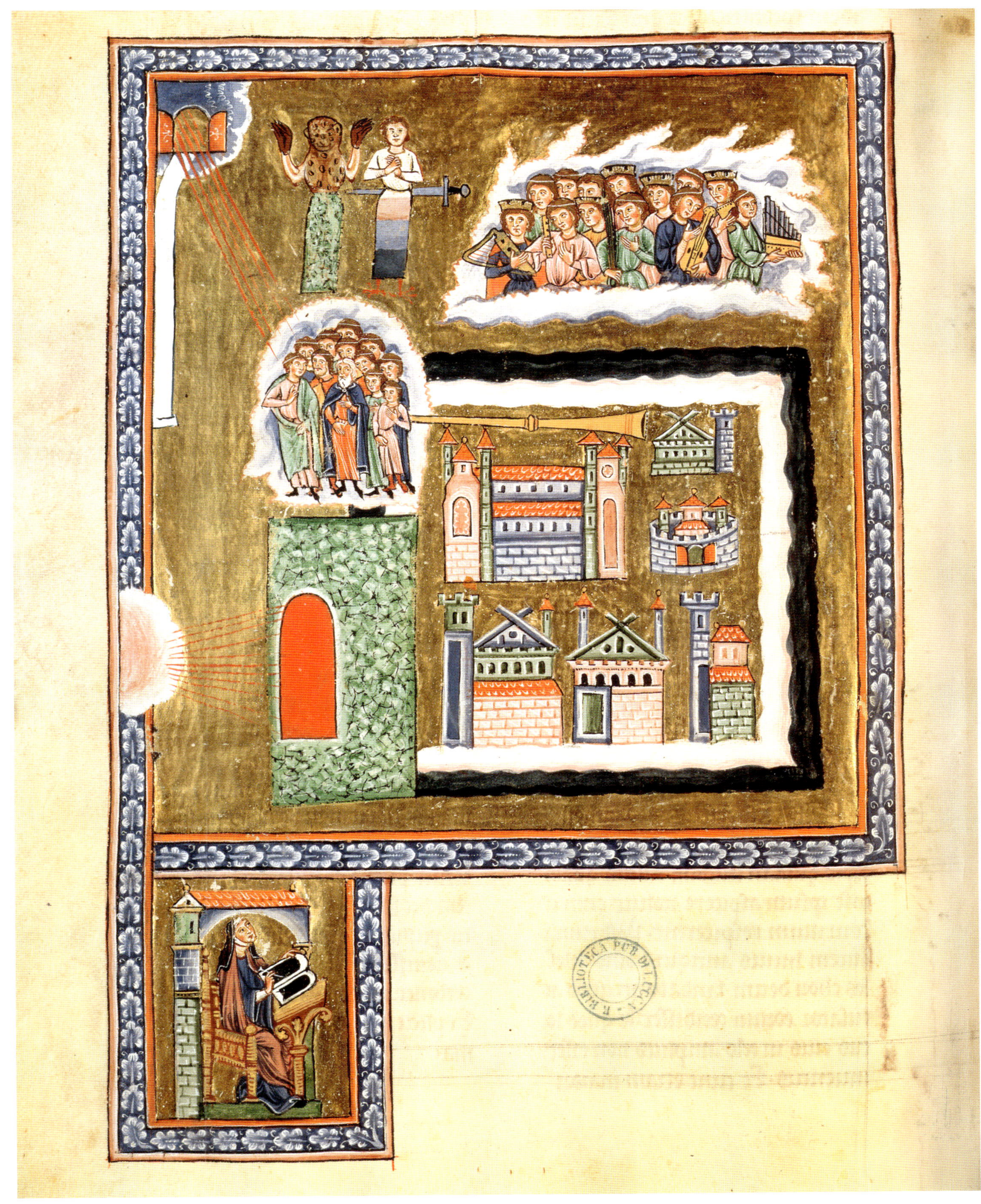

Grammar

III.3

The Fountain and the Three Images
The Spirit of God, Divine Love, Humility, and Peace

The living fountain is the Spirit of God, which he distributes unto all his works. They live because of him and have vitality through him, as the shadow of all things appears in water. [...]
As water makes what is in it to flow, so too the soul is the living breath ever streaming in a human being, and it makes him to know, to think, to speak, and to work as if by streaming forth (III.3,2, 388).
All that God has done, he has accomplished in Divine Love, Humility, and Peace, so that humans, too, should lovingly desire Divine Love and embrace Humility and hold also onto Peace, and should not go to ruin with him mocked these virtues in his first origins (III.3,3, 390).

The prophecy announces the vision, near a city[1] of a FOUNTAIN OF THE PUREST WATER [4]: it is the Spirit of God from which the purity of the living God and rivers of beatitude flow. The FIRST *IMAGO*[2] is Divine Love [1], *suffused with a purple fulgor* because it burns like purple in heavenly love. The SECOND *IMAGO*[2] is Humility [2], *suffused with a candid[3] (white) fulgor* because she has cast off earthly filth through the candour of rectitude. They stand in the fountain, *as if rooted there, like trees that sometimes seem to grow in the water*, meaning that they are not separated from divinity, in the same way that the root is part of the tree, because God, who is Divine Love, maintains humility in all his works and judgments. Divine Love and Humility, who descended upon the earth with the Son of God, bring him back to heaven. The THIRD *IMAGO*[2] is Peace [3], *and stands outside the fountain*, on the ROUND, PERFORATED STONE[4] [5]. This means that Peace, who dwells in heaven, also defends earthly undertakings that lie outside the heavenly realm. *Its face shone so brightly that it reverberated upon my face:*

this means that Peace, which manifested through the Son of God, cannot be on earth as it is in heaven. Appearing before the three images, as if in a CLOUD[5] [6], are the blessed hosts of saints who are *gazed upon lovingly* by the three images, meaning that *it is through works of charity and humility that one reaches the glory on high of the heavens [...]. Thus the Church, adorned and endowed with the virtues described above, was led to the King's bedchamber (III.3,3, 392).*

[1] City: divine predestination (II.1, III.1–2, III.4–5).
[2] *Imago*: Divine Love (I.1); virtues (III.1), before and after the flood (III.2); Wisdom and God (III.4); Divine Love (III.5).
[3] Candid: men (I.4); the Son of God (II.1); blessed spirits (III.1); as far as the navel (III.2); mercy (III.5).
[4] Stone: mountain (III.2).
[5] Cloud: men (I.2); blessed and damned (I.4 and III.1); prophets (III.2).

THREE IMAGES

FIRST *IMAGO* [1]
Divine Love

SECOND *IMAGO* [2]
Humility

THIRD *IMAGO* [3]
Peace

FOUNTAIN OF THE PUREST WATER [4]
Spirit of God

ROUND, PERFORATED STONE [5]

CLOUD [6]
saints

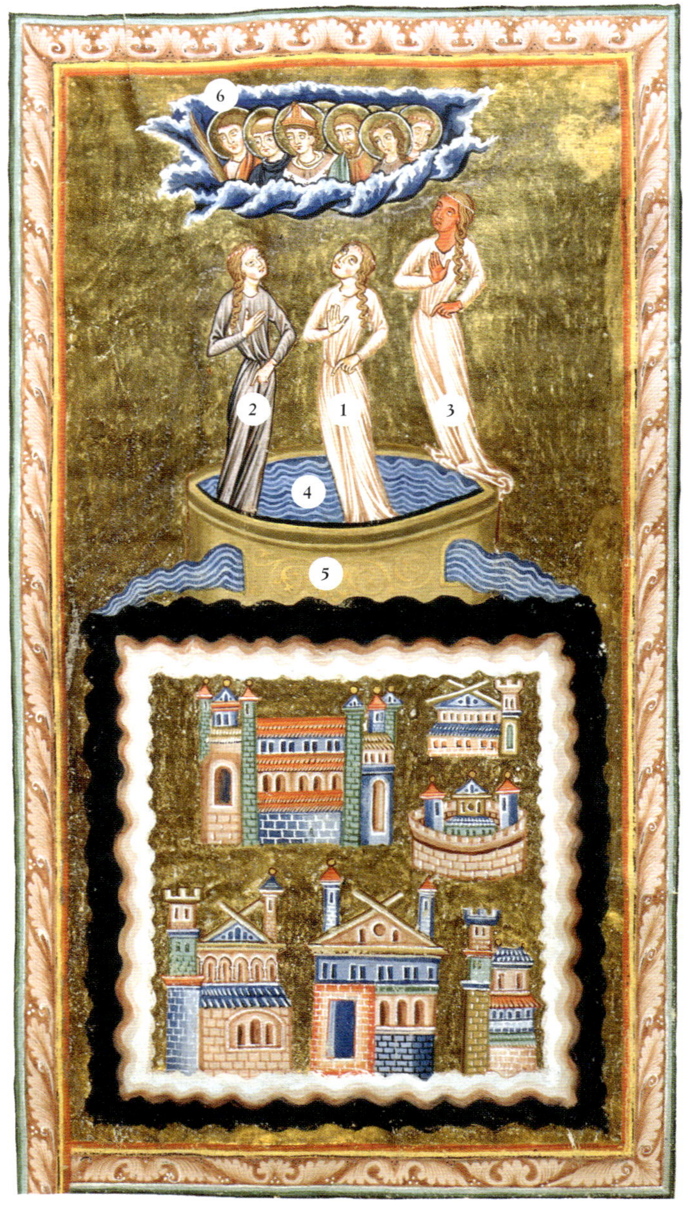

Part III.3 – Vision 8 – Chapters 4 – Fol. c. 132r

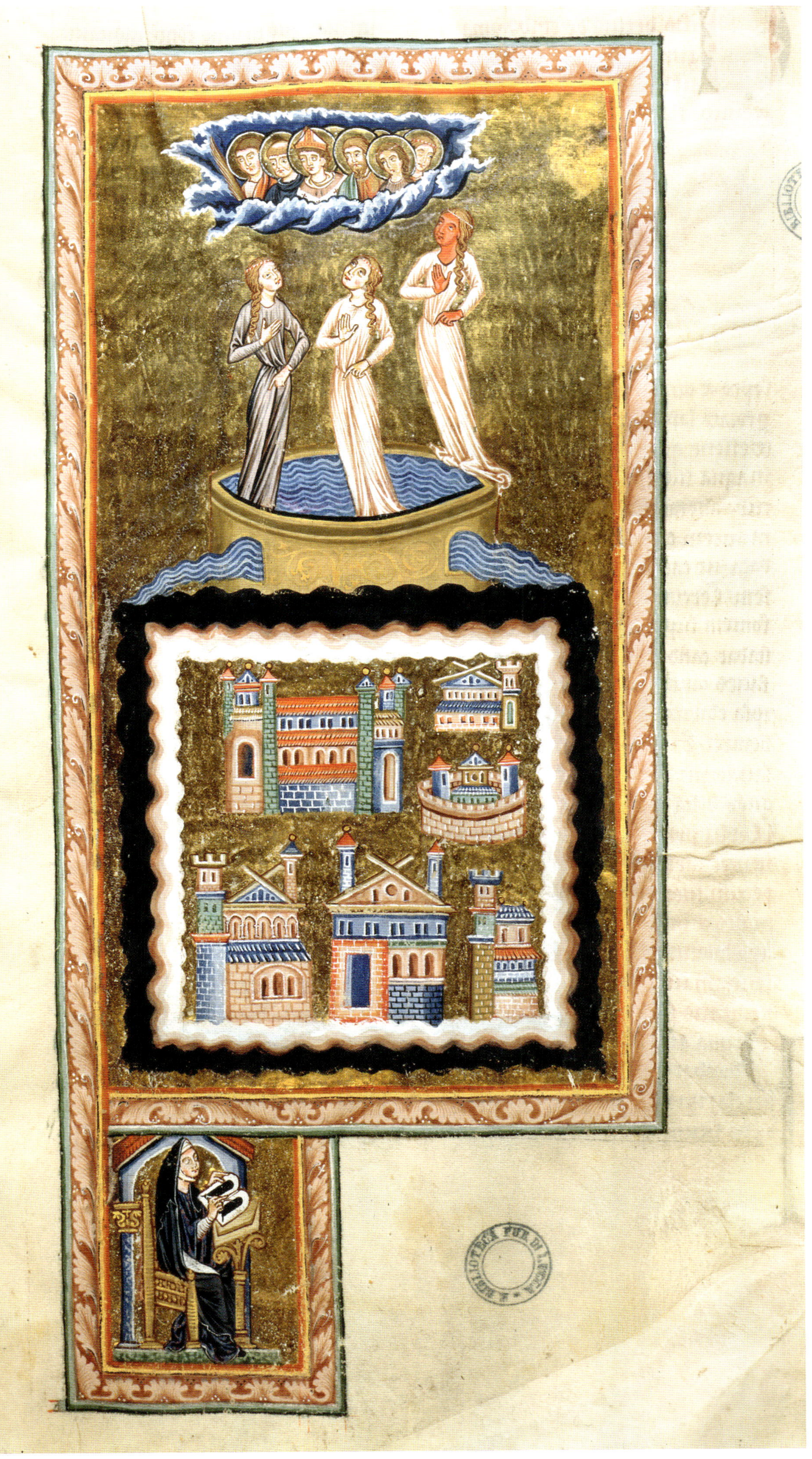

III.4

Wisdom and God and Victory over Darkness

For when foolishness comes to an end and justice arises, the Wisdom of true beatitude is revealed. Her beginning and end surpass human understanding (III.4,2, 396).

On the north side of the city[1] two images appear. In the eastern corner, the IMAGO[2] [1] is Wisdom; *its face and feet shine with a fulgor*, it is the light of divine foreknowledge. Its *robe is made of white silk*, the whiteness and gentleness of the love of God, which embraces and reveals the mystery of the incarnation of the Son of God in the beauty of virginity. It has a *green tunic*[3] *adorned with coloured pearls*, and gives life to all creatures so that they may serve humankind like the pearls adorning this garment. It wears *earrings, necklaces, and bracelets of the purest gold, set with precious stones*, so that all creatures may obey and be mindful of the precepts that it has laid down. The OTHER IMAGO[2] [2] reveals God's opposition to the violence and wicked thoughts of the ancient serpent. It *stands upright and has a strange and wondrous form*,[4] signifying the majesty of God who is invincible, wondrous, and unknowable in his mysteries. *At the top, where the head should be, there shines a ful-gor*; this is God's excellence, which no one can see as long as they are living. *In the middle of its belly is the* HEAD OF A MAN [3] *with white hair and a beard*, signifying that God made Man in his image and likeness. *The feet are like lion's paws*, because God, through his Son, draws to himself the works of men and judges them. It has SIX WINGS[5] [4–6]; they are the six days' works, in which man praises God and looks after himself with his help. The first TWO WINGS [4], *which rise upwards from its shoulders*, represent the love of God and neighbor, and are the image of the heavenly army. A further TWO WINGS [5], *extending from the shoulders down to the head*, represent the Old and New Testament, and *widen towards the bottom*, showing how the prophets announced the Son of God in the Old Testament and the Church's children in the New. The last TWO WINGS [6], *going from the loins to the heels*, refer to present and future life. *They are opening out as if preparing for flight*: they precede the end of the world in the midst of terrors and prodigies, while the diabolical gullet spews the taste of sins and of fleshly desires, and divine protection defends men and suppresses the attacks through a single man. The *rest of the body is entirely covered by small quills resembling fish scales more than feathers*. It signifies that the Son of God was born in holiness and with a nature utterly unlike that of other humans. On the two descending WINGS [5] there are FIVE MIRRORS[6] [7–11], each bearing the name of a luminary: Abel, Noah, Abraham, Moses, and the Son of God. The image has *its back turned to the north* in order to conceal from the friends of the north what it has done through the Son of God. Lastly, in the west there is the DEEPEST DARKNESS[7] [12], representing places of punishment with the various kinds of tortures; in the northern corner is the DARKEST FIRE [13] with sulfur and darkness; this is the abyss of punishments and the lake of perdition.

[1] City: divine predestination (II.1, III.1–3, III.5).
[2] *Imago*: Divine Love (I.1); virtues (III.1), before and after the flood (III.2); Divine Love, Humility, and Peace (III.3); Divine Love (III.5).
[3] Tunic: Divine Love (I.1); first *imago* (III.2); Divine Love (III.5).
[4] Form: Hildegard (Prologue); Divine Love (I.1); wings (I.1).
[5] Wings: Divine Love (I.1 and II.1); dove (III.1).
[6] Mirror: divine foreknowledge (III.1).
[7] Darkness: space of the ancient enemy (II.1).

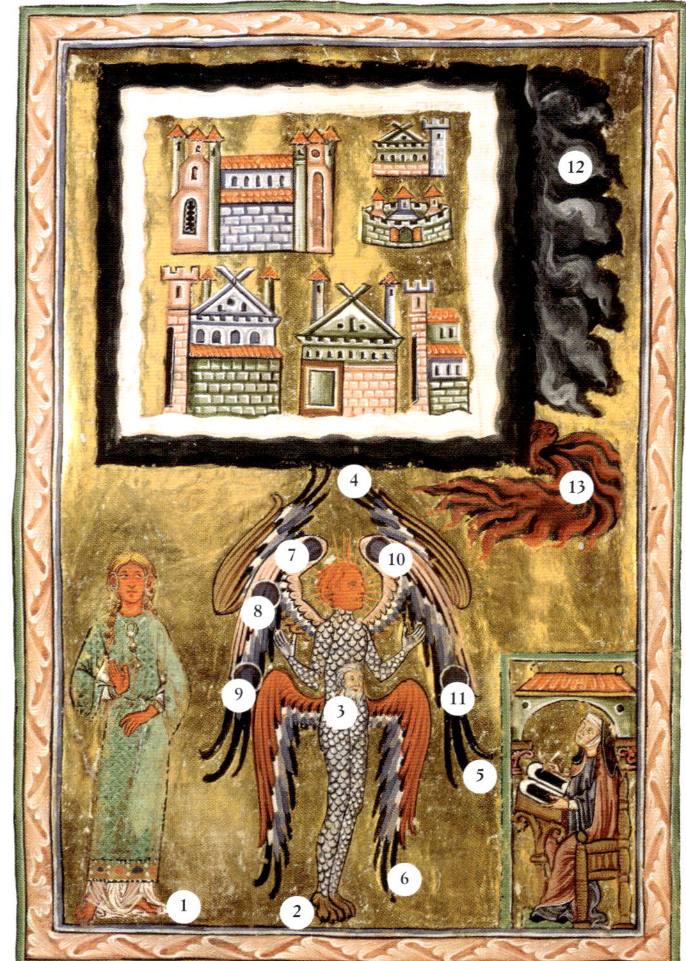

Part III.4 – Vision 9 – Chapters 14 – Fol. c. 135r

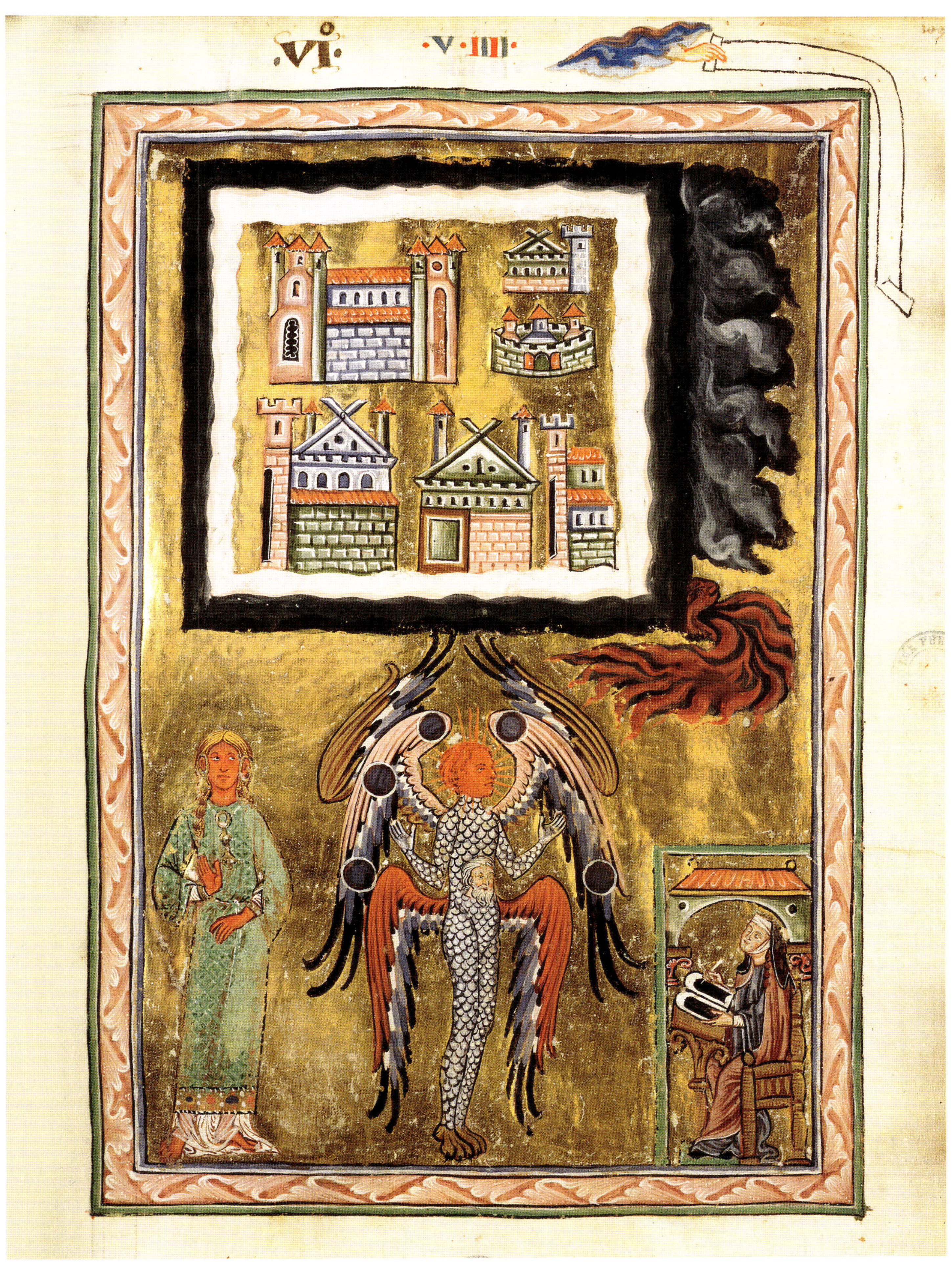

Grammar

III.5

The Wheel/God, Divine Love, and Divine Foreknowledge

Let almighty god be praised in all his works, before the time and into time, for He is the first and the last (III.5,38, 478).

The journey in the city[1]/building ends in the east, near the MOUNTAIN[2] [1] of the first vision where a WHEEL[3] [2] now appears, representing the power of God. *With no beginning and no end*, of *a wondrous size*, like a *candid* [4] *cloud*, it means that God can do all things and that he is merciful. A DARK LINE[5] [3], as *thin as a human breath*, divides the wheel into two equal parts: this is the perfection of the will of God who separates the temporal from the eternal. The HALF ABOVE THE LINE [5, 6] represents time before the beginning and after the end, eternity; this is divided by another LINE WHOSE COLOR IS LIKE A GLOWING AURORA [4]: it indicates the fullness of the perfection of God, who takes charge of the justice of the world in every time. The LEFT SIDE [5], which is *green*, shows how God maintains in the viridity of his will the creatures whom he has endowed with bodies so that they might work; the RIGHT SIDE [6], which is *red*, indicates that at the end of time, God will bring to perfection

that which he has caused to live. The HALF BENEATH THE LINE [7], which is of a *pale color intermingled with blackness*, indicates the fleeting time of things that have a beginning and an end. In the middle of the WHEEL [2] appears the IMAGO[6] [9] *referred to earlier as Divine Love* (I.1), *seated on top of the line*: it is Divine Love, joined to God's will in peace. Its *ornaments* reveal the virtues that are at work in humans in different moments. Its *face* shines like the sun, teaching us to fix the attention of our hearts upon the true sun, Christ. Its *tunic*[7] gleams like purple so that humans, clothing themselves in mercy, may provide succor to anyone asking them for help, as far as possible. Around its *neck* it has a golden necklace with precious stones: this invites humans to accept the yoke of submission embellished with the virtues of the blessed. It wears *sandals* that produce flashes of light so that the paths taken by humans may be lit by the truth and so that they may follow Christ and be an example of rightness in faith to others. It holds a *perlucid*[8] (*transparent*) CRYSTAL TABLET [10] bearing an inscription: *God's foreknowledge and Divine Love agree in unity*. As Divine Love observes the tablet, the line begins to move, mean-

ing that God gave life to all creatures. The line makes two movements. With the FIRST MOVEMENT [A], it reaches the left side and the external part of the wheel turns into water: this is the moment of the judgment in the flood. With the SECOND MOVEMENT [B], just over half of the wheel [8] becomes *red*, the time of justice after the flood; *luminous* and *transparent*, the time of the repression of idolatry and of good works, from Noah to Moses, and the time of prophecy; finally, *agitated* and *turbulent*, the coming of the Son of God and the end of time.

[1] City: divine predestination (II.1, III.1–4).
[2] Mountain: judgment (III.1); Dio (III.2).
[3] Wheel: God/firmament (I.2–4).
[4] Candid: men (I.4); the Son of God (II.1); blessed spirits (III.1); as far as the navel (III.2); fulgor and garment (III.3).
[5] Line: sun (I.2).
[6] *Imago*: Divine Love (I.1); virtue (III.1), before and after the flood (III.2); Divine Love, Humility, and Peace (III.3); Wisdom and God (III.4).
[7] Tunic: Divine Love (I.1); first *imago* (III.2); Wisdom and God (III.4).
[8] Lucid: fire and clouds, and air (I.2); splendor (III.2).

MOUNTAIN [1]

WHEEL [2]
power of God

DARK LINE [3]
perfection of God's will

LINE WHOSE COLOR IS LIKE A GLOWING AURORA [4]
fullness of the perfection of God

HALF ABOVE THE LINE [5, 6]
time before the beginning and after the end [eternity]
   LEFT SIDE [5]
   the creation of creatures and maintenance of their viridity
   RIGHT SIDE [6]
   at the end of time, God will bring the creatures to perfection

HALF BENEATH THE LINE [7]
the fleeting time of worldly things that have a beginning and an end

HALF BENEATH THE LINE AFTER THE MOVEMENT [8]

IMAGO [9]
Divine Love

CRYSTAL TABLET [10]
God's divine foreknowledge

[MOVEMENTS]
   [A] THE LINE REACHES THE LEFT SIDE
   the flood
   [B] A STRETCH BEYOND THE MIDDLE OF THE HALF
   from the flood to the Son of God

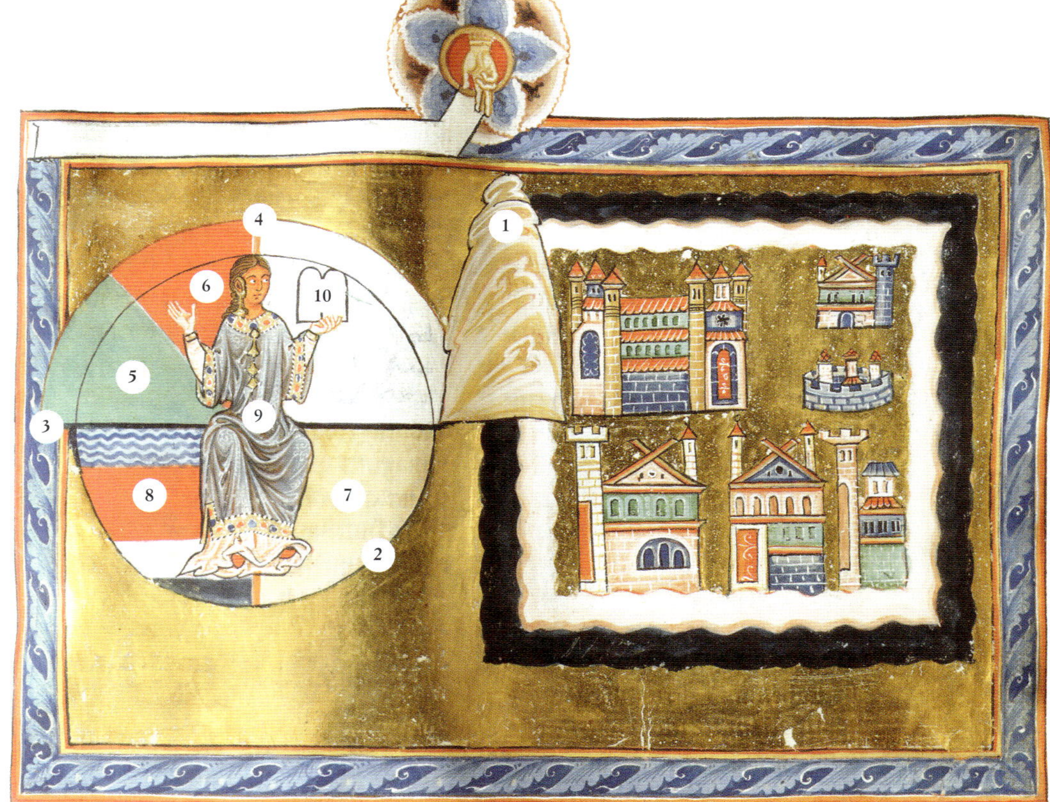

III.5 – Vision 10 – Chapters 38 – Fol. c. 143r

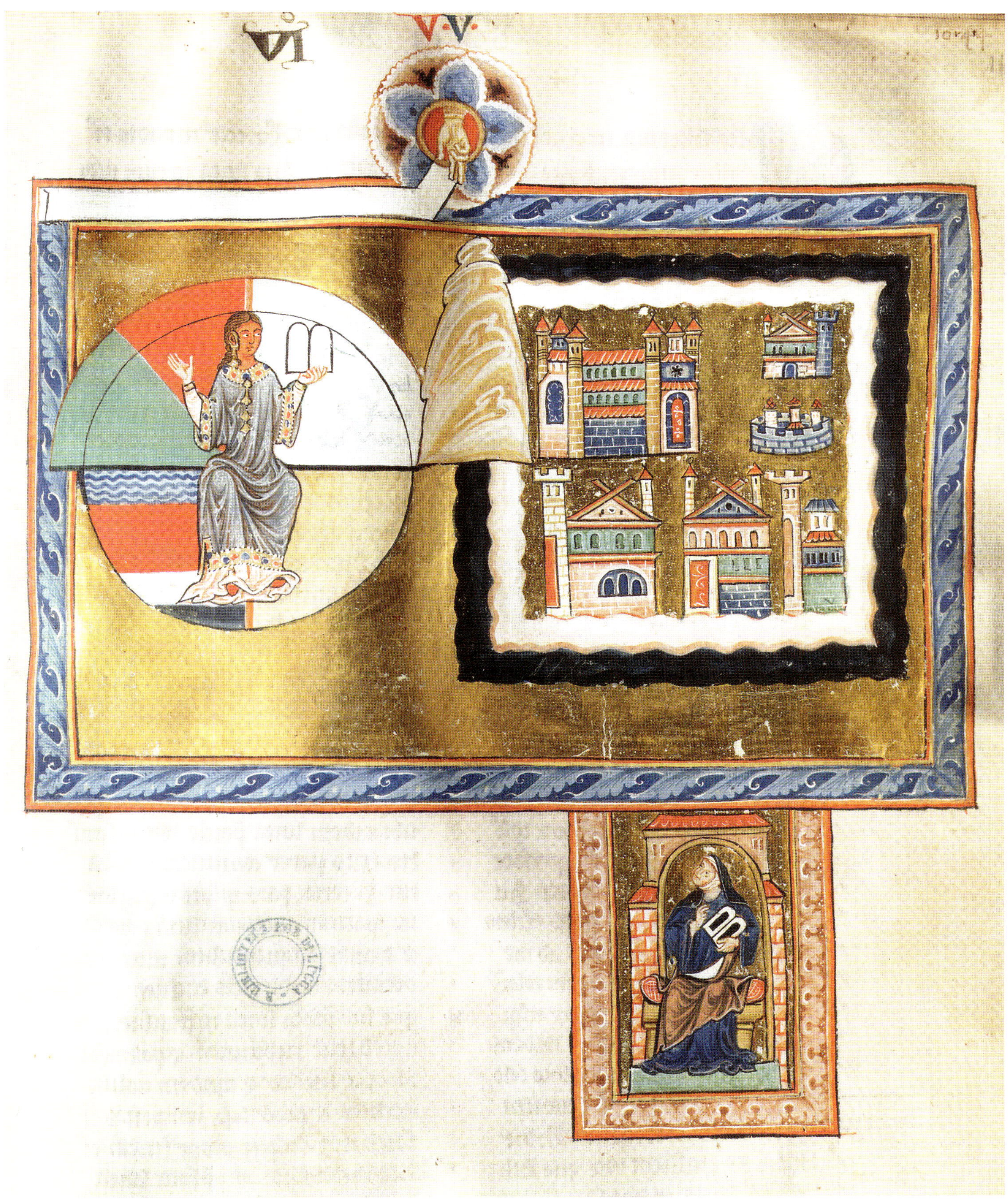

Grammar

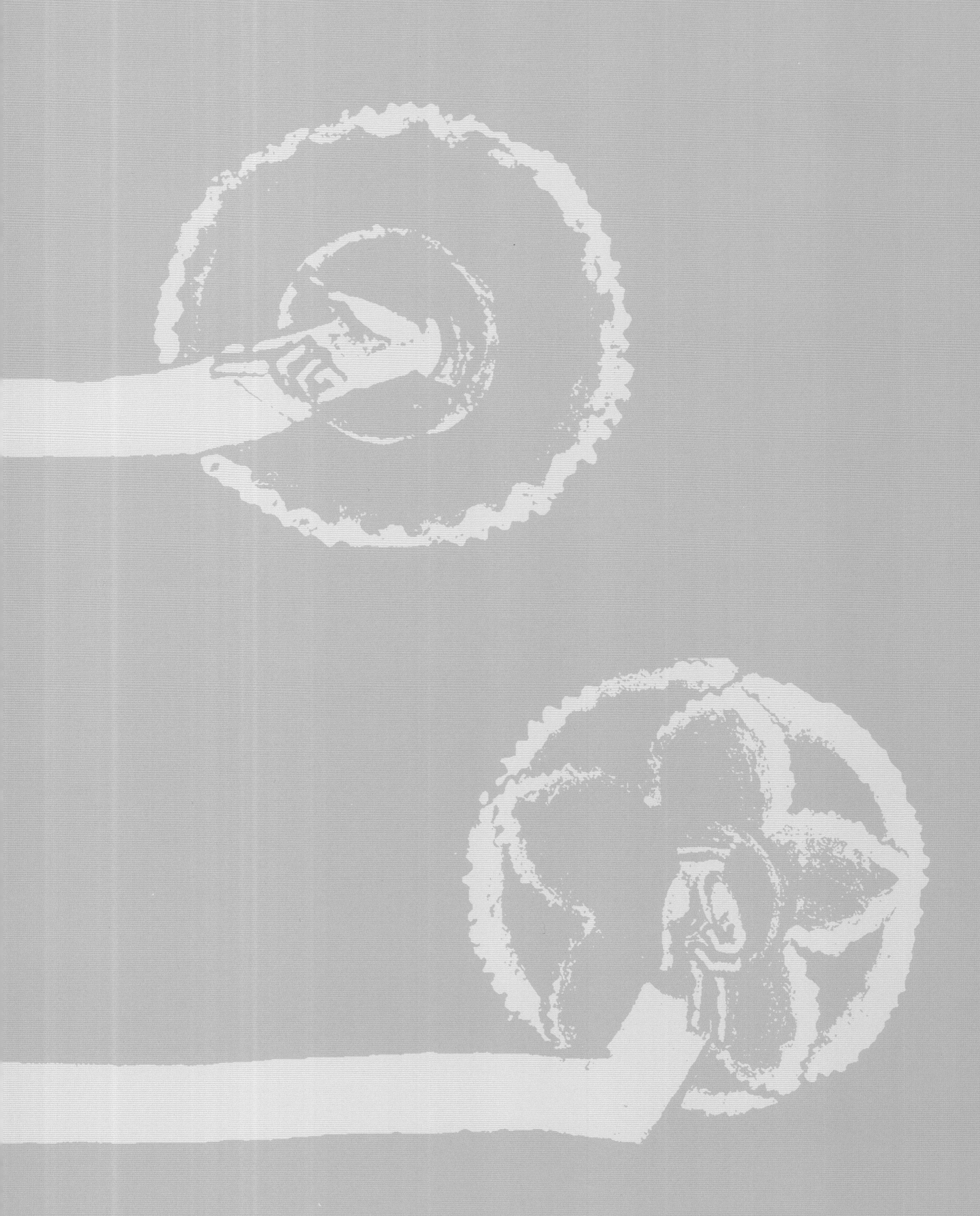

The Journey

In the first vision in *Scivias*, *Lux vivens* invites man, still ignorant of faith, to look upwards and take God, and only God, as a guide for his journey, offering him the gift of the virtue of the Fear of God, an image made up of eyes, that must be imitated to enter the dimension of the poor in spirit and thereby be filled with holiness. And this is when it reveals to man the creation/firmament in the form of an *egg, instrumentum*, inviting him to pass through the various layers—the *water* of the Baptism, the *air* of faith, the black of the *fire* of darkness before once more reaching the light of the bright *fire* of the sun—and to become a new man. On this journey, he meets the Sun/Christ; sees his birth, death, and resurrection; and the Moon/Church, which illuminates the pure ether of faith with its reflected light. After being washed by the water, floating in the air, and being strengthened by the vigorous power of the fire, man is ready to continue along the path of edification until he reaches the prophetic vision of God's final battle against the Antichrist, of the Last Judgment, and of his ultimate destiny. The man emerging from *Scivias* is an adult in his faith, who has encountered the Spirit in the sacraments, has walked in the brotherhood of the Church, has edified himself by observing the dangers represented by vices and by acquiring virtues. This journey was deepened and enriched by the detailed account of the long path of edification in Hildegard's second theological work, the *Liber vitae meritorum* (Book of the Rewards of Life). At this point, man, now living knowingly in faith, is presented with the vision-narrative of the *LDO*. He is ready to meet God face to face and to complete the final stretch of his journey, following the footsteps of Christ.

He is a self-aware man, a man to whom God can now reveal himself in his fullness, in the wonderful and magnificent Divine Love (*Caritas*) that holds man *in his breast*, in his heart, the same heart where he keeps his Son, the Lamb. Through his perception of the heart beating with life in his *breast*, man is able to experience the divine mystery of God/Divine Love whose *breast* holds man and Christ, God made man. They are both surrounded by the whole, perfect wheel of creation, above which flies the winged figure of Divine Love, image of life and Wisdom, no longer the primordial *egg* but a perfect *globe*. The man who has received the gift of Wisdom is now allowed to see the firmament from a remote point far beyond the skies. But on occasion his humanity still leads him to forget. It is for this reason that the journey that begins in *LDO* is a journey of conscious redemption, the final stretch, on the great *way* of *virginitas*, following the footsteps of Christ. The *way* that will lead him to heaven, upwards, towards the east, the place where the sun is born, where Christ was born, and where he himself was born. Unlike *Scivias*, where the narrative proceeds swiftly without dwelling on the description of details and roughly outlining the elements through forms and colors, there is change of perspective in the *LDO*, with images explained by means of the precise language of Wisdom, which orders things by means of *number*, *weight*, and *measurement*. Each element is now described in terms of its measurements, its proportions, its relationship with the other elements, its place in the cosmos and in the terrestrial space and in the human body. Doing so requires new systems of different coordinates—cosmological, and relating to human and terrestrial geography—because the cardinal points no longer suffice.

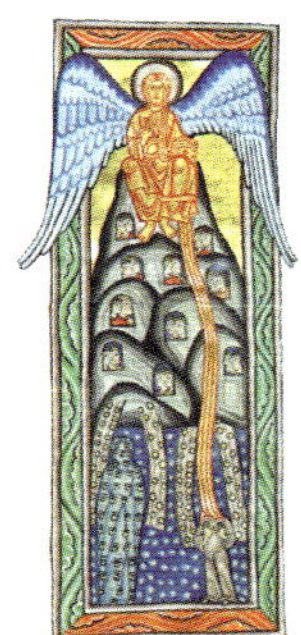

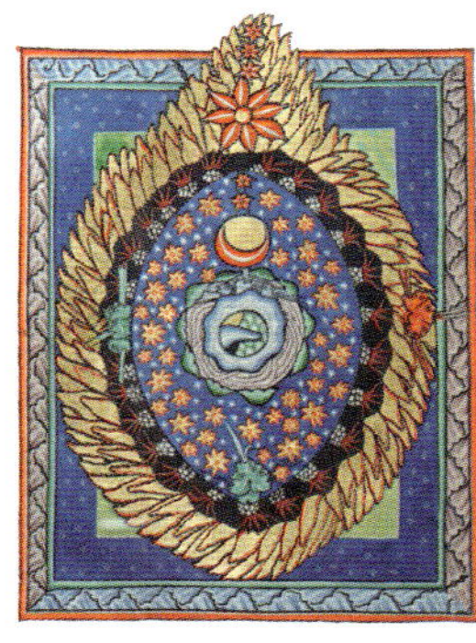

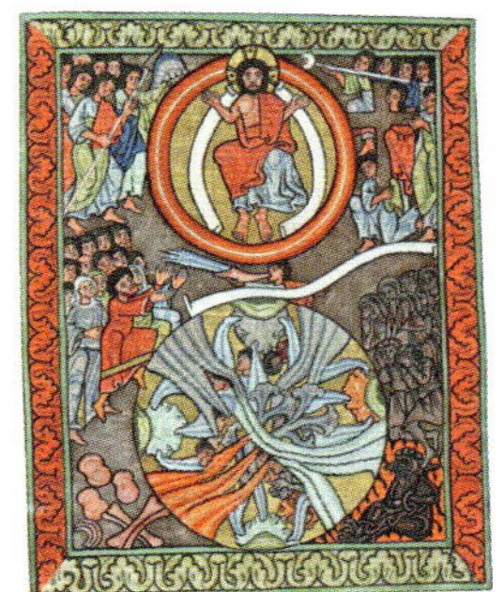

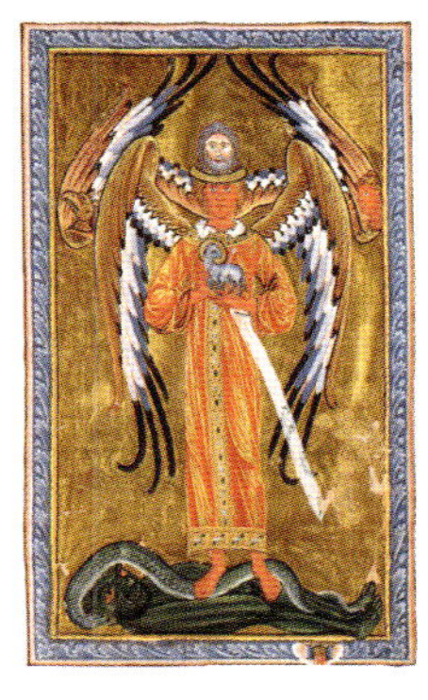

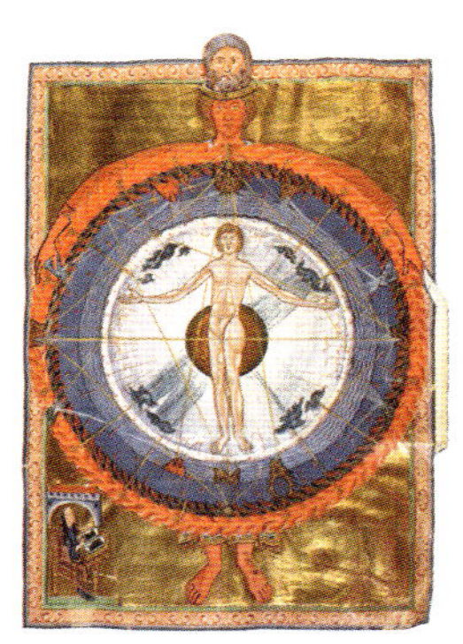

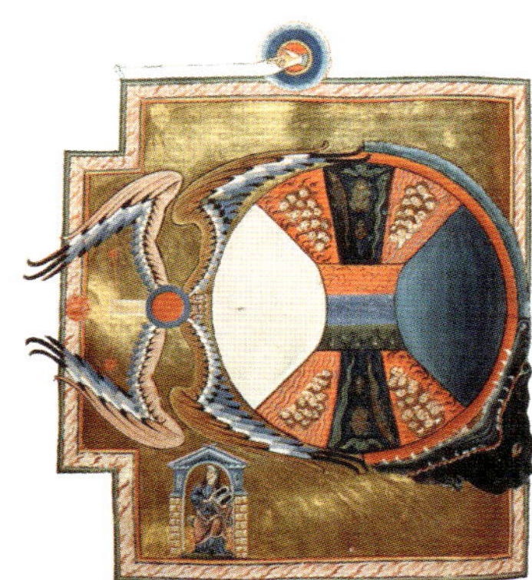

The Mystic Marriage

And I saw as if in the middle of the southern sky an image, beautiful and wonderful in the mystery of God, like a human in form (I.1,1, 33).

And behold, in the midst of this wheel, sitting upon the line I again saw the image that had previously been identified to me as Divine Love; but she appeared now with different trim than I had seen previously. For her face shone like the sun, while her tunic gleamed like purple; she had a golden necklace set with precious stones around her neck, and she wore shoes that reflected her brightness like lightning (III.5,1, 416).

Scivias and *LDO* both open with a *winged human form* and end with the *imago* of a *seated woman* in a circle. Placed at the beginning and end of the work, they are the Alpha and Omega of human history. They are the intense images of a *mystic marriage*, of the symbolic re-unification of the male and female, which takes place in *Scivias* through the marriage of Christ and Mary, and in the *LDO* through the figures of the bridal couple found in the male and female faces of Divine Love.

The image of Divine Love, separate and united, becomes the image of reference for man in experiencing an eternal, circular, divine love that is always in movement and inseparable in its human path of love for one-self and for others. A nuptial fusion that invites man to go on a journey of integration of the self in a union where the bridal pair is both separate and united. In a process leading to the profound integration of the two-fold earthly dimensions of man-woman; male-female; inside and outside the human being.

The images show the two winged figures with male features, one seated on the *mountain*, the kingdom of God, and the other embracing the *wheel*/firmament in his breast. One shows man the kingdom of God seen from the earth, the other, creation seen from a far-off point in the firmament. The two female figures are both placed in the circular *wheel*, the image of the fullness of God. The symbols in their hands represent his manifestation: the globe/creation, the lily/Trinity, and the tablet of divine foreknowledge. They both have their arms open like the Church in a sacerdotal act of offering and praise. Moreover, the *image of the woman Divine Love* in the wheel alongside the *mountain* is also a clear summary of the entire human path. Man is now capable of seeing the *wheel*, the image of the firmament in its entirety and perfection, while the *mountain* is the image of the kingdom of God, recalling the starting point of the journey in the first vision in *Scivias*.

In addition to the images, we are also guided by the text in our perception of these precious internal threads. The wheel on which Divine Love is seated in the *LDO* is described in a similar manner to the *candid cloud*. In *Scivias* this expression refers to the complex passage bringing together in a female line Eve/*candid cloud*, Mary/Church/Wisdom/*candid cloud*, and the wings of divine justice/zeal of God. Lastly, the word *aurora* describing the Virgin Mary, dawn of the new world, returns in the description of the circle *glowing like the aurora* which embraces the wheel of Divine Love while in *Scivias*, it identifies the power of God surrounding the Building, a place of human passage and growth. We might conclude that the final female image of Divine Love distills the journey of redemption carried out through the candid cloud and the *aurora*, Eve/Mary, in a journey imbued with Wisdom, protected by the Power and Justice of God, that leads towards Salvation and towards the eternal nuptial embrace of Divine Love.

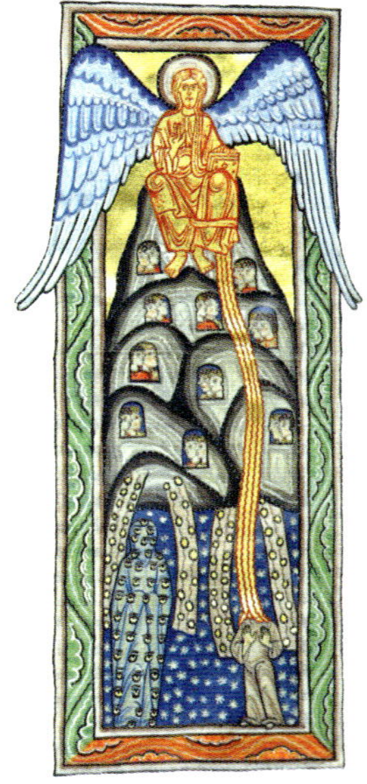
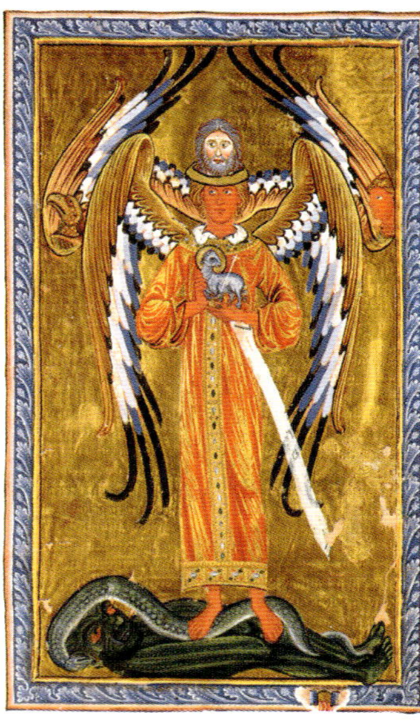
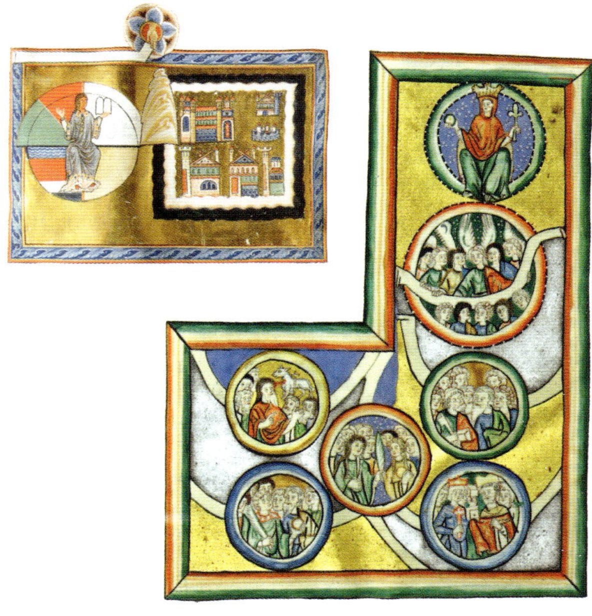

Light and Darkness

There arcs this line—the path of the sun, avoiding the northern region. For the sun does not immerse itself in those parts, but holds them, as it were, in neglect. God has deprived them of access to the sun, for there the ancient seducer chose for himself the seat of his dwelling place (I.2,11, 59).

When the Son of Man shall come in his glory, and all the holy angels with him, then shall he sit upon the throne of his glory. And before him shall be gathered all nations: and he shall separate them one from another, as a shepherd divideth his sheep from the goats. And he shall set the sheep on his right hand, but the goats on the left.

Then shall the King say unto them on his right hand: Come, ye blessed of my Father, inherit the kingdom prepared for you from the foundation of the world […].

Then shall he say also unto them on the left hand: Depart from me, ye cursed, into everlasting fire, prepared for the devil and his angels (Mt: 25,31–34, 41).

To him who conquers I will give the hidden manna, and I will give him a white stone, and upon that stone a new name, which no one knows except him who receives it (I.2,11, 60).

The journey of man, embraced by the image of the mystic marriage, takes place within the *globe*/sphere. An *instrumentum* described as a wheel within which *Lux vivens* extends a *line*, the *path of the sun*, dividing the wheel longitudinally into two parts, southern and northern, one of *light* and one of *darkness*.[1]

Moreover, the text also specifies that the north is the place beyond which *the sun does not go*, the place the ancient seducer has chosen for his dwelling. Thus the faithful man is asked to *avoid anything harming his soul*, and to oppose the *devil's devices* by choosing good. Those winning the battle against the *serpent*, causing him to flee, will receive from God a small *candid* (white) stone bearing a new name, their name of regeneration in Christ, *the bread of life descending from heaven*, to reach *eternal blessedness*.

The distinction between *light* and *darkness* also represents the choice that man must make in life, illustrated by the passage from Matthew in which we read that Christ, the Sun of Justice who comes from the east to judge the living and the dead, will divide the blessed from the damned, placing the former on his right hand, corresponding to the zone of light, the south, and the latter on his left, the part of darkness, the north.

The image of the judgment of the end times in *Scivias* (III.12) and the image of the wheel in the *LDO* both belong to the same eschatological reality, which guides man on his journey along the paths of edification towards the reunification of self and the integration/*virginitas* towards the eternal nuptials.

[1] The miniaturist has chosen to represent the image of II.1 horizontally, with the wings to the left, to emphasize the distinction between light and darkness, forging continuity with the image of the winged figure of Divine Love in I.1.

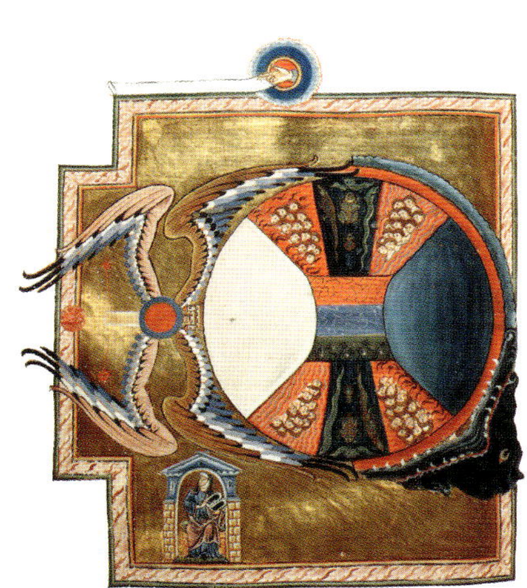

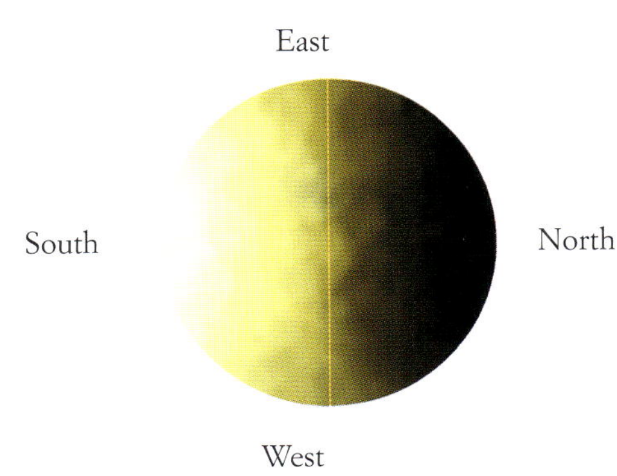

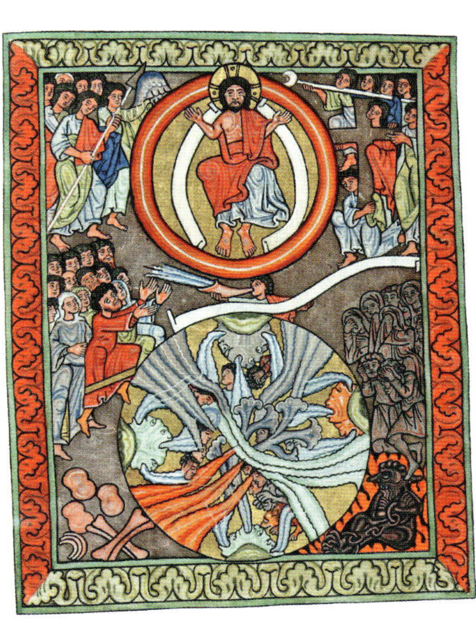

The Celestial Spheres. Divine Love and Man

And I saw as if in the middle of the southern sky an image, beautiful and wonderful in the mystery of God, like a human in form [...]. And these faces [head of an eagle and human face, in the upper wings of the image] were turned towards the east (I.1.1, 33).

Flying around the circling circlet with my upper wings—with wisdom—I have ordered all things rightly (I.1.2, 34).

And I saw that the firmament, together with everything attached to it, had as great a density from its top to the top of the earth as the earth had from pole to pole (I.4,1, 130).

And so man faces the east, gazing as the west does to the east; and extending his arms as south and north are divided from each other, he points his right arm to the south and his left to the north (I.4,48, 175).

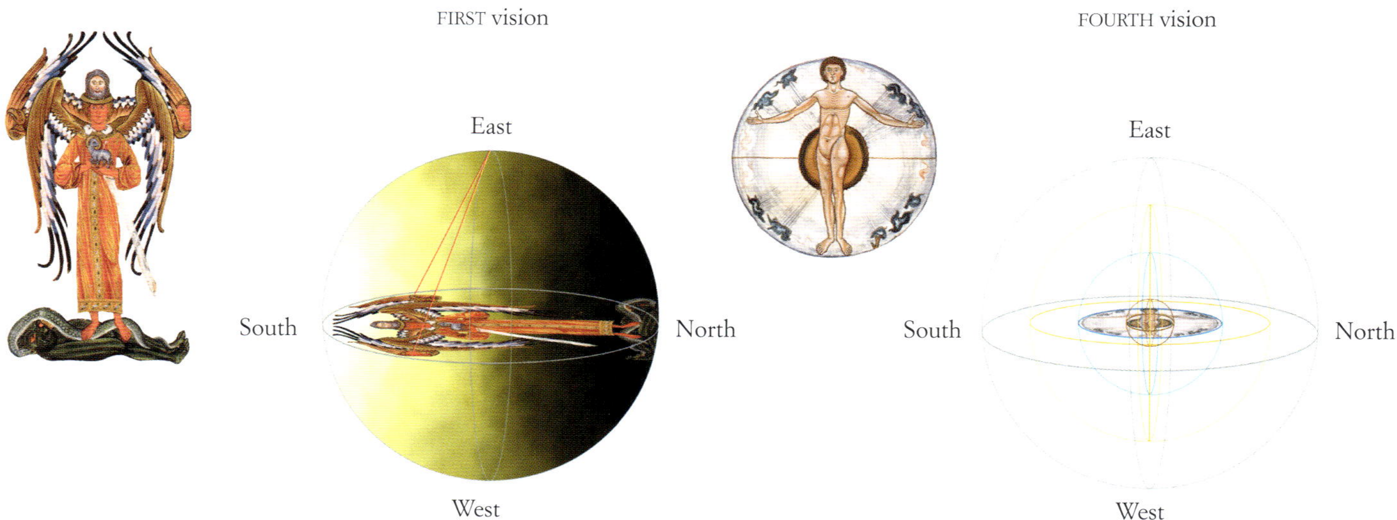

In the *middle of the southern sky*, in the bright part of the heavens, is the *human figure* by means of which God/Divine Love manifests himself. The *eastwards-turning* gaze of the two faces in the upper wings of the image allows us to put the figure in the correct position: the upper wings reach the point corresponding to the position of the sun in the south, exactly where Hildegard places the sun to the right of the image of the man (see page 78). The text underlines this by repeatedly referring to the sun in its description of the face and tunic of the figure, and of the lamb: *her face was of such beauty and radiance that I could more easily look at the sun than at her*; and again: *She was clothed with a robe like the brilliance of the sun, and in her hands she held a lamb, shining like the light of day* (I.1,1, 33).

God/Divine Love manifests with the fulgor and clarity of the sun and the *splendor of the light of the day*, manifestation of the Sun/Christ and of the light of the Father and of the fiery energy of the Spirit. The image does not remain still but *moves around the circle, flying around it with its upper wings*. The circle is the *wheel/instrumentum* that the vision places in the breast of the figure, the same image that Hildegard claims to have once described in the form of an *egg*, now as a *wheel*, but which is actually a *globe/sphere* (I.2,3).

Today, using perspective, it is possible to represent what Hildegard describes in the wheel of the second vi-

sion by means of a series of concentric globes/spheres—corresponding to the concentric circles described in the text—embraced by the winged figure; this allows us to reconstruct the image of *globe/sphere*, which she indicates as such. This reconstruction uses a three-dimensional model of a transparent sphere, which allows us to grasp how the location of the cardinal points—which appear on modern maps with the north to the top and the east to the reader's right—can be represented in models with a different order that changes according to the position from which we observe the sphere. This explains the apparent inversion of the north with south in the miniature, pointed out by other authors.

The three main circles of the wheel are shown in the sphere: *lucid fire* (yellow), *strong air* (blue), and *globe*/earth (brown). In the wheel, which is divided into light and shade, illuminated and enlivened by the fiery energy of Divine Love, we can make out the human figure within the *strong air* and with the terrestrial globe in the middle. The position of the latter is described in the fourth vision, where *the firmament with everything attached to it* and with *a density similar to that of the earth* is seen, as in the first vision, from a very distant perspective point. Inside, the position of the human figure has been reconstructed through the direction of its gaze and the position of its arms: *the man faces east, gazing as the west does to the east, extending his arms, with the right arm pointing south and the left to the north*. It reflects a dense theological meaning: the man turning eastwards, towards the place of birth of the Sun/Christ, observes the light of the rising sun like a star guiding his path. If we juxtapose the two drawings of the first and fourth visions, the two figures of Divine Love and of the man form a cross. The monster being crushed by Divine Love is thus located in the north, while the human figure and the earth remain divided between light and darkness, indicating that humankind must still choose between good and evil. The miniaturist has represented the figures of Divine Love and of the man in the wheel frontally, as they were seen by Hildegard in her first two visions. The three-dimensional reconstruction allows us to observe the two images in a single representation, in which Divine Love and the human figure are shown two-dimensionally, from above and from the east, lying across a section of the wheel. By rotating the two figures around the north/south axis, we can see Divine Love or the human figure frontally, as they appear to Hildegard in her visions and as they are represented in the two miniatures of the first and second visions.

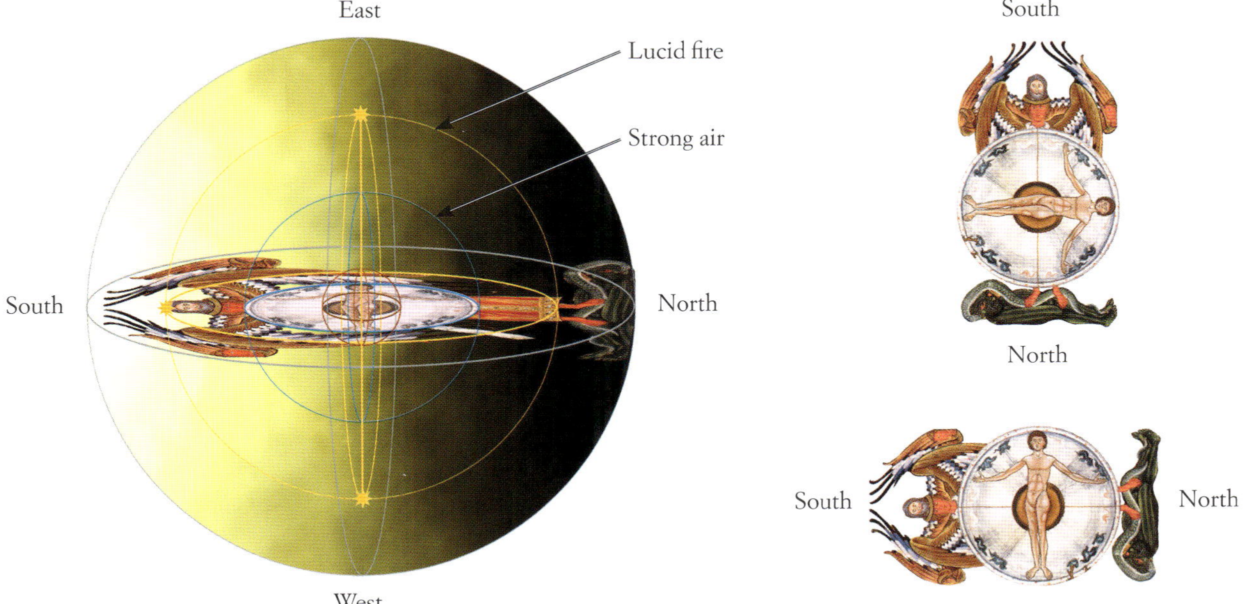

The depiction of the winged Divine Love at the top of the first miniature reflects the decision of the miniaturist to portray the winged figure frontally in all its beauty. As we have seen, he orients the single vision that comprises the second part with the wings towards the right of the image, facing southwards, seemingly interrupting the continuity of the two figures, linked by the position of the wings, evoked by the indentation in the frame (see pages 103 and 127, where the mirroring of the image is also explained).

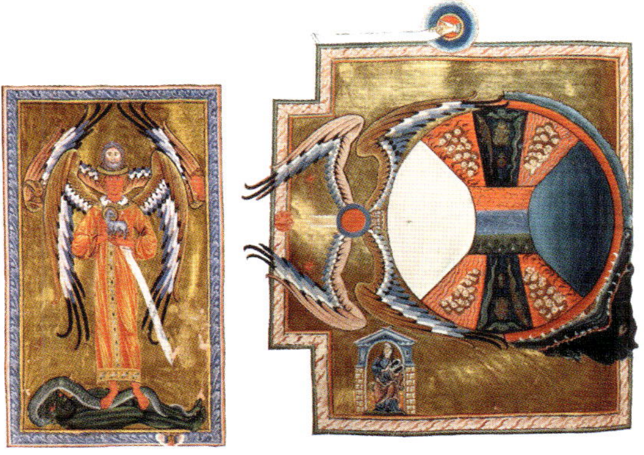

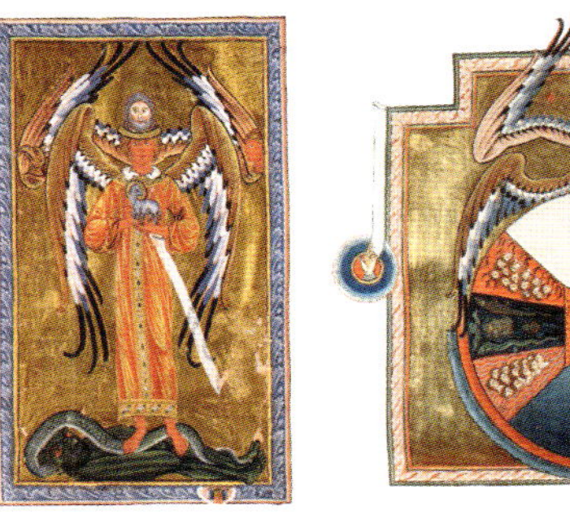

The Human Being in the Middle of the Wheel

In the middle of the wheel there also appeared the image of a human being, whose crown reached above and whose feet stretched below the circle of strong, bright white air. The fingertips of the right hand were extended from the right side, and the fingertips of the left hand were extended from the left side, to that circle, marking it out from here to there in its circumference, because the image had its arms thus extended. […]

Furthermore, facing these parts there appeared four heads—as it were the head of a leopard and a wolf, and the head of a lion and a bear (I.2,1, 49).

For above the crown of that image, […] I saw as if the leopard's head blowing a breath from its mouth (I.2,17, 64).

Moreover, beneath the feet of the human image […] there appeared as if the head of a wolf producing a breath from its mouth (I.2,20, 68).

But to the right of this human image […] you look upon as if the head of a lion (I.2,23, 72).

Furthermore, to the left of this image […] there appears as if the head of a bear (I.2,28, 79).

The sign of the sun is marked out in an ordered fashion above the crown of that image […] marked out in its own circle along the image's right side and then beneath its feet (I.2,37, 89).

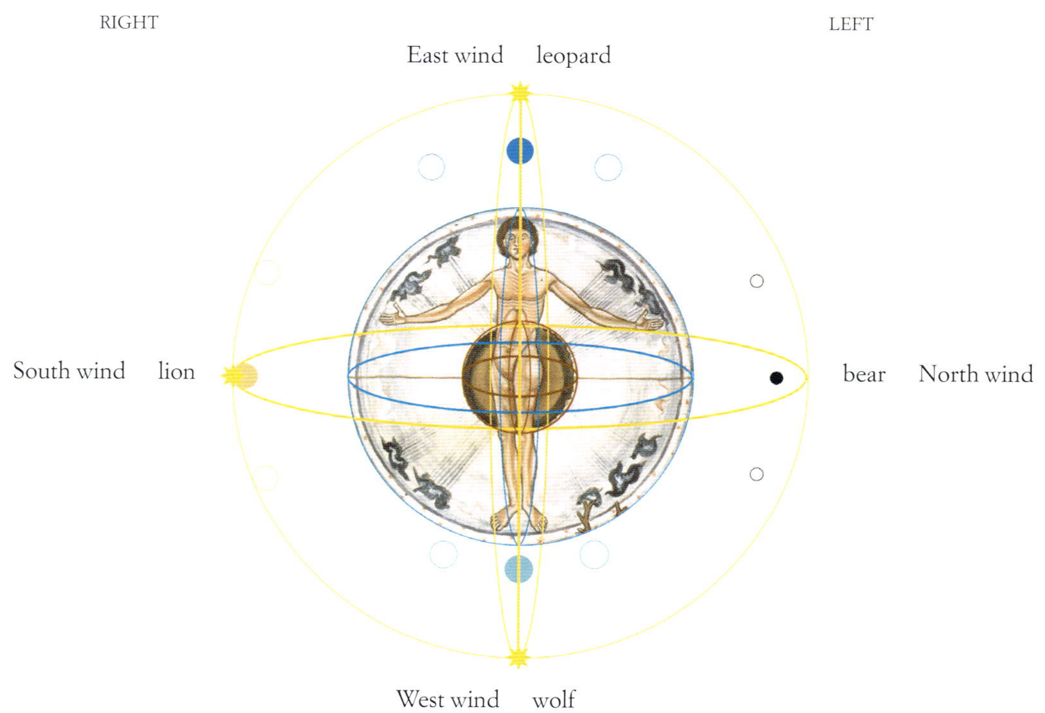

In the second vision, the human figure in the middle of the wheel is seen frontally, in a standing position with its arms outspread. At the four points where its hands and feet touch the circle of *strong air* in the wheel, there are four animal heads blowing winds: *east*, *west*, *south*, and *north*. The human figure and the wheel are therefore seen as if the *globe/*sphere were a cross-section. There is no sense of depth and the terms of geographic orientation (*south*, *north*, *east*, and *west*) are replaced by *above*, *beneath*, *right*, and *left*. The vision focuses less on the position of the human figure with respect to the vast sky in which the figure of Divine Love is placed, and more on describing the position of the elements of the wheel and of the figure, and on the relationships and influences linking the elements of the firmament, and of the human body and soul.

In this frontal, earthly vision of man, the miniaturist traces the line of the sun horizontally, apparently contradicting the previous description of the vertical division of the sphere carried out by the line of the sun, which divides it by going from east to west, as specified in the text.

All of this can be explained by the fact that, in this case, as we have seen, astronomical or geographic coordinates have been replaced by a frontal, earthly vision of the human figure.

Therefore, the representation of the line of the sun inserted into this scene also crosses the figure transversally, reflecting the reality experienced by man every day, as a dweller of the earth, when he sees the sun rise from a point of the horizon and set in the opposite point, always along the line of the horizon. The following pages contain a hypothetical reconstruction of the image of God embracing with his wings of wise love the sphere set into his breast that holds man. This reconstruction was carried out in accordance with the description of the single elements, following the observation of the images and exchange of ideas with the other members of the research group, bringing together points of view and perspectives that were historical, philosophical, theological, and astronomical. As a result of this process of observation and interchange, we returned to the description, in Hildegard's own words, of her experience of the vision in a letter to Guibert of Gembloux. In the letter, penned by the now elderly Hildegard to her last secretary in the same period as the *LDO*, she writes, *In these visions my spirit rises, as God wills, to the heights of heaven and into the shifting winds, and it ranges among various peoples, even those very far away* (*The letters of Hildegard of Bingen* 1998, 23). These words show us how the vision led her beyond the dimension of the earthly vision, beyond that of heaven, moving her through space to a point lying beyond the sphere/globe of the firmament, to its *heights*. And this shows us that what Hildegard is seeking to reveal to us is a far-reaching cosmological vision, of great modernity, that leads her to reconcile multiple viewpoints and perspectives in a single great vision. She attempts to describe this complexity by drawing upon different semantic levels. At the first level, she refers to an immense, unfathomable firmament seen from a distant perspective, beyond the heavens, using noteworthy expressions such as the ones opening the first and fourth visions—*in the middle of the southern sky* or *you see [...] the firmament, together with everything attached to it*; at the second level, she introduces the terms indicating geographic coordinates, such as *east* and *west*, *east wind* and *west wind*, by means of which she attempts to describe the position of the figures within the sphere; followed by the terms indicating coordinates close and near to the human figure, *above/beneath* and *right/left*, with which she seeks to describe the location of the man in the sphere, referring to the elements of his body, hands, and feet; finally, through the description of the wind blowing and the gaze of the figures, she indicates the directions, which do not seek to define precise points but movements starting in one point and ending in another. Our reconstruction is, of course, a preliminary one, which will hopefully be followed by further reflections and studies. What is interesting is that the apparent inconsistencies identified during an initial examination of the design of the miniature actually derive from the deliberate decision to depict the figures from different points of view, through various changes of perspective and observation of the same reality. The miniaturist chose to alternate frontal visions, not located in the wider geographic and cosmological space, with clearly oriented visions. The limits imposed by the two-dimensional page meant he could not include all the perspectives in a single vision. He chose instead to remain close to the choices made by Hildegard when observing her first and fourth visions from beyond the firmament, while dwelling upon the wheel in the second vision from a human perspective. In his drawing, the miniaturist conveys the essence of the vision and its strong symbolism, using a similar approach to the one used for the *Scivias* miniatures. In fact, this approach is typical of the medieval style, in which symbols and their stratification evoke complex contexts that readers can only fully grasp through a detailed, extended, and informed reading that will take them step by step into the heart of the message. This perspective is unfamiliar to modern viewers who are used to realistic interpretations of images that sacrifice beauty and fluidity in their search for exhaustiveness, as well as streamlining the complexity of the vision—as revealed by our reconstruction, which, though accurate, is certainly far from poetic.

Let us conclude with a final passage from Hildegard's letter to Guibert of Gembloux, in which she evokes the vastness and splendor of her immense vision: *The light that I see is not local and confined. It is far brighter than a lucent cloud through which the sun shines. And I can discern neither its height nor its length nor its breadth. This light I have named the "shadow of the Living Light,"* [umbra viventis luminis] *and just as the sun and moon and stars are reflected in water, so too are writings, words, virtues, and deeds of men reflected back to me from it [...].*

I can by no means grasp the form of this light, any more than I can stare fully into the sun. And sometimes, though not often, I see another light in that light, and this I have called "the Living Light" [Lux vivens]. *But I am even less able to explain how I see this light than I am the other one. Suffice it to say that when I do see it, all my sorrow and pain vanish from my memory and I become more like a young girl than an old woman* (*The letters of Hildegard of Bingen* 1998, 23).

The light (*lumen*) speaking to her now in the *LDO* encapsulates the voice of *Lux vivens* heard in *Scivias*, whose cognitive dimension guides man into the wider space that he is now capable of grasping. We have shifted to the farthest boundaries of the firmament, entering wider space and approaching the vision of the divine. The time of the vision appears to expand with our gaze; Hildegard describes it as a sensation of lightness and youth, weightless and timeless dimensions close to the next experience beyond the firmament of the eternity of Paradise.

Divine Love

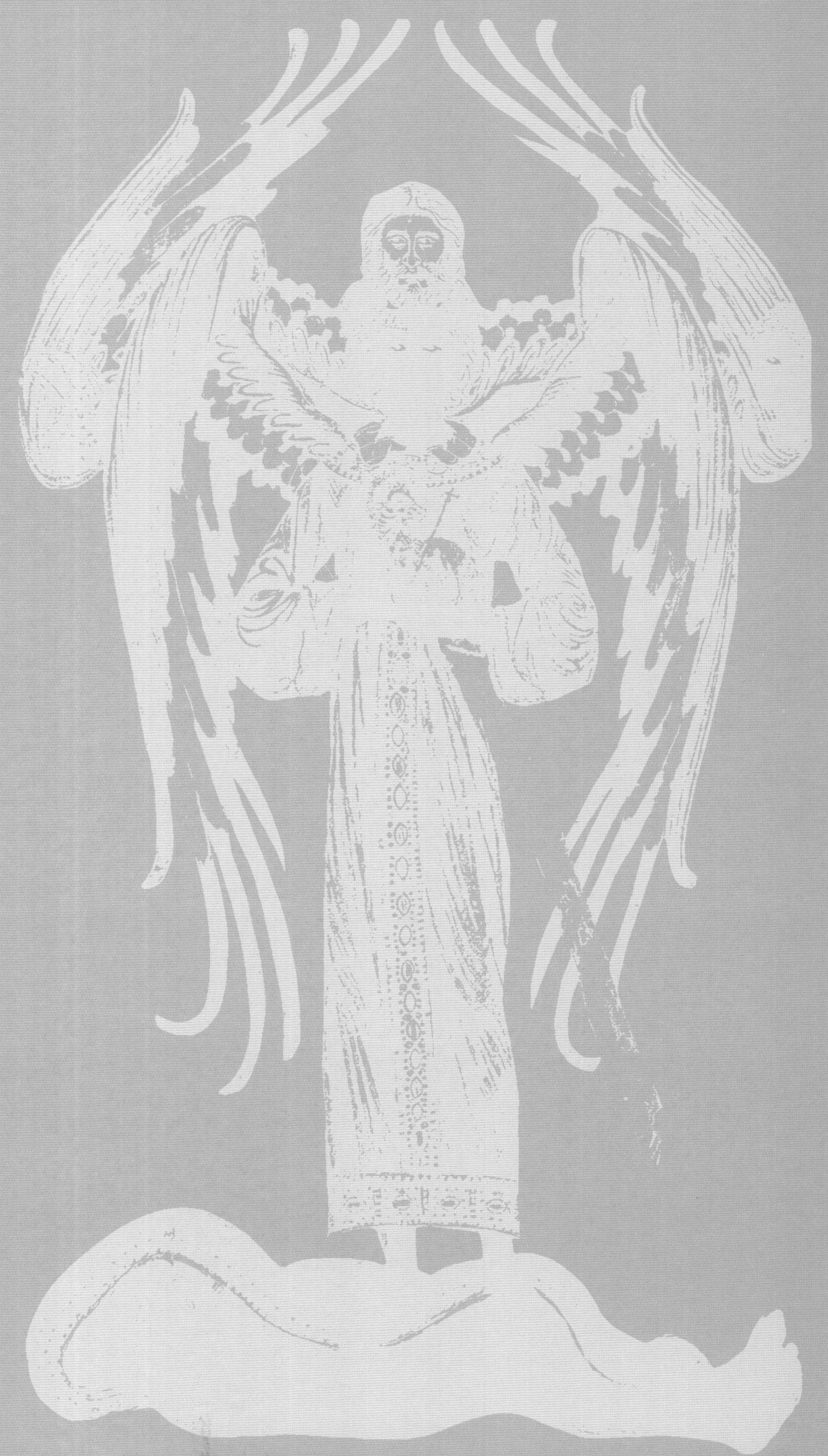

An Almost Human Form and Wings. *Imago Dei*

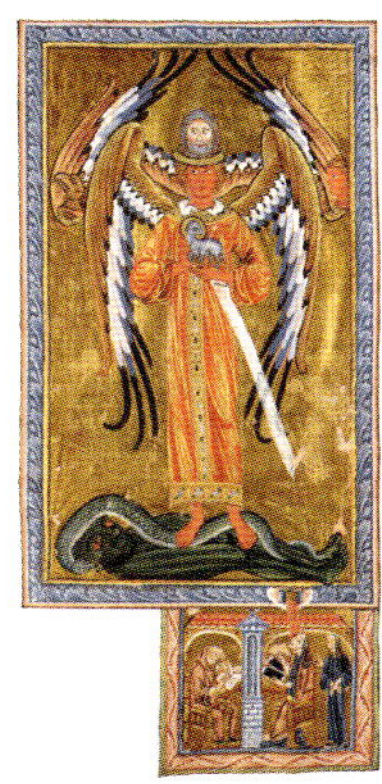

I am the supreme and fiery force, who sets all living sparks alight and breathes forth no mortal things, but judges them as they are. Flying around the circling circlet with my upper wings—with wisdom—I have ordered all things rightly (I.1,2, 33–34).

The opening vision of the *LDO* shows God's fiery energy, strength and *vis* (force). This energy breathes life into creation, where everything comes alive like *living sparks* to emphasize that each thing contains the particles of that originary fire. The account prefigures the wheel in the second vision, where it describes the wings propelled by the energy of fire: *flying around the circling circlet with my fiery wings […] I have ordered all things rightly*, with Wisdom. The circle embraced by the divine wings is all of creation, and *as a circle surrounds and contains all that lies inside of it, so holy divinity contains and exceeds all things infinitely, for no one can divide or overcome it in its power, or bring it to an end* (II.2,2, 55).

The wings of God fly around the circle of creation: on the one hand, they order it rightly through Wisdom; on the other, they govern it with justice that observes and distinguishes each thing. Thus God's fiery force is a creative, ordering, and preserving force. In the vision the fiery energy materializes as an *imago almost like a human form*, an image that clearly evokes the concept of *imago Dei* (image of God), which manifests at the beginning of the work *almost in the human form*, thus synthetically revealing the ontological relationship between God and Man. This is a relationship of love that begins on the sixth day of the Creation, when God gives life to man, making him in his image and likeness, *imago similitudinis*, and continues through history, when God himself assumes *the human form* and descends to earth in the *form* of the Son of Man, Son of God.

God's becoming Man represents their most complete union in the relationship of love. This winged figure of quasi-human form appears three times to Hildegard, who describes it in her three theological works. In the first vision of *Scivias*, it appears as *he who sat on the mountain*, with a pair of wings symbolizing divine justice. In the *Liber Vite Meritorum* (*The Book of the Rewards of Life*) it is *a man so tall that he reaches from the summit of the clouds down to the abyss*, and has a wing on each shoulder (I.1). The image becomes more detailed in the second vision (I.2), in which two more wings, one on his back and one on his chest, are seen. Each wing on his shoulders contains an open book that recounts the encounter between God and humankind: from the command given to Noah to the Law written on stone; the story of Jacob and of the people of Israel; the coming of Christ narrated at the beginning of the Gospel of John; and the gift of prophecy, indicating the Wisdom and Knowledge in the writings of philosophers and other wise ones, which show the ways of justice to follow to combat evil (I.1 and I.2). In the last work, the *LDO*, the winged figure appears almost in *a human form* with two pairs of wings, one above and the other below, symbolizing the love of God and neighbor (I.1). The same wings appear in the only vision in part two (II.1): an image of God's protection that envelops the earth.

The wings are the symbolic image that connects God/Man to the space that they themselves embrace. This space has a different form in each of the three works: in *Scivias* it is like a *mountain*/Kingdom of God, and an *egg/instrumentum*/firmament; in the *Liber Vite Meritorum*, the *four parts of the world*; and in the *LDO*, a *circle/wheel*/firmament/world.

These are limited representations, according to Hildegard, who points out that neither the form of the *egg* in *Scivias* nor that of the *wheel* in the *LDO* bears a resemblance/likeness to the form of the world, since the latter is *whole, round, and whirling*, and only a *globe* could imitate that form in its every part (*LDO*, I.2,3, 55). To conclude, a consideration concerning the sapiential terms: the word *globe* is the same word with which, in *Scivias*, precisely within the context of the *instrumentum/egg*, the *Lux vivens* (Living Light) indicates the Earth/Man as a *sandy globe*; the Moon/Church as a *globe of incandescent fire*; and the Sun/Christ as a *globe of glowing fire*. Thus, the image of the *world/wheel* in the *LDO* is linked to the three *globes*—sun, moon, earth—the Trinity reflected in creation, embraced by the wings of Wisdom and the generative and protective Love of God.

On the following pages, the various elements are represented and compared with the ones in *Scivias* that form the reconstruction of the plate on page 67.

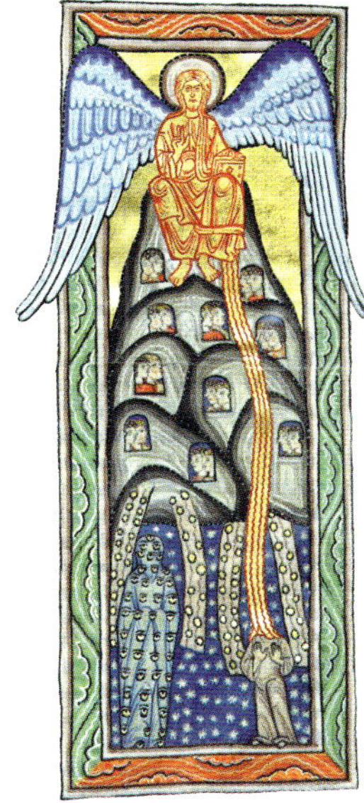

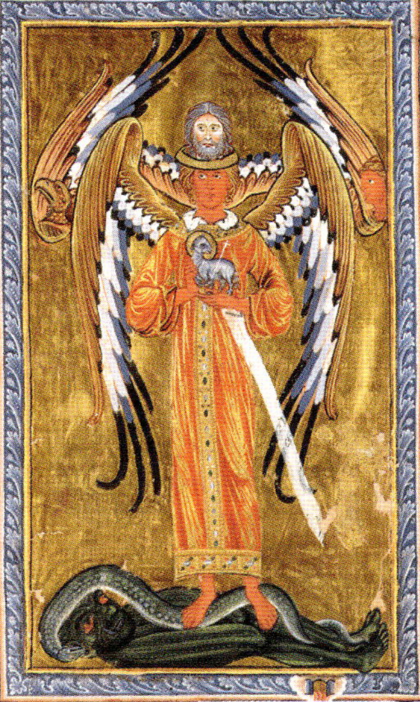

An Almost Human Form and Wings/Divine Love

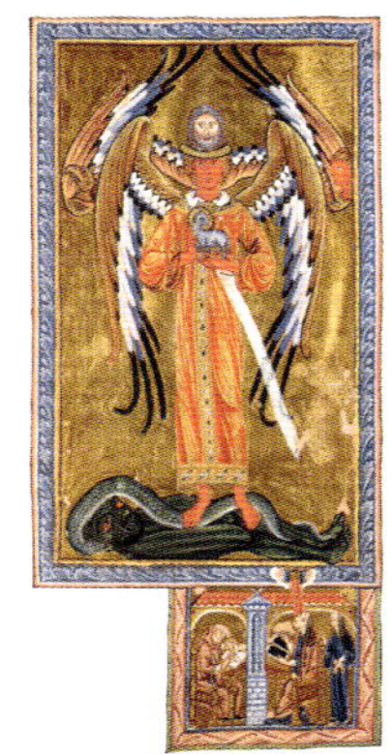

In the middle of the southern sky
Purgatory

And I saw as if in the middle of the southern sky an image [...] like a human in form [Divine Love] *[...]. And these faces were turned towards the east* (I.1,1, 33).

In medio australis aeris: these opening words admirably condense the profound meaning of the work. The main theme, as we have seen, is the path of purification of the soul. Hildegard describes the places of penitence within the wheel as being located where *they are purged, after they have been stripped of their bodies, the souls* (II.1,6, 272); thus the term "purge" is linked to a place (see *Il libro delle opere divine* 2003, 1228, note 14). Returning to the description of the geographical place where the figure appears, we find a close connection with the Purgatory that Dante later places in the same southern sky in the complex geography of the afterlife that he created in the *Divine Comedy*.

The concept of Purgatory and its location in the geographical space of the *australis aeris* thus seem linked to a conception that gradually evolved throughout the Middle Ages, which, narrated by Hildegard and present in other medieval authors, was systematized by Dante in his great work.

The positioning of the figure of Divine Love in *medio australis aeris* means that it is in the bright part of the globe, where the sun reaches its maximum splendor at noon. Sun and Divine Love come together in the maximum splendor of light: an expression of the ardent outpouring of the love of God that vitalizes and enflames everything.

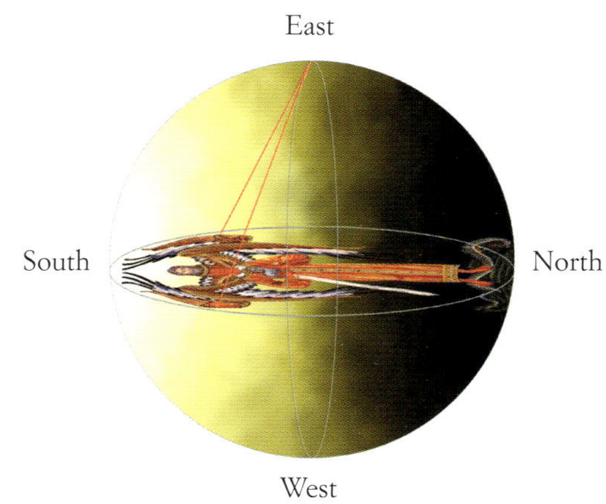

The wings
The law of love

And from each side of the figure's neck a single wing came forth, [both] rising up to join together above the aforementioned circlet [...].

Furthermore, from each shoulder of this image, a single wing stretched forth down to her knees (I.1,1, 33).

In *Scivias*, at the beginning of his journey, Man finds himself before a paternal God enthroned on a mountain, an authoritative presence, who *sees* into his heart and whose wings, as light *as shadows*, embrace him and gently *exhort and admonish* him with *ineffable* divine *Justice*.

In completing the journey along the *ways*, the human being grows in virtue by listening to the dialectical sparring match between vices and virtues described in the *Liber Vite Meritorum*, where God again appears in human form with four wings, representing the transition from the ancient to the new law.

In the *LDO*, Man arrives at the encounter with God no longer as an immature son who needs the authoritarian guidance of his father, but as the son of a father who gave him everything out of love, even his own Son, who lovingly *brought to himself the righteous and the sinners and lifted them both by the shoulders—because they had lived rightly—and by the knees—because*

he had recalled them from the way of injustice—and made them consorts of the citizens of heaven (I.1,10, 40).

The way of Wisdom thus leads to obedience of the mature law of love: *love God and thy neighbor*. A law that comes from and always tends toward God, like the wings pointing to heaven. In these wings, there are two heads: on the right, the head of an eagle, since *when in the soaring heights of triumphant submission, [...], he [Man] is made lofty in the blessedness of divine protection* (I.1,5, 37); on the left, a *human countenance, for it is not according to herd animals but according to what human nature teaches them that they begin to live in moral integrity* (I.1,8, 39).

Returning to *Scivias*, in the vision of the Wall (III.6) we find the same wings turned upward in the figure of the angel held by the virtue of Compassion in her lap. The virtue of devotion and obedience, she is flanked by the two other virtues of Temperance and Generosity, and followed by the three neotestamentarian virtues of Truth, Peace, and Blessedness. The combined images from *Scivias*—The Kingdom of God (I.1) and The Wall (III.6)—contain the two elements of the lower and upper wings with which we can reconstruct the wings of the image of Divine Love (see page 67). The iconography of the wings enables us to see the transition from the God of Justice (*Scivias*, I.1) to the God of Love (*LDO*, I.1) through the experience of Compassion whose gifts are Truth, Peace, and Blessedness.

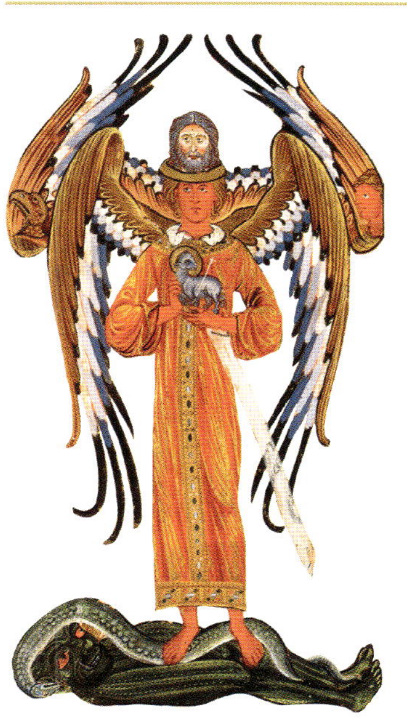

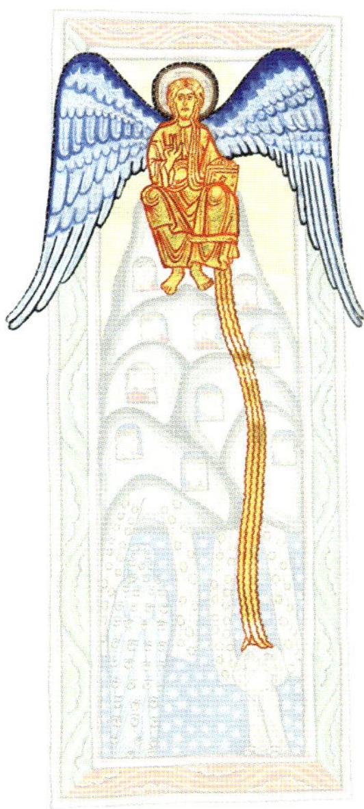

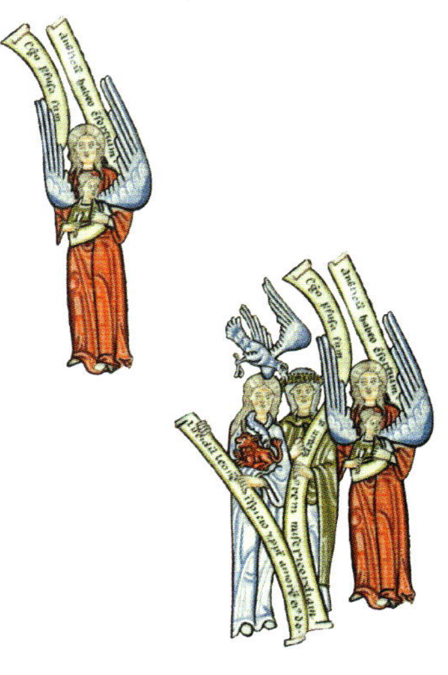

The lamb and the face of the father
The gentleness and benevolence of God

Above that head, moreover, in the same circlet appeared another face as of an old man, whose chin and beard touched the crown of the [lower] head (I.1,1, 33).

And in her hands she held a lamb, shining like the light of day (I.1,1, 33).

Above the face of the image of Divine Love, there is the face of an old man, enclosed in a circle formed by the upper wings: *the all-surpassing goodness of divinity, which is without beginning and end, brings aid and comfort to the faithful [...]. For divinity holds fast the lofty reaches of supreme Love [, which touch those of the younger head,] by arranging and protecting all things, as when the Son of God in his humanity led lost humankind back to heavenly thin*gs (I.1,4, 37). Divine Love is manifested in the works of the Son of God represented by the Lamb, image of the *gentleness of true faith*, so that the faithful may fly *upon the wings of the winds, that is, upon the heavenly harmo-ny* (I.1,11, 41). The face of the old man and the Lamb appear at the end of *Scivias*, in the account of the time of peace when, after the tumult of the Last Judgment, heavenly harmony reigns in the Quiet and Jubilation of the Heavens (III.12). The faithful arrive there after sur-mounting the wall of Speculative Science in the square Building (III.2) which, like the Lamb in the *LDO*, *shines like the light of day*. After being greeted by a *human [...] face*, crossing the Wall of the light of day, and follow-ing the path of edification through faith—a gift of the

Lamb—they finally see God the Father's *head with white hair* when they come face to face with him in Paradise at the great celebration where the harmony of heaven reigns supreme. And this is where the *LDO* journey begins.

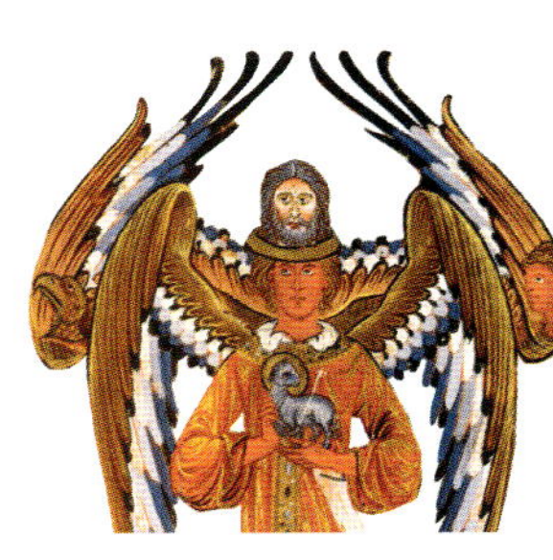

Rhetoric

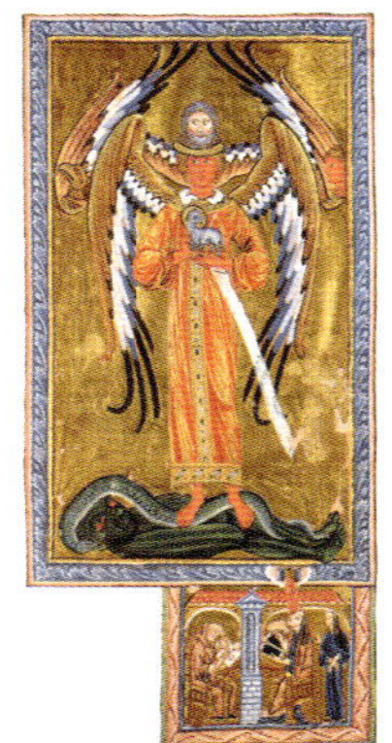

The circle as aurora
The catholic faith

And a great circlet of golden color surrounded her head (I.1,1, 33).

The golden circlet around the head of the human figure represents *the catholic faith, spread throughout the whole world and rising in the first dawn of exceptional brilliance, [which] embraces the excellence of true Love's abundance with every devotion, as when God redeemed humankind in his Son's humanity and strengthened them by pouring the Holy Spirit into them. So one God is understood in Trinity, who without temporal beginning before the ages was God in divinity* (I.1,4, 36–37).

    In *Scivias*, this *circle like the aurora* appears in two images: the Synagogue (I.5), where it surrounds the head of the *imago of a woman* and represents the *prefiguration of the incarnation of the Son of God*; and the square Building (III.2), which it surrounds, symbolizing the *power of God*. The color of the aurora refers to Mary/*aurora*, who gives birth to the Son of God. True faith is born in Man after Christ has come to earth and, through his death, shown humanity the *way.* This is depicted in three images: the death of Christ on the Column of the Trinity

(III.7); Faith, in the Column of the Savior (III.8), and the building of the Church in the Tower of the Church (III.9). In the *LDO*, faith becomes visible in the first vision through the certainty of the presence of the Lamb/Son of God, and through the crown of Divine Love that connects him with the benevolence of the Father.

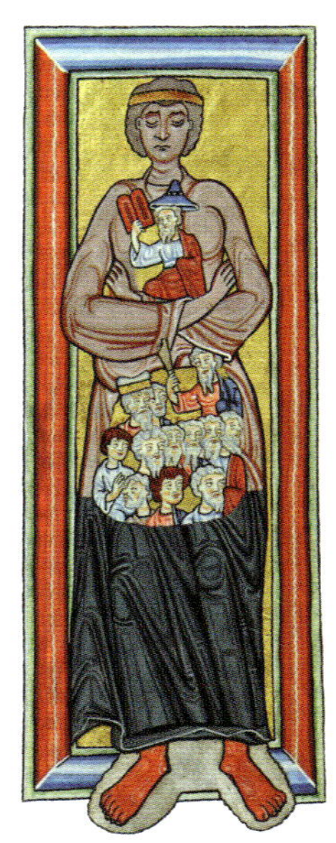
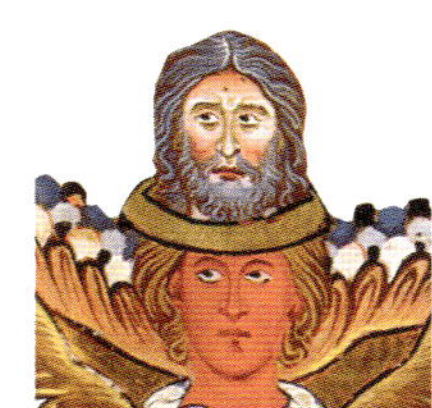
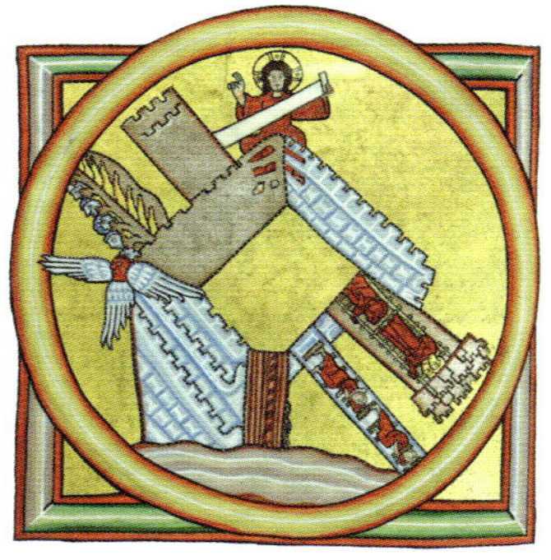

The monster and the serpent
The devil and discord

Moreover, she was treading with her feet a monster, dreadful in appearance and venomous and black in color, and also a serpent that had fixed its mouth upon the right ear of the monster (I.1,1, 33).
    True Love […] bruises discord's injury, which is misshapen by its excessive vices and horrifying because of its many perversities, and poisonous in deception and black in perdition. Likewise, she bruises the ancient serpent as he lays traps for the faithful, for upon the cross the Son of God reduced him to nothing (I.1,12, 41).

The winged figure that treads the monster is the image of God, who with the Benevolence, Faith, Divine Love, and Meekness of the Son immolated like a lamb on the altar, conquered the Ancient Serpent, bringer of discord. The same image of the monster is found in *Scivias* in the vision of the Ancient Serpent (II.7a) in which, enchained by the power of God, it is trampled by *men dressed in white*. These men have received faith through Baptism and the sacraments, and are united in the Church born with the Crucifixion of the Lamb. They are illuminated with the radiance of *tongues of fire*, representing the justice of the Holy Spirit. Thus ends the story of evil that began when the devil, spawned by the *loathsome cloud* that spread out from the pit of hell, resorted to diabolical

trickery and assumed the *sinuous form* of the serpent to assault the *candid cloud*, Eve. The devil's envy *sows deceit and discord*, and will do this *until the end of time* (I.1,12, 41–42). In fact, in the *LDO* the serpent *fixes its mouth upon the right ear of the monster* and stretches its *tail* all the way down to its feet, because even if evil is bound in chains and vanquished, it continues to work on humankind through the sense of hearing. This is what is shown in the opening vision, in which Man is reassured by the defeat of evil, and he is exhorted to remain vigilant.

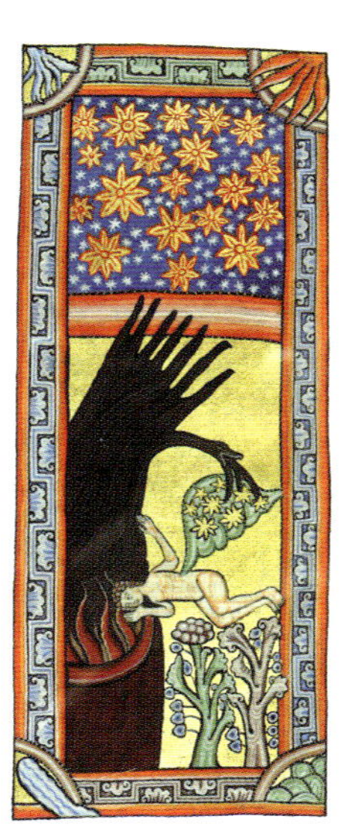
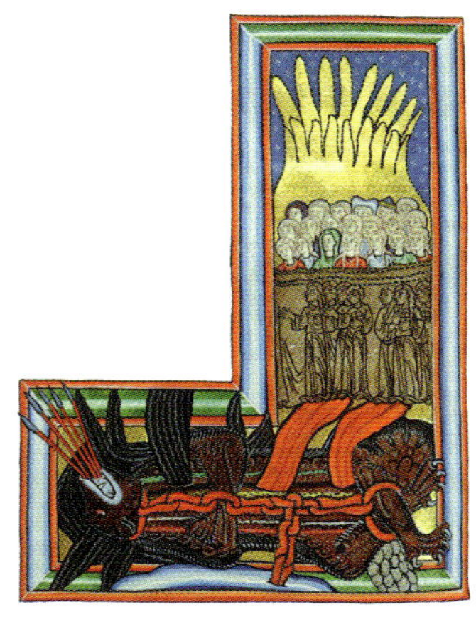
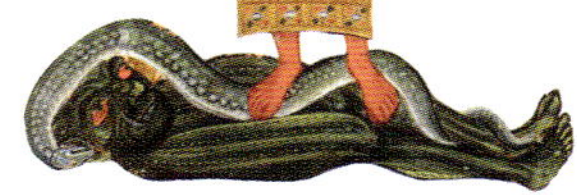

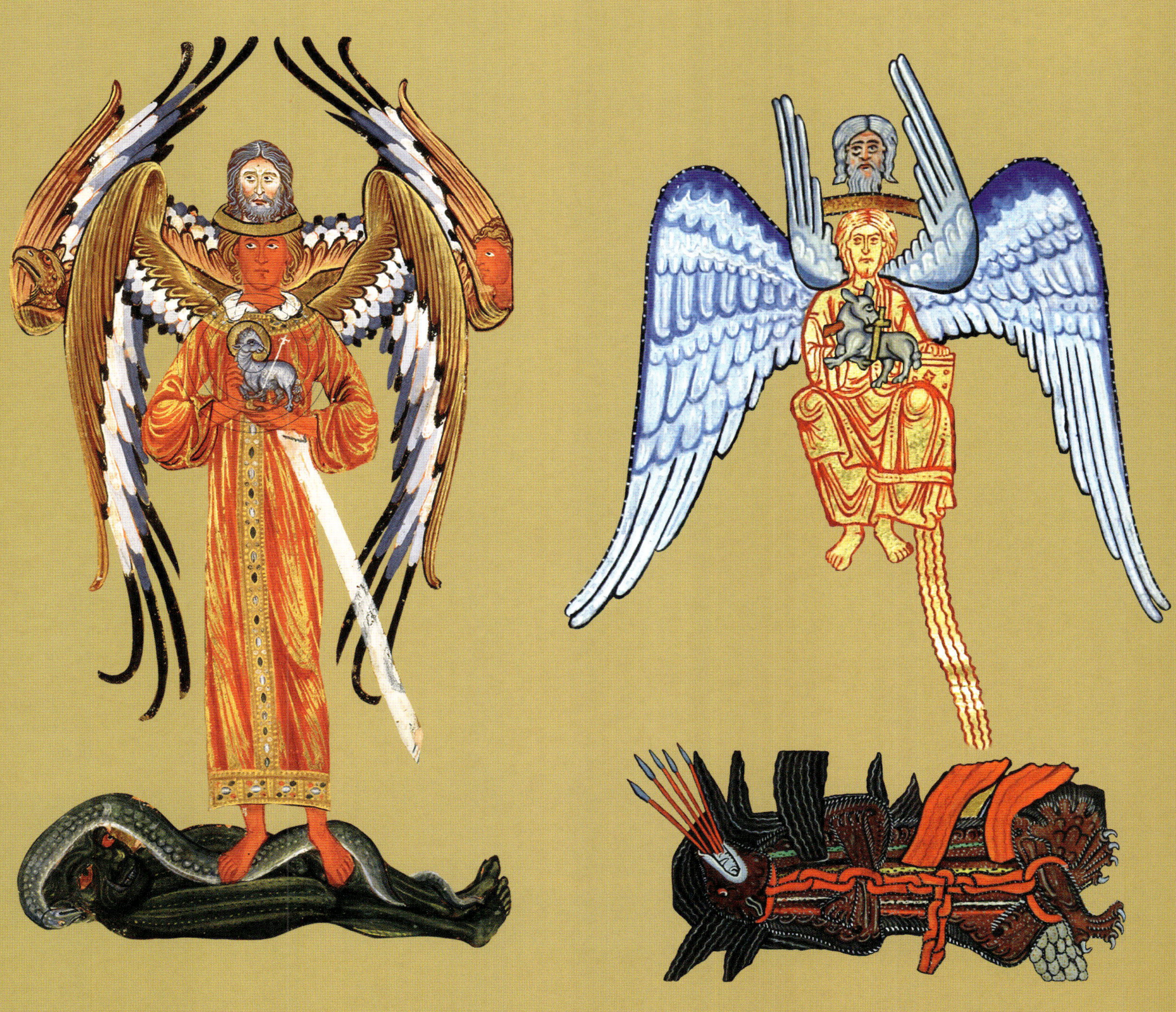

The complete reconstruction of the winged figure using the iconographic elements from Scivias.

The Wheel

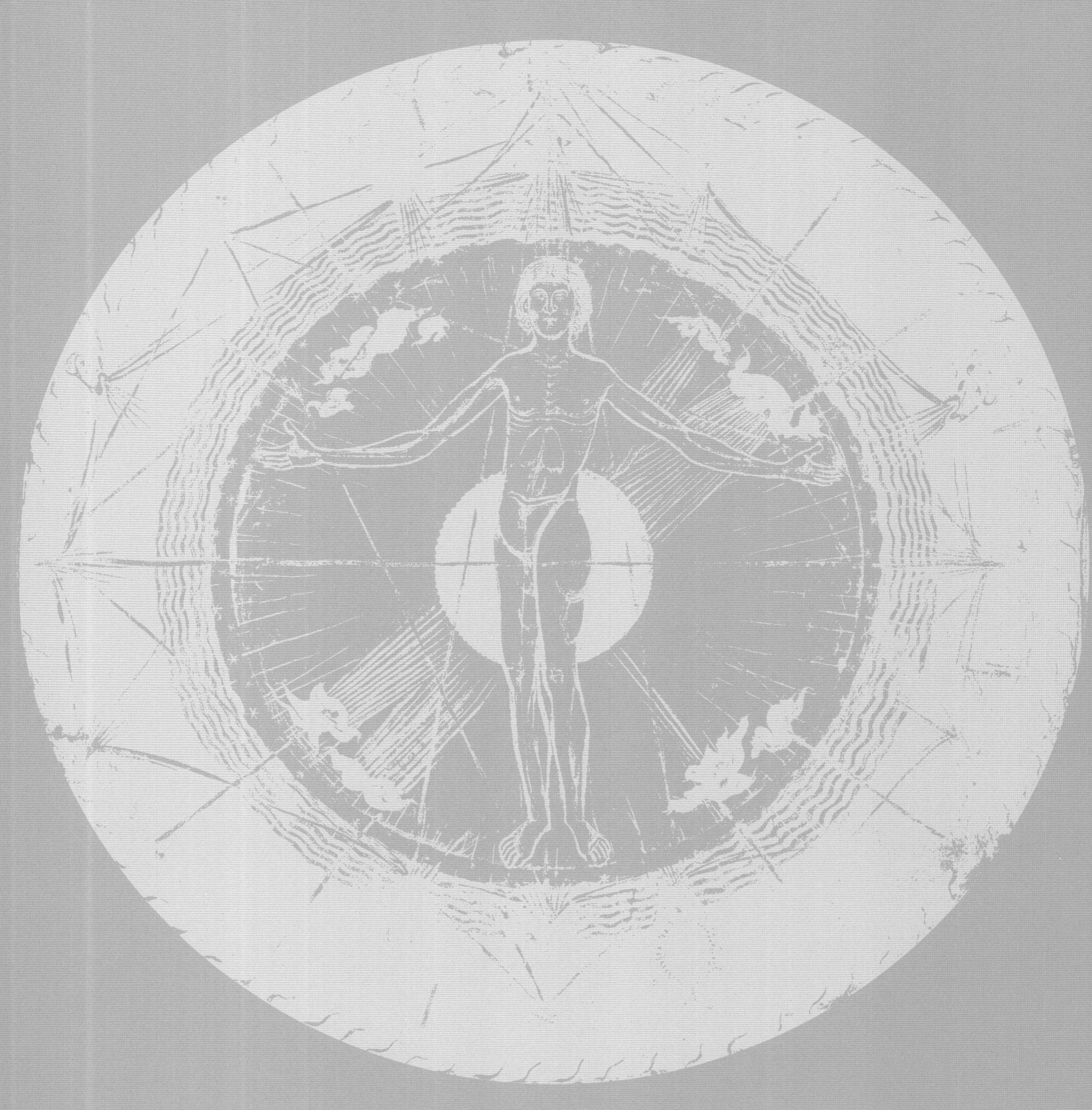

Instrumentum: Egg, Wheel, Globe. *God and Creation*

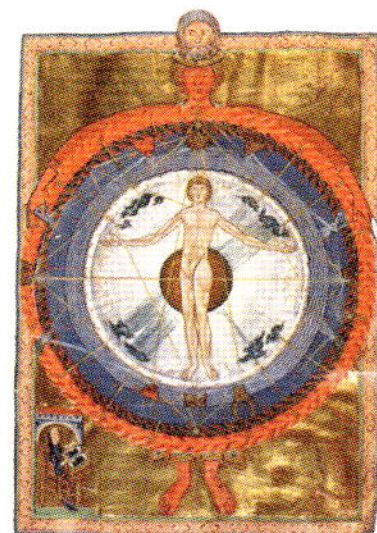

Then, upon the breast of the aforementioned image […] there appeared a wheel, wonderful to see, together with its signs and symbols. This wheel was nearly like that instrument that I had seen twenty-eight years before, signified in the shape of an egg (I.2,1, 46).

But now, the circumference and correct proportion of these elements is shown only in a wheel, though neither of these holds a complete likeness of the figure of the world in every detail, because it exists everywhere whole, round, and whirling. Rather, a globe that is whole and whirling better imitates the form of the world in its every part (I.2,3, 55).

The wheel, *instrumentum*/device, appears upon the *breast* of the image in human form of God/Divine Love. The vision of the form of the world, circular and in perennial movement, unfolds in God's heart: *the body of the world remains indissoluble with its circular movement.* Previously described as an *egg*, this form now appears to Hildegard as a *globe*/sphere. Modern man is instinctively drawn to distinguish God and creation, objectifying them as two distinct representations. The vision leads us to understand that God and creation are actually a single, whole unity: *And as a circle surrounds and contains all that lies inside of it, so holy divinity contains and exceeds all things infinitely, for no one can divide or overcome it in its power, or bring it to an end* (I.2,2, 55).

God takes human form in order to become known to man and is described by means of an *almost* or *similar to* or *how* or *form of*. *Lux vivens* explains and illuminates Hildegard telling her that the image in the *form of man* is God/Divine Love and that God/creation is *like a wheel. Indeed, in its foreknowledge and operation, divinity is like a wheel, whole and utterly undivided, for it has neither beginning nor ending, nor can anything grasp or surround it, for it is outside of time* (I.2,2, 54–55).

The Elements of the Wheel and the Form of Man in Its Middle

Second vision

Firmament, world, earth

The form of the world (I.2,2, 54).

I saw, and behold the east wind and south wind, together with their collaterals, moved the firmament through the blasts of their strength and made it to revolve above the earth from east to west (I.3,1, 106).

And I saw that the firmament, together with everything attached to it, had as great a density from its top to the top of the earth as the earth had from pole to pole (I.4,1, 130).

Then I saw the round of the earth divided into five parts (II.1.1, 264).

Within the wheel appears the *figure of the world*. Within the world is the earth's globe and the body of man with his five senses.

The vision leads us to look into God's heart as if we were embarking upon a journey from the vast universe through the heavens of the firmament and were able to glimpse the earth, and in it, man, and in him, his body and soul.

The measurements of the wheel/world in the second vision correspond to the circumference of the earth in the fifth vision, in which the earth is made in the image and likeness of the world/firmament/God just as man is made in the image and likeness of the Son of Man and Son of God.

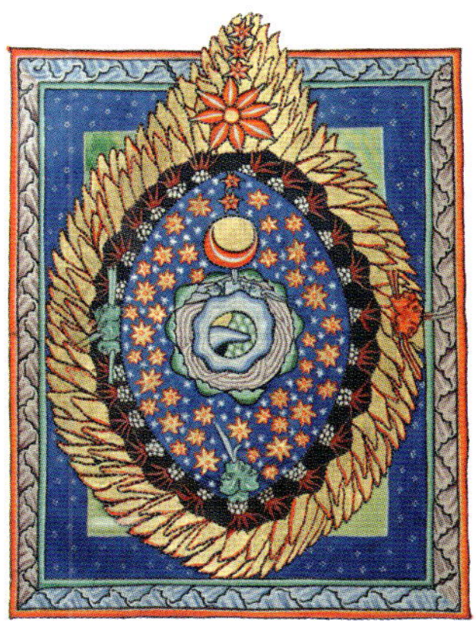

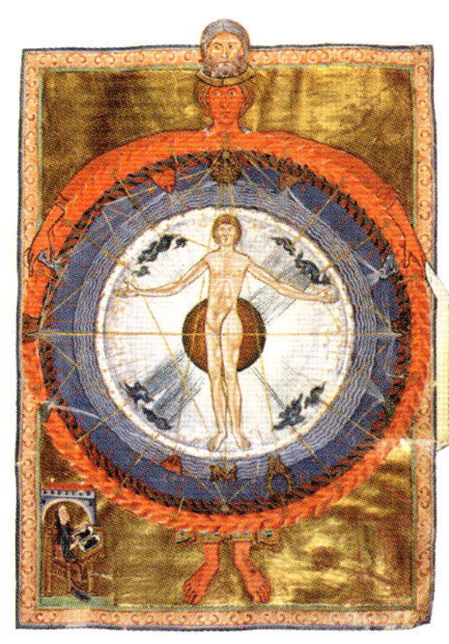

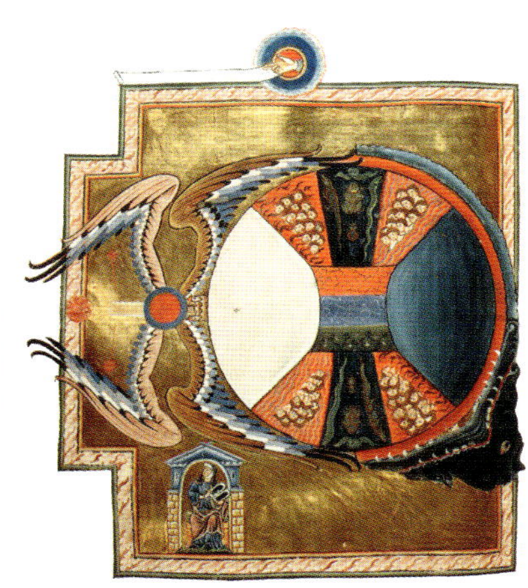

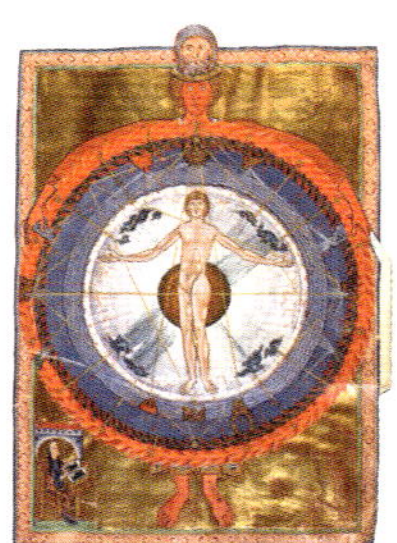

God, the wheel, and man
In the heart of God, in the heart of man

Then, upon the breast of the aforementioned image [...] there appeared a wheel, wonderful to see (I.2,1, 46).

In the middle of the wheel there also appeared the image of a human being (I.2,1, 49).

This signifies that humankind exists within the structure of the universe, in its middle as it were. For humankind is more powerful than the other creatures that exist within that structure (I.2,15, 62).

Right from the beginning, we are told that man and the world lie *in pectore*, in God's breast/heart, and the fourth vision adds that *so God did in his Word when he created all things, for the Word, which is the Father's Son, lay hidden within the Father, like the heart hidden within a person. And God made Man's form according to his image and likeness* (I.4,14, 139).

All of this amplifies the meaning of the opening words of the vision—*upon the breast*—and leads us through the various passages informing us that man's heart is kept in his breast just like the Son of God in his Father; man is made in the image and likeness of God; all of creation is born from the Word/Son concealed in the father. And this is a marvellous distillation of love. The world lies in God's breast; in the middle of the world, surrounded by the circles of the elements, is man; in the middle of man is his heart. In the same way that God holds his Son in his heart.

Forming a continuous line of creation of love, the expression *in pectore* conceals the infinite mystery that reveals that man's heart lies in God's heart. And a sign of this can be found in the vision of the Omnipotent (III.1a) opening the third part of *Scivias*, which describes the filthy mud surrounded by precious stones that can be seen in God's breast. The mud is man who is kept in God's heart and who, by imitating the virtues and the blessed—the precious stones surrounding him—may once again shine in his original grace. All of this suggests that *Scivias* contains the indications for a path to be followed and that in the *LDO* we will find its end destination.

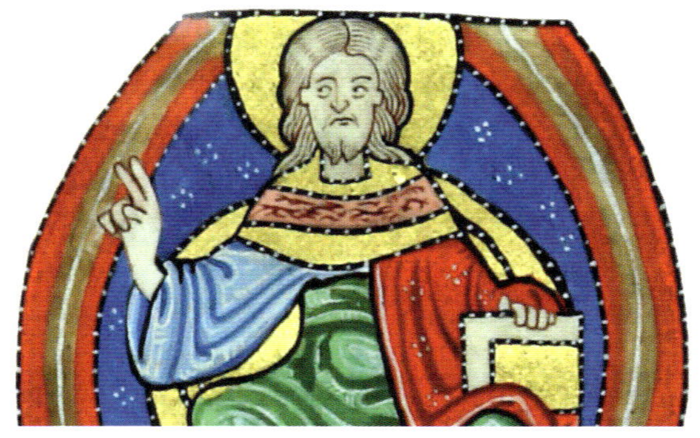

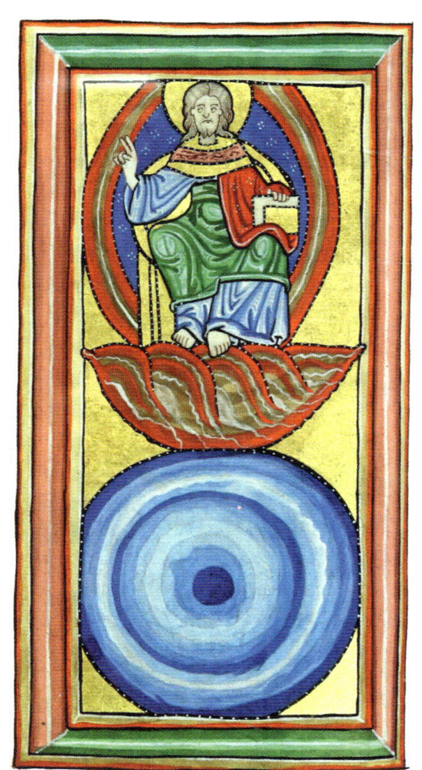

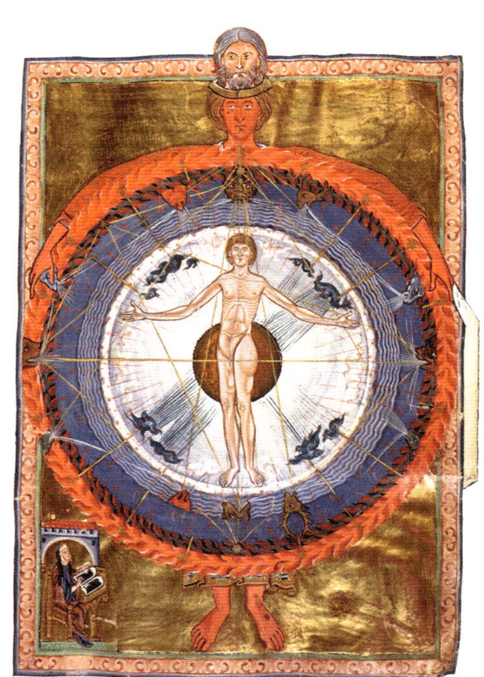

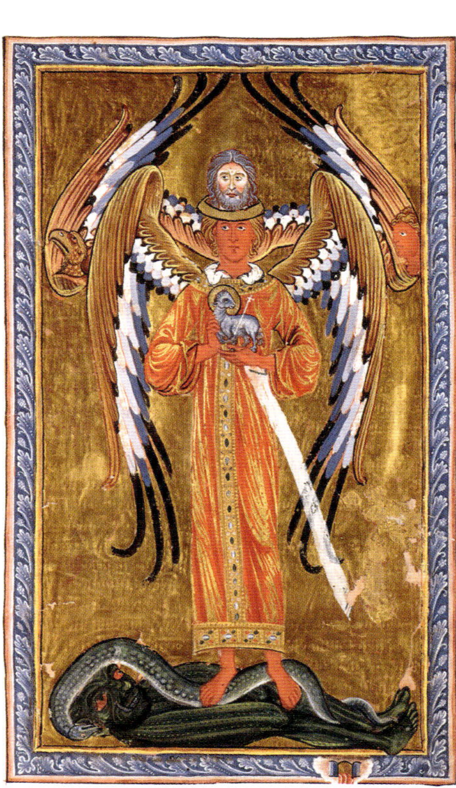

The circles of the wheel/egg/globe
One great vision

This wheel was nearly like that instrument that I had seen twenty-eight years before, signified in the form of an egg. […] But when the instrument described above was laid out in your earlier visions in the shape of an egg, this was to show that only the division of the elements was signified in that likeness […]. But now, the circumference and correct proportion of these elements is shown only in a wheel (I.2–3, 54–55).

The wheel in the *LDO* and the egg in *Scivias* are two visible forms of the same vision, which, as time passes, reveals different aspects to man. At the beginning of his journey, the man sees an egg and is capable of perceiving its elements in terms of form and colour. After reaching the end of his journey through the wheel in the *LDO*, he is able to perceive more subtle and more specific aspects, and can grasp its message of wisdom—*number*, *weight*, and *measurement*—contained in the language of numbers and of proportions.

The image can be reconstructed by drawing the circles of the wheel using the measurements provided in the *LDO* and then referring to the chromatic description of the egg in *Scivias*. This allows us to discover the similarities—in the images and not just in the text—between the egg *instrumentum* and the wheel *instrumentum* through the two-dimensional representation of a section of the three-dimensional figure of the globe.

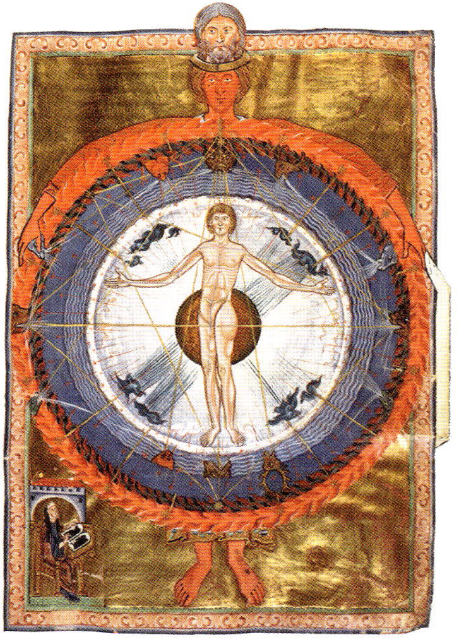

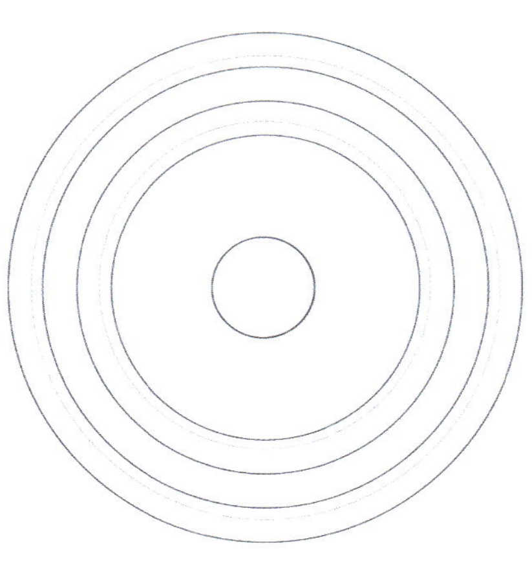

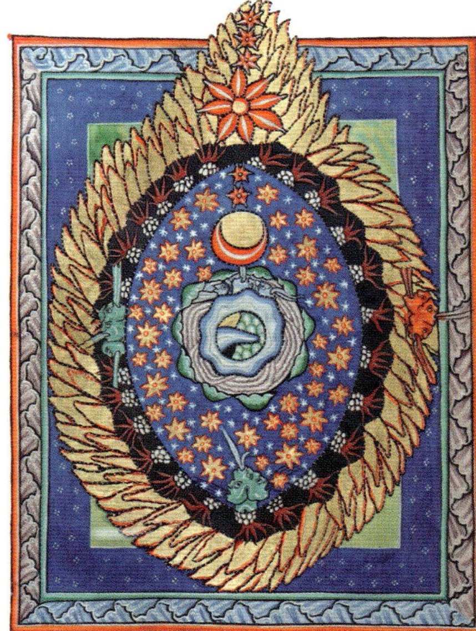

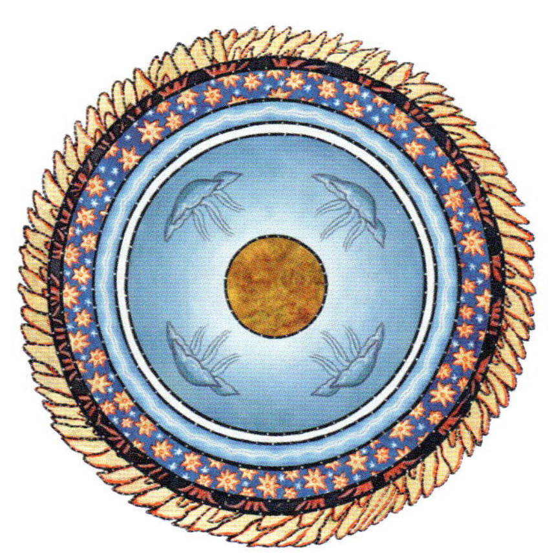

Given that the description of the elements (lucid fire, dark fire, pure ether, etc.) is the same both for the egg in Scivias *and for the wheel in* LDO*, we coloured and redesigned the wheel in* LDO *with the colours and elements of* Scivias *to create a computer-generated image.*

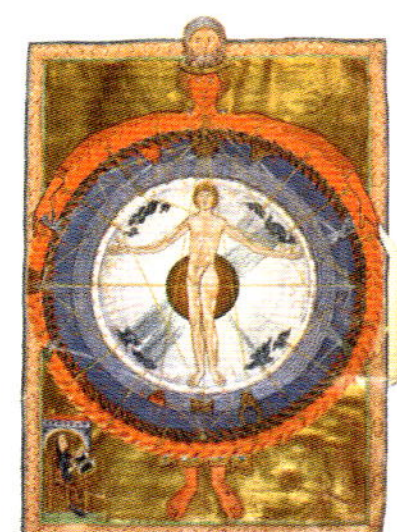

The circles
The Trinity

Along its outermost circumference there was shown a circle in the likeness of bright fire, and beneath this circle there was as if another circle, of black fire [...]. And these two circles were joined to each other as if they were a single circle. [...] Beneath the circle of black fire there was another circle, in the likeness of pure ether, which was everywhere of the same thickness as the previous two circles of fire. [...] Beneath the circle of pure ether, there was shown another circle of watery air, and its round thickness was as great as the thickness of the circle of bright fire. And beneath that circle of watery air there was shown another circle as of strong, bright white air [...] and it appeared everywhere in its circumference to be of the same thickness as the circle of black fire. These two circles were also joined together, so that they appeared as if they were a single circle. [...] There was also marked out in the middle of the thin air's sphere a globe (I.2,1, 46 and 48).

The measurements of the elements of the wheel are based on a series of proportional relations. Starting at the external circle—following the description of the vision—the *lucid fire* is double the thickness of the *dark (black) fire* (2:1) and both circles are joined together (2+1=3) (A). The thickness of the *ether* is equal to that of *lucid fire* and *dark fire*, so 3 (B). The same ratio is found in the two circles of *watery air* and *strong air*, whose sum is once again 3 (C). There are three concentric crowns: one with *dark fire* and *lucid fire* (A); one with *ether* (B); and one with *watery air* and *strong air* (C). Each of the three elements—*fire, ether,* and *air*—has a value of 3 and their combined value is 9. The circular crown occupied by the three elements (C') has the same diameter as the globe (A'), which is equivalent to the distance between the globe and the *strong air* (B') (see page 100). Finally, the wheel is divided into 3 large spaces, each with a value of 9: the space of the *globe* (A'), the space *from the globe to the strong air* (B') and the space *from the strong air to the bright fire* (C').

The result is a veritable hymn to the Trinity, composed through forms, numbers, and ratios, and contained in the constituent parts of creation.

Turning back to *Scivias*, if we place the outer circle of the wheel on top of the silver outer circle of the miniature of The Three Persons (II.2), we will notice other surprising coincidences. In fact, the middle circle coincides with the yellow of the glowing fire of the Spirit and the circle of the earth globe with the middle of the body of the sapphire-colored figure of man. Clearly, both visions were constructed on the basis of the same proportions.

In particular, the silver outer circle referring to the Father brings to mind the words in the vision of *Scivias* describing how the Trinity appears as three flames—*stone, flame,* and *word*—and how the silver circle of the Father has three qualities: *moist greenness, palpable strength,* and *glowing fire.* We can therefore gain a sense of the profound correspondence in terms of measurements and meanings connecting these three qualities to the three elements—*watery air, ether,* and *fire*—of the wheel in the *LDO* onto which they are superimposed.

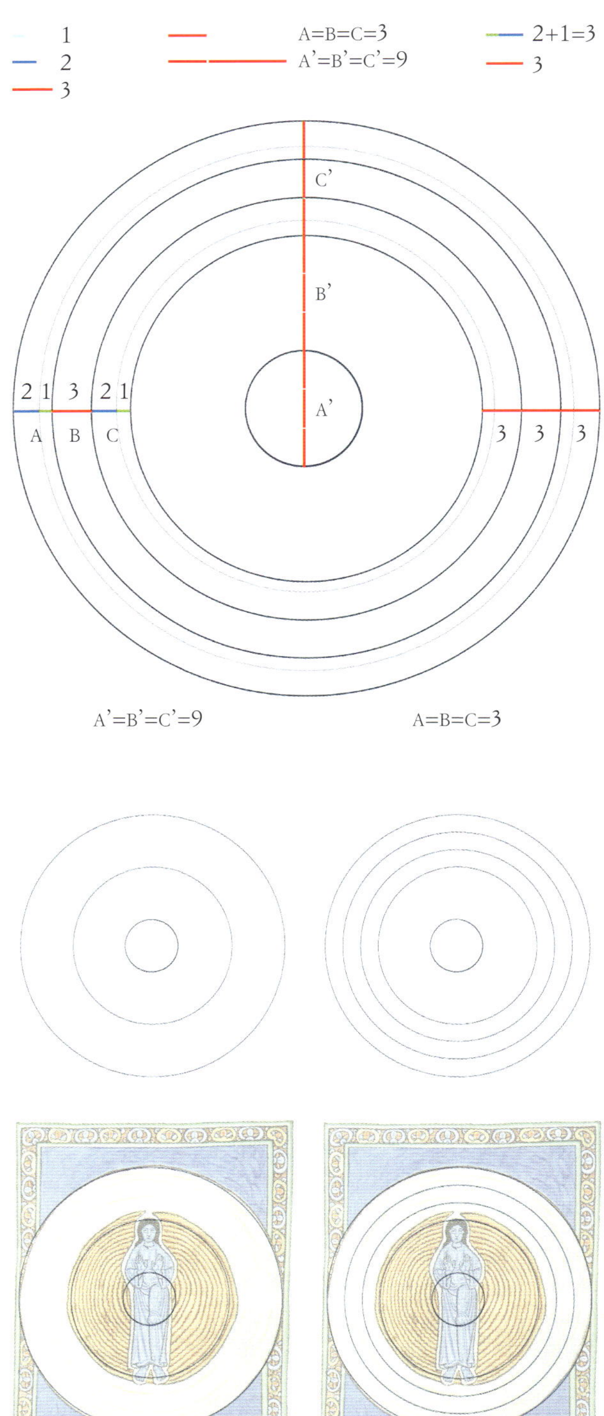

The line of the Sun/Christ
Light and darkness

And there stretched a line as if from the beginning of the eastern part of that wheel to the end of its western part, and it faced the northern part, separating, as it were, the northern region from the other regions (I.2,1, 48).

For from the first dawn in the east, where the sun first rises as the days begin to get longer, to the final sunset in the west, where the sun cannot go any farther, there arcs this line—the path of the sun, avoiding the northern region (I.2,11, 59).

The description of the circles of the elements is followed by the description of the *line of the sun* that divides the *wheel/body of the world* into two distinct parts: *light* and *darkness*. Man is called upon to fulfil his choices in the path within creation by discerning between *light* and *darkness*. The division of the wheel is made by the *line of the sun*, which starts in the east and ends in the west. The path of the sun coincides with the places symbolizing Christ's birth and death, represented in *Scivias* in the vision of the Building (III.2). On the top, in the east, is Christ the Cornerstone; on the bottom, opposite him, is the Column of the Trinity (III.7), red with the blood of Christ's death. The line of the sun crosses the east/west axis, going from top to bottom. As we have seen in the pages dedicated to the one great vision, this reconstruction seems to be partially contradicted by the miniature showing the line in a horizontal position.

The globe
Earth/man

There was also marked out in the middle of the thin air's sphere a globe (I.2,1, 48).

For the earth exists within the midst of the atmosphere like the honeycomb amid the honey (I.4,80, 203).

The breadth across this globe was as great as the depth of space from the top of the outermost circle to the final layer of clouds, or from the final layer of clouds to the top of this globe (I.2,1, 48).

All of the belly's inner organs cling to the navel, just as the rest of creation looks to the circumference of the earth. For the navel is the strong point of the belly, just as the earth's compass is the refuge for all other creatures (I.4,76, 200).

The earth/globe is placed in the middle so that it may be *tempered* by the other elements and *continually receives from them viridity and strength as sustenance* (I.2,13, 60). Similarly, man is also placed in the middle so that he may orient himself towards the *right discernment* with *devotion* through the *active life* and *right desires*.

However, if we rotate the figure around its south/north axis, the line appears in a vertical position. It is evident that the miniaturist deliberately chose to depict the wheel frontally, unshackled from its geographic and cosmological coordinates. Far from being inaccurate, this is a representation revealing the complexity of the orientations, which, as we have seen (page 58), can only be represented in a single image by means of a three-dimensional reconstruction.

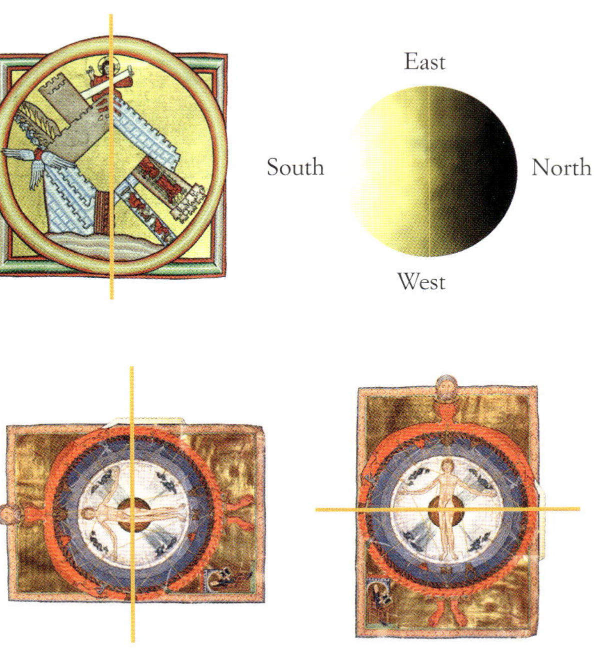

The earth/globe is placed in a proportional relationship with the elements of the firmament because the Creator has ensured that this should not be undone. In the same way, the faithful should look to God in order to maintain their equilibrium, overcoming the instability of their minds and the weakness of their flesh. The text cites the words of St. Paul inviting men to avoid *grumbling* and to *shine as lights, holding fast the words of life* (I.2.13, 61). The firmament divided into five parts is correlated to the five parts of the human body (see page 98). In particular, the earth/globe corresponds to the middle of the man's body with the navel becoming the middle of man, of the earth, and of the firmament.

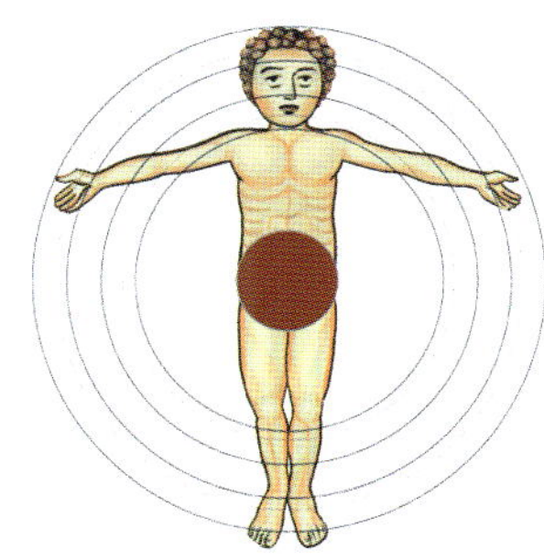

Rhetoric

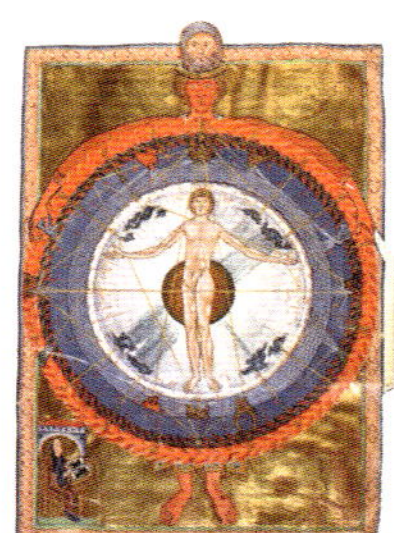

Man in the middle of the wheel
Body and soul

In the middle of the wheel there also appeared the image of a human being, whose crown reached above and whose feet stretched below the circle of strong, bright white air. The fingertips of the right hand were extended from the right side, and the fingertips of the left hand were extended from the left side, to that circle, marking it out from here to there in its circumference, because the image had its arms thus extended (I.2,1, 49).

The man inside the wheel/firmament is described as *imago hominis* or image of man. The use of the word *imago* is linked to the concept of *imago Dei*; in fact, the fourth vision states that God created humans in his image and likeness.

Returning to the superimposition of the wheel and vision of The Three Persons (II.2) in *Scivias*, we should note that the outer crown coincides with the silver circle of the Father, the inner crown with the yellow of the glowing fire of the Holy Spirit, and the *imago hominis* inside the wheel with the *sapphire-colored figure of man/* Christ. The image of the man described in the *LDO* is therefore closely correlated to Christ, the manifestation of God in the flesh.

The man is placed in the middle of the firmament *because he is the most powerful of all creatures* and his greatness lies in the *virtues of his soul*; he is connected to the higher and lower elements, and his hands operate within them. His strength is inner strength and *just as man's heart is hidden within his body so is man's body surrounded by the strengths of the soul*. This sequence— heart, body, soul—is the image of the relationship of the Trinity.

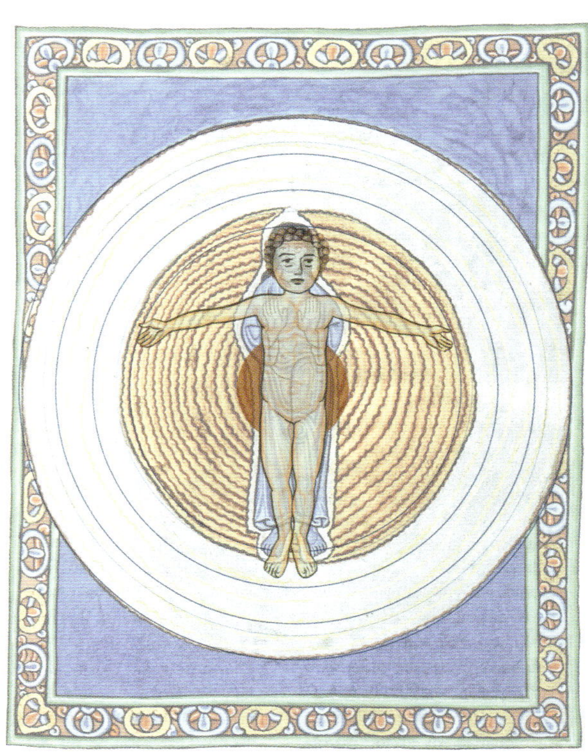

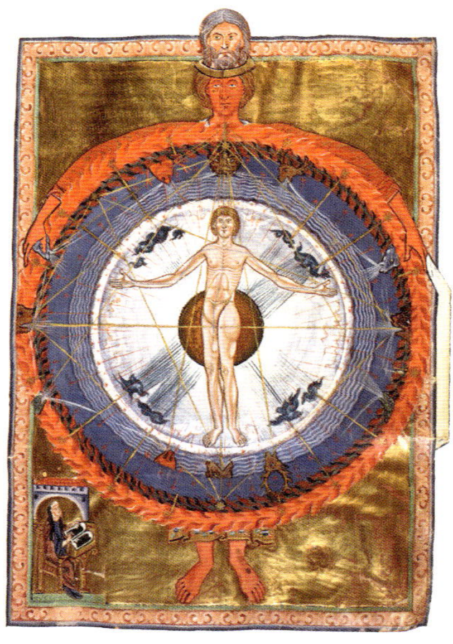

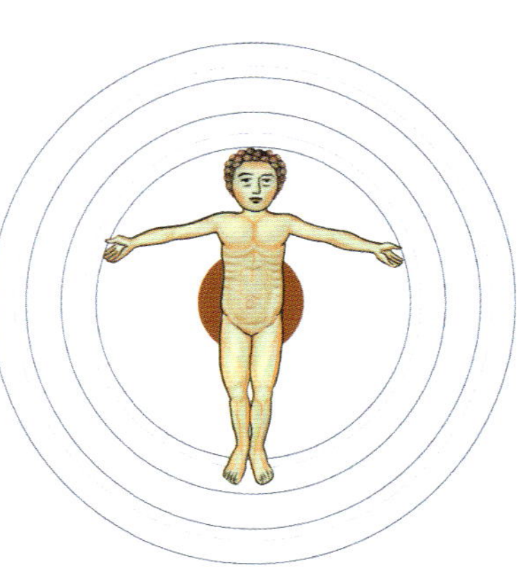

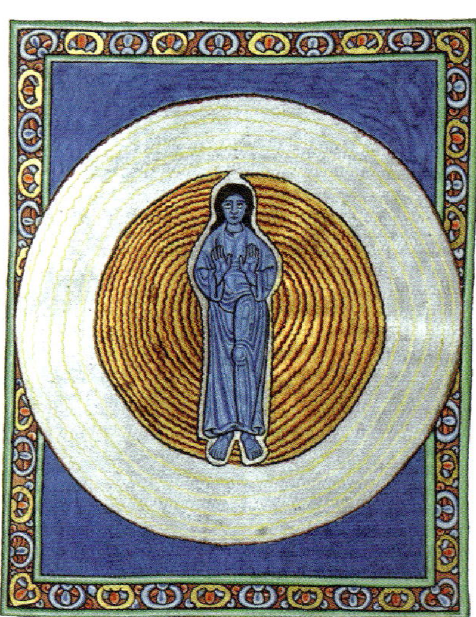

The winds: the powers moving the world
The solstitial lines

Furthermore, facing these parts there appeared four heads—as it were the head of a leopard and a wolf, and the head of a lion and a bear (I.2,1, 49).

All of these heads also breathe into the aforesaid wheel and onto the image of a human being, for these winds temper the world with their blasts and with their ministry preserve the health of humankind. For the world could not subsist, nor humankind live, if they were not quickened by the breaths of these winds (I.2,18, 65).

The winds are the *pillars of the world*. Each wind blows from one of the elements: *lucid fire, dark fire, ether*, and *watery air* appear in the form of animals and indicate the four cardinal points. The description begins at the top, with the east wind, following the direction of the extreme

points of the cross: top/*leopard*, bottom/*wolf*, right/*lion* and left/*bear*. Each wind has two collateral winds. There are 4 principal winds and 8 collateral winds, or 12 winds in total, recalling the Vitruvian division (see page 96).

The winds are also present in the vision of the Firmament (I.3) in *Scivias*. Here they indicate the initial phases of man's journey towards the knowledge of the *word of God* against the *Devil's rage*, with the *power of faith*/air and *purified with the water of Baptism*. In the *LDO* we learn that shortly before the definitive moment of the judgment, man receives the virtues through the blast of the four winds emitted by the four animal heads: respectively, *Fear of God, fear of hellish punishments*, and the certainty of *God's Judgment* that promises *physical suffering* if he fails to do good. During this journey he receives the support of the virtues coming from the breath of the collateral winds of *trust, faith, patience* and *prudence*, represented by the figures of the *crab, stag, lamb*, and *serpent*.

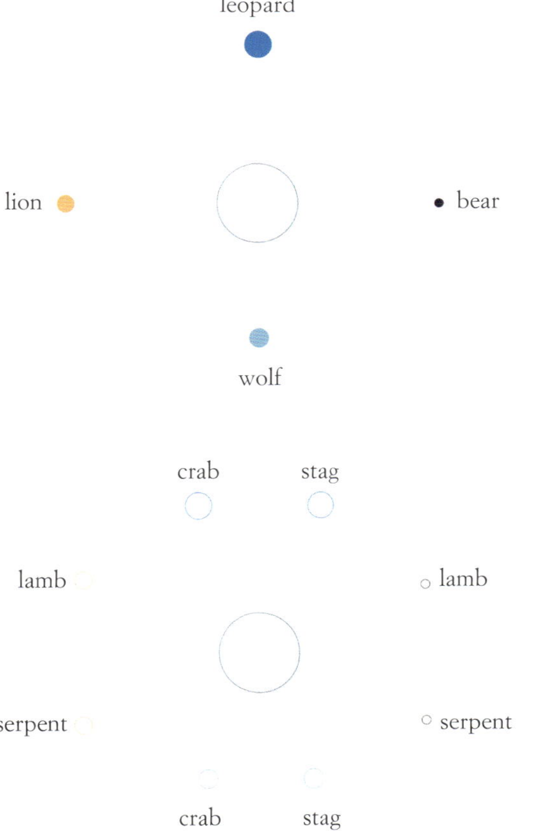

In her description of the line of the sun, Hildegard names the solstices (I.2,1, 52).

In medieval cosmology, the crab and the stag, which are images of Christ, are associated with the two solstices. Thus, the ideal and hypothetical solstitial lines going past the head of the crab and the head of the stag, to the left and right of the line of the sun, are indicated by a blue and red line: a deduction suggested by the name of the collateral winds and by their position, a hypothesis awaiting further investigation.

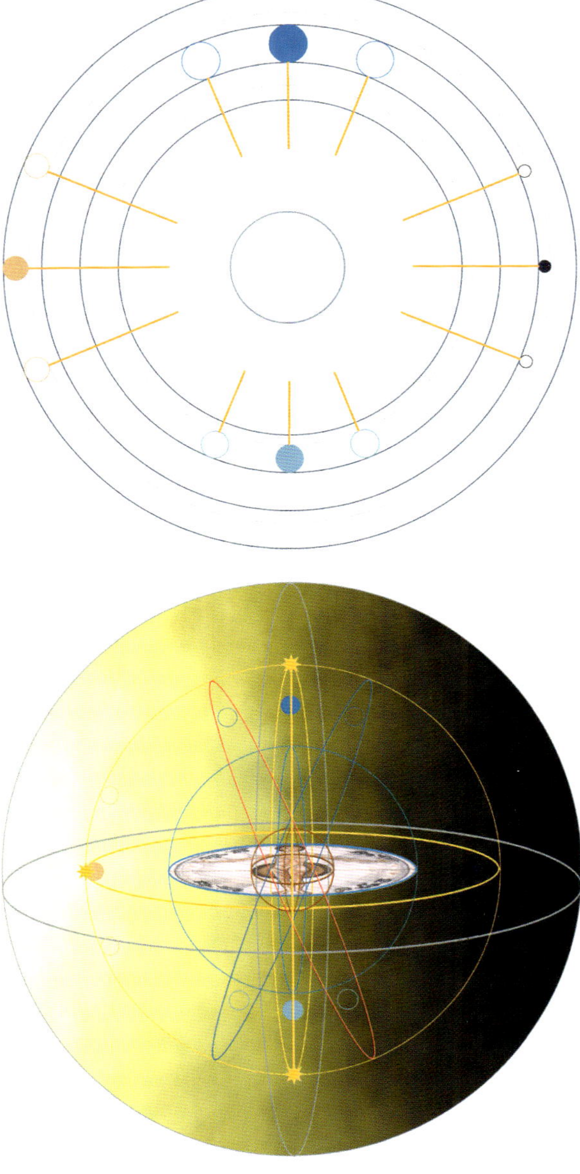

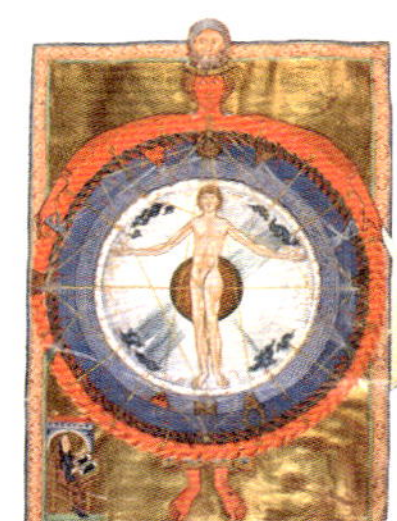

The position of the winds in the egg and in the wheel
*The two perspectives from the earth/man
and from the firmament/God*

In the *LDO*, the winds are described in terms of their position relative to the human figure; the direction in which they are blowing; and the element in which they are placed. *Scivias*, on the other hand, describes them in terms of the order in which they appear; the element in which they are placed; and the direction in which they are blowing. This wealth of detail highlights similarities and differences, and indicates a change in perspective. While it may seem that what has changed is the positions of the winds or the spatial orientation in which they are placed, what has actually changed is the point of view from which we are observing the egg/wheel/globe. It is similar to what happens when we look at our hand, turn it and then observe it from the other side: our fingers remain in the same place but first our thumb is on the right and then it is on the left; first the fingers point up, then they point downwards. This change in

perspective can be analyzed by considering three aspects: the order in which the winds are named (A); the element in which they are placed: lucid fire (Lf), dark fire (Df), ether (E) and watery air (Wa) (B); and the direction in which they are blowing (C).

Underneath, we have placed the wheel, with south to the left and the east on top according to the three-dimensional reconstruction on page 58; in the middle is the egg shown in the same position as in *Scivias*; on the right, the different angle and perspective from which the wheel/globe must be observed in order to see the winds compared to the order, elements, and direction in which they are visibly blowing in the egg.

I believe that three-dimensional reconstructions are necessary in order to fully appreciate the symbolism and dynamics of Hildegard's visions. As she herself wrote, the *instrumentum* egg/wheel is like a revolving sphere, which we are invited to observe from different viewpoints—from inside the earth, from outside the firmament, and from different angles—transferring the vision into a concrete real dimension.

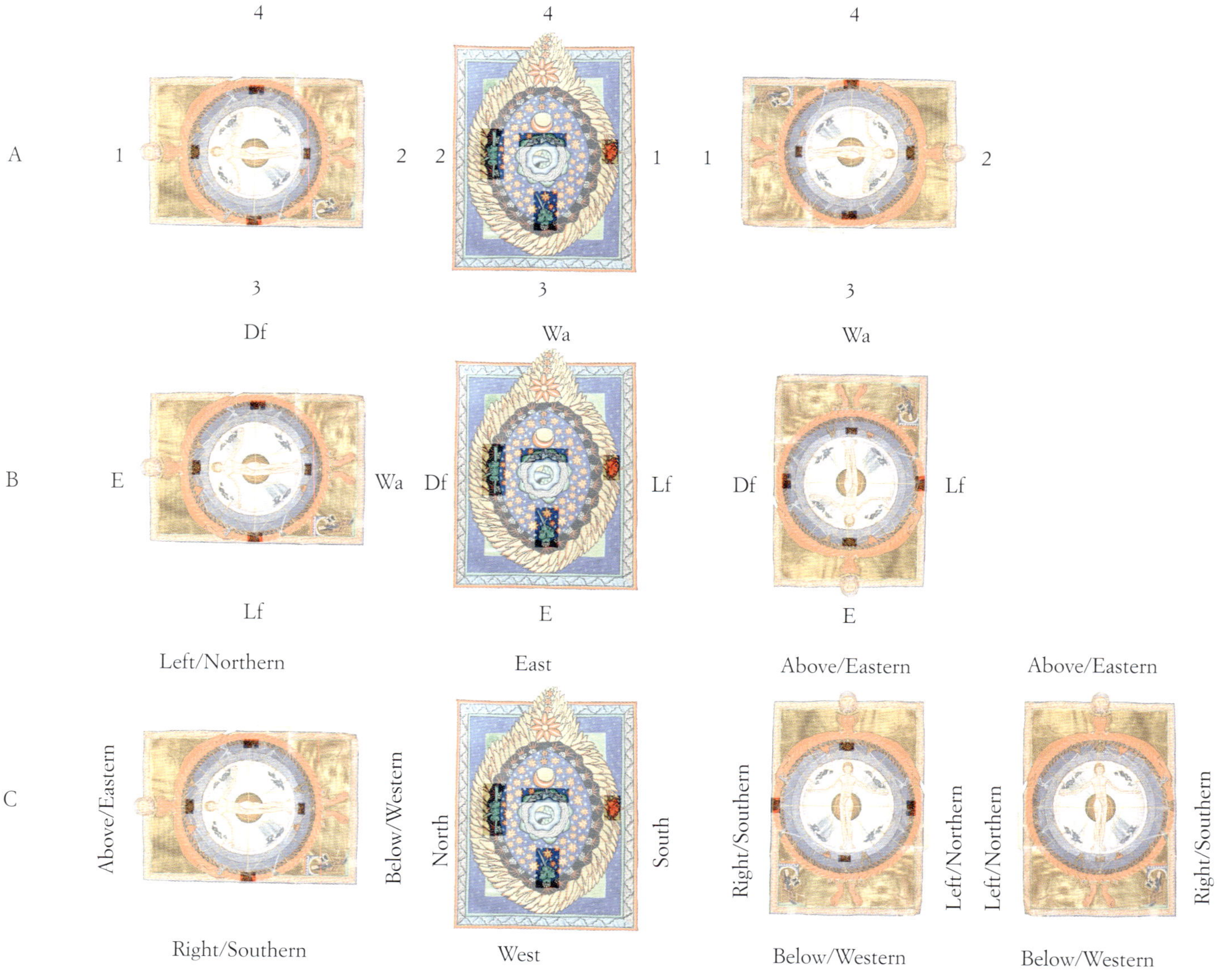

Rhetoric

Breaths and rays of wind. The moon and its orbit
Blessedness

*All of these breaths with one accord and with the common
zeal of their powers' exhalation call forth humankind
to blessedness. For although they each work in different
ways, they all tend toward a single blessedness (I.2,18, 66).*

*From the sign of the moon a ray beams as if over each
eyebrow and over each ankle of the image. This shows
that a salutary breathing forth comes to humankind
[…] to direct the strength of their inner spirit's footsteps
towards the path of rightness, so that as they walk in the
truth, they might secure eternal blessedness (I.2,36, 95).*

The four winds and their eight collateral winds emanate
breaths and rays that create a powerful movement of
edification in which one virtue follows another. There
are sixteen rays altogether. The breaths form an ellipti-
cal orbit whose position with respect to the earth suggests that this design was created by the movement of
the moon.

This hypothesis seems to be borne out by the fact
that the gift of the breaths and rays of the wind lead
to a single Blessedness and that the moon is the main
guardian of the path leading towards the former. With
its light and its movement in the sky during the lunar
month, it lights up the way for man on earth to reach
eternal Blessedness.

Thus the design emerging from the meticulous,
detailed description of the breath of the winds, recalling
the design of the lunar orbit around the globe, seems to
take shape in the symbolic description in the text, joining other visible astronomical movements represented
in the wheel.

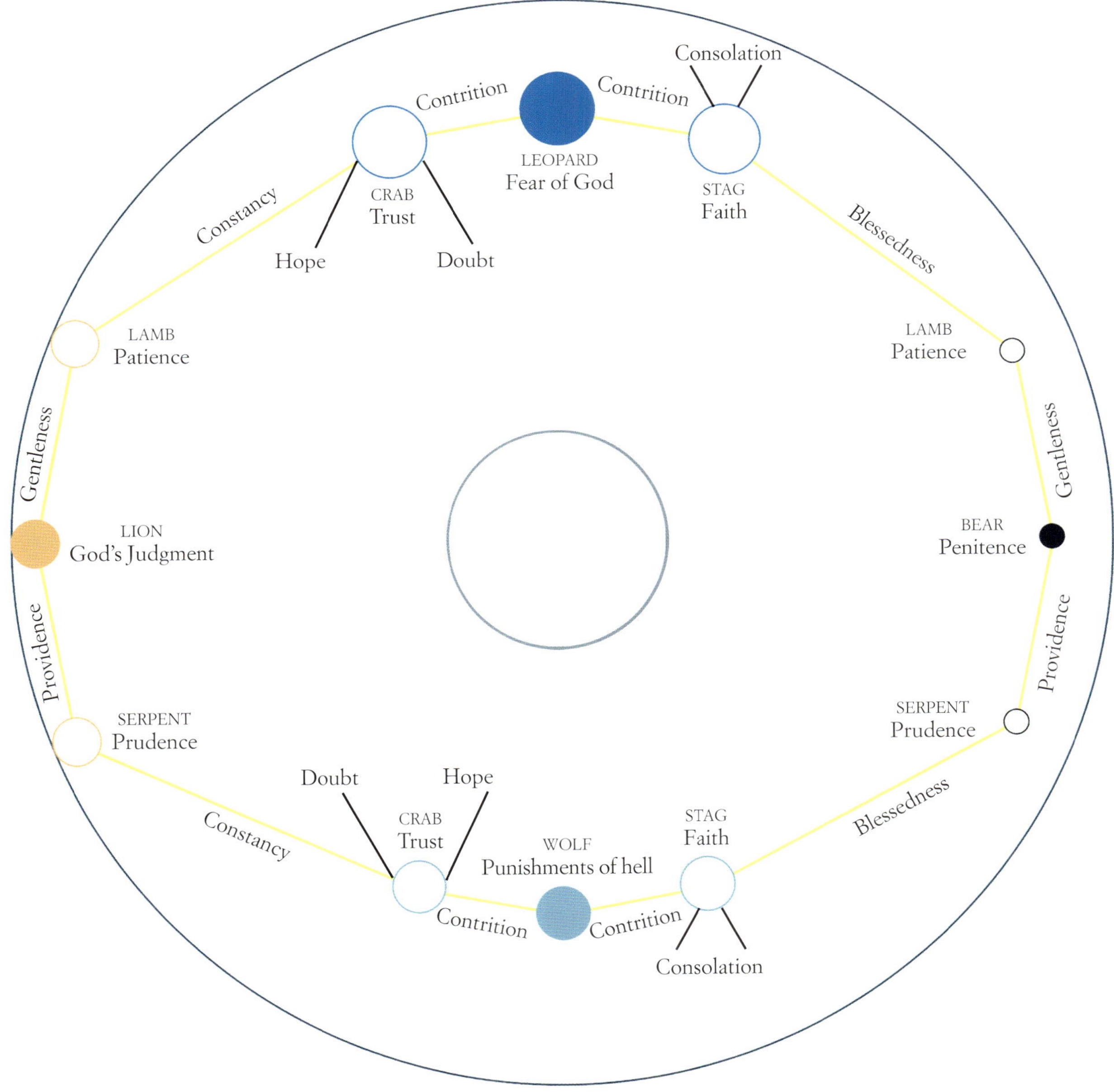

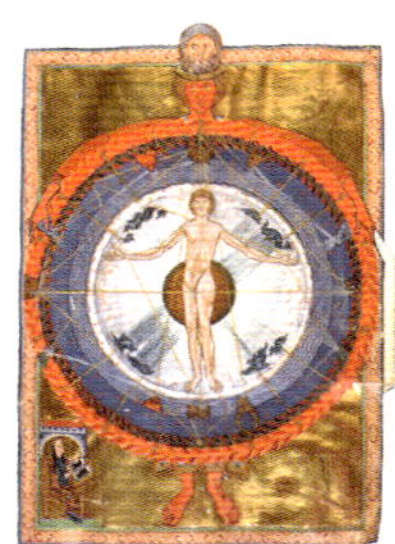

The planets and the three positions of the sun
The seven gifts of the Holy Spirit and the three ages

But there were also marked out above the head of this image seven celestial bodies, one above the other: three in the circle of bright fire, one also in the circle of black fire laid beneath that, and finally three in the circle of pure ether laid beneath that (I.2,1 51–52).

Furthermore, as described above, the sign of the sun was marked out in an ordered fashion above the crown of that image, with its rays to each of the places described—and in the same way it appeared at those places, marked out in its own circle along the image's right side and then beneath its feet (I.2,1, 53).

The seven planets represent *the seven gifts of the Holy Spirit in the three ages before the law, under the law, and in the Gospel*. The sun, Omnipotent God, is placed in the dark fire, showing that it has *fought and conquered its enemies through its power*. The three planets below, including the last one, which is the moon, are placed in the pure ether and *moreover, the three established in the circle of pure ether laid beneath that demonstrate that the three persons of the divinity are truly to be worshipped by humankind in the good and submissive disposition of pure repentance, when one completely submits oneself to God* (I.2,33, 90).

Yet again we can notice that there is a different viewpoint to *Scivias*, in which the seven planets were (from the top): the manifestation of the Trinity, the Sun/Christ, the Old and New Testament, and the Moon/Church. Man must walk along the path from the middle of the earth to the lucid fire, allowing the Church to guide him, through the reading of the Holy Scriptures, to be able to contemplate the Sun/Christ and the Trinity. In the *LDO*, the planets show the gifts of the Holy Spirit, which illuminate and guide man towards repentance through the law, God's judgment, and adoration. It is interesting to note that the sun in *Scivias* is located in the lucid fire and symbolizes Christ who illuminates man's path and crushes the dark fire between the ether of the faith and the divine action of the lucid fire, while in the *LDO* the sun is in the dark fire, and represents omnipotent God/judge conquering evil. In the third vision, the seven planets are shown in an inclined position to represent the movement of the firmament as we will see on page 84.

The sun is depicted in three different positions—east, south, and west—so as to delineate the movement describing its orbit: *For in breathing forth, the spirit of fortitude pours out its mystical gift described above with equal measure and flow as upon a person's intention, so that it also inspires his perfect deeds and examples, by which he edifies his neighbors, in complete blessedness to desire the holiness of a right beginning* (I.2,37, 95–96).

The miniaturist places the point of the sun in the east above the image, and the point of the sun in the west below the image, as described in the text. However, he slightly raises the point of the sun in the south with respect to the central point on the right side (see image below), thus ensuring that the point of the sun in the south does not coincide with the point in which he has begun the line of the sun, described by Hildegard as the line that crosses the wheel, going from east to west. This slight shift allows the two perspectives to exist side by side (see page 73).

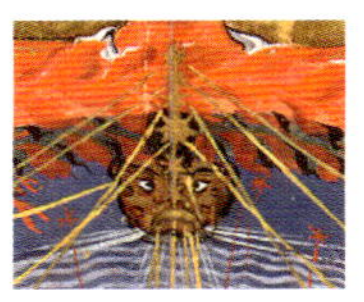
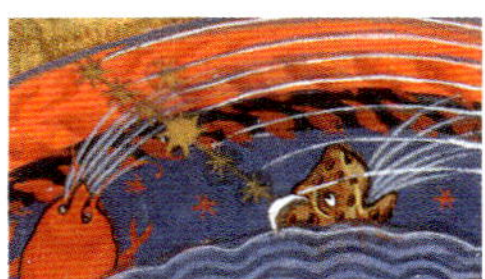

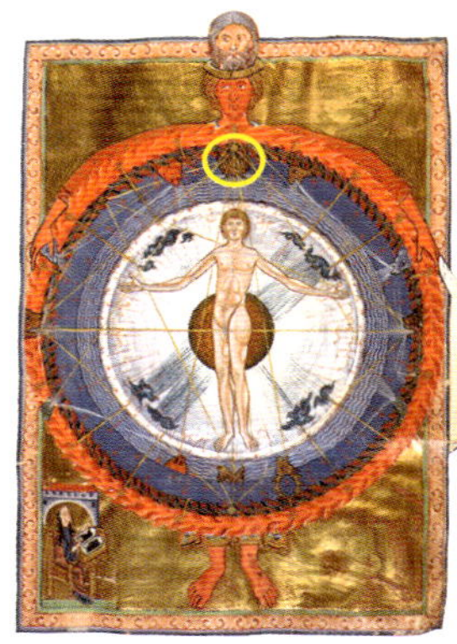
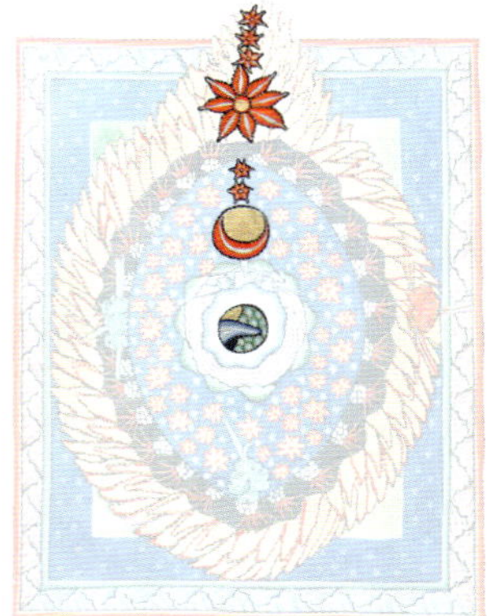

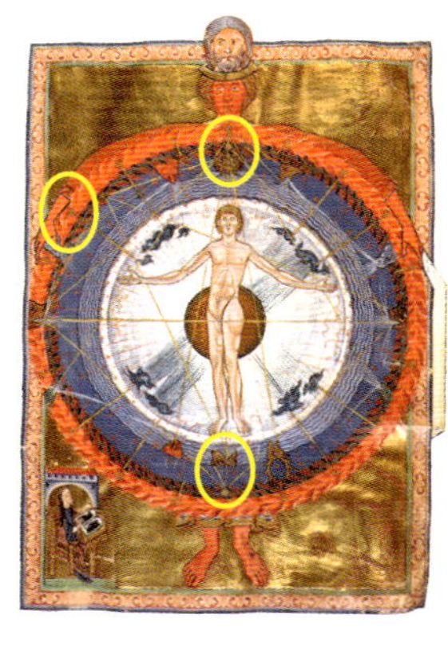
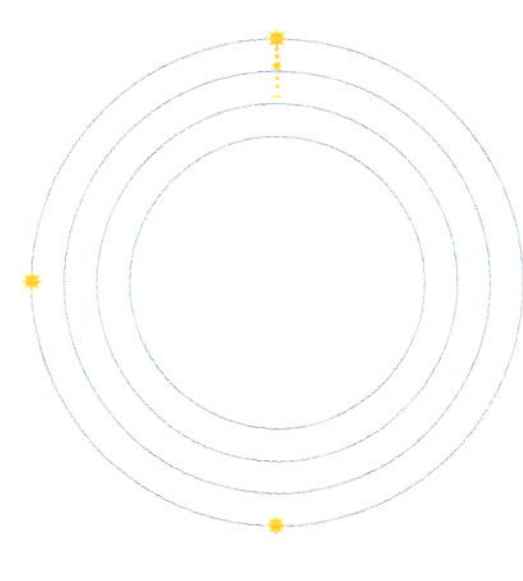

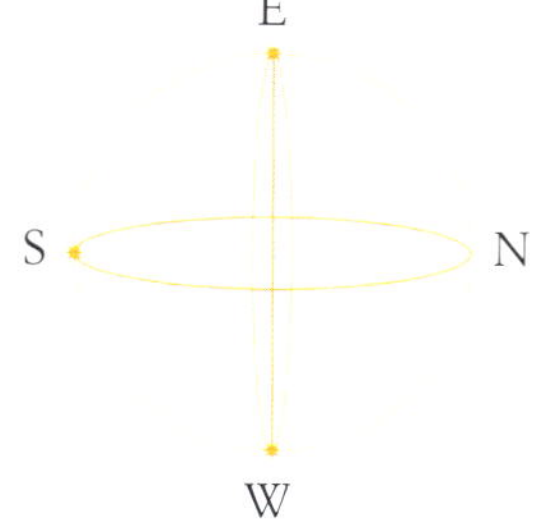

Breaths and rays of the planets. *The seven gifts of the Holy Spirit. The sundial and the Passion of Christ*

The planets represent the seven gifts of the Holy Spirit: *Wisdom, Understanding, Counsel, Fortitude* (sun), *Knowledge, Piety*, and *Fear of God* (moon). Rays extend from each planet, joining them to the sun, to the moon, to the parts of the figure of the body of the man, to the heads of the animals, with the exception of the head of the bear, which indicates that they avoid *any bodily distress that is not undertaken solely because of God* (I.2,35, 93).

The Spirit exhales its breath through these rays, engendering a virtuous movement of growth in the man. For example, the first ray departing from the highest planet and reaching the sun causes man to grow in holiness: *the virtues spring from [...] the spirit of wisdom [highest planet] [...]. From them, a holy breathing forth descends to the sign of the sun—to the spirit of fortitude—to which it allies itself, so that the fortitude of holiness might enter wisely into the faithful, lest they foolishly presume to undertake a task they cannot complete* (I.2,34, 91).

It is interesting to note that the total number of rays is 26, the same as the number of visions in *Scivias*. It also indicates the presence of God, YHWH, whose numerical value is 26. The first column of the table shows that nine rays emanate from the higher planets—three from each planet—evoking the Trinity and its internal division. Seven rays go from the sun, omnipotent God, again alluding to the seven gifts of the Spirit. Ten rays depart from the lower planets—six from the planets and four from the moon—a possible reference to the days of creation and to the earth/man.

In the table columns (C) 4 to 8 indicate: the planet from which the ray departs (C4); its gift (C5); the place reached (C6) and its characteristic (C7); and, lastly, the effect produced (C8). Numbers 1 to 3 indicate: the number of rays from 1 to 26 (C1); the total number of rays from 3 higher planets, from the sun, from 2 lower planets, and from the moon (C2); the number of rays (C3) (see section above).

1	2	3	4	5	6	7	8
1					Sun	Blessedness	Fortitude
2		3	Upper planet 3	Wisdom	By the right foot of the crab (leopard)	Fear of God	Trust
3					By the right antler of the stag (leopard)	Rectitude	Faith
4					Sun	Intelligence	Fortitude
5	9	3	Middle planet 3	Intellect	Lamb's head (lion)	God's Judgment	Patience
6					Towards the line, towards the northern part, above the lamb's head (bear)	Patience	Justice
7					Sun	Tempers	Fortitude
8		3	Lower planet 3	Advice	Serpent's head (lion)	No excessive practices of mortification	Prudence
9					Five rays as far as serpent (bear)	No despair	Justice
10					Leopard's head	Fear of sinning	Fear of God
11		3			Lion's head	Abandoning sinners	God's Judgment
12					Wolf's head	Freeing oneself from habit of sinning	Punishments of hell
13	7	1	Sun	Fortitude	Moon	Strength in Fear	Fear of God
14					Human skull	Intention	
15		3			Left heel	Good deeds	
16					Right heel	Good deeds	
17					Sun	No foolishness	Fortitude
18		3	Upper planet 2	Knowledge	Crab (wolf)	Corporal mortification	Trust
19					Left horn of the moon	Setting aside temporal concerns	Fear of God
20	6				Sun	Defence from evil	Fortitude
21		3	Lower planet 2	Compassion	Stag (wolf)	Flee punishments of hell	Faith
22					Right horn of the moon	Advances in prosperity	Fear of God
23		2			Eyebrow	Inner sight	
24			Moon	Fear of God	Eyebrow	Inner sight	
25	4				Heel	Inner fortitude	
26		2			Heel	Inner fortitude	

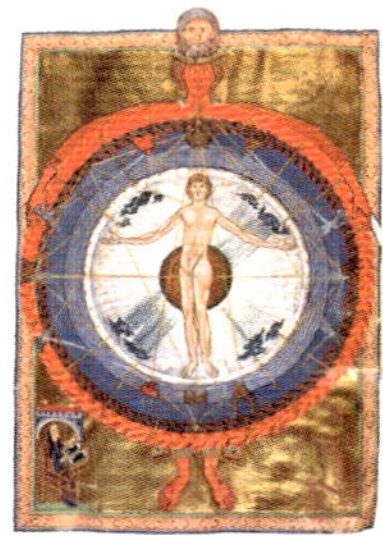

The fine golden threads representing the rays in the miniature are rather difficult to distinguish so we redesigned them on the basis of the description. Their stylized transcription has revealed an image strongly reminiscent of a sundial. In the Middle Ages, the sundial divided the day into "canonical" hours regulating the Benedictine prayer "hours." Many 12th-century churches feature sundials in the shape of circles/wheels held in front of a figure closely resembling the image of Divine Love with the wheel on its breast. Famous examples can be found in Piacenza cathedral (1122–1233) and in Stoke Minister in England (11th century), featured in *Gnomonica Italiana* (year II, n. 5, June 2003). These natural clocks were developed by observing the shadows cast by the sun and their movement during the course of the day. Sundials have a gnomon set vertically into the flat plate (dial), which casts a shadow indicating the changing hours of the day. Hour-lines are marked on the dial to make it easier to read the time.

The reconstructed image of the wheel with golden rays resembles the dial of a sundial with its hour-lines. The gnomon appears to be situated at the top, in the point from which the lines depart. The symmetry of the hour-lines is broken by a single line, shown in red in the design, which is generated by the *ray*/breath that goes from the *sun* to the *lion*/judgment of God, to the right of the figure.

The head of the lion, southern wind, coincides with the position of the noonday sun in the middle of the southern sky. The lion breathing God's Judgement therefore coincides with the image of Christ, Sun of justice. The red line indicates the noonday hour, described in the Gospels as the time when the Passion of Christ began. Although there is no reference to a sundial in the text, the image emerged through an analogy with the reconstructed design of the rays. We might cautiously hazard the opinion that this hypothesis is supported by the fact that the wheel in the reconstruction seems to be more evidently a device revealing astronomical movements linked to theological symbolism, a mirror of manifestations of the divine in creation.

The rays extending from the three upper planets and the two lower planets

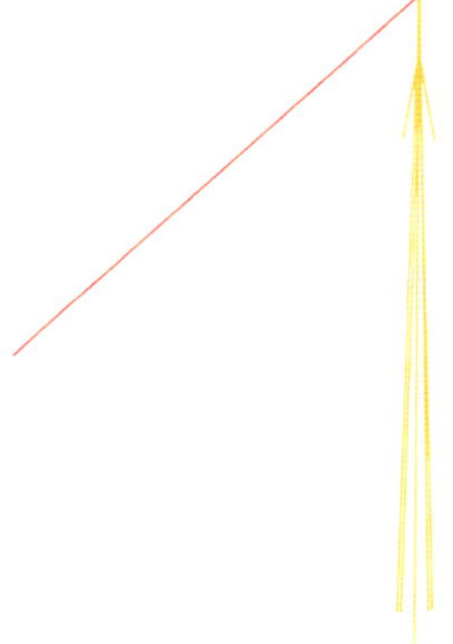

The rays extending from the sun and the moon
The red line indicates the ray going from the sun to the lion

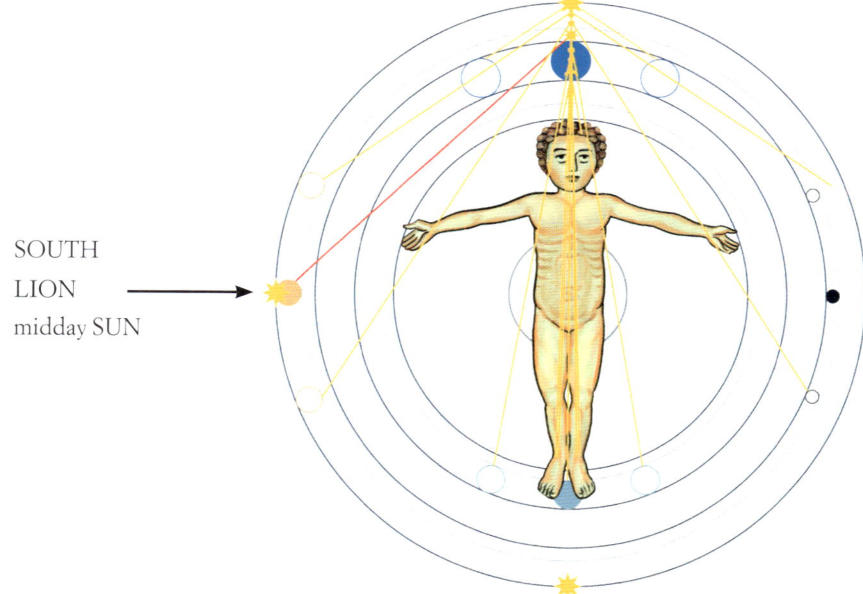

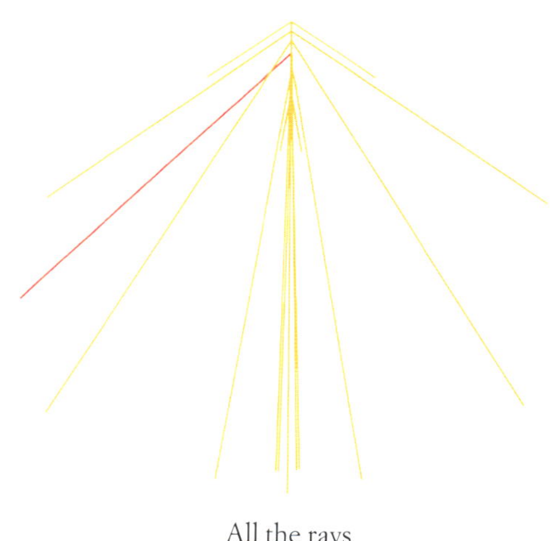

All the rays

The sixteen fixed stars: *the Doctors*
The eight beatitudes and the judgment

And in the circumference of the circle in which the
likeness of bright fire was seen, there also appeared sixteen
principal stars: four between the head of the leopard
and lion, four also between the head of the lion and wolf,
four between the head of the wolf and bear, and four
between the head of the bear and leopard (I.2,1, 53).

The sixteen fixed stars *strengthen each part of the fir-*
mament with their powers and temper the four winds.
They are the doctors who taught and continue to teach
that the *ten commandments of the law* are to be fulfilled
throughout *the six ages of the world*, and who exhort
humankind to live in the Fear of God and also to fear
the judgment that God pronounces in the *four parts—*
east, south, west, and north. Its extending to four parts
is reminiscent of the Science of God spreading in four
directions as in the vision of the Journey of the Soul
(1.4) in *Scivias*. When this Science reached humankind
they were invited to enter the Building (III.2) to complete the way of salvation. Illuminated by the Science
of God, human beings are called upon to abide by the
commandments while awaiting judgment.

    The stars are divided into two groups of eight. The
first group, located near the heads of the principal winds,
stretch their rays toward the thin air, strengthening the
whole firmament, *just as the veins descend from one's head*
all the way to one's feet. They represent the *eight beati-*
tudes that inspire human beings, enflamed by the love
of God and neighbor, to yearn for heavenly things. The
other eight stars direct their rays toward the dark fire, *lest*
it spew forth unchecked the fury of its heat, to show humanity that even minor sins will be judged (I.2,39, 97–98).

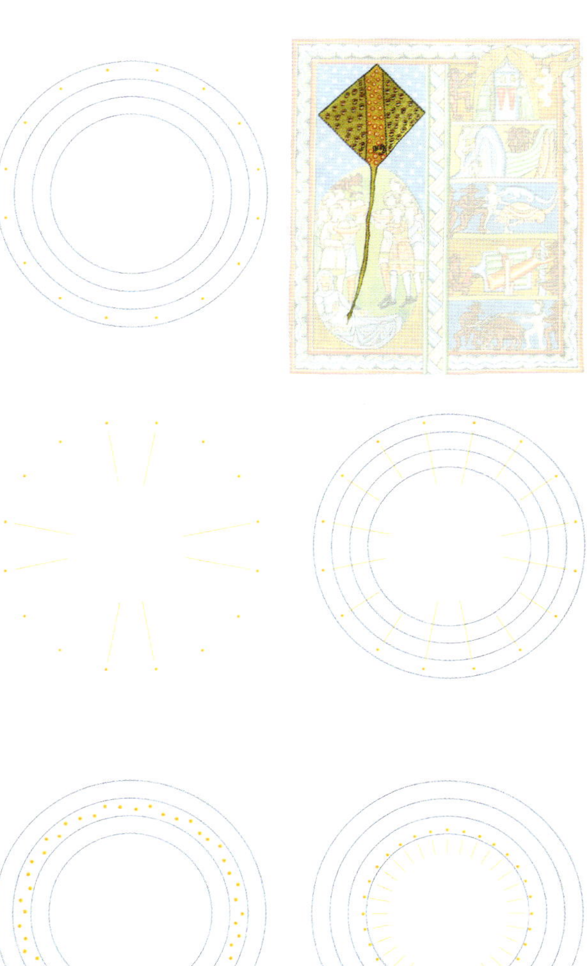

Stars in the ether and stars in the strong air
Penitence and discernment

Both the circle of pure ether and the circle of strong,
bright white air were as if full of stars that emitted
their radiance to the clouds opposite them (I.2,1, 53).

The function of these stars is to strengthen the elements in
which they exist and to prevent the clouds beneath from
crossing the boundary defined by God. They indicate that
the integrity of true repentance, as well as the integrity of
discerning holy works, thrives in the manifold brilliance of
rationality. They preserve the manifold powers of beatitude and *fashion the minds of the faithful […] so that all the*
works that they do appear rational before God (I.2.43, 101).

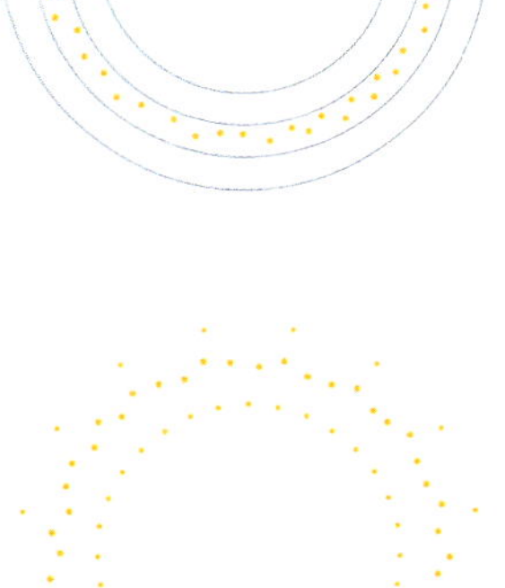

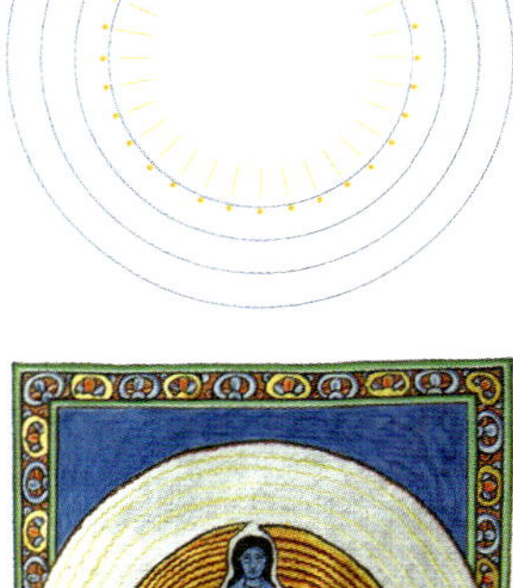

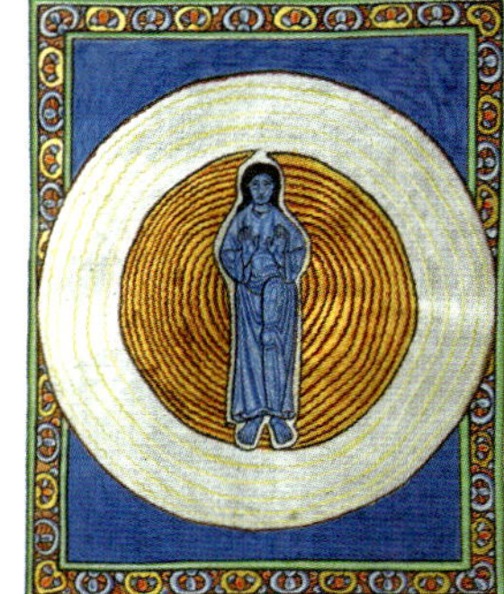

The Trinity of stars
Law, penitence, and discernment

The stars of the ether and the strong air, together with
the fixed stars, form three concentric circles, redesign-
ing yet again the Trinity and its division into three concentric circles. They combine the *law*, *penitence*, and
discernment in a single image.

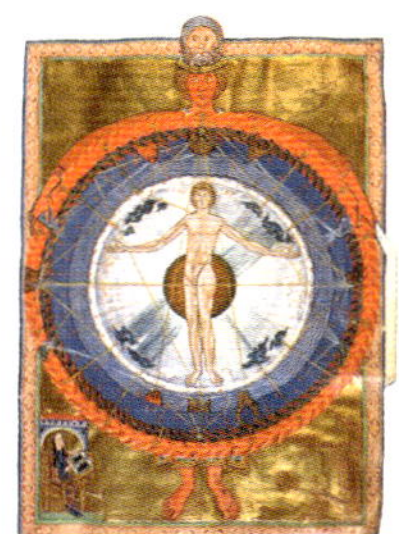

Clouds and tongues
Old and New Testaments

And then, in the right part of the aforesaid image, these clouds brought forth from themselves as if two separate tongues and directed certain rivulets from them into the above-mentioned wheel and toward the image. Furthermore, on its left, two tongues a little distance apart turned themselves from the signs of the clouds and onto the wheel and toward the image as with rivulets that flowed from them (I.2,1, 54–55).

Two great walls, the *tongues*, emerge from the *clouds, both on the right and left.* They symbolize *defensive forces that preserve everything that exists in the world, man and the other creatures.* They represent the two testaments, *one according to the flesh, the other according to the spirit. They fill up the whole world with their testimonies* and *the dew of their teaching enables man to overcome temptations.*

It is interesting that, as in the miniature of the Tower of the Law (III.3a) in *Scivias*—where reference is made to the law of the Old Testament—the term *propugnaculum*, meaning a tower designed for defense purposes, is used. In the *LDO*, the Old Testament is evoked through another semantically related term: *munitiones*, "defensive walls,"

to describe the tongues that emerge from the clouds. Both words are used by Vitruvius in *De Architectura*.

The 4 principal winds, the 16 stars and the 4 clouds with tongues constitute the 24 points in the wheel that could indicate the 24 hours of a day and refer to the 24 elders surrounding the throne of God in the Book of Revelation (Rev 4:4).

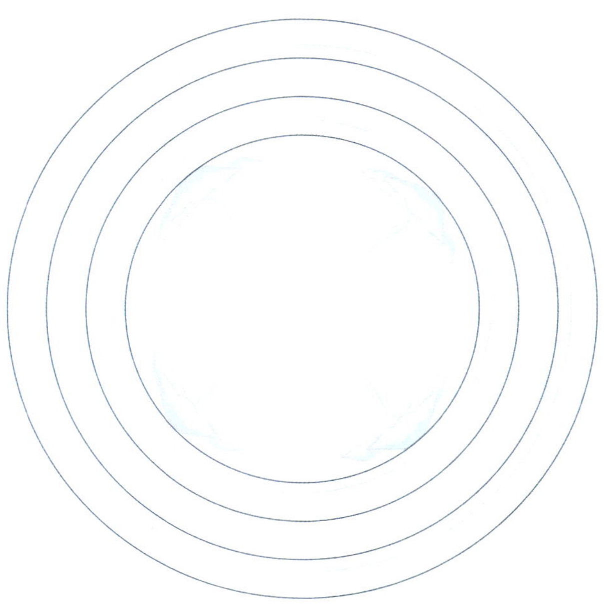

Threads
Harmony

I also saw that from the mouth of the image first mentioned, upon whose breast appeared the wheel, a light brighter than daylight came forth like threads, by which are rightly and distinctly measured the signs of the circles and the signs of the other figures that could be seen within the wheel, as well as the individual signs of the limbs of the human form—that is, of the image that appeared within the wheel, as revealed in all of the foregoing and subsequent words of this vision (I.2,1, 54).

The last element in the wheel to be described are the golden threads that came forth from the mouth of the figure/Divine Love, who has the wheel in its breast/heart. They are threads of light *brighter than the day.* The brightness of this higher light brings supreme order to the cosmos and mankind by combining everything with the right balance; it encompasses and exceeds even the light manifested by the Lamb/Christ, light of the day (see page 65). *For from the virtue of true Divine Love, in whose knowledge the circumference of the world exists, proceeds her elegant plan of order, shining above all things and containing and constraining all things (I.2,46, 103).*

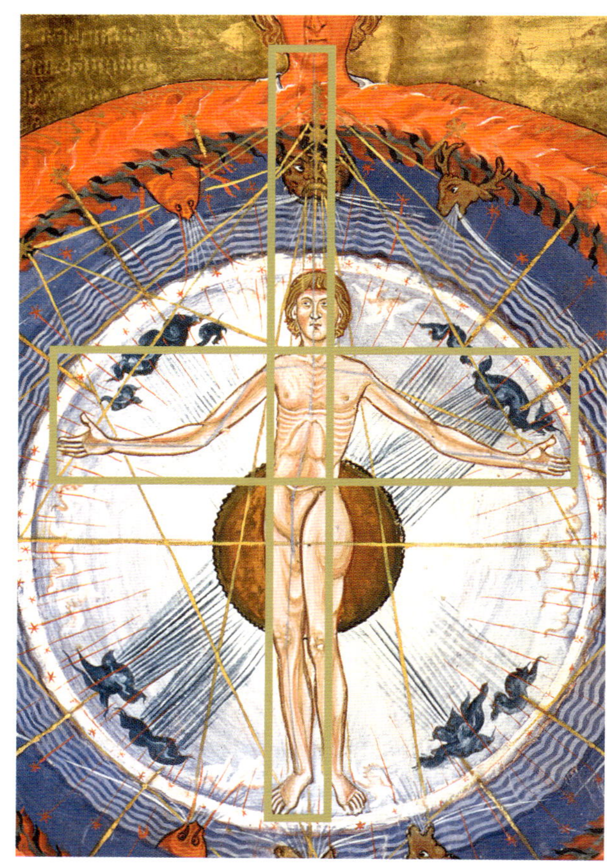

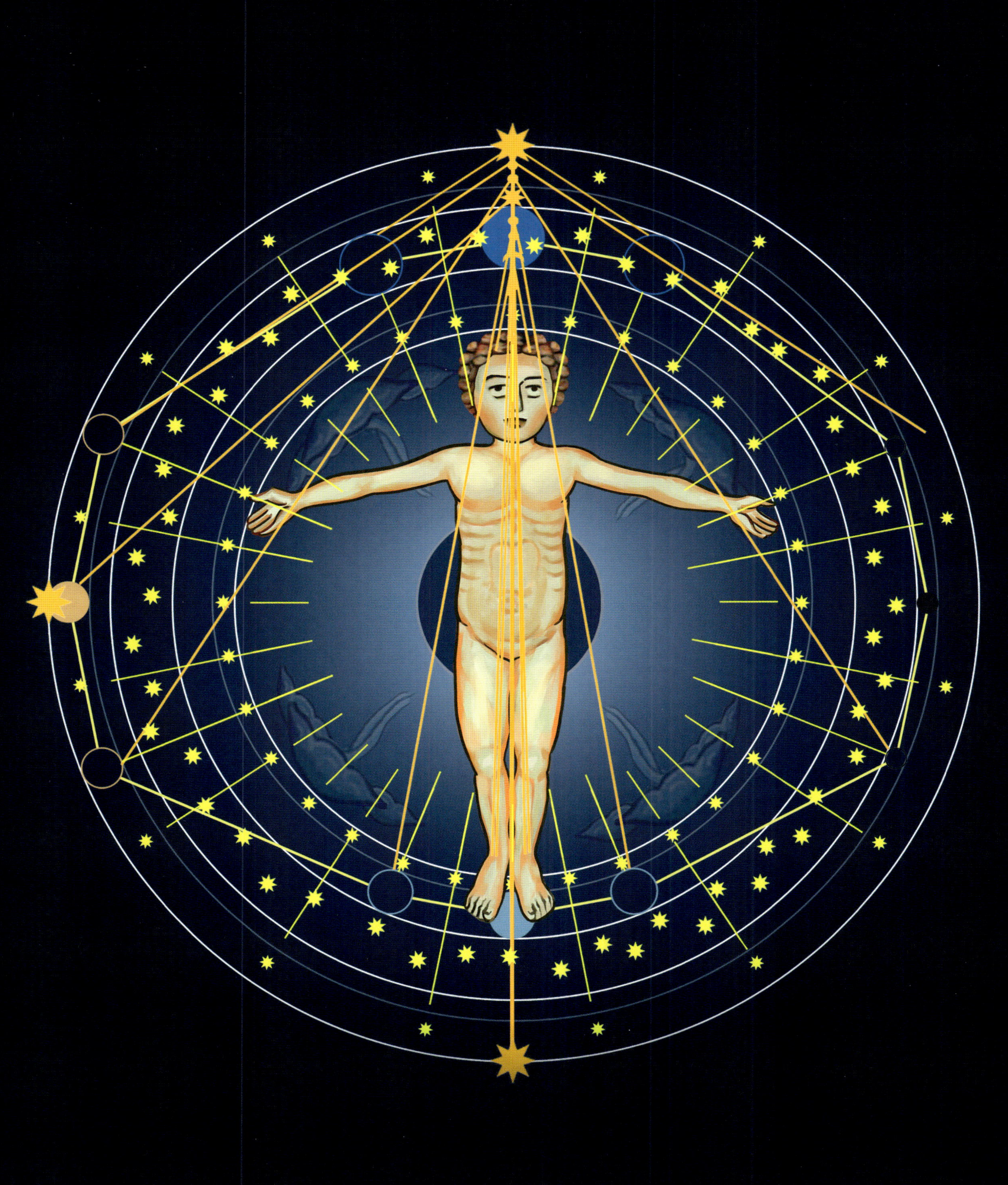

Winds and Movements. The Visible Motions of the Firmament

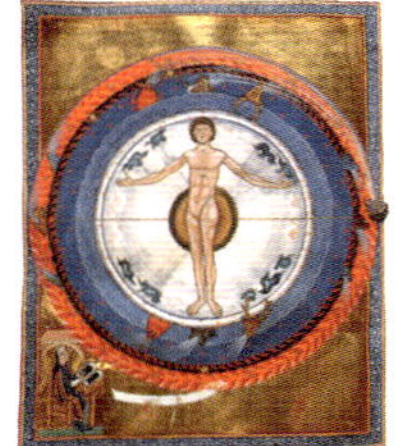

Third vision

I saw, and behold the east wind and south wind, together with their collaterals, moved the firmament through the blasts of their strength and made it to revolve above the earth from east to west. There, the west wind, the north wind, and their collaterals received the firmament and, pushing it on with their blasts, drove it back under the earth from west to east. I saw also that from the day on which the days begin to lengthen until the day in which they no longer lengthen, the south wind with its collaterals lifted the firmament up in the southern region and towards the northern, as if by propping it up. Then, from the same day in which the days begin to shorten, the north wind with its collaterals—because they shrink from the sun's radiance—forced the firmament back by pushing it bit by bit from the north towards the south […]. But I also saw that in the upper fire there appeared a circle that enclosed the firmament all around from east to west. From this circle a wind rushed forth from the west and forced the seven celestial bodies to go from west to east, opposite the revolution of the firmament. As with other aforementioned winds, this one did not send its blasts into the world, but instead tempered the course of the celestial bodies, as described above (I.3,1, 106).

The winds cause five motions that drive the firmament/wheel: the first and second winds make it rotate clockwise, and complete a whole rotation; the third and fourth winds shift it up and down along the transverse axis; the last wind makes the planets revolve counterclockwise to the firmament. This description recalls the motions of the sun and the other planets visible in the sky.

The first two winds seem to describe the *rotation* of the Earth, which causes the alternation of day and night; the third and four winds, the *revolution* of the Earth, which creates the alternation of the seasons between the two extremes of the summer and winter solstices, that is June 21, when *the days begin to shorten*, and December 21, when *the days begin to lengthen*. The last movement is that of the planets which are forced in the opposite direction to the firmament and seem to indicate a *retrograde motion*. The movement of the firmament is similarly indicated in *Scivias* when the Omnipotent One (III.1a) emanates a *rotating circle* that moves *from east to north, from west to south, then to the east again*. It is the circle of the *power of God*, which by traveling from east to north manifests God's justice that combats the confusion created by the devil in the north, and by moving from west to south manifests the light that is reborn from darkness and kindles ardor in the hearts of the faithful through justice in the south. This motion is similar to that of the first two winds in the *LDO*, which, from the east—place of God's justice—instill in mankind the fear and rectitude necessary to overcome sin (west) and to return, purified, to the origins.

The description of the motions that move the firmament in vision three, clearly shows that the *instrumentum/wheel/*firmament is a veritable machine through which it is possible to describe all the cosmological movements, which provide an image of the manifestation of the perfect ordinance of God's creation.

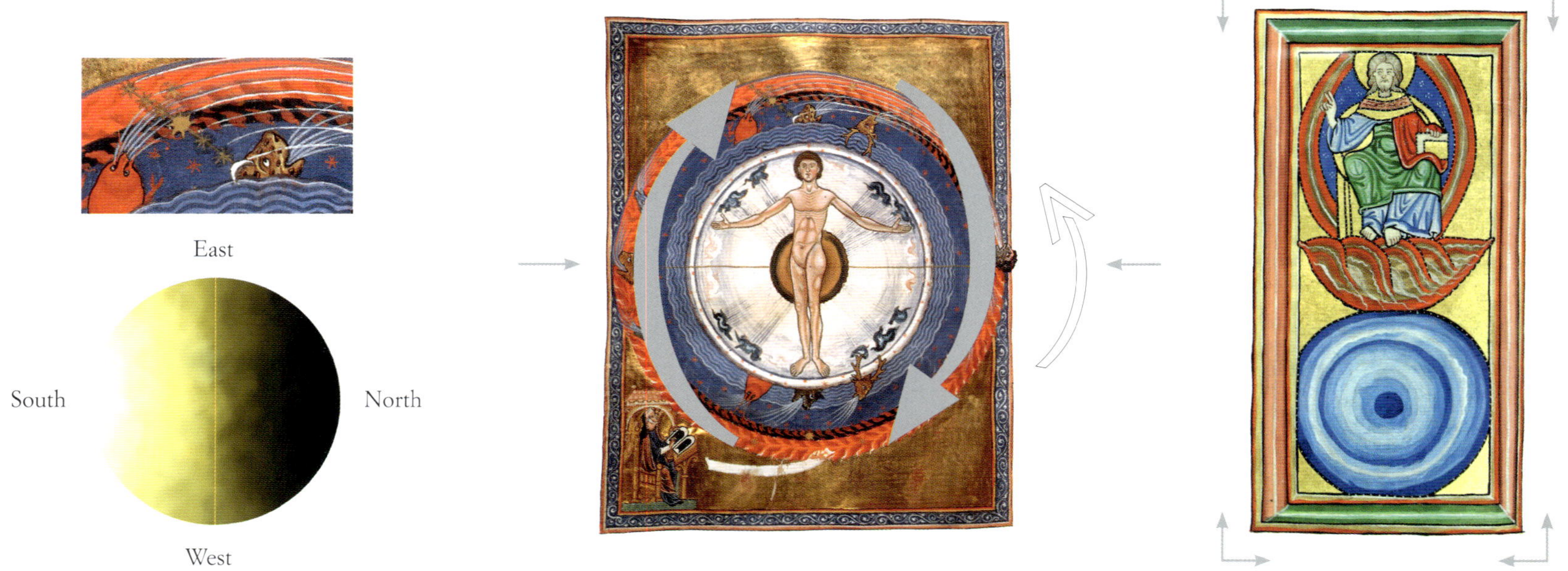

Rhetoric

The Firmament's Influence on Man

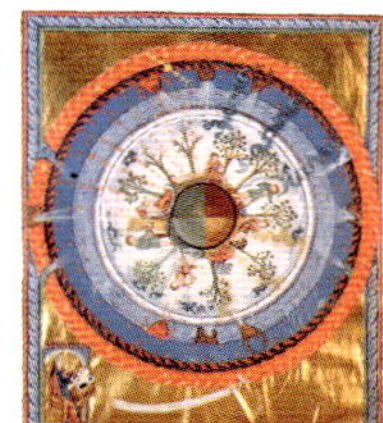

I saw also that the firmament's upper fire was sometimes moved to emit from itself ember-like scales upon the earth that caused pockmarks and ulcers in humans, animals, and the fruits of the earth. I saw also that from the black fire, a certain mist sometimes descended to the earth to wither the earth's viridity and suck dry the moisture of its fields. [...]

And I also saw that from the strong, bright white air, another mist sometimes stretched down to earth, casting a great pestilence upon humans and beasts, so that many were then exposed to various infirmities, and many met with death. [...] I saw also that from the thin air, moisture bubbling forth upon the earth roused the earth's viridity and made all the fruits to sprout and grow (I.4,1, 130).

For when with the sun's descent there is cold upon the earth, the thin air sends forth snow that, as it flies, is strewn upon the earth, for the water drops are converted by the upper cold into snow. But in the heat of the sun's ascent, this air exudes moisture falling over the earth like honey from the comb, which sometimes melts into a sweet rain because of the pleasant east wind (I.4,7, 134).

It also bore certain clouds above, which sustained all the things above and were strengthened by all those things above. In that air I also saw a certain cloud of brilliant white that was as if fixed at either end to the other clouds of the firmament, and whose middle stretched up like a curved bow to remain in the aforesaid air (I.4,2, 132).

When the body and soul of man troubled by sin are no longer in accord, the elements of the firmament/God are unleashed. A centripetal motion strikes the Earth/Man, arousing the same terrible fear experienced by a human being when caught in the eye of the storm, buffeted on all sides, without shelter. God's mercy bestows upon man both *dew* and *rain*, perceived as grace due to their abundance that makes the land fertile and verdant. The vision also enables us to observe *clouds* as mirrors that reflect the movements of the planets and of the moon and sun, through which mankind is permitted to contemplate and draw inspiration from God's works. In particular, the *candid cloud* that appears is heaven's recompense for the holy works of men. The vision represents in detail what each element causes to descend on earth, except for the ether and watery air, which serve to mitigate the effects unleashed by the other elements.

The iconographic elements in Scivias were utilized in this representation of the atmospheric phenomena caused by each of the elements illustrated in the vision, as they were for the wheel.

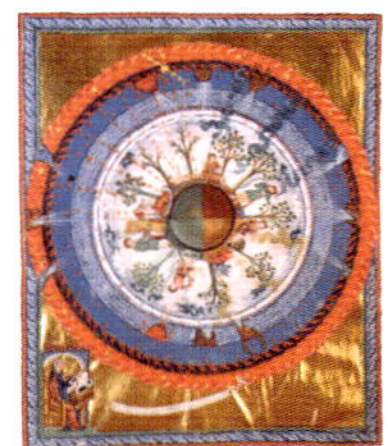

The elements inflicted on the Earth by the firmament take the form of *scales* of *lucid fire*; *mist* from the dark fire and from the white air; *snow*, *dew*, and *rain* from the watery air. Let us look at these in more detail. The sparks like leprous *scales* are sent by the lucid fire and indicate the punishment for sins of concupiscence and fornication. Indeed, they form to dry up the central part of a human being's body. *These humors also cause the moisture in a person's navel to flee, so that it sometimes dries out and hardens. The person's flesh then becomes scaly and full of sores like a leper's, though he does not in fact have leprosy.* (I.3,1, 111).

In *Scivias* the same scales indicate the wounds inflicted by the woman/Church on men who commit fornication. They are visible in the space between the navel and the genitals of the female image of the Church in the vision of the End Times (III.11).

The dark *mist* discharged by the *dark fire* creates havoc in man and on the earth. In *Scivias* it is emitted by the fiery smoke of hell in the second vision and causes sin in humans. It is vanquished by the power of God, whose thunder decapitates its black head in the End Times (III.11). In the *LDO* this same power is emanated by the *lucid fire*.

The *mist* that proceeds from the *white air* brings pestilence as retribution for sins committed through a lack of discretion and discernment. This is where purifying grace in the form of *snow* and *water* intervenes, which in the Scriptures bears witness to the Word of God, along with *dew*, bearer of God's blessing through the Christ. This process is summed up in the following: *But in his Son, God washed away the scales of sin's conception in a bath that the devil cannot strip from humankind, for he knew not how a virgin could conceive that Man who dissolved by water all appetite for sin* (II.1,38, 322).

In fact, it is the Spirit that through faith (*ether* in *Scivias*) acts in man and leads him to repent (*ether* in the *LDO*). This is attested by the holy life that begins with Baptism (*watery air* in *Scivias*), and is represented by the holy works (*watery air* in the *LDO*). Apropos of this Hildegard evokes the theme of dew, tracing it back to Jacob and describing it thus: *the most pleasant and temperate heat of the sun, it spreads upon the earth the dew of blessing that Jacob gave to his son* (I.4,7, 135). And also Hosea's prophesy: *I will be as the dew unto Israel: he shall grow as the lily, and cast forth his roots as Lebanon* (Hos 14:5).

The forth vision ends with a description of the *candid cloud* whose middle stretches down *like a curved bow*. The description and form of the *candid cloud* references the vision of the Omnipotent (III.1) in *Scivias* and represents human wisdom. This is borne out by the *LDO*: *Likewise, as just described, the minds of some people are so established in the order of right desire [...] as my servant Job shows, saying: "And the just man will*

hold to his way, and the clean one will add strength to his hands." [...] For the just person takes hold of wisdom (I.4,9 and 10, 136).

In chapter 11 we read that *God placed the firmament as the footstool of his throne, and it has the form of a circling circle in likeness to God's power, which has neither beginning nor end, for no one can discern where a revolving wheel begins and ends* (I.4,11, 137).

Here, God is described as surrounded by the circle of God's power that is similar to a wheel—exactly as he is depicted in *Scivias* in visions 1 and 2 of part three. In the first vision, we see the Omnipotent One, namely God, encircled by an oval which, in the second, widens out into an actual circle that surrounds the whole Building, like the wheel that encompasses the world.

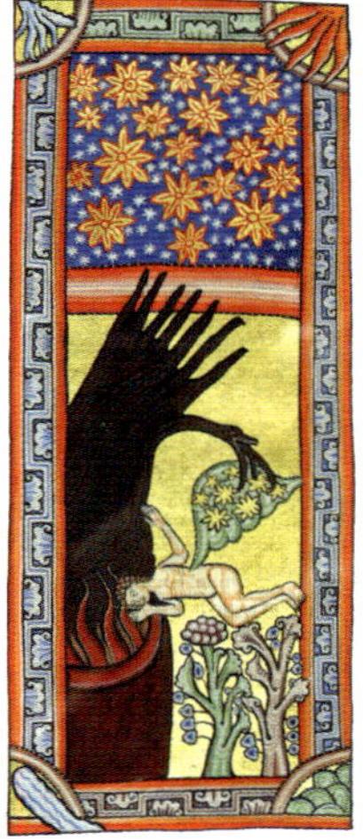

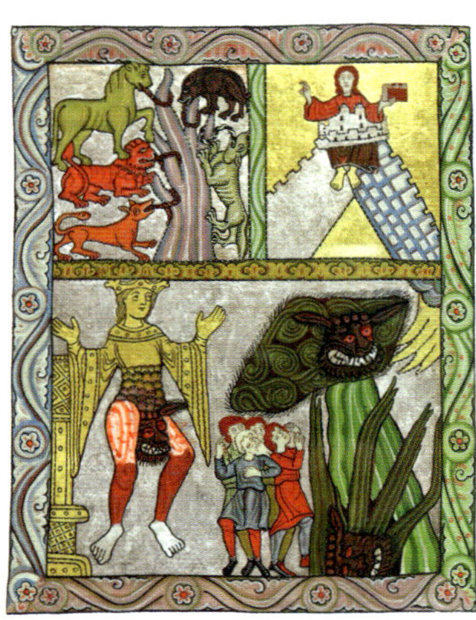

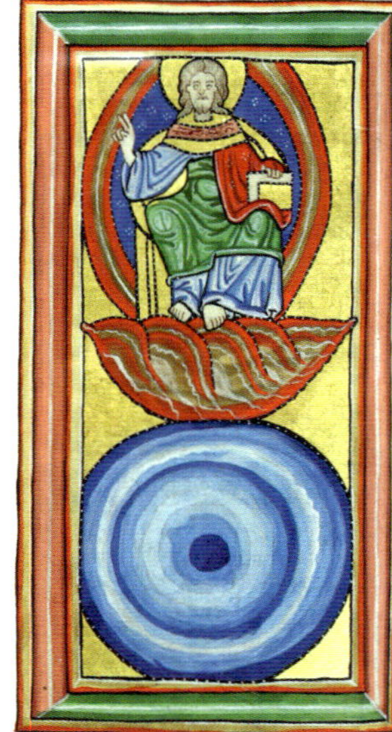

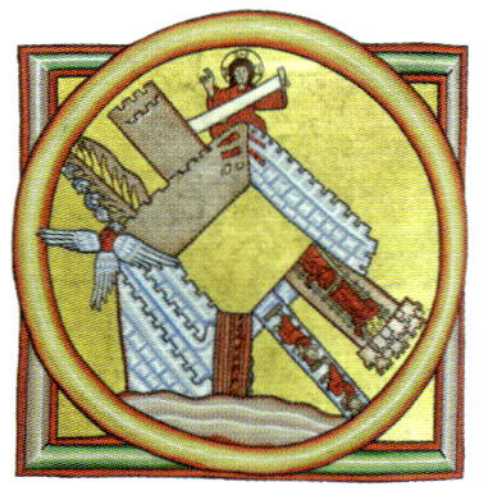

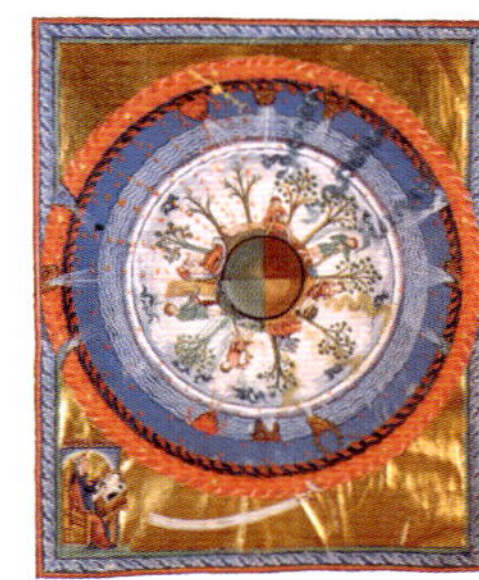

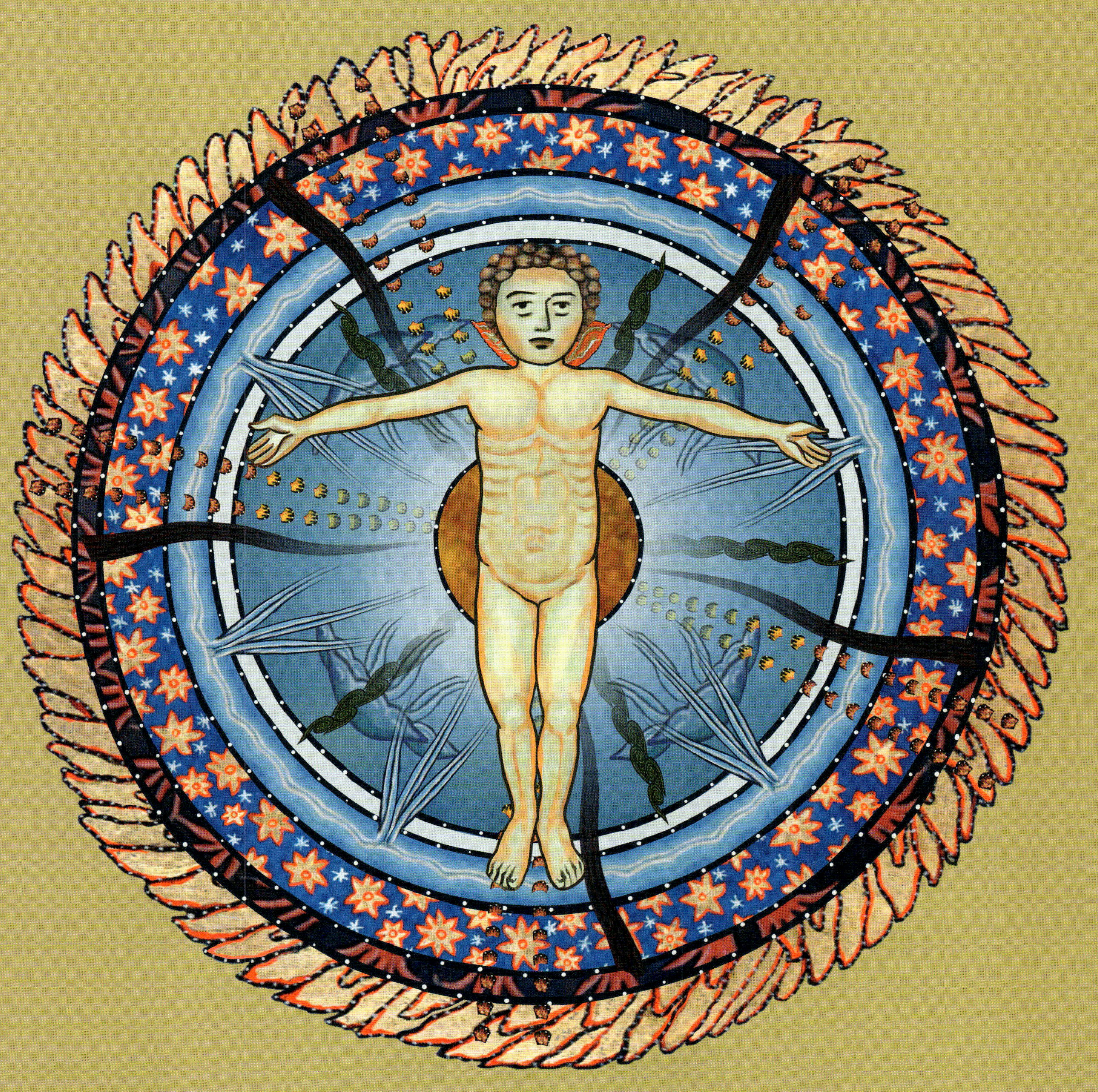

Man

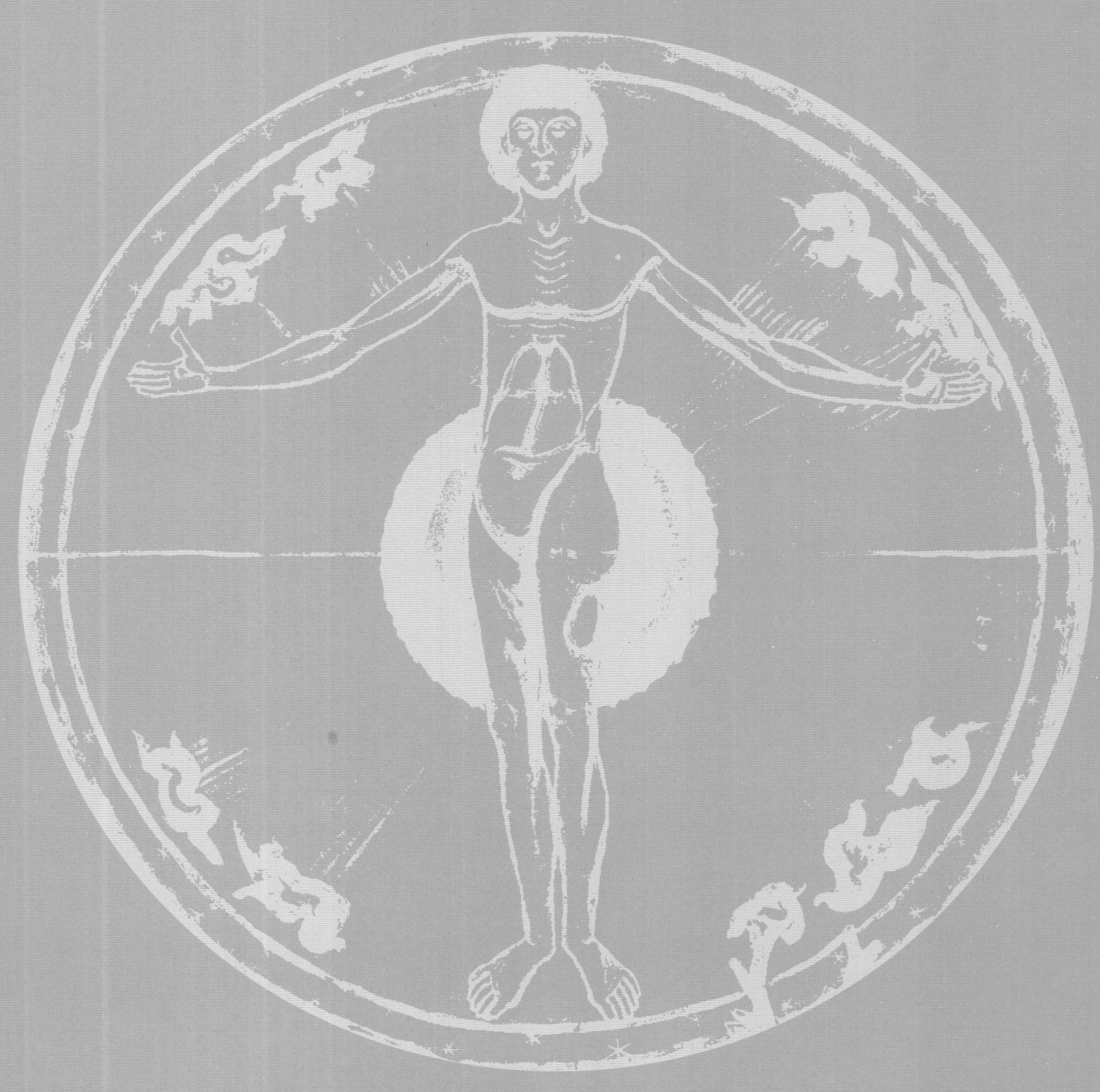

Man in the Middle of the Wheel

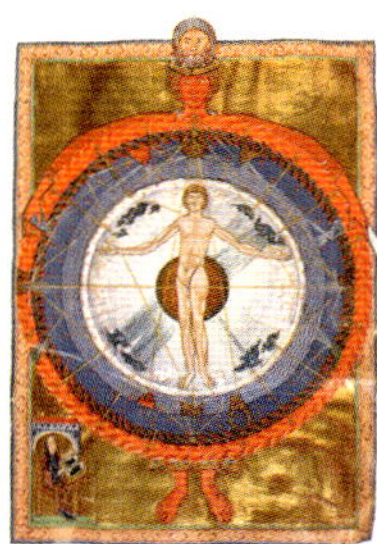

In the middle of the wheel there also appeared the image of a human being, whose crown reached above and whose feet stretched below the circle of strong, bright white air. The fingertips of the right hand were extended from the right side, and the fingertips of the left hand were extended from the left side, to that circle, marking it out from here to there in its circumference, because the image had its arms thus extended (I.2,1, 49).

Then I also saw that the humors that are in a human person are moved about and changed by the various qualities of the winds and air when the latter run and swirl around each other, and the humors receive those qualities (I.3,1, 108).

[…] so too all these things were signified in the human form, though not in the same order or achievement as in the elements above (I.4,14, 140).

During our journey from firmament to man, in these pages we have brought together the descriptions of the wheel appearing in visions I.2, I.3 and I.4. The same visions also refer to the presence of the man within the wheel, focusing, in particular, on the position of the man in the wheel (I.2); the influences of the movements of the firmament on man's humors (I.3); and, lastly, the correspondence between the parts of his body and the firmament (I.4). Moreover, in the single vision of the second part, in which the five senses are described, the image of man coincides with the wheel/earth/man.

The only chapter dealing with the human figure in the second vision is chapter fifteen, which provides a systematic description of the wheel, of its elements, and of the figures dwelling in it, including the human figure situated exactly in the middle of the wheel, in the thin, strong white air, in the space in which everything is *vivified and supported* by the breath of air of the Holy Spirit. Man is placed in the middle because God has given him power over all creatures. The faithful man who is aware of the Knowledge of God (an image full of eyes) is capable of seeing the presence of God in all the creatures surrounding him. His length and breadth are equal to the diameter of the inner circle of thin air: his head touches the top and his feet the bottom, and his hands the right and left sides, meaning that he is capable of reaching both the higher and lower elements thanks to the virtue of his soul, and he can operate to the left and to the right with his hands. This is possible because the powers of his body are circumscribed by the powers of his soul just *as the human heart is contained within the body* (I.2,15, 63).

In the third vision, we find a brief description of the movements of the firmament followed by a long account of the influence of the winds on man's internal humors. It concludes with the vivid image of a man whose inner humors are reconciled: *This signifies that, if a person's thoughts are neither too hard and ferocious nor too slick and easy-going, but are arranged decently and well in an honest morality in regard to both humankind and God, they lead that person with a gentleness that is restful for the body and refined in the conscience. So as this person flees the world's favor, he does not fall away onto either the right or the left, but supported by the many virtues, yearns for the joys of heaven, as it is written in the Song of Songs. […] for thus had God joined himself to the earth, that humans might look upon him in human form, and the angels might see him perfectly, Man and God* (I.3,19, 128 and 129).

In the fourth vision, the turbulence of the firmament casts sparks, mist, or snow and rain onto the earth/man in response to human actions so that man, who has long been blind, may become aware, through his wounds or sins, that it is not possible to live without God. Man is therefore called upon *to gaze upon almighty God as if upon a seal […] so as not to be torn away from God by any shock* (I.4, 11, 137), and to open his heart to the knowledge given to him by the candid cloud, the final element of the vision. This marks the start of a long description of the soul and body and of the way they are ordered according to precise forms and measurements, and in close relation to the firmament that God has placed *as the footstool of his throne* (I.4.11, 137). God has shaped man from the muddy earth according to his image and likeness. He has given him the five senses that are like *a ladder with ascending steps*. Through his senses—*the eyes for seeing, the ears for hearing, the nose for smelling, and the mouth for speaking*—man *sees, recognizes, discerns, categorizes, and names all parts of creation* (I.4,14, 140) and can walk along the paths of goodness and repentance. And this is shown in the single vision in the second part where the wheel/body of the world is divided into five parts corresponding to the five senses of man and to the five places of purification through which he must pass in order to reach the way of *virginitas*, following the footsteps of Christ, which will lead him to the eternal blessedness of Paradise.

The Winds in the Firmament and the Humors of Man

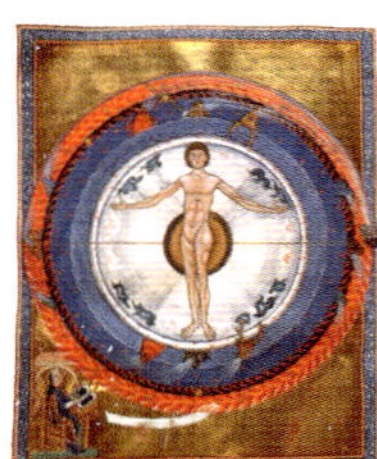

Third vision

*But again you see that, when any of the winds of
all the aforementioned qualities is stirred […]so that
in that place it emits its own blast after the air has
been mutually stirred and tempered by it, […] by that
blast, it grants to humankind a bit of its mutability
in their humors* (I.3.8, 118–119).

The Holy Spirit breathes its gifts into man through the
winds. By moving the air, the winds enter the human
body and set the humors in movement. Sometimes
the influence of the winds is weaker causing man to
become mutable, either continuing along the path of
goodness or giving in to adversity.

PHYSIOLOGY

When the movements are positive in a man's body, the
humors move in the following way.

The liver is on the *right side*, which produces heat
and is the seat of justice. It receives knowledge from
the brain and guides man in judging good and evil, op-
erating through discernment and discipline. It obtains
information through the sense of hearing, which may
introduce things that are good or even things that are
disgraceful. The right side is where a movement begins, going from the hearing to the brain, liver, heart,
and lungs. Hearing allows good or evil to enter man,
where it is gathered and processed by the knowledge
of the brain. The thoughts then reach the liver, which
heats the entire right side and develops the right judgment through right discernment and discipline.

The resulting judgment moves towards the cold
left side of the body containing the heart and lungs,
leading man to profess his faith with a sincere heart
and to bear the burden of existence.

The navel, which lies in the *middle* of the body, is
like the head of the bowels and has the task of maintain-
ing the body's equilibrium, by curbing the cravings of the
bowels, the lust of the loins, and the longings of the kidneys in order to channel desire towards good works rather than actions motivated by sin. When man succeeds in
quelling his longings through modesty and chastity, all
of his organs bring strength to the kidneys, transmitting
it to his calves, giving him strength and causing him to
persevere in continence and justice. This strength rises to
his genitals which produce holiness as an offspring/fruit.
Finally, man is enhanced and receives support from the
strength of the muscles in his arms and forearms, calves
and thighs. Just as the belly holds together the bowels so
does abstinence hold together the virtues.

EXCESS OF RECTITUDE AND ABSTINENCE

When man takes the path of rectitude without moderation, he is driven to despair, his lust increases and
only true abstinence can restore his balance and bring
him back to the true path of rectitude. These are the
movements in the body.

The nerves and veins beneath the knee touch *the
calves*, undermining their strength, and through this
endeavour they reach the *liver* and then the *brain*. Believing he lacks strength, the man falls into despair.

When the veins of the kidneys touch the *left calf*
more, they lead to lust, while the *right calf* is comforted
by the sense of justice of the liver; thus man continues
to walk in the path of righteousness and continues to
pursue true abstinence. Justice rises from the *liver* to
the *kidneys*, once again conquering lust and causing
fatness to disappear.

PATHOLOGY

When the humors are stirred up in a man's body, this
causes either a withering or excess of humidity. In
both cases, the man becomes infirm.

ARID AND DRY

Ungodly thoughts and hardness of heart make the *liver* arid, and cause headaches and sore eyes as well as
withering the marrow. Man will meet with a wasting
disease when the moon is waning. His sins will putre-
fy; his body will harden due to drought, and his *navel*
and flesh will become scaly and full of sores like a leper. Bad examples stir up his loins, which will wither
and become covered in scabs.

Useless thoughts and things, a lack of constancy
and abstinence cause the *kidneys* to wither, the *marrow
of his bones* and the *veins of the flesh* to suffer. Man will
therefore languish, enduring a life of weakness.

EXCESSIVE HUMIDITY

Sometimes such thoughts cause a man to think himself
wise while other times they flood into his *chest*, rising
to his *brain* and poisoning him. They may descend
to his *stomach*, causing a fever. When a confusion of
thoughts reaches his restless *heart* and the man feels
foolish, an excess of phlegm in his *ears* will poison his
lungs. He coughs and struggles to breathe, feeling a
pain in his *heart* that descends, causing pleurisy. When
a man is immoderate and lewd, excessive humidity
enters his navel, leading to agitation and causing him
to fall into a frenzy. This agitation reaches his *loins*,
making him upset and sorrowful. Lastly, the seduction
of pleasure causes his *kidneys* to become excessively
moist, poisoning his *calves*. The man will then overin-
dulge in food and drink, and fall victim to fatty leprosy.

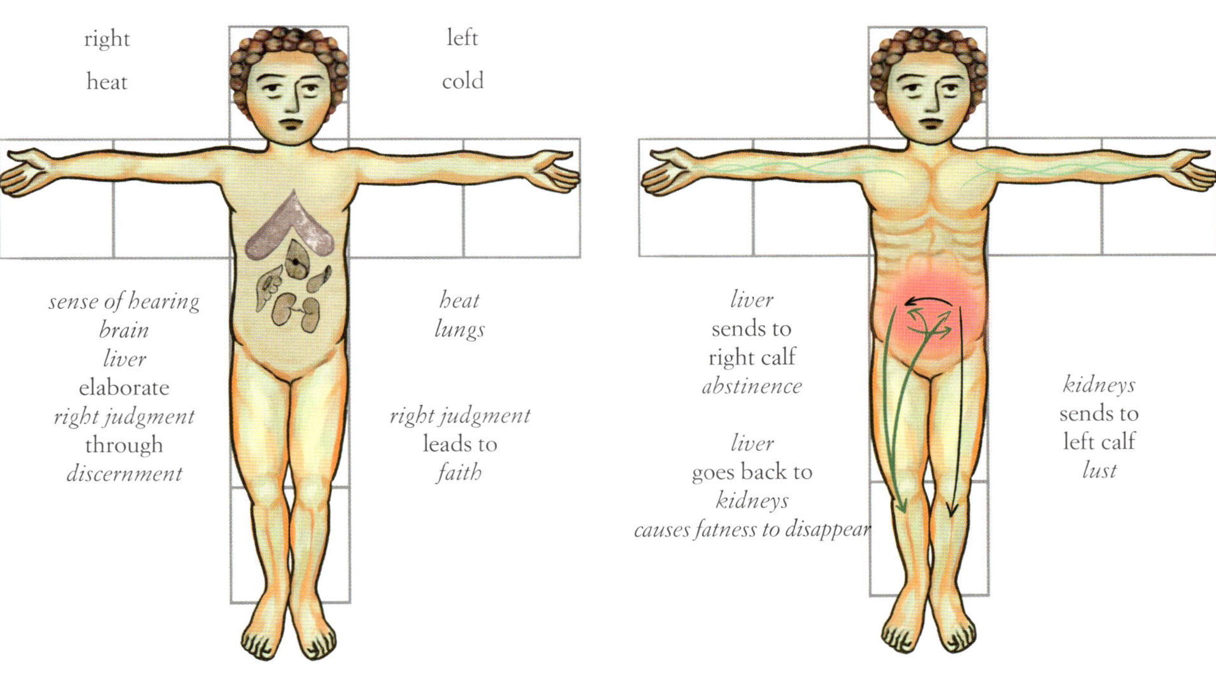

PATHOLOGY

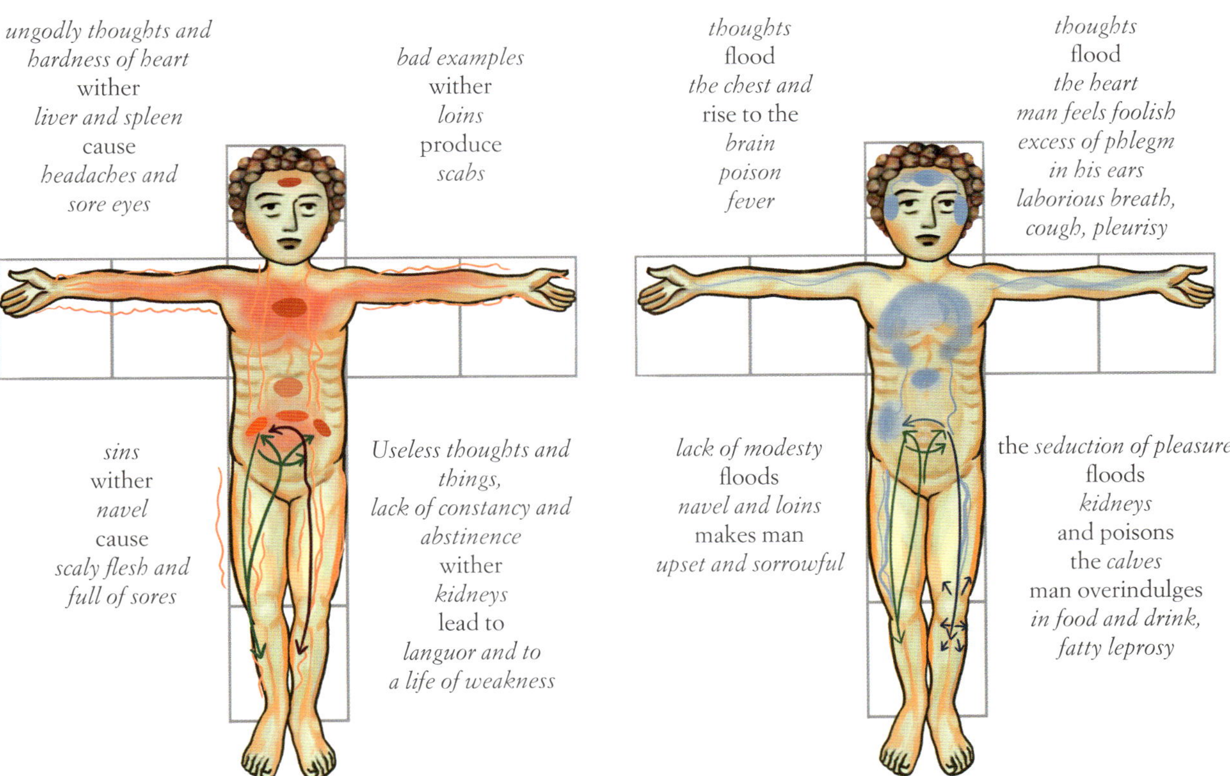

The image of the human figure has been reconstructed on the basis of the three images of the man/Christ found in Scivias, in The Fall (I.2) and The Crucifixion (II.6a).

The Body of Man and the Firmament

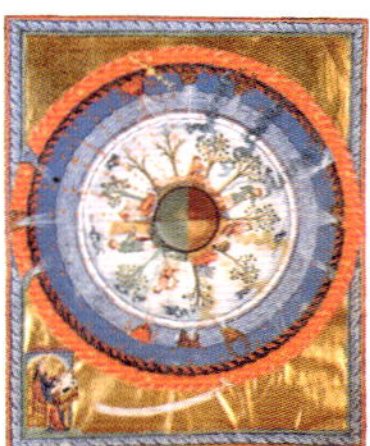

God formed Man and brought him to life with a living breath, which is the soul. He joined him together with flesh and blood and strengthened him with a heap of bones, as the earth was strengthened by stones—for as the earth cannot exist without stones, so neither could Man exist without bones. The firmament also cannot have the sun, moon, and stars absent from the established places in which they complete their courses, for these heavenly bodies could not possibly be confirmed without being assigned their own locations. Therefore, all of their placements were established in proper measure so that the circle of the firmament's wheel could rotate properly; so too all these things were signified in the human form, though not in the same order or achievement as in the elements above (I.4,14, 140).

The head and the four senses
The beginning of the soul's operation

The top of the head signifies the beginning of the soul's operation, which acts like the air flying into the body to satisfy its desires. Through the four steps that are the four senses—*sight*, *hearing*, *smell*, and *taste*—it perceives external information, allowing it to discern the requests of the body thanks to *rationality* (I.4,15, 140).

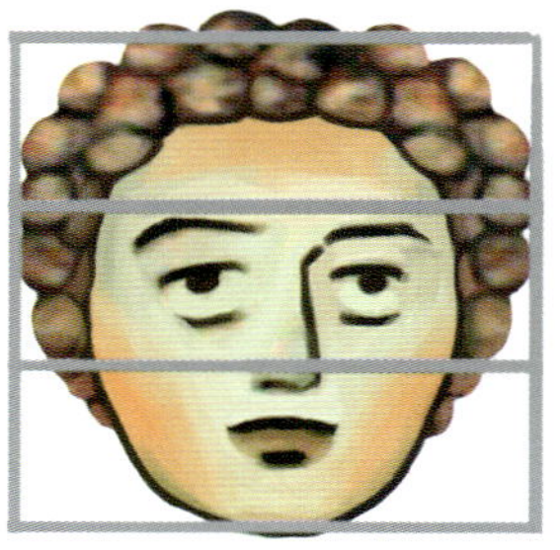

The length and breadth of man
The knowledge of good and evil

For a person's length in stature and breadth with arms and hands extended equally from the chest are equal, just as the firmament has an equal length and breadth [and represent] the knowledge of good and evil (I.4.15, 141).

The roundness of the human head and of the firmament
The ordering rationality

In the roundedness of the human head is shown the roundedness of the firmament, and in the right and equal dimensions of the head are shown the right and equal dimensions of the firmament (I.4,16, 141).

Thus, as long as body and soul live together, they experience this powerful conflict together, for when the flesh delights in sin, the soul suffers (I.4,16, 142).

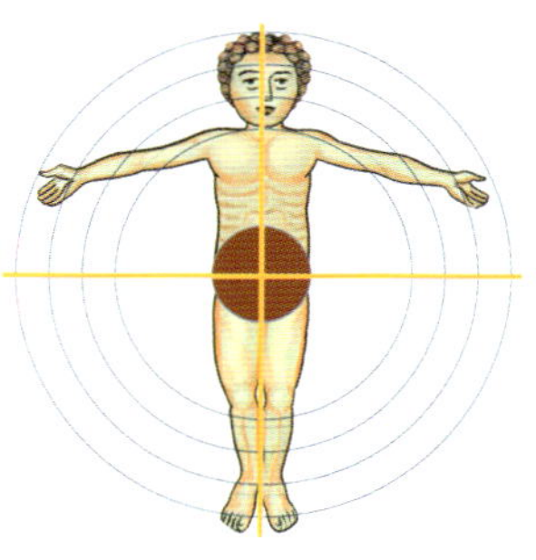

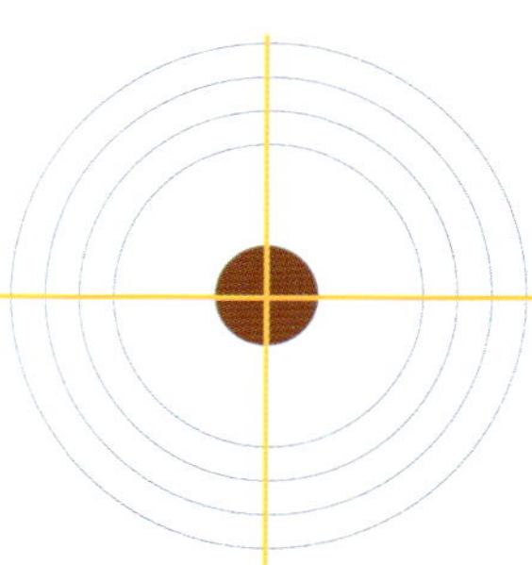

Man's body can be superimposed on the firmament, with his head corresponding to the upper elements; his head in turn may also be superimposed upon the whole firmament. The figure reveals the manifestation of *God's ordering rationality*, which affects man's head and body as it does the firmament.

Even if the soul sometimes sins, the uniformity of the firmament leads it to repent and to feel ashamed and it is like the moon that is sometimes bright and sometimes dark.

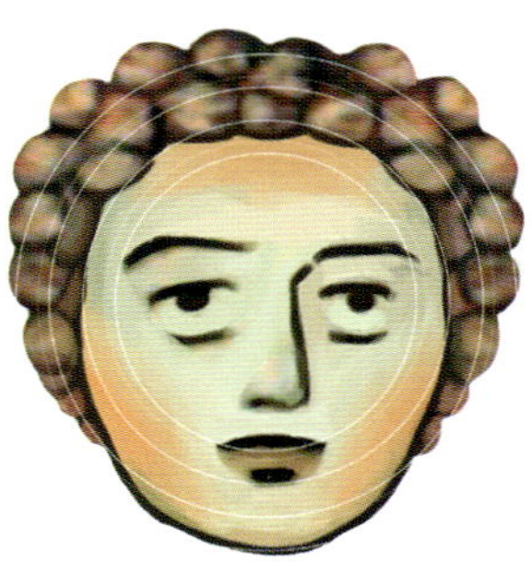

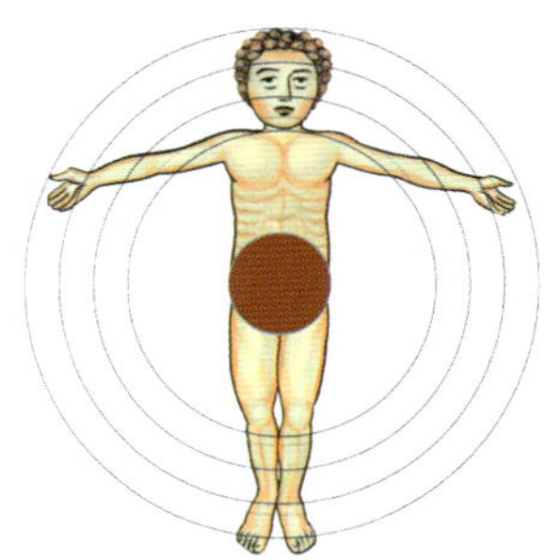

The head and the three spaces of the firmament
Comprehension, intelligence, movement

We have seen the measurements of man's body placed in relation to those of the firmament, with his head occupying the space of the upper elements. Specifically, we read that his *head* occupies the space that goes from the *lucid fire* to the *white air* and in particular that: the *lucid fire* and *dark fire* occupy the part going from the *top of the skull to the forehead*; the *ether* goes from the *forehead to the end of the nose*; the *watery air* and *strong air* go from the *nose to the throat*. As we have seen on page 72, these three spaces evoke a Trinitarian model and are linked to the three powers in the soul: *comprehension, intelligence*, and *movement* (I.4,17, 142).

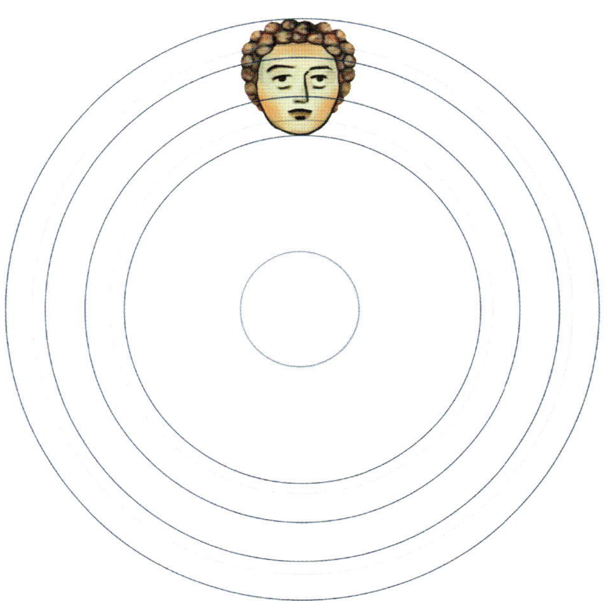

The thickness of the head and of the firmament
Spirit, knowledge, and sensation

But the equal thickness of the elements, together with their attendant constitutions, is signified also in the right and equal dimensions from the top of the human head forward to the eyebrows and on either side to each ear, and then back again to the beginning of the neck (I.4,17, 143).

The concept of depth refers back to the concept of globe/sphere expressed at the beginning, and therefore to a three-dimensional form, once again confirming that the wheel should be seen as a section of the globe. The three measurements described represent the powers in the soul: *respiration, knowledge*, and *sensation* (I.4,17, 143).

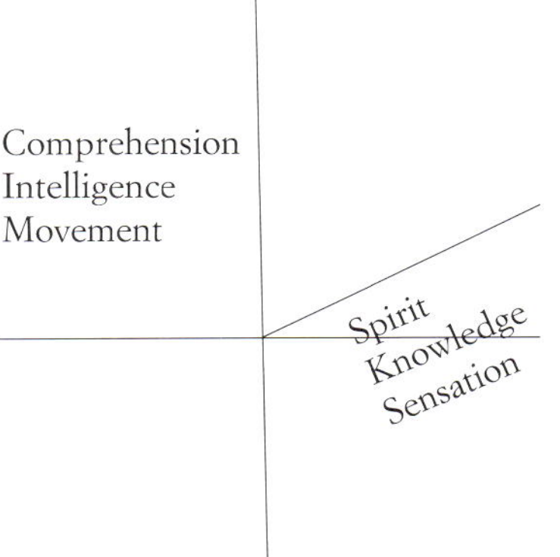

Man's lips
Praise to God

Man's *upper and lower lips* are equal in size to each other and to the *dark fire, which purifies in God's vengeance* and to the *strong, bright white air*, which moderates its effect. They therefore divide the watery air into two equal parts, creating a tripartition, sign of the presence of the Trinity.
　　This means *that a person ought to praise God with his mouth with equal fervor both in upper (celestial) and lower (earthly) matters, casting away from himself the evils of both soul and body* (I.4,18, 144).

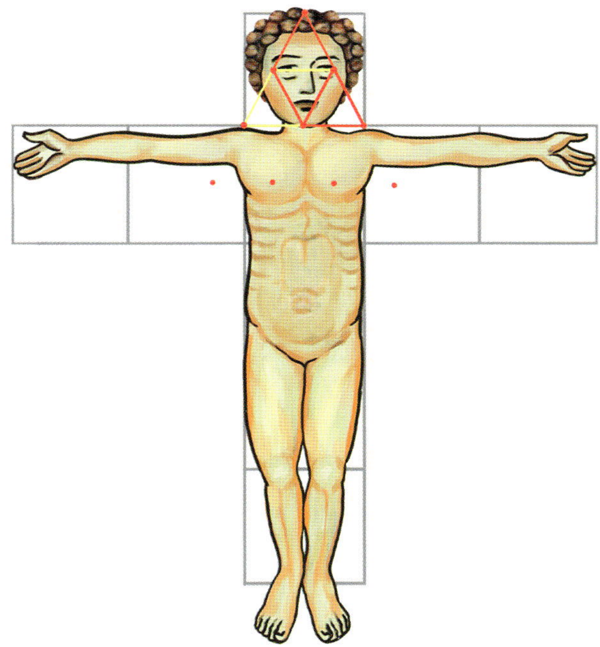

Ear/ear, ear/shoulder, shoulder/throat
Discretion

The relationship between the distance between the *ears*, between *ear* and *shoulder*, and between *shoulder* and *throat* means that man must *[perceive] God's commandments with the ears, [impose] them faithfully upon the shoulders* and, lastly, *[ingest] them as if down the throat*. In so doing, he must *keep in all things a balanced and discerning moderation* (I.4,18, 144).

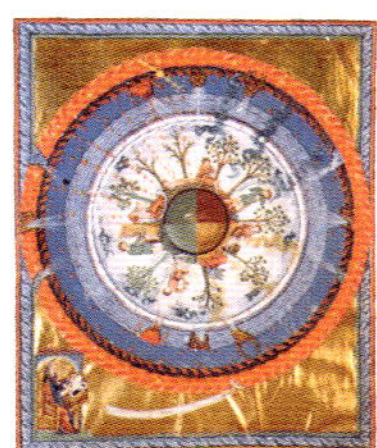

Reconstructing this image, we can begin with the known distance between throat and shoulder (1), which corresponds to exactly half of one of the five squares into which the figure is divided.

If we shift this measurement (1) to the line of the ears dividing the head horizontally, we can obtain the position of the ears seen from the back as specified in the description (2). We can then connect the point of the ears to the shoulder (3). The result is a series of equilateral triangles produced by these three equal measurements.

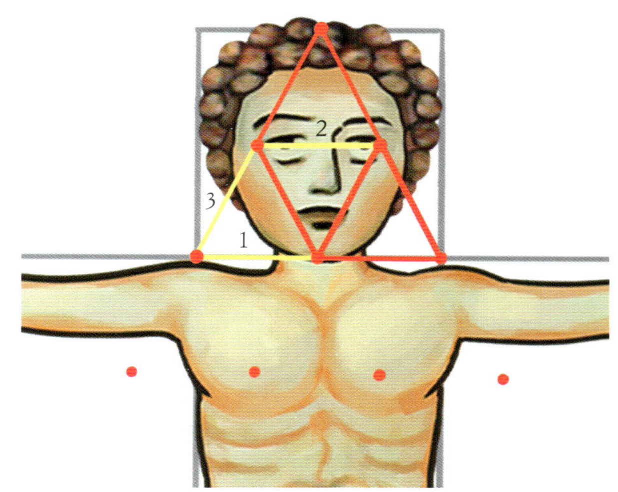

At this point, if we include some previous information, a new scenario will unfold. Let us examine it step by step. The initial description of the head as a *circuenti rota* uses the word *vertex* "crown", followed by the more generic *summitas*, "top." *Vertex* is closely linked to the language of geometry and our studies of *Scivias* show that Hildegard uses words to draw attention to the area of knowledge that she intends to draw upon, in this case, geometry. The figure shows us a sequence of equilateral triangles forming a larger triangle, revealing a marked similarity to the image of the Pythagorean tetractys. This connection seems to be confirmed by the location of the points with respect to the elements of the firmament: the vertex in *fire*, the two bottom points in *ether/air*, and the three points in *watery air/*water. Finally, if we complete the figure of the tetractys, we can see how the four points closing the Pythagorean triangle all lie on an imaginary line situated halfway between throat and navel, marking the boundary between the waters and dry land, as we will later see in the single vision of the second part. The arrangement of these elements is the same as that of the Pythagorean tetractys described by Philolaus. Again, this aspect requires further in-depth studies and analysis using critical texts.

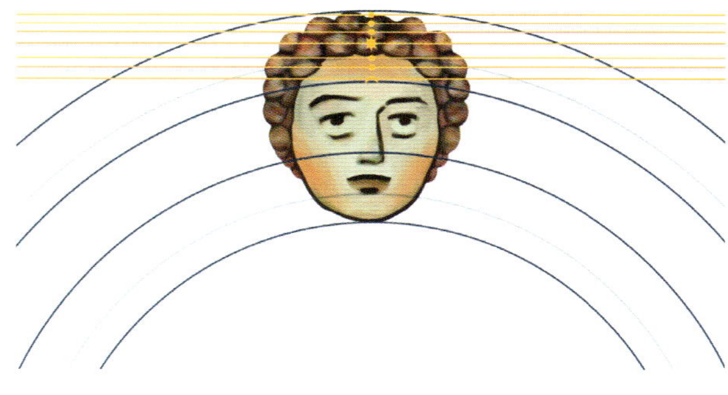

The seven spaces from the head to the forehead and the seven planets:
The seven gifts of the Holy Spirit

From the uppermost top of the brain's vessel to the final edge of the human forehead can be discerned seven equally spaced divisions, signifying the seven celestial bodies that are equidistantly placed in the firmament (I.4,22, 147).

As we have seen, the planets represent the seven gifts of the Holy Spirit. In the second vision, they occupied the space of the two fires and of the ether, while now, in the fourth vision, they occupy a space coinciding with that of man's forehead, which corresponds to *lucid fire* and *dark fire.* It is as if the firmament were now being seen from a great distance and we were in the presence of a profound sky, the empyrean, while in the description of the second vision, the viewpoint came closer. This changed perspective corresponds to

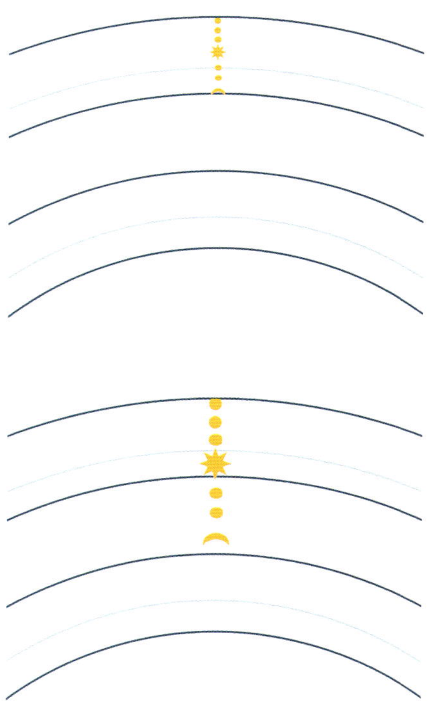

Rhetoric

a change in the position of man, who is initially described as being in the wheel and is now superimposed over the entire wheel.

Bearing in mind this dual vision, we can reconsider the representation of the planets in the egg/firmament in *Scivias*. In the first image, we caused the position of the planets of the egg to coincide with the *LDO* circles, which occupy the same position described in the second vision of the *LDO*. In the second image, we positioned the egg, causing its planets to coincide with the position described in the fourth vision of the *LDO*. We were surprised to note that the *Scivias* egg remained small and suspended high up, becoming even smaller in the second image, again confirming that the viewpoint in the *LDO* is further away. This is also supported by the projection of light of the egg on a plane, underlining how the two different positions of the planet come together in the cone of light and also how the image of the wheel emerges from the projection of light of the egg/firmament on a plane. In *Scivias*, the same projection of light generated the circle around the Building (III.2) from the mandorla/egg around the figure of the Omnipotent (III.1). That projection revealed a cup and plate, recalling the offering of the Eucharist on the altar (Salvadori 2019, 174). We find an important reference to this in the *LDO*, which compares the firmament to a "well-turned bowl" or *crater tornatilis*. We also read that the sun moves through the firmament and *emits its brilliance like wine poured from a bowl*. In conclusion, the images of the Omnipotent (III.1) and of the Building (III.2) in *Scivias* are closely connected to the winged figure/Divine Love and to the wheel in the *LDO*, both images of a firmament seen from different viewpoints, representations of the victory over evil through the offering of the sacrificed lamb evoked by the Eucharistic gifts.

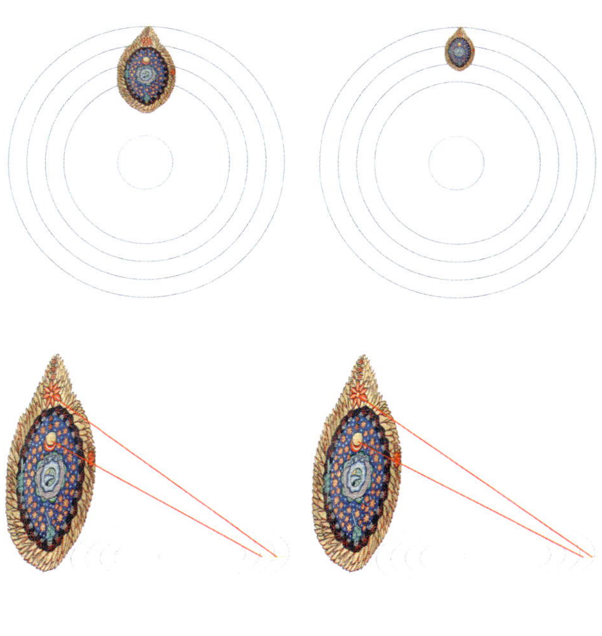

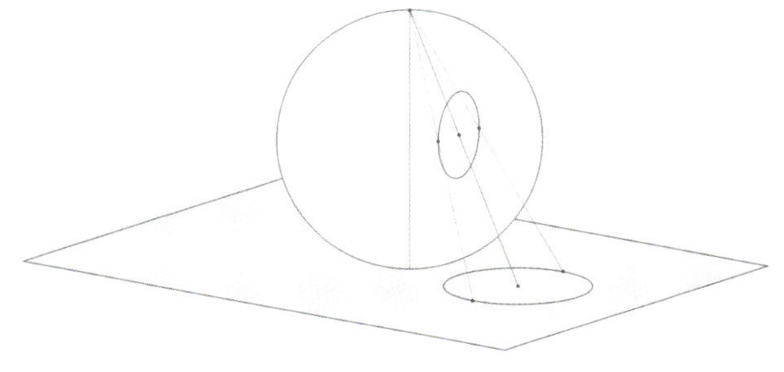

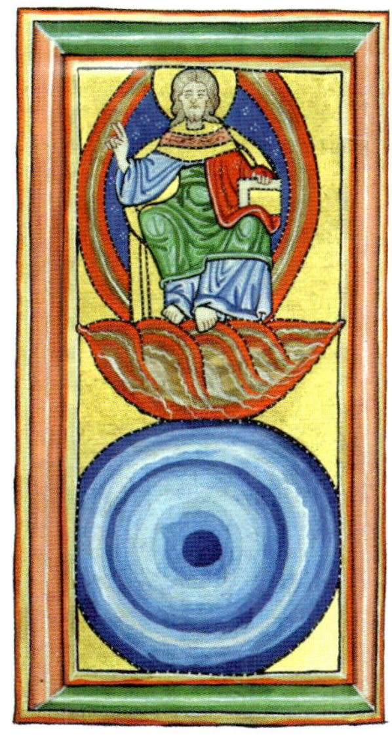

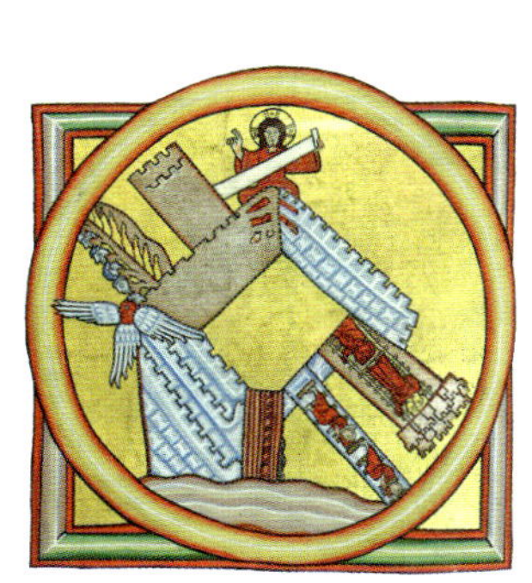

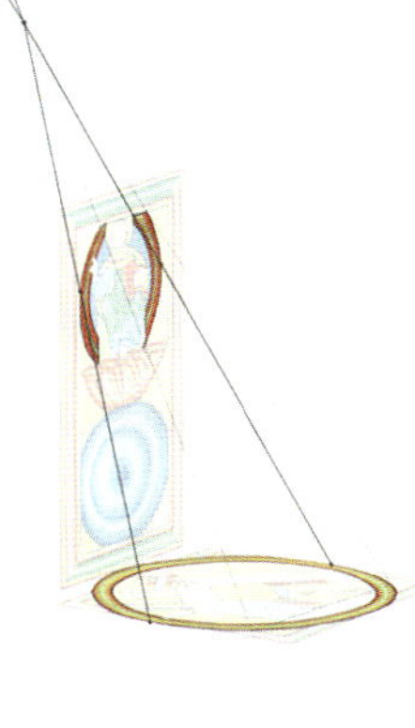

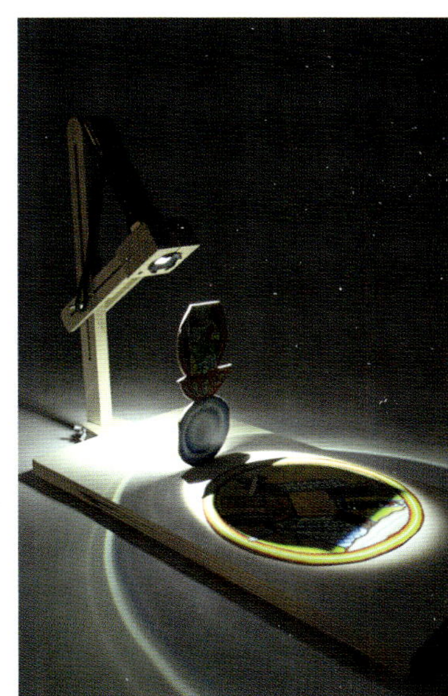

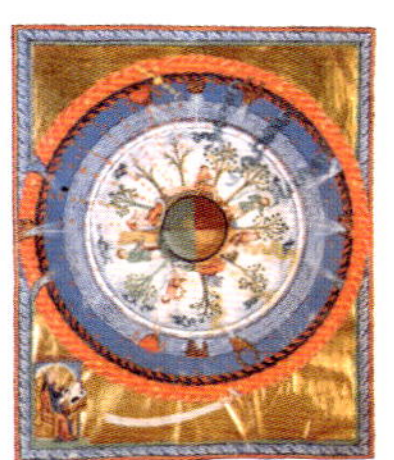

The man facing east
God is the east of man

And so Man faces the east, gazing as the west does to the east; and extending his arms as south and north are divided from each other, he points his right arm to the south and his left to the north (I.4,48, 175).

The soul operates in man with the power of the four elements. Thanks to the knowledge of good, it recognizes that its direction is towards God/east. The south wind is the wind of good deeds while the north wind reminds man that he will be chastised in the places of punishment (north).

The soul is diffused throughout the entire body, just as the windiness of the winds roams throughout the entire firmament (I.4,50, 178).

Cardinal points, human body, and rotations
The works of man and the choice of good and evil

For the human person governs and upholds himself completely with his arms and legs (I.4,51, 178); just as the winds uphold the firmament so does his soul flying in his body support the works of the body through the choice between good and evil.

In the left elbow is signified the principal east wind, [...] in the right elbow is demonstrated the principal south wind (I.4,52, 179).

The right leg's knee [...] demonstrates the principal west wind; [...] the left leg's knee also denotes the principal north wind. (I.4,93, 217).

Here the collateral winds to the right and left of the principal winds are situated in the forearms and arms, and in the upper and lower part of the leg. This means that the north/south and east/west axes are located in the right and left sides of the body, respectively. The two images must be superimposed in order to make the axes cross. By positioning the cardinal points in the right order, we obtain a cross created by rotating the figure around an ideal centre that coincides with the head. Continuing with this rotation, we obtain a geometric form with twelve sides. There is a clear reference to the image of the winds in *De Architectura* by Vitruvius. The text reads: *God signified the constitution of the winds in the human person: there are twelve major joints—the elbows of the arms, the shoulders and hands, the knees, the hips, and the feet—as too there are twelve winds* (I.4,93, 217).

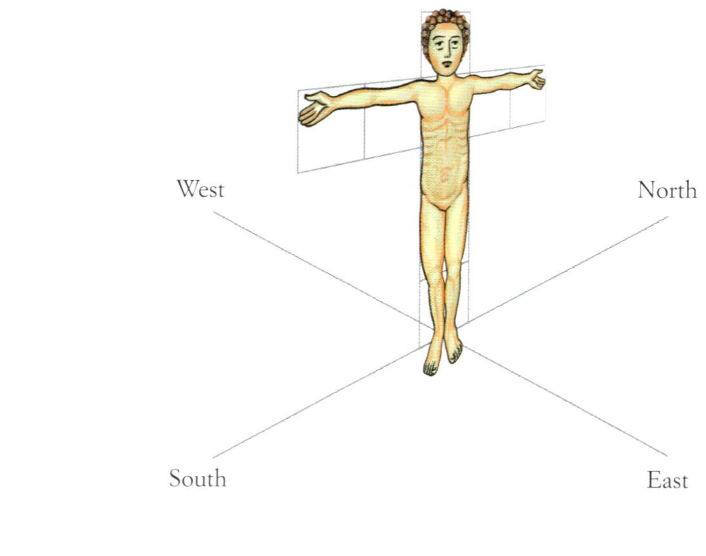

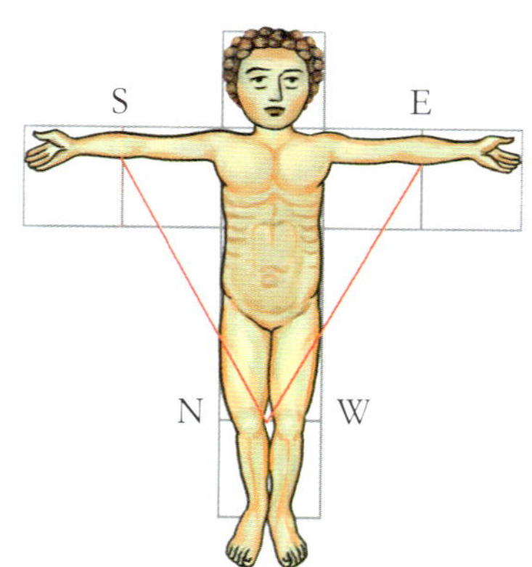

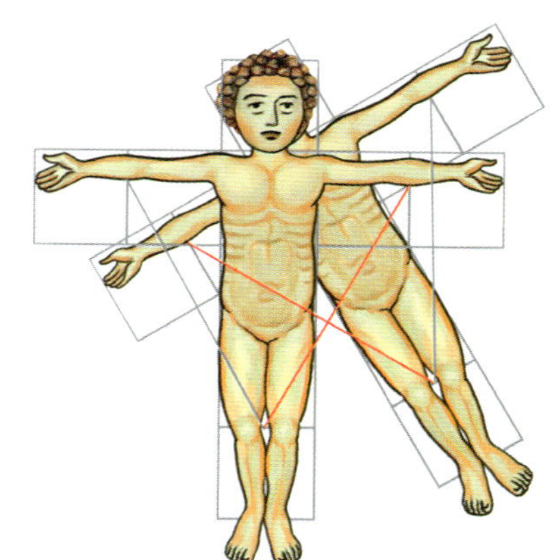

Rhetoric

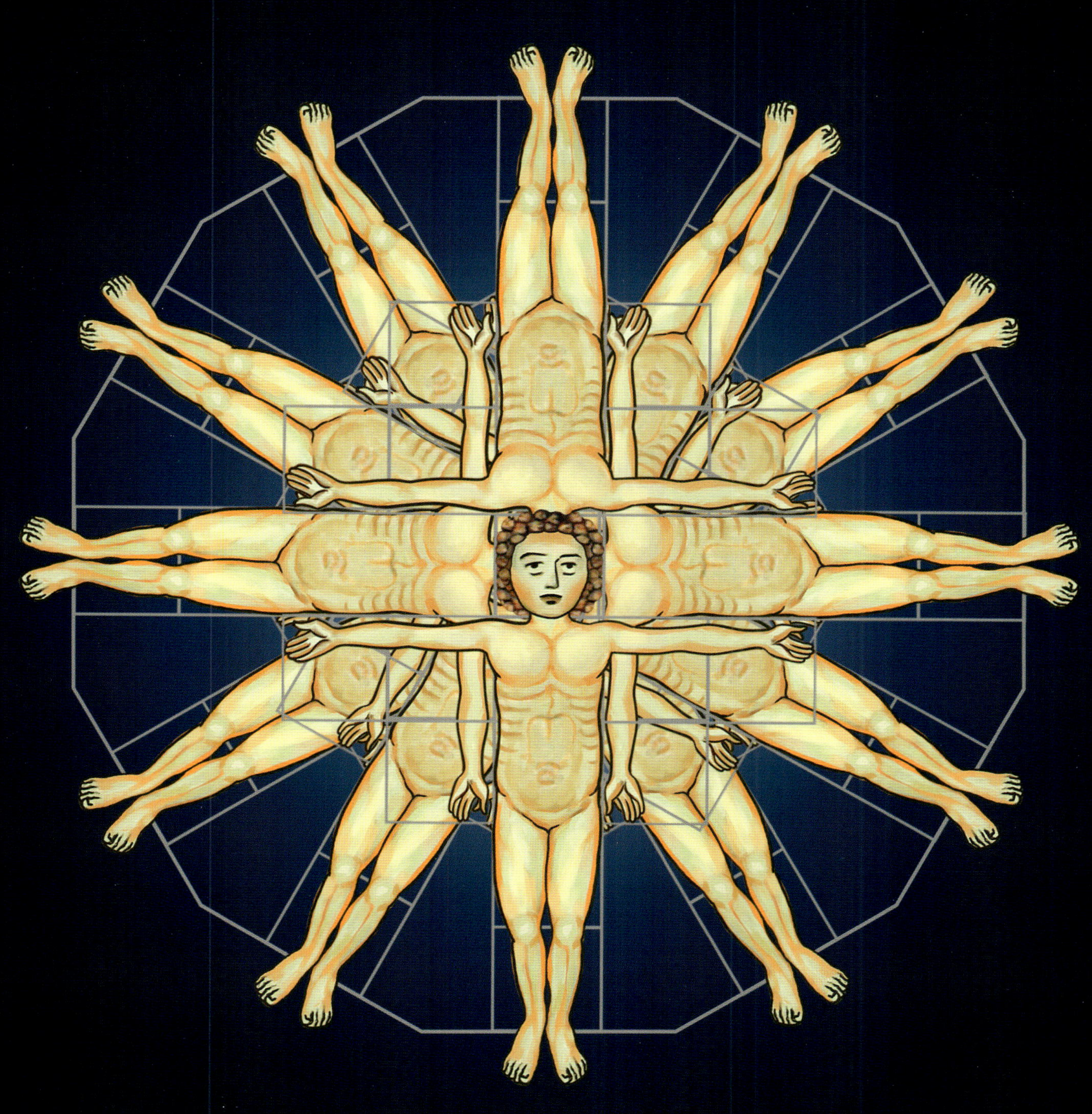

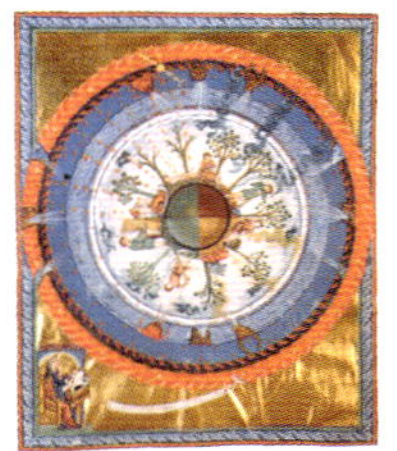

The measurements of man and of
the firmament. The five spaces
Body and soul

---

*And there is an equal measurement from the top of the
human head to the bottom of the throat, and from the
bottom of the throat to the navel, and from the navel to
the place of discharge. Likewise, there is also an equal
measurement from the top edge of the firmament to
the lower layer of the clouds, and from the lower layer
of the clouds to the top of the earth, and from the top
of the earth to its bottom* (I.4,53, 179–180).

From the top of his head to the lowest point, a man's
body is divided into five spaces. The firmament has the
same measurements as the man and each of its parts
corresponds to a part of the man. The man is therefore
made in the image and likeness of the egg/wheel/globe/
firmament/God. This is confirmed by superimposing the
Wheel (I.2) onto the vision of The Three Persons (III.2)
in *Scivias* (see page 72): the proportions of the human
figure in the wheel and the sapphire-colored man/Christ
(III.2) and the crucified Christ (II.6) all coincide. Even
the measurements of the arms of the human figure in the
middle of the wheel and of the Crucifix are the same.

• The first space: represented in the head of the man
are the *three powers of the soul—comprehension, intelligence*, and *capacity of movement*—which are joined
by three other powers—*respiration, knowledge, and
sensation* (I.4,17, p. 142)—the final two are the ones
that regulate *labor* and *rest* (I.4,19, p. 145).
   *The soul mounts into the brain and into the heart,
into the blood and into the marrow, and throughout the
entire body to fill it up* (I.4,19, 145).
   We should note that this is the same description used
to recount the infusion of the soul in *Scivias* (I.4) and of the
flame of the Spirit upon Hildegard in the *Protestificatio*.
• The second space: *But the space between the bottom
of the throat and the navel also signifies the atmosphere,
which descends from the clouds all the way to the earth
and tempers the earth's creatures with its natural energy.
For indeed the soul, a living spark and rational breath of
the divine power, permeates the entire body to give it energy. It encircles it with its love, motivating it to each task;
and although the body may have been born with an appetite for sin, the soul compels it to cooperate* (I.4,57, 182).
• The third space: *The belly, which is contained by the
ribs and other bones that do not have marrow's sap, signifies the soft and fruitful earth, which is interspersed
with stones. […] the soul maintains the body in its every task, as the soft and fruitful earth is made firm by its
inset stones* (I.4,69, 193).
• The fourth space: *For the measurement from the
place of discharge or the thigh to the knee signifies that*
the force of sexual desire is aroused at the devil's primal
seduction* (I.4,92, 216).
• The fifth space: *The measurement from the knees to
the ankle is the same as that from the place of discharge
or the thigh to the knee. The measurement of this limb
[…] signifies the ocean* (I.4,92, 215).

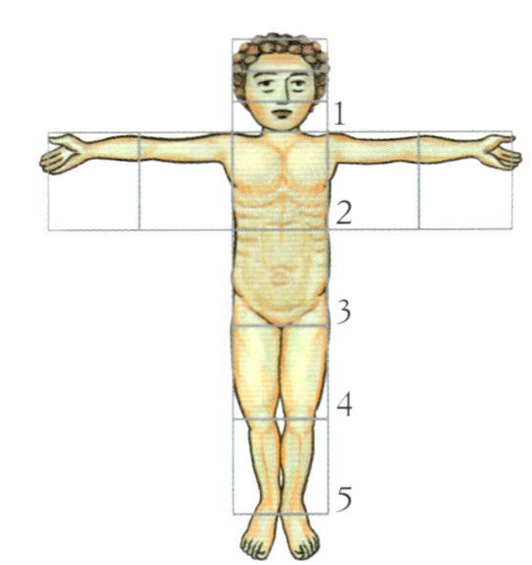

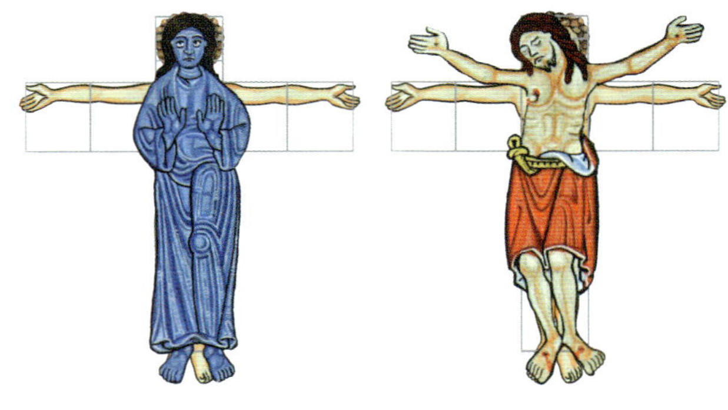

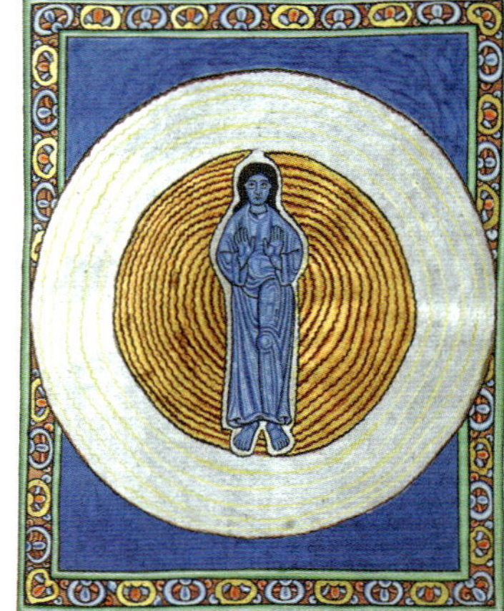

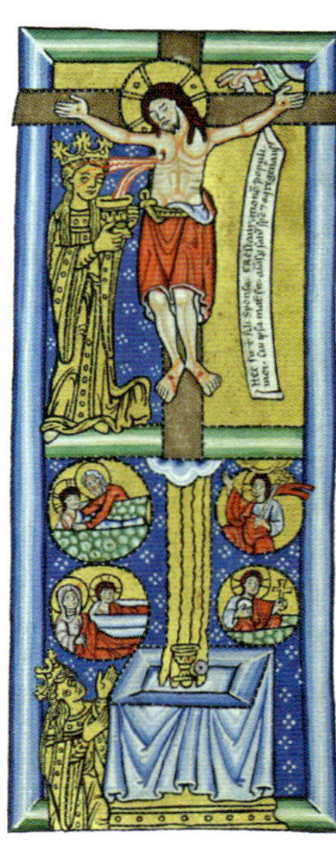

Width of the measurements of man and the firmament
Pride and repentance

*But there is also an equal measurement from each
shoulder to the elbow of each arm, and from each elbow
to the end of the middle finger of each hand* (I.4,55, 180).

The measurement *from the shoulder to the elbow* signifies the works carried out through *pride*, from the
elbow to the fingers the works by means of which man
will, through repentance, cancel those committed
through presumption.

Hand and foot
Works and the sequel of God

*The hand also has the same measurement from its
wrist to the tip of the middle finger as from the ankle
to the end of the big toe […]* (I.4,55, 180).
   *Then […] he turns away from deeds wicked
and contrary to the soul, and instead does good
works—signified by the hand—and runs upon the
ways of God—shown by the feet* (I.4,55, 181).

Breadth/thickness of man/earth and of the firmament
Desires of the flesh and abstinence

*The measurement from one thigh across to the other
in front is also of the same length as that from the navel
to the place of discharge, for the breadth across the
earth is of the same length as the thickness of its depth*
(I.4,56, 181).

The desire of the flesh is represented by the depth
while abstinence is represented by length and breadth.
The two measurements of length and breadth form
a cross as if to say that faith in Christ, who defeated
death on the cross, will guide man towards victory
over his carnal desires.

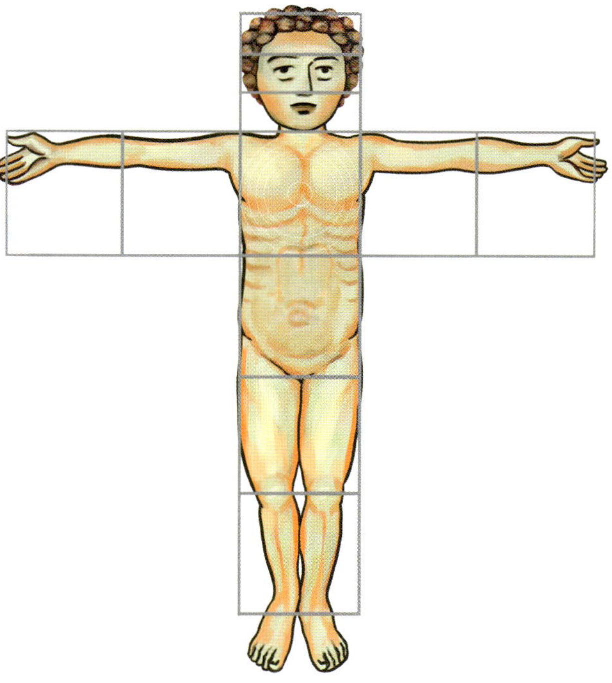

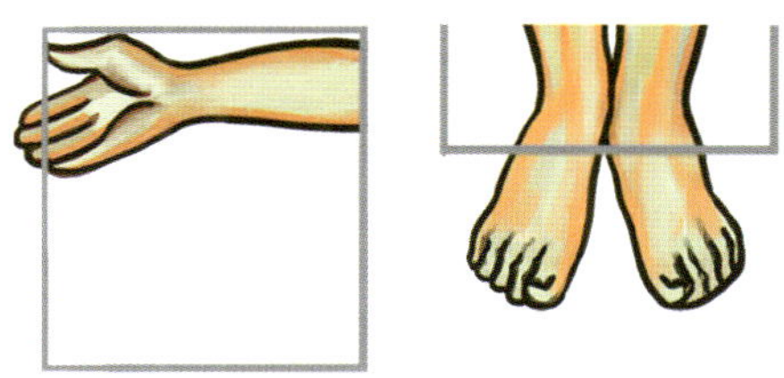

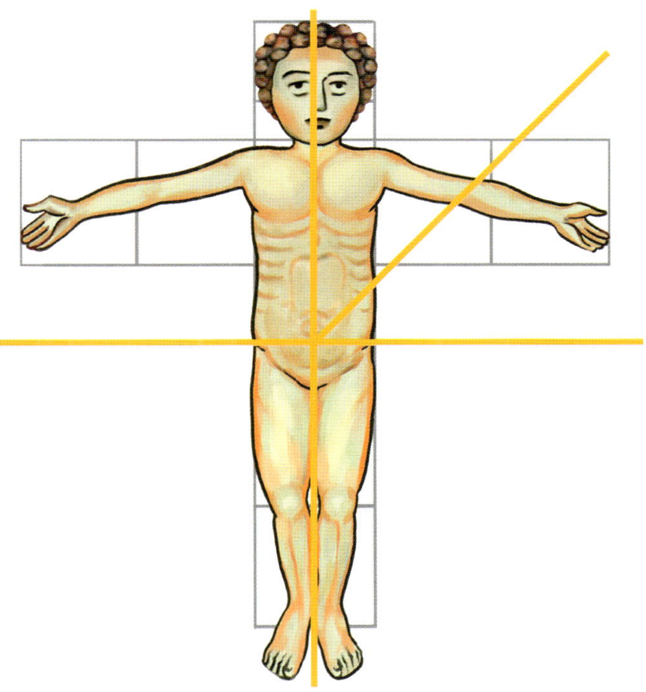

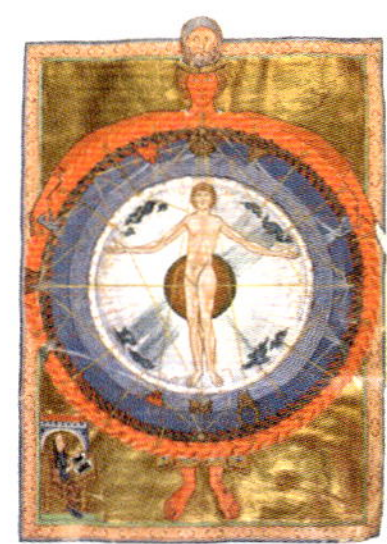

The heart of God and man

The human *figure/form* is described three times: in the first vision as the huge winged figure *quasi hominis formam*, God/Divine Love; in the second vision as a human figure (*imago hominis*) in the middle of the wheel; in the third vision its measurements coincide with the external diameter of the wheel/firmament and we read, *For a person's length in stature and breadth with arms and hands extended equally from the chest are equal, just as the firmament has an equal length and breadth* (I.4,15, 141).

Man's measurements guide us both in defining man within the wheel (second vision) and in giving him the same proportions as the firmament (fourth vision). In the first, the man divided into five spaces is located in the thin air while in the second, the same man with the same five spaces is situated in the wheel and his head occupies the space of the outer circles.

Each of the figures is divided into exactly five parts and, like a matryoshka doll, each part is in proportion to the others, from the smallest to the largest. This difference in size can be mathematically represented by a ratio of 3/5: in fact, the large figures like the wheel are 5/5, the other occupying the inner space of the wheel is 3/5 and the globe/earth/man is 1/5.

So if the man's heart is in a 1/5 of the figure, just like the lamb is in a 1/5 of the winged figure and the wheel is in the place of the lamb, we can see that man's heart is in God's heart.

[...] so God did in his Word when he created all things, for the Word, which is the Father's Son, lay hidden within the Father, like the heart hidden within a person (I.4,14, 139).

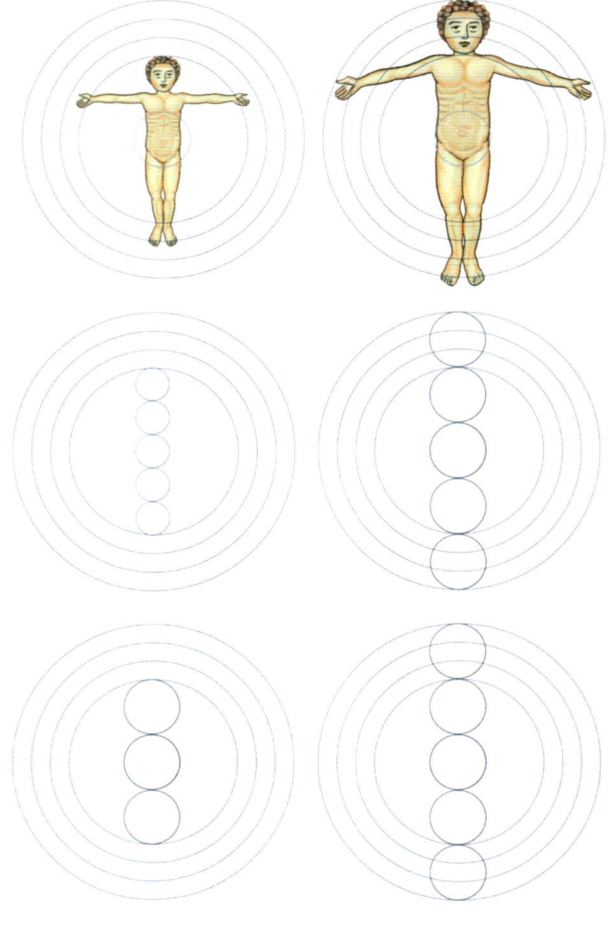

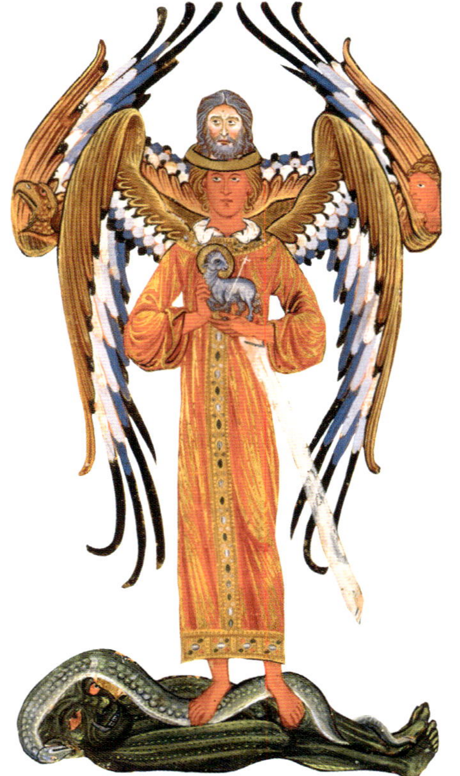

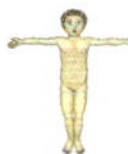

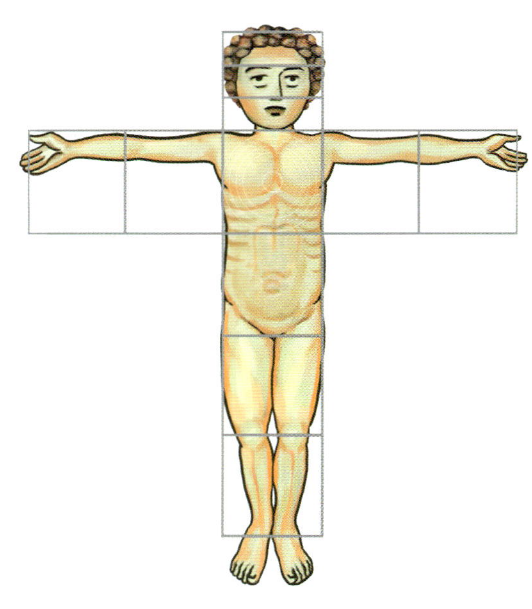

Rhetoric

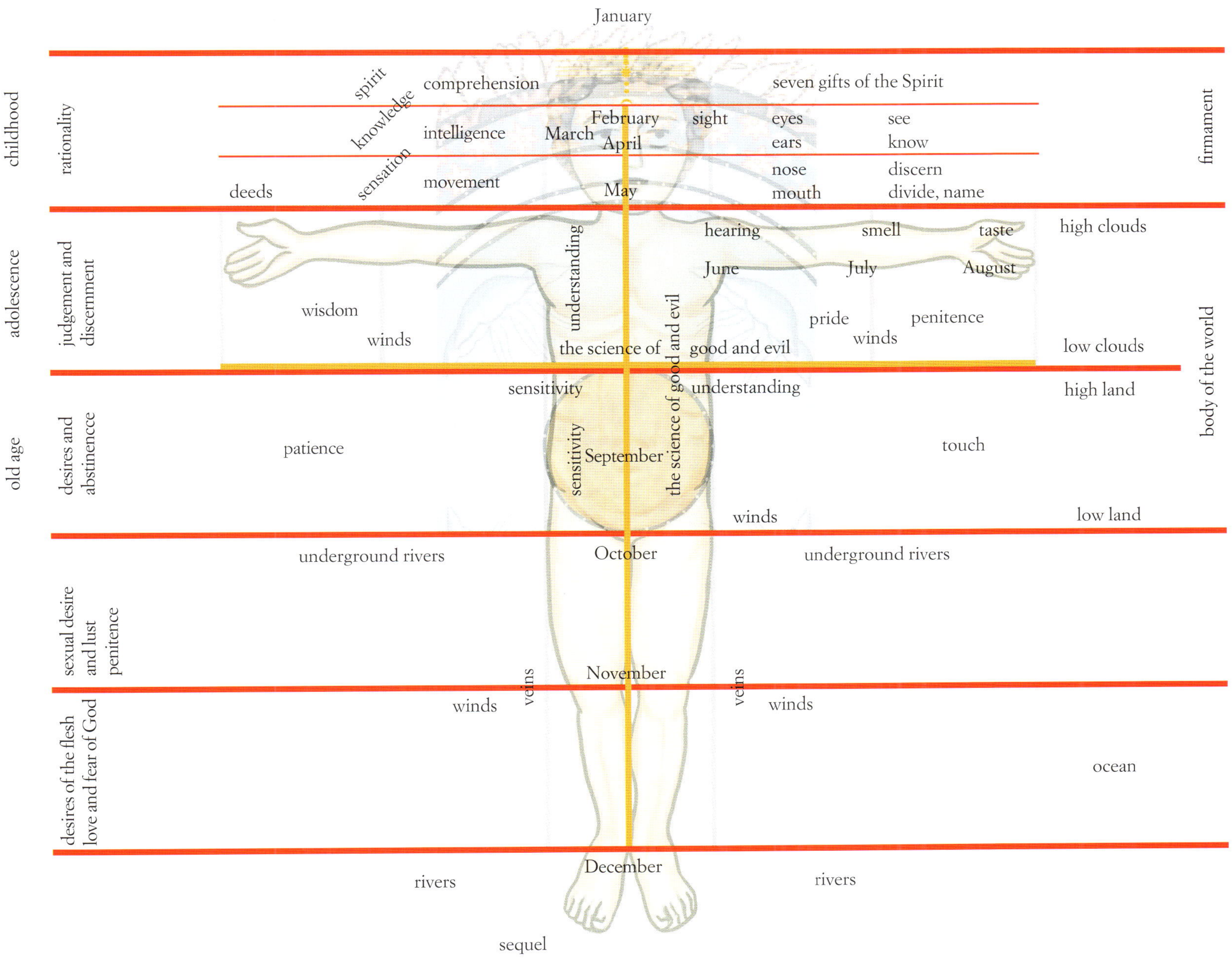

January
childhood
rationality
spirit
knowledge
sensation
comprehension
seven gifts of the Spirit
intelligence
February
sight
eyes
ears
see
know
March
April
nose
mouth
discern
divide, name
deeds
movement
May
firmament
hearing
smell
taste
high clouds
adolescence
judgement and discernment
understanding
June
July
August
wisdom
pride
penitence
winds
the science of good and evil
good and evil
winds
low clouds
body of the world
sensitivity
understanding
high land
old age
desires and abstinencce
sensitivity
patience
September
the science of good and evil
touch
winds
low land
underground rivers
October
underground rivers
sexual desire and lust
penitence
veins
November
veins
winds
winds
desires of the flesh
love and fear of God
ocean
December
rivers
rivers
sequel

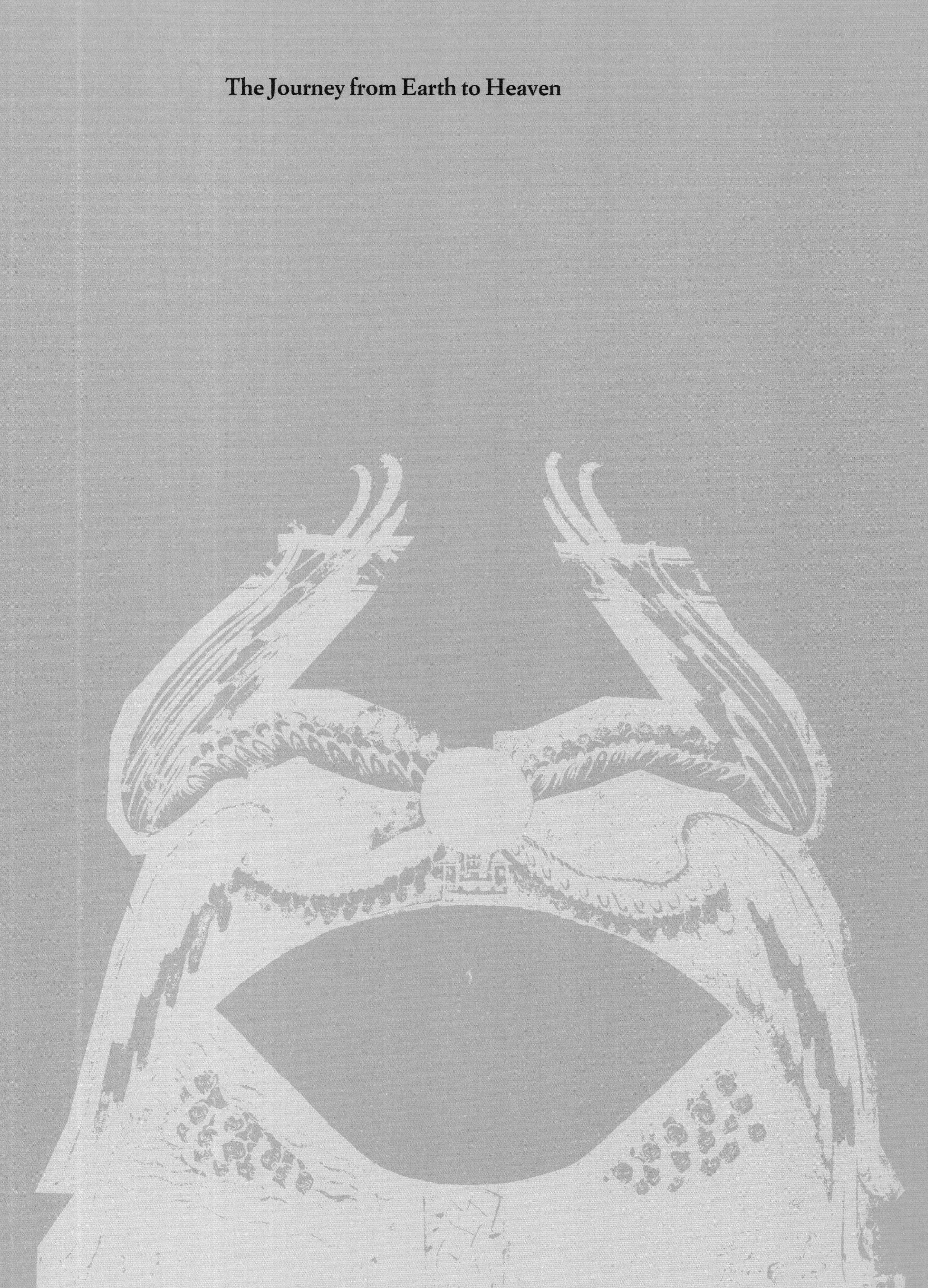

The Journey from Earth to Heaven

Single Vision. *The Journey from Earth to Heaven*

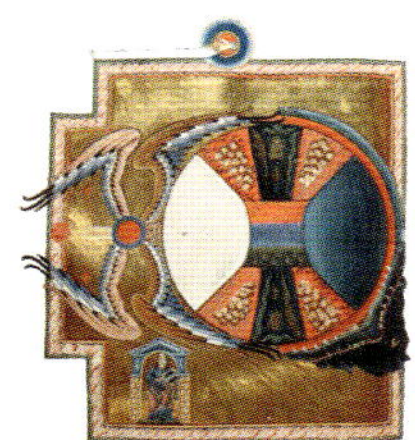

God suspended the sphere of the earth amid the other three elements, so that it could not slip away or be unloosed in any way. In this he shows that he is wondrous and powerful, because he only renders human flesh and bones to dust in order to restore them at the Last Day to their full integrity (II.1,2, 267).

The first part, with its long, detailed account of creation and man kept in God's heart, is followed by the single vision in the second part. This shows us the close-up internal vision of the winged figure of Divine Love (*Caritas*). The circle of the earth is none other than the interior of the wheel set into the breast of Divine Love, and the star and globes of the figure are the symbolic image of the Trinity, which made itself visible in the two human faces and in the golden circle of the winged figure. The focus of this vision is the theme of judgement and of the end times, and it illustrates the complete journey from earth to heaven.

The earth is now shown divided into the two zones of *light* and *shadow*: in the bottom left-hand corner of the image, we can make out endless, terrifying darkness that seem on the point of devouring the round body of the world/earth/man, while on the right, beyond the bright part of the earth, we see the *way* leading to God. A way of self-integrity that leads towards the splendid southern sun, towards blessedness. The passage quoted above, which opens the vision, reveals the Last Judgment in all its strength. In just a few lines, it describes the moment in which the earth/*orb* is judged and the subsequent moment when the bones of the dead are returned to men's bodies so that they might rise to heaven with their bodies and souls. This passage recalls the end times depicted in vision III.12a in *Scivias* with the *orb* being shaken by the judgment in the middle: on Christ's *right*, in the light, the bones of the dead are recomposed in the blessed up on high; on his *left*, in the darkness, there are infernal flames and demons; and above, the gray damned swaddled in eternal death. The single vision in the *LDO* not only portrays the moment of judgment but also includes merciful Divine Love offering man the possibility of repentance. The world is divided into five places that are both the five places of "purgatory" and man's five senses.

In fact, through his senses, man is called upon to use his discernment to live righteously. When man chooses good works, he is guided on the *way* indicated between the *globes* of Divine Love and justice and of the Holy Spirit.

This is the *way* of *virginitas*, the *way* following in the footsteps of the Son of God, a journey during which we are called upon to recognize the gift God has given to each human being with their soul, lighting them like a *living spark*.

The *candid star* above illuminates the *way*, inviting us to follow its rays, the footsteps of Christ, in order to join God definitively. The ceaseless praise of blessed men in the *building* placed between the earth and the heavens reveals the real possibility of this journey to the men who are traveling. The *building*, which is the prefiguration of the New Jerusalem, tells us that everything dwells in God forever and forever in Divine Foreknowledge. Man is therefore called upon to show his trust and to praise God ceaselessly.

Orientation towards the south and towards the east
The judgment, the journey

The single vision/figure of a man/Divine Love is oriented in the *middle of the southern sky* as described at the beginning of the work, with the south to the left of the reader. This clearly illustrates the division of the earth into *light* and *darkness* to the *right* and *left* of God but in order to observe man's journey from earth to heaven we need to rotate the image with the wings on top towards the east in the same position as Divine Love, mirroring it on the vertical axis. The miniaturist has clearly grasped this second view (see page 127).

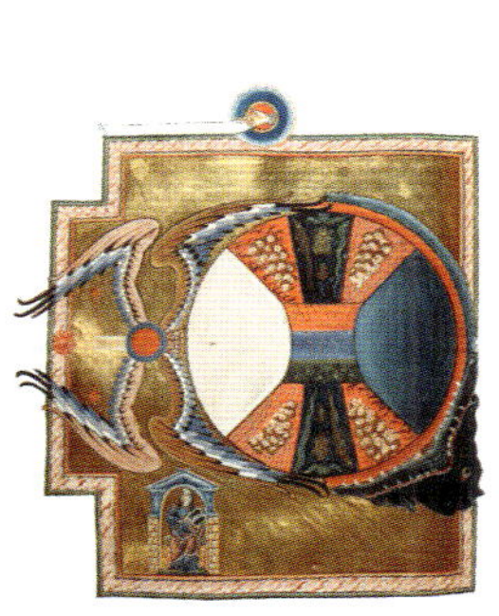

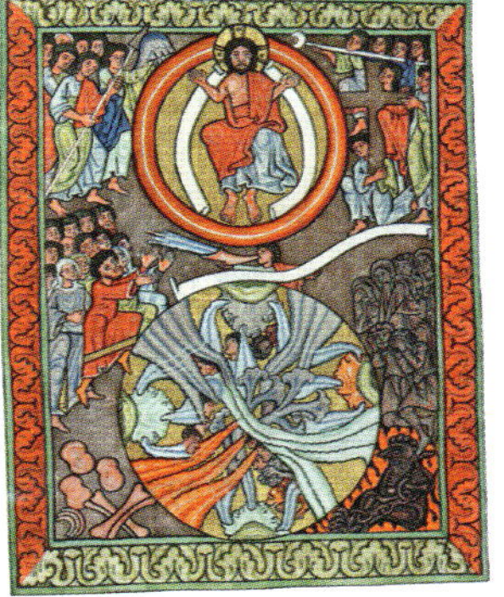

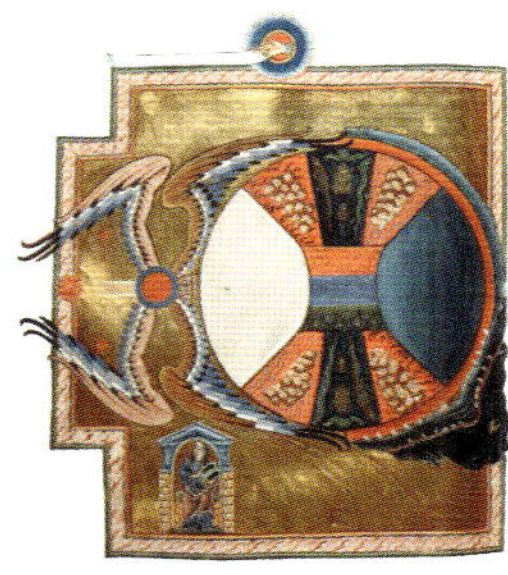

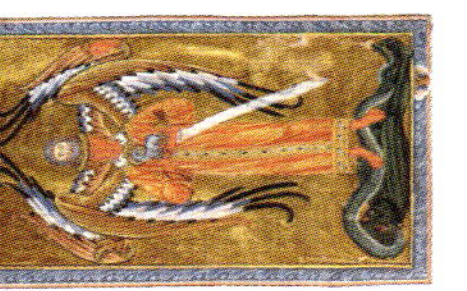

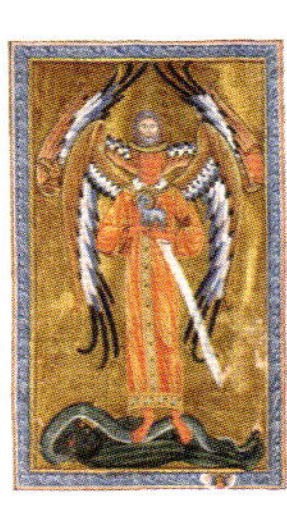

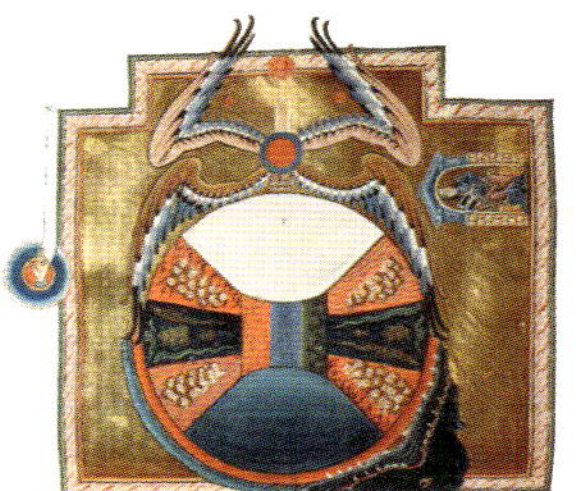

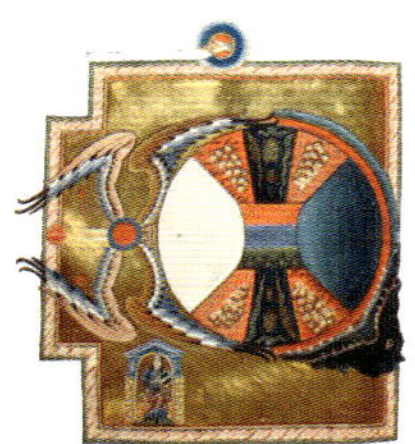

The round earth divided into five parts

Then I saw the round of the earth divided into five parts, so that one part was to the east, one to the west, the third to the south, the fourth to north, while the fifth in their middle. The extent of the eastern part and the extent of the western part were of equal dimension, and each had the form of a drawn bow. The extent of the southern part and the extent of the northern part also were of a single measure, equal in length and breadth to the previous two parts—except that, because the inner edges of the previous two parts curved around, these two appeared as if truncated as they bent inwards. So they too imitated the form of a drawn bow, except that their inner edges were truncated.

For each of these parts—the southern part and the northern part—was further divided into three parts […].

But the fifth part of those described, which was in the middle of all the others, appeared in squared form and was flooded in one place by heat, in another by cold, but in another by a temperate air (II.1,1, 264 and 266).

Thanks to the precision of its reconstruction of the earth and of its division into five parts, this first long section of the description is key to our understanding of the entire *LDO*, allowing us to make some remarks relative to constructive aspects.

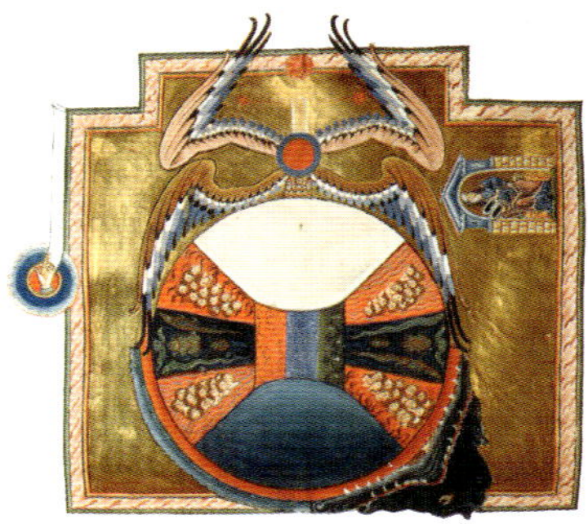

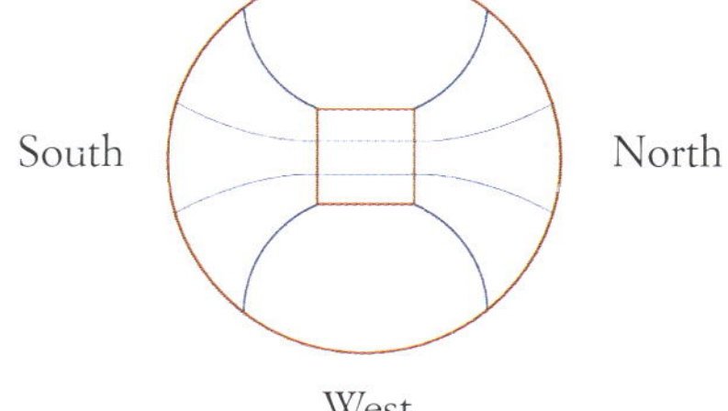

The five parts of the orb
The Last Judgment and End Times

Our journey through the images in *Scivias* has revealed the presence of a single constructive arrangement in which clear geometrical references can be identified. In the two miniatures of the Judgment and Paradise (III.12a and III.12b), the dimensions of the red circle surrounding Christ the Judge are the same as those of the middle circle in the second vision (shown in red here) and the dimensions of the nimbus of Christ the Judge are the same as those of the inner circle of the lamb in the middle of the Father (shown in yellow here). If we superimpose the two miniatures, causing the circles of the nimbus and of the lamb to correspond, we will see that the red circle of Christ the Judge and the circle of the blessed in Paradise coincide with the two arcs of the circles dividing the circle of the Father and the circle of the blessed. The superimposition emphasizes the mandorla, *vesica piscis*, framing the saints and the blessed bearing the three lily crosses. The same image returns in the circle underneath, where a second mandorla appears, containing the sun, moon, and stars, immobile in the eternity of Paradise. It is interesting

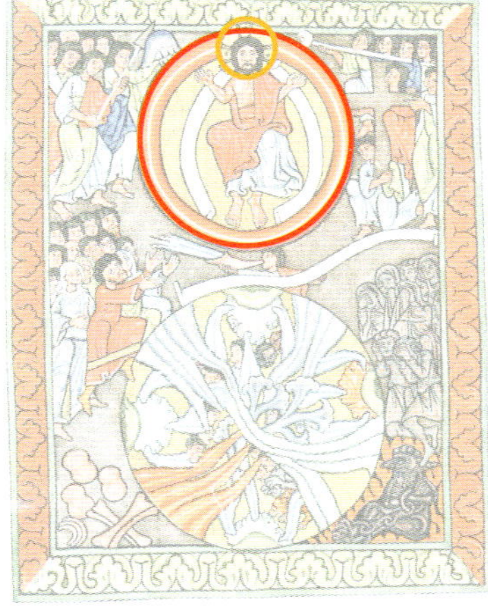

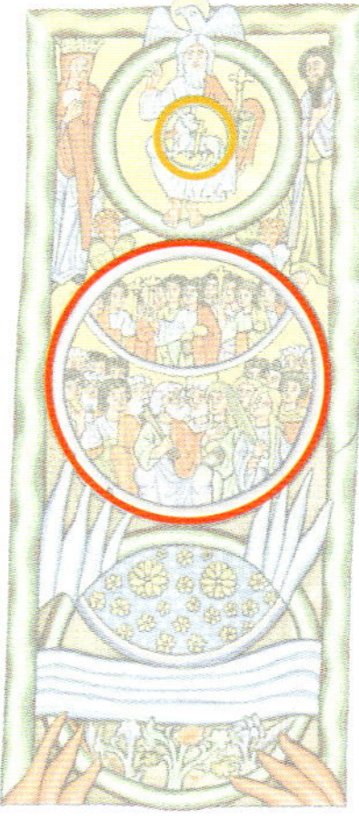

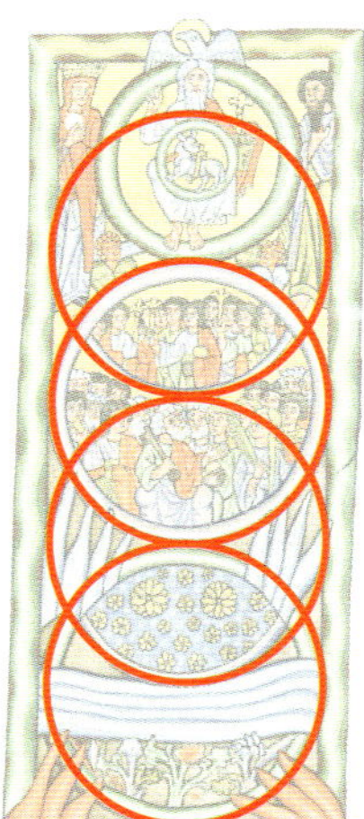

to note that the stars in the heavens are star men on earth who have reached the heavens where they have become saints.

These two mandorla forms recall the description of the two drawn bows dividing the earth into *light* and *darkness* (east/west). The circle containing the two mandorlas has the same diameter as the earth and the two mandorlas coincide with the eastern and western part of the vision.

By duplicating the diagram obtained and rotating it horizontally, we obtain the other two parts into which the earth is divided (south/north). By joining the two diagrams, we obtain the circle of the earth with its four divisions and the square in the middle.

The intersection of the two diagrams illustrating the internal division of the earth reveals a four-lobed flower formed by the overlapping mandorlas. The symbolism of the *vesica piscis*, or mandorla, evokes the fish outline symbolizing Christ *Ichthys*. The flower created recalls the Flower of the Apocalypse.

The correspondence between the images of the Judgment and Paradise in *Scivias* and the *LDO* vision is clearly very close, underlining the eschatological framing of the whole work.

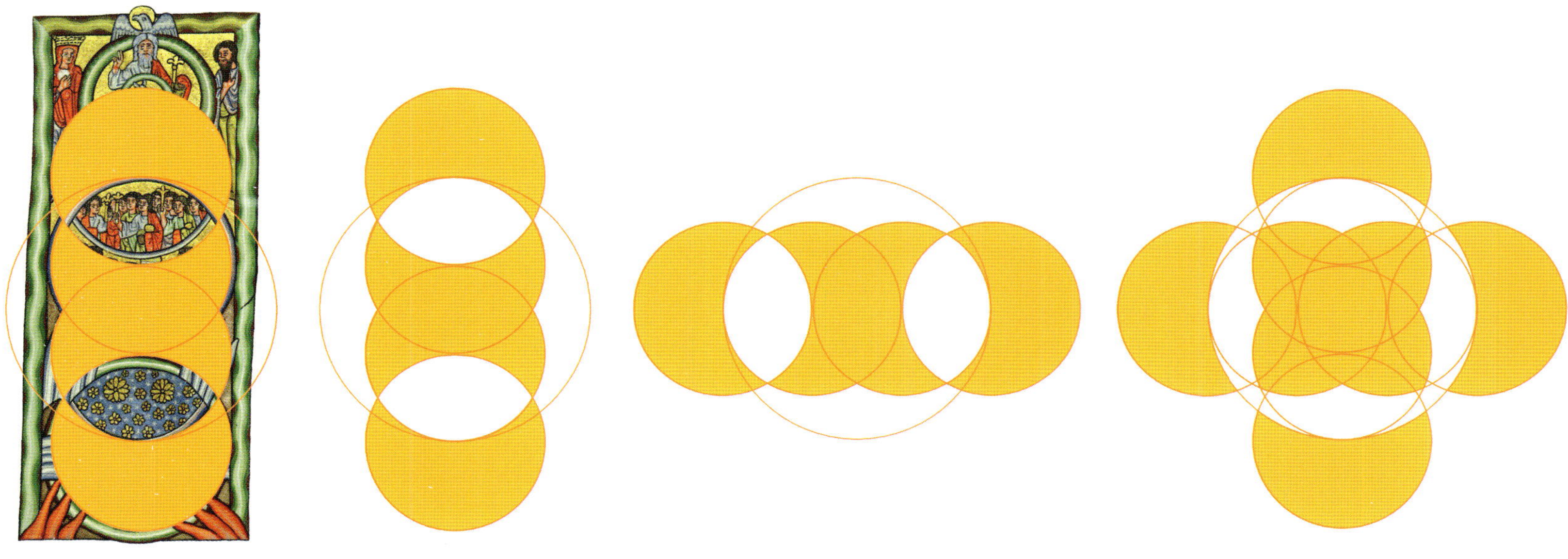

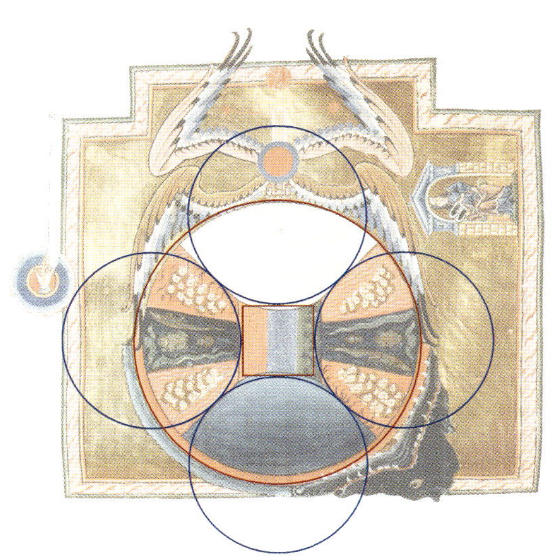

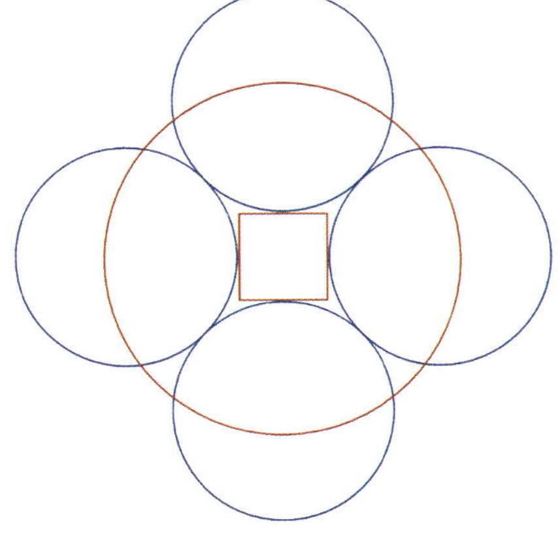

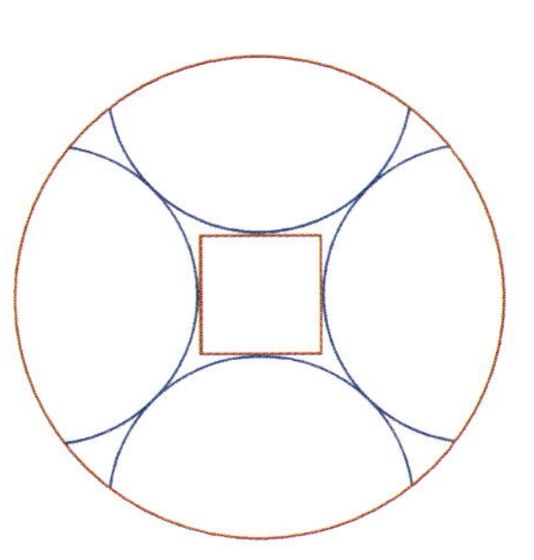

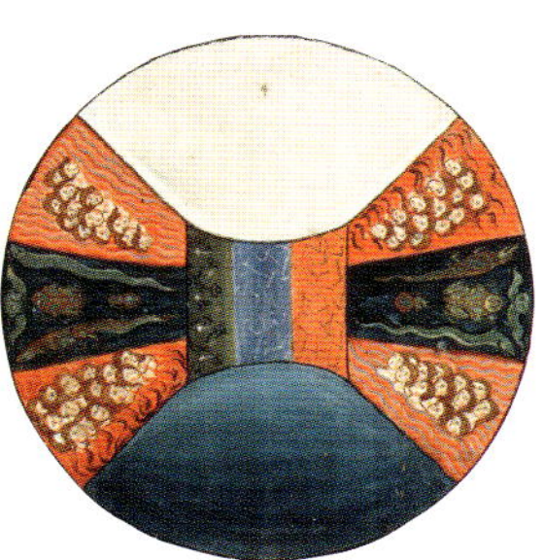

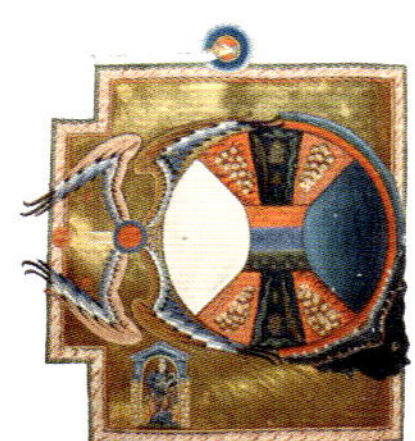

The red and sapphire globe
Christ. Divine Love and Justice

*But toward the east and above the aforesaid round
of the earth, I saw at a certain height a red globe
surrounded by a circle of sapphire color* (II.1,1, 266).
*This is because in the eastern region—signifying
the origin of justice—God's jealousy, which surpasses
human understanding and dwells in the height
of heavenly secrets, is revealed in his power with the
justice of Divine Love* (II.1,10, 279).

In the celestial space above the circle of the earth is the
first element taking the form of a *red globe* surrounded
by a *circle of sapphire color*, God's jealousy or zeal, justice, and Divine Love. It corresponds to the youthful
face of the winged figure/Divine Love in the first vision,
which has lost its human appearance.

The *red and sapphire globe* recalls the *sapphire-colored man* in *Scivias* who is the incarnation of the Son, in
the vision of the Three Persons (II.2). The description

of the vision of the Trinity and of the *sapphire-colored
man* is followed by the chapter on *John the Divine Love
of God*, with a long passage from the first letter of John
describing the mission of the Son of God/ *sapphire-colored man* sent to purify men from their sins. Christ/the
sapphire-colored man is carried by the *globe in the east
where justice rises* in the End Times (III.11).

The position of the globe with respect to the circle
of the earth is determined precisely by the indications
given in the vision (see page 131). By superimposing
the circle of the earth and the globe onto the images of
the Final Coming and of the Quiet and Jubilation in the
Heavens of *Scivias* (III.12a and b), we can see that the
globe is in the middle of the breast of Christ the Judge
and beneath the feet of God the Father.

In this regard, it is interesting to recall the passage
from Exodus 24:10, identified in the critical edition of
Scivias, concerning the description of the sapphire-colored man: *And they saw the God of Israel. Under his feet
was a work like a pavement made of sapphire, as clear as
the sky itself.*

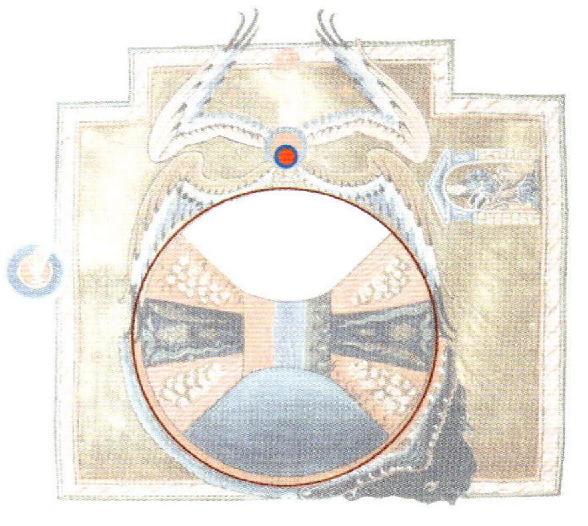

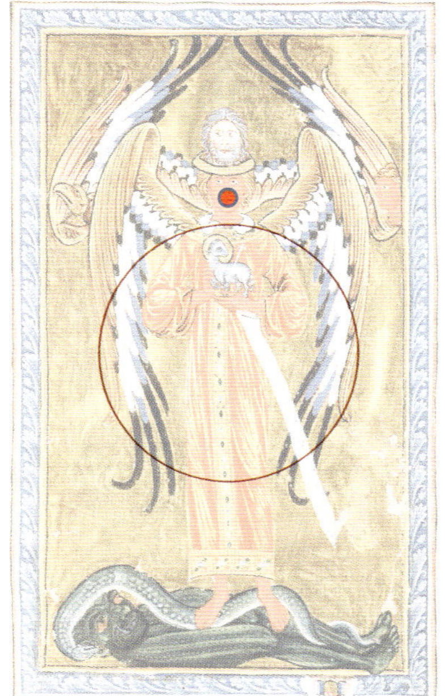

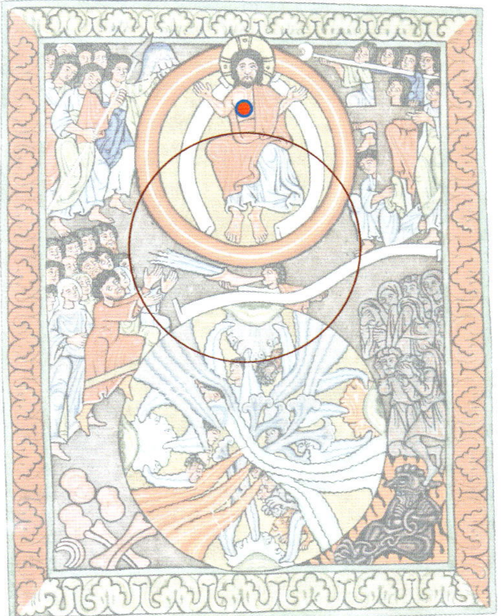

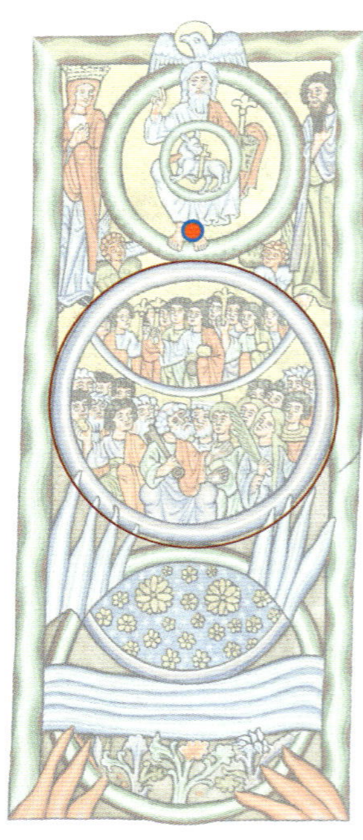

Wings
Protection and true tenderness

One of these [wings] on each side extended out and up from each side of that circle, so that as each curved around, they looked upon each other at their tips. But the others descended from each side down to the middle of the aforesaid round of the earth, so that each of these wings touched the round's middle by embracing it along the outside of the firmament (II.1,1, 266).

Extending out from the globe of Divine Love and Justice are the wings with which God protects men, embracing what is in the heavens while also defending what is on earth in an embrace of protection and true tenderness. These are the same wings we saw extend out from the winged figure in the first vision.

The red circle
God's zeal

And from that midpoint, a red circle, stretching itself like a bow, surrounded the whole outer part of the west, as well as certain segments that were outside that round, by twisting itself from the tip of the southern wing around the west and all the way to the tip of the northern wing (II.1,1, 266).

The red semicircle surrounding the wheel/earth and extending to the midpoint of its circumference is God's zeal, by means of which he supports those who adore him and justly judges *those who walk beyond the perimeter of good works, and those who are outside the integrity of the true faith (II.1,11, 280).*

The description of God's zeal strongly evokes the winged head representing the zeal of God in the building of *Scivias*, which is red, and placed halfway up the circle with the central wing dipping downwards. All of this is strongly reminiscent of the red semicircle in the bottom half of the wheel. It is interesting to note that in the *LDO*, God's zeal is followed by a description of the building, as if to underline the connection between the two figures present in both works.

The building/city
Song of glory to God

[…] the city built of living stones directs its gaze to [God's] judgment, glorifying him (II.1,11, 280). Moreover, from that round between the wings in the east appeared as if an edifice, climbing up to the aforementioned globe (II.1,1, 266).

The city of living stones directs its gaze towards God's judgment, glorifying him. It is situated on the external perimeter of the circumference of the earth, wrapped in the wings of divine protection. The circle of the earth coincides with the circle of the building of *Scivias* (III.2), and is therefore located at the beginning of the seven *white steps* leading to the Son of God (III.10)—we know from our previous study that these two miniatures are united. The *city of living stones* is, in fact, the start of a journey that ascends from the earth, leading men to the heaven of blessedness, following the footsteps of Christ, on the way of *virginitas*, in the certainty that everything has been ordered by divine foreknowledge.

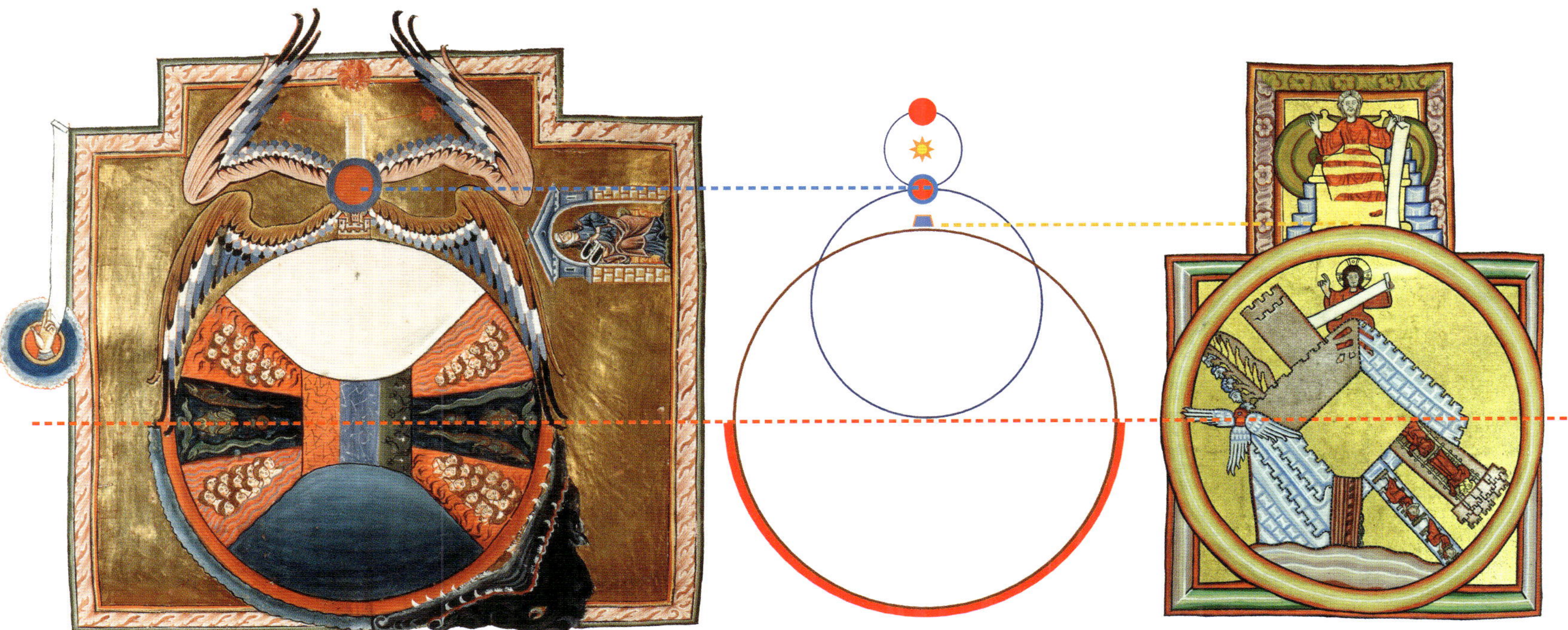

 Rhetoric

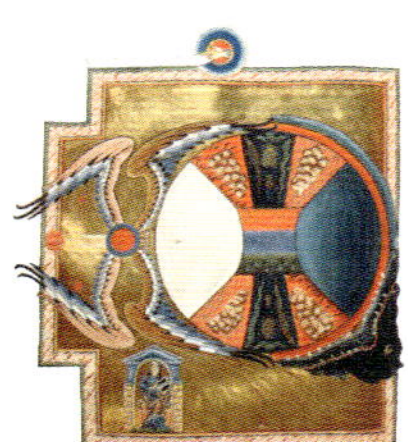

The way. *Virginitas*

And from that globe all the way up to the midst of the aforesaid wings, there stretches as if an avenue, above which beams as if a brightly shining star. For from the judgments of God's power to the perfection of his protections runs a way, upon which virginity flourishes when the incarnate Son of God appears, born of the Virgin. Him the greatest multitude follows mightily with reverent devotion as it loves virginity and seizes perfection (II.1,12, 280).

Confirming what emerged from the previous super-imposition, it is clear that the *way* extending to the middle of the wings coincides exactly with the middle of the throne on which the Son of God is seated. In the text of the *LDO* we read: *for from the judgments of God's power to the perfection of his protection runs a way, upon which virginity flourishes when the incarnate Son of God appears, born of the Virgin* (II.1,12, 280). In *Scivias*, we find the theme of *virginitas*, described here as an ascending path, expressed by the figure of a young woman in the breast of the standing woman/Christ surrounded by men and women (II.5). *Virginitas* reaches the height of its expression in Christ. Like precious stones, the virgins and virtues surround the filthy mud/man in the breast of the Omnipotent One (III.1a), anticipating the image of God/Divine Love with the wheel and man in his breast, emphasizing the parallels between *virginitas* in the heart of the Church and *virginitas*/Christ in the heart of God. And yet again from the *ways* of *Scivias* to the *way* of the *LDO*.

The candid star
Son of God

[…] above which [avenue] beamed as if a brightly shining star (II.1,1, 266).

The *candid* (*brightly shining*) *star* represents the Son of God who illuminates the *way* of *virginitas*, showing men the footsteps they should follow. A *star* shining in the east to safely guide men on their journey.

The fiery globe and the rays
Holy Spirit

And then, between those wingtips, as if a fiery globe appeared, casting from itself certain rays [...]. Also between that first set of wings and on either side of the aforesaid avenue, particular and distinct rays of stars were seen, from the first globe, around the indicated star, all the way to the fiery globe (II.1,1, 267).

The *fiery globe*, the Holy Spirit, casts rays to the star, the Son of God; the rays then return to the Holy Spirit indicating that the men who imitate Christ are protected on all sides by the strength of the Holy Spirit, a strength that returns to God. The description of the heavenly elements above the circle of the earth ends here. It is clear that the *sapphire globe*, the *star*, and the *red globe* coincide with the faces and the golden circle of the winged figure of the first vision.

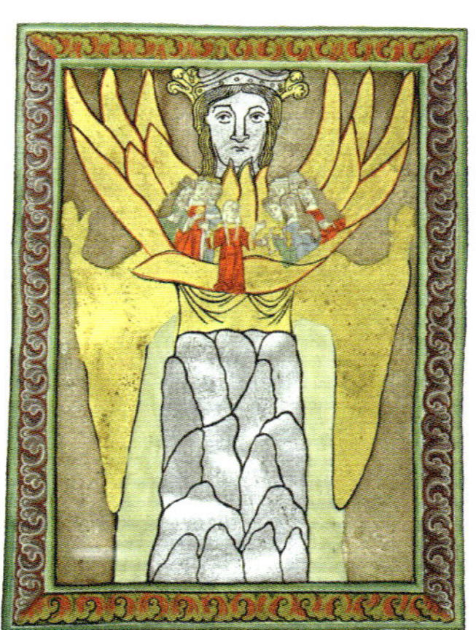

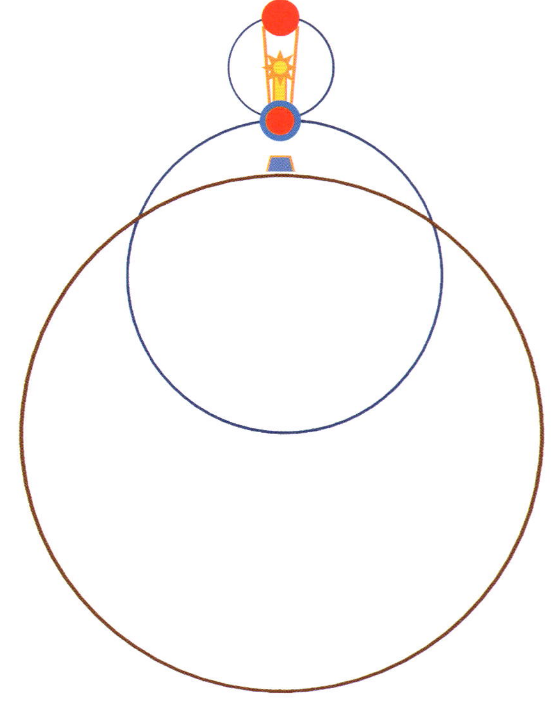

The faces and the wings. The red/sapphire globe,
the candid star, the fiery globe. The sun and the
three torches
The Trinity

We can therefore see that the red/sapphire *globe*, Divine
Love and justice, coincides with the sun/*globe of glowing fire* of the egg/firmament (I.3) of *Scivias*, Christ, Sun
of justice. And that the sandy *globe*/earth in the middle
of the egg is inscribed in the square in the middle of the
earth in the *LDO* vision. While at the top, the red globe
of the Holy Spirit coincides with the highest point of the
wings and the extreme limit of the egg above the torches
of the Trinity.

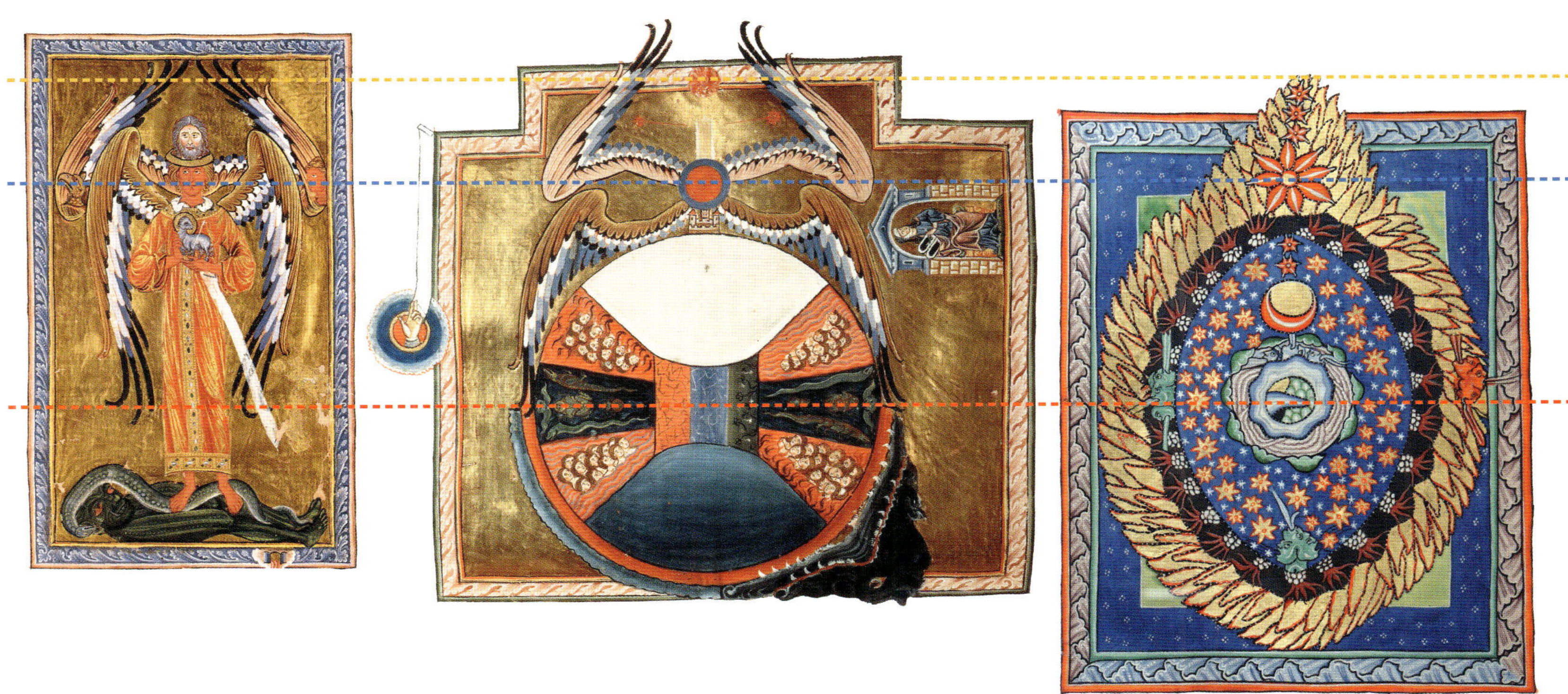

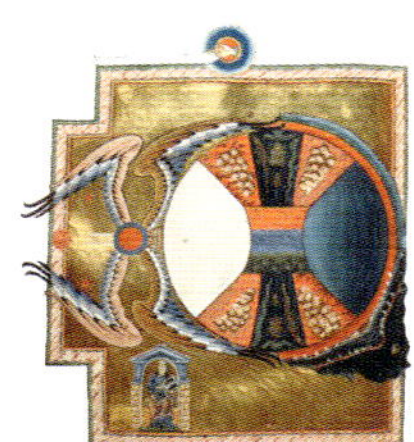

The darkness and the mouth
The hell

But to the west, beyond the earth's round, darkness appeared that stretched itself like a bow from each part of that round to its middle, where the aforesaid wings came down. Within it, between the western and northern points, there was another darkness, denser and sharper, with a form as of a mouth's horrible and devouring gullet, to which clung, like its mouth and jaws, the worst darkness of all, densest and endless, beyond the other darkness. For I knew that this darkness was infinite, though I did not see it (II.1,1, 267).

The darkness is the space that formed due to the evil rebellion of the fallen angel, and is the place where the ancient enemy *rejoices to keep torments over the souls surrendered to oblivion* (II.1,13, 281).

The entrance to hell is like a horrible open *mouth* devouring souls. Beyond the *darkness* lies further *darkness* not visible to man's gaze because his intellect may not discern it as long as he lives in his body, just as his soul may not recognize his merits as long as he lives. In *Scivias*, in the third miniature of the Journey of the Soul (I.4c), there is a division between darkness and light both at the top and bottom of the figure; on the bottom, between left and right, and on the top, between top and bottom, reflecting the position of the single vision seen according to its two orientations. Also visible is the gaping mouth of hell, as in the second miniature of the Ancient Serpent (II.7b).

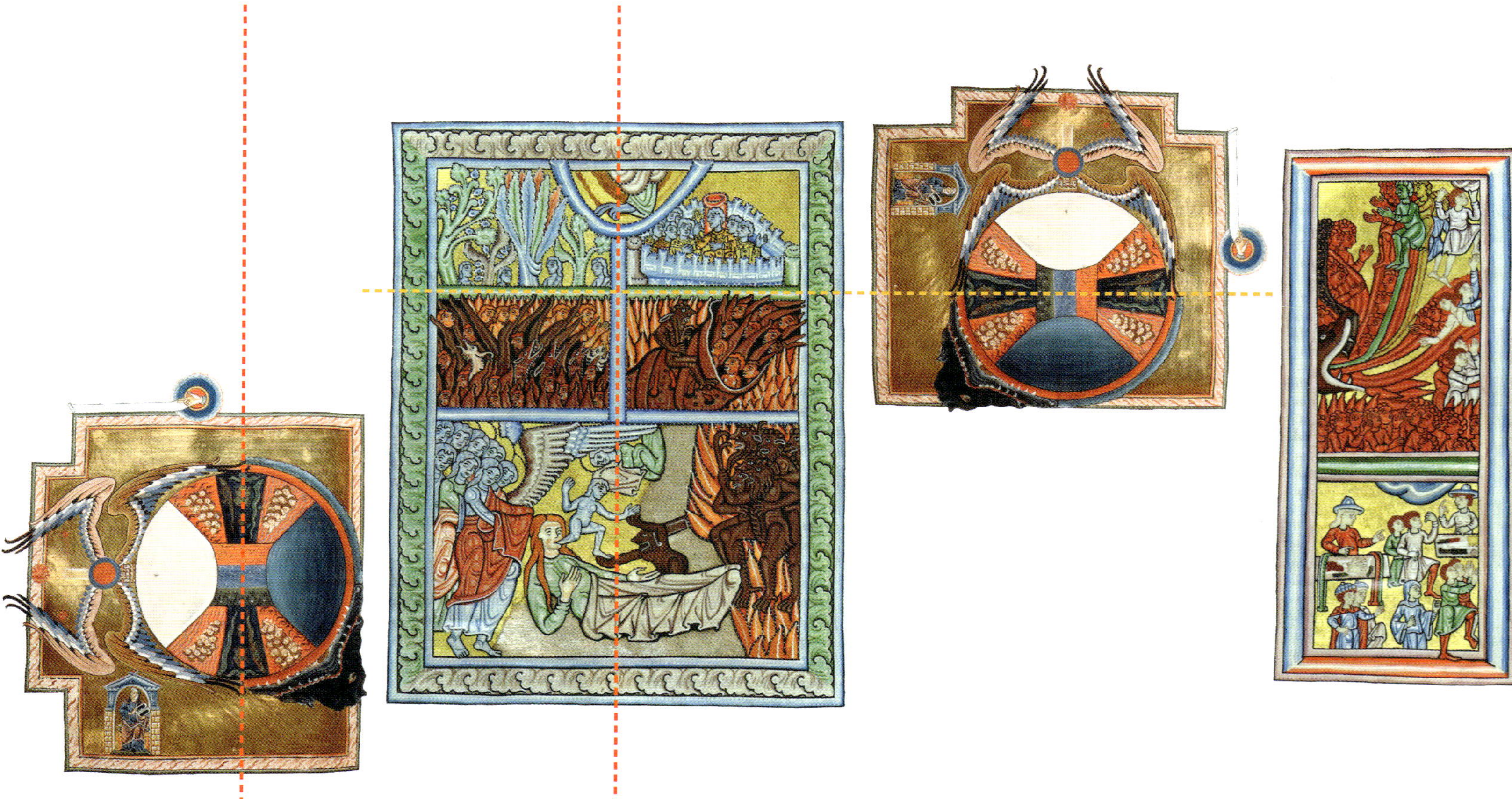

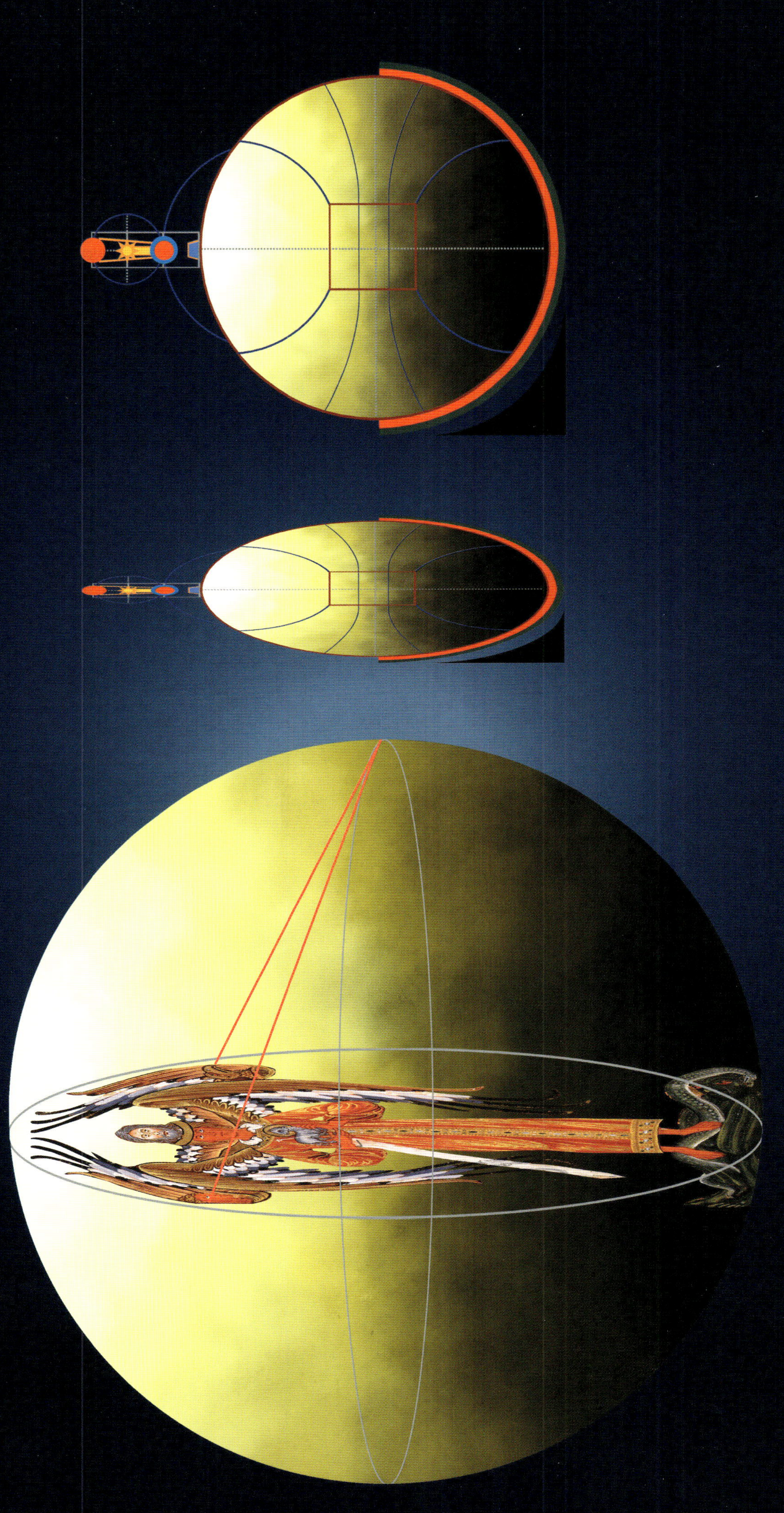

*Complete reconstruction
of the vision and its location
in the cosmos.*

The Building

And again I saw as if the squared instrument of a great city, surrounded as with a certain radiance and a certain darkness, as with a wall on either side; and adorned also with certain mounts and images (III.1,1, 348).

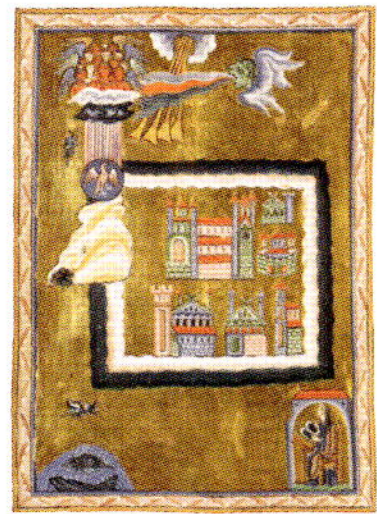

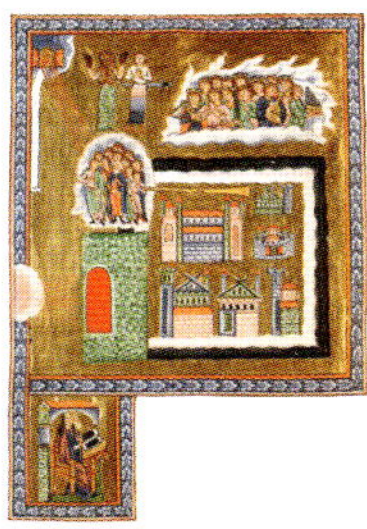

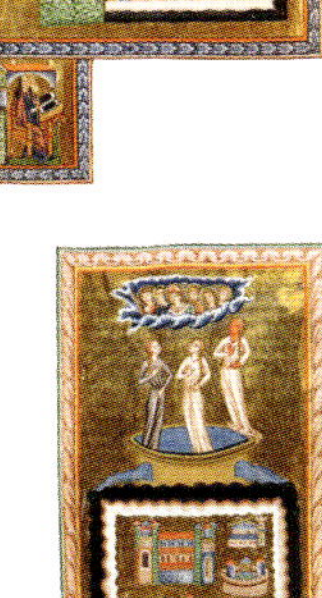

The *building* is the image of divine foreknowledge, showing man that everything has always dwelled in God and will return to him. In the building we hear the *symphony* of the blessed, a foretaste of the Heavenly Jerusalem that invites man to show his trust and praise God ceaselessly, completing the journey begun in *Scivias.* This journey is distilled in the words succinctly describing the city for the first time, underlining the differences with Hildegard's vision of the same building some years earlier, described in her first work. There is a transition from a sideways/oblique vision to a clear, frontal vision, from the *urbs*, city of men, to the *civitas Dei*, animated by the singing of saints, from the vision of architecture with earthly forms to mountains and images, from its foundations on the rock of the Fear of God to its location between earth and heaven at the bounds of the circumference of the body of the world.

Instrumentum

The city is described as an *instrumentum quadratum.* In Hildegard's work, *instrumentum* refers to the egg, the creation, and the wheel, the cosmological device revealing God's harmonious order in the firmament.

From *rectangular* to *square*

In *Scivias*, it was described as *rectangular* and placed *obliquely*, now it is *square* and seen *frontally*. At the start of the journey, humankind had to progress from virtue to virtue in order to become the living stones used in building the Church. Before, humans were not able to see directly, now they hear the voices of the saints praising God and prepare for the contemplation of eternal joy.

From *urbs* to *civitas*

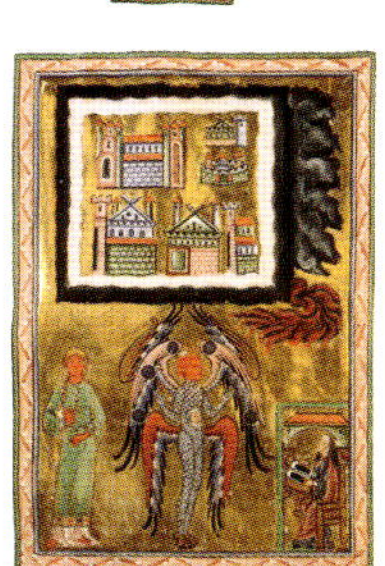

Having *left the urbs*, man enters the *civitas Dei*. This is the final stage before the arrival in the celestial city. The walls of the building are described as light and darkness. There are *faithful* and *unfaithful* men, facing each other at the eschatological moment of the end of time.

From architecture to the vision

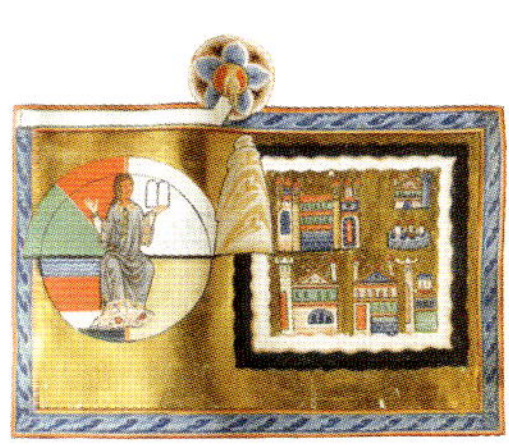

The *urbs* in *Scivias* was a city with towers, pillars, walls, and a multitude of men who proceed, accompanied by the virtues. The architectural elements lose their function in the *civitas* in the *LDO*, turning into *mountains* and *images*. Man has now arrived at the contemplation of the divine.

The three elements. *Mountain, fountain, wheel*

At the beginning of the journey, the man finds himself in front of the mountain of judgment as he was in *Scivias*. And he will again be welcomed by the mountain af-

ter crossing the entire city. Subsequently, the *fountain* of pure water with the three virtues will be the place of purification announced in the first vision of *Scivias*, the fountain of glory reached by those carrying out good works and becoming a living stone of the Church and of the celestial city. The fountain in the *LDO* and the Tower of the Church (III.9) in *Scivias* are both in the south, the place of the blessedness of the splendor of the sun. The journey ends in the wheel, alongside the mountain. After passing through the darkness and becoming infused with the beauty of knowledge, man may return to God's heart.

The three splendors. *Knowledge, Order, and Prophecy*

Three splendors illuminate the building. The first, divine foreknowledge, appears out of mirror on top of the mountain; the second, which comes from the door of the mountain, is the image of the order of pure divinity; while the third shines down from above, illuminating the way with the light of prophecy. The three splendors give the *knowledge of God*, *order*, and *prophecy* to the world. All three are situated up on high in the east. A powerful image of the action of the Trinity.

The eight *Imagines. The time of history. The three virtues. Justice, Wisdom, and Divine Love*

The *time before and after the flood*, *Divine Love*, *humility* and *peace*, the *justice of God*, *wisdom*, and *Divine Love* are eight divine images, *imagines Dei* of the city of God in which man's inner historic journey takes place. A journey supported by Divine Love, Humility, and Peace, strengthened by Wisdom, towards the justice and embrace of Divine Love/God. Eight images that now offer themselves to the man to guide him in completing this journey. They are eight like the *stars*/humans gathered in the *candid cloud*/Eve who are called upon to shine in the sky as blessed spirits, luminous stars, a representation of the transformative arc.

The five clouds. *Humankind, prophets, believers, saints. God*

Humankind floats in the building in the form of clouds and stars, taking on different features: humankind before the start of the journey, the prophets, the believers, and the saints. Finally, the cloud turns into the *wheel* of God embracing everything. *Lux vivens* emphasizes the brightness of the cloud/humankind and of the cloud/wheel/God. Eve and Wisdom, the *candid cloud*, resonate in *Scivias*. A wonderful synthesis signifying that humankind, made in the image and likeness of God, and emanating from him, is called upon to return to him thanks to the gift of prophecy that guides men towards the south where the Sun/Christ shines, and where the bride of Divine Love awaits.

From east to west. The path through the building

In the single vision of the second part, the building was placed on the circumference of the earth and viewed from a very distant perspective. Now the building appears close up and we can make out the details of the walls and of the figures dwelling in it as well as the movements taking place there. The third part of the work is entirely devoted to its description, going straight to the heart of the matter.

The miniatures depict the different sides of the building. Each one also contains an overview so as to show the position within the building of the elements described in the vision. In *Scivias*, on the other hand, the description opened with a general plan and the ten visions in the third part depicted each element alongside a detail of the building so as to help readers understand where they were located.

In the following pages, we will compare the general elements of the building, highlight the shared elements linking the various figures, describing each side in detail. Lastly, we will include photographs of a 3-D reconstruction. The diagram is a general plan showing the following:

• in the four sides:

east: the mountain with the gate and the mirror; the cloud/humankind, the wheel, the crystal tablet; the three splendors;
south: the fountain and the three virtues; the cloud/believers and the cloud/saints;
west: darkness;
north: God's Judgment and victory over darkness;
• in the four corners:
east/south: the time before and after the flood and the cloud/prophets;
south/west: void;
west/north: the blackest fire with sulfur;
north/east: Wisdom.

The path running around and through the building proceeds in the same direction as in *Scivias*, beginning in the east and moving counter-clockwise according to the movement of the firmament, before returning east. The Roman numerals in the diagram refer to the vision in which the elements described appear. Lastly, we should remember that north and south are inverted in the orientations of the two buildings in *Scivias* and in the *LDO*.

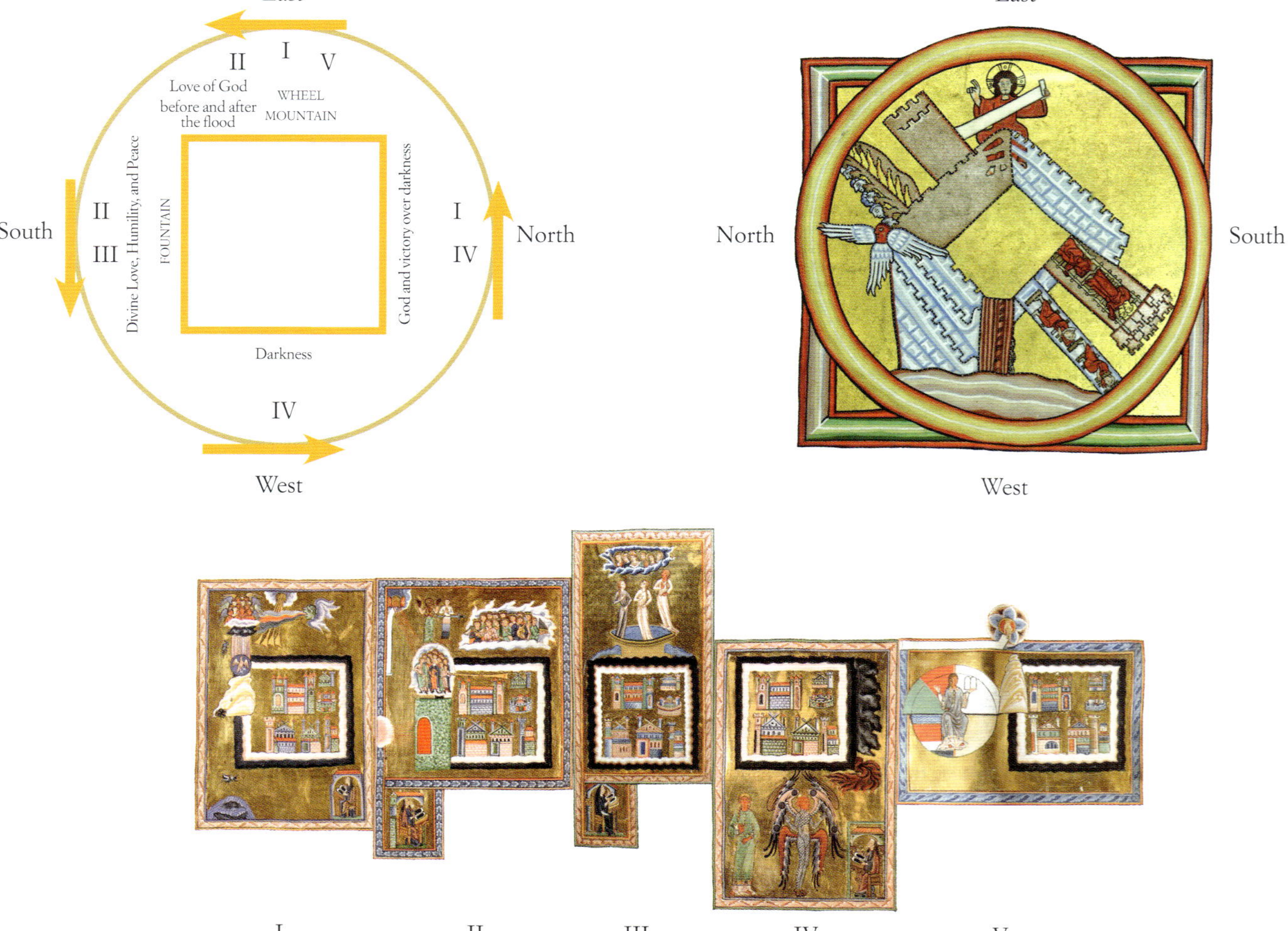

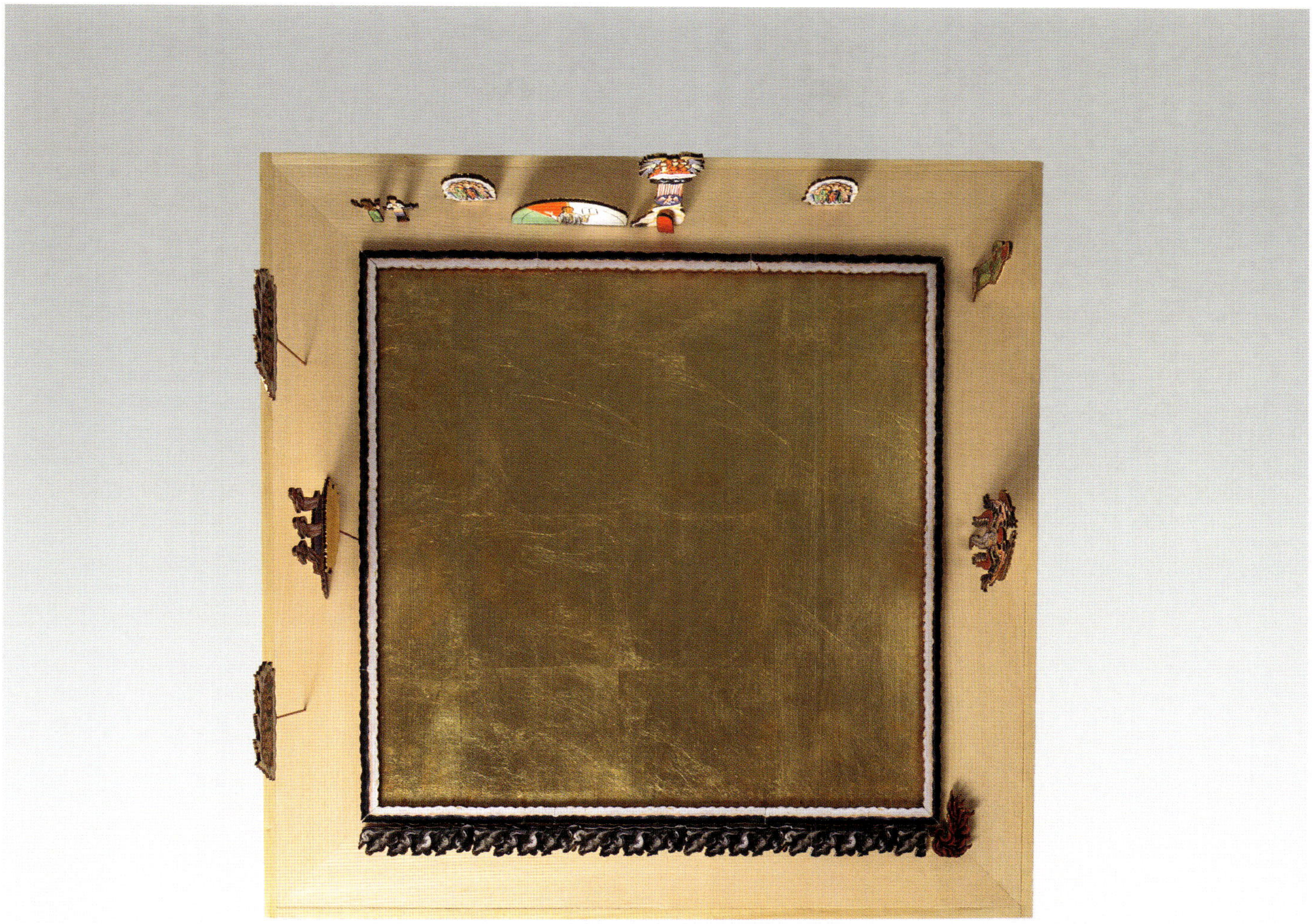

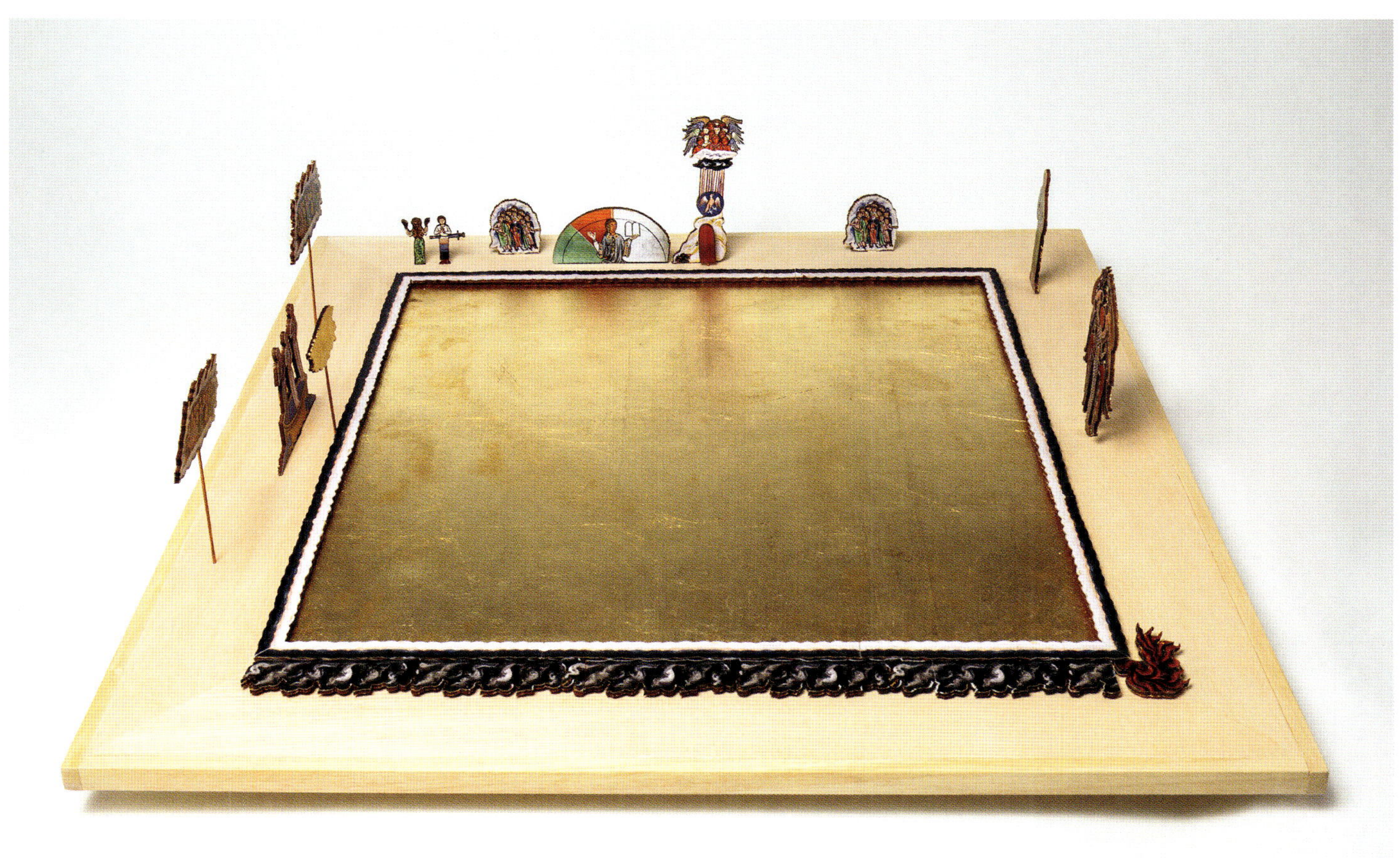

          Rhetoric

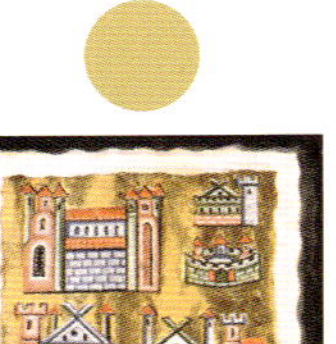

The mountain. *The justice of God*

I saw also amid its eastern stretch as if a mountain, great and tall, of hard white stone, its form like that from which fire is belched (III.1,1, 348).

Then, near the mountain that I spied as if amid the eastern stretch, as described above, I saw as if a wheel of wondrous size, in the likeness of a shining cloud and turned toward the east (III.5,1, 416).

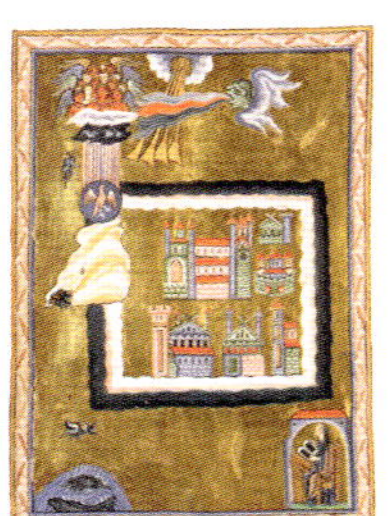

The *mountain*, which is situated in the middle of the eastern side, is described twice, in the first and in the final vision of the third part: the start and end of the journey. It represents the Justice of God, *heaven and earth were founded upon him and he upholds the firmament together with all creation, as a cornerstone secures the entire edifice* (III.1,2, 350).

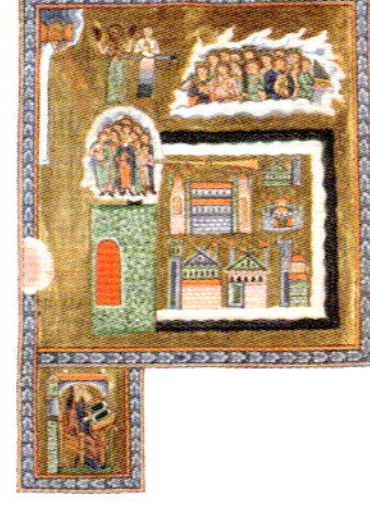

It is interesting to note that in the *LDO* the faithful on their journey are offered a vision from a frontal contemplative perspective in which they see God of Justice/*mountain* supporting the firmament and Christ as the door, while in *Scivias*, God is seated on top of the *mountain*/kingdom of God and Christ is on the topmost corner of the edifice with a perspective looking upwards from below, from the earth to God.

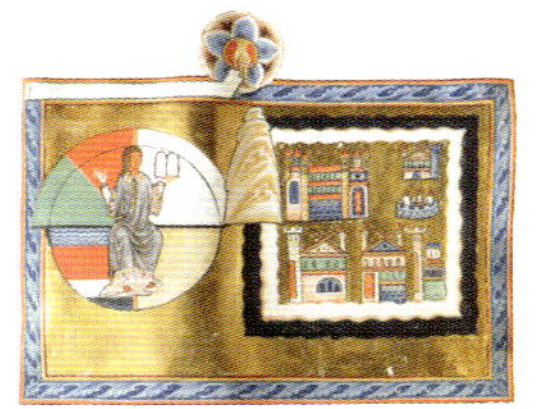

The mirror and the crystal tablet.
Divine Foreknowledge

At its summit gleamed as if a mirror (III.1,1, 348).

But there also appeared before the face of this image as if a tablet, transparent as crystal (III.5,1, 416).

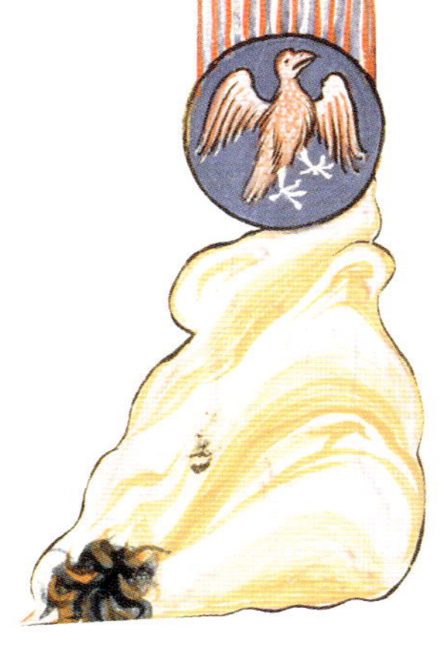

Divine Foreknowledge is present in the *mirror*, which is situated on top of the mountain in the first vision, and in the *perlucid (transparent) crystal tablet* held by the figure in the wheel placed alongside the mountain in the last vision. Justice and Divine Foreknowledge, described in terms of their close relationship, accompany the beginning and end of times.

The gate. *Christ the Cornerstone. Rising sun*

After this, I spied in the eastern corner—where the east begins—as if a marble stone, like the mountain great and tall, a monolith in which only a gate as of a great city appeared hewn out; and a certain bright splendor coming from the rising of the sun completely flooded this gate, but did not extend beyond (III.2,1, 357).

The second vision again describes the eastern side with the *mountain* and the *mirror*; specifically, *the eastern corner—where the east begins*, thereby determining a precise point in the eastern space, the cardinal point, and describing the gate providing access to the mountain.

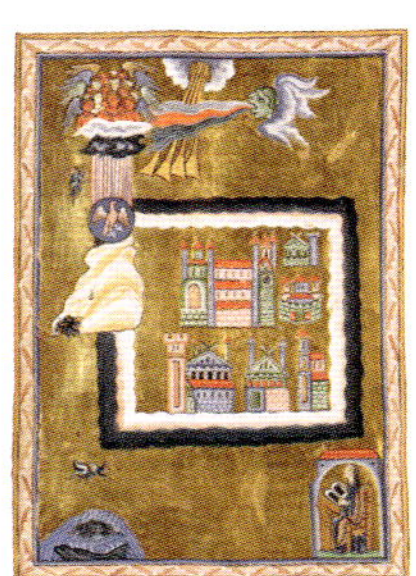

I

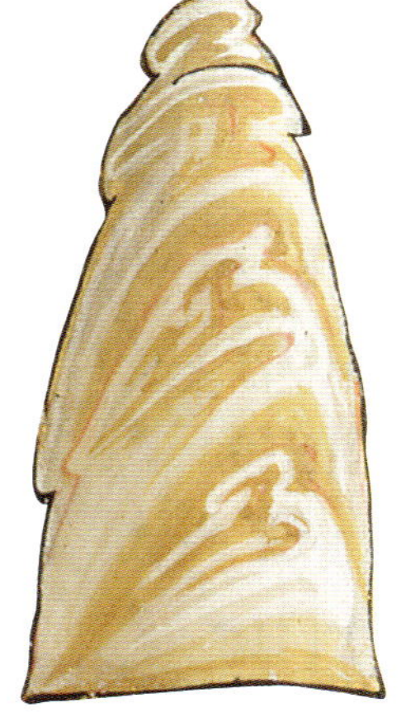

V

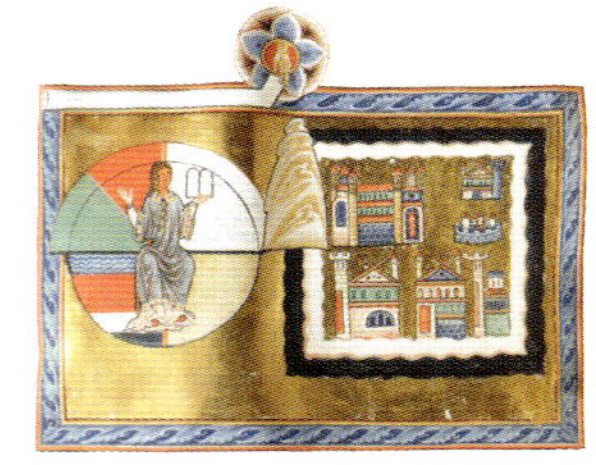

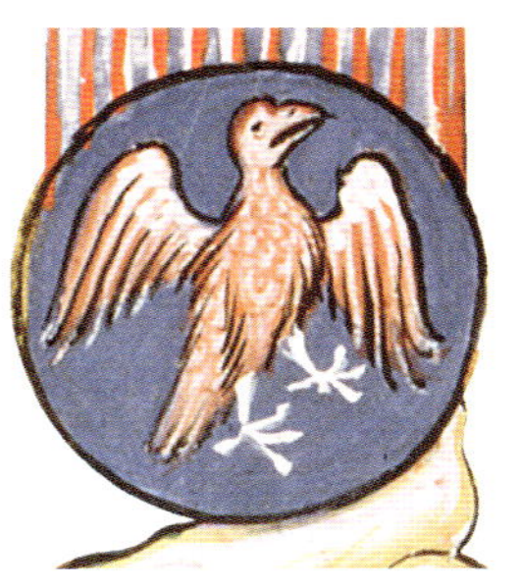

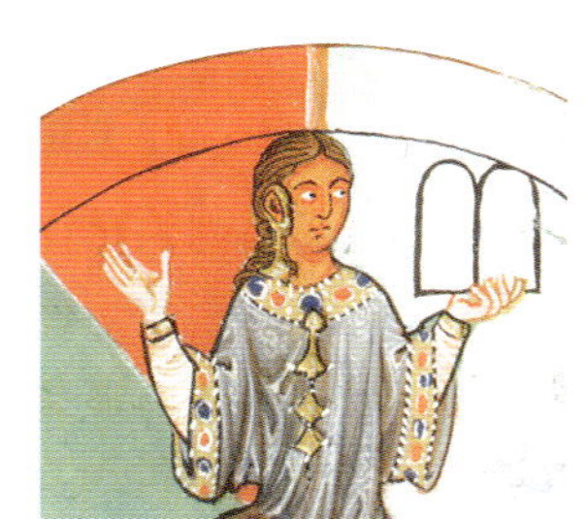

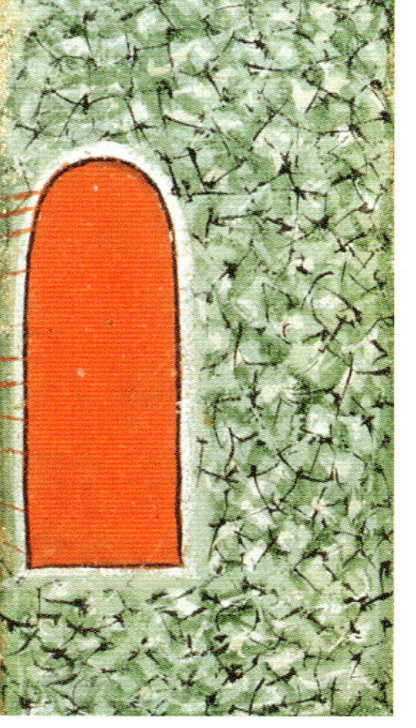

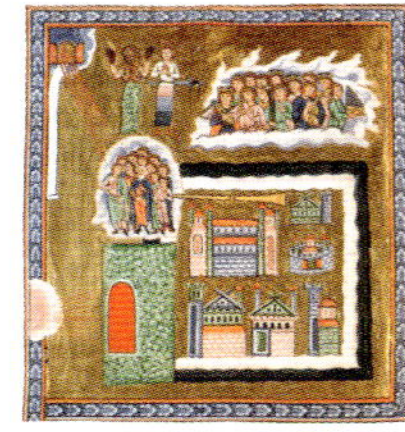

II

The gate recalls Christ, the cornerstone and the dawn of the new day. The lucid splendor emanating from the gate lights up man's path, inviting him to enter the city thanks to the divine order of all things. The *urbs* in *Scivias* was entered via a wall described as *a splendor shining like the light of day*, almost *splendor lucidus ut lux diei est*. These words evoke the words describing the light emanating from the gate in the *LDO*, *quam splendor quidam lucidus ab ortu solis*. The *lucid splendor* indicates God's action on earth through the aurora/Mary, dawn of a new day, of a new era, and of a new alliance born in Christ.

Candid cloud and angels. *Humankind and celestial spirits*

For in that radiance [emanated by the mirror on top of the mountain] appeared in the southern direction as if a cloud, shining white above but black beneath. Above it flashed as if a vast multitude of angels […] all of them were stirred by a wind as if it blew upon burning lamps (III.1,1, 348).

Humankind is gathered in the *candid cloud* as in *Scivias*, in which humankind in the form of eight stars was gathered in the *candid cloud*/Eve. The *LDO* describes angels flying above humankind, like *burning lamps* lighting up their *way*. Similarly, in *Scivias,* the path is lit by *living lamps*, celestial spirits to be emulated.

Wind and fire. *Judgment and hell*

And that wind raised up its voices in its wrath and cast by it fire into the aforementioned blackness of the cloud, […] but soon, it blew upon it and caused it to fall apart and dissipate like thick smoke (III.1,1, 348 and 350).

The wind, the Spirit of God, blows and judges with the burning fire of vengeance, thereby forming a fire in the dark part of the *candid cloud*, the unfaithful, whom the wind casts northwards into the mouth of hell. Similarly in *Scivias*, we see the *shining star*/Lucifer being quenched in the darkness. There, the fall of Lucifer took place before man began his journey through the edifice, and in *LDO* it is similarly described at the beginning of man's pilgrimage.

Gleaming clouds. *Glory of God*

And so the shining white part of the aforesaid cloud gleamed even brighter than before, and no one could resist at all the wind that had cast down the cloud's blackness with the three tones of its voices (III.1,1, 350).

Lastly, the candid cloud gleamed even more brightly than before, shining in glory. Splendid peace before judgment strikes.

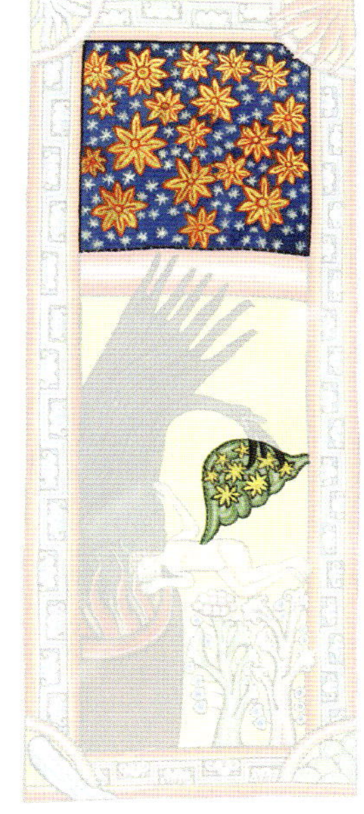

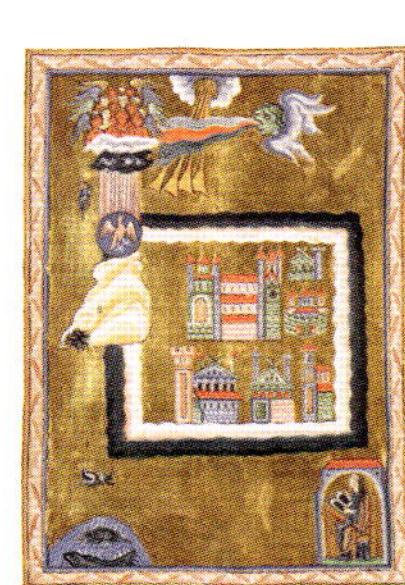

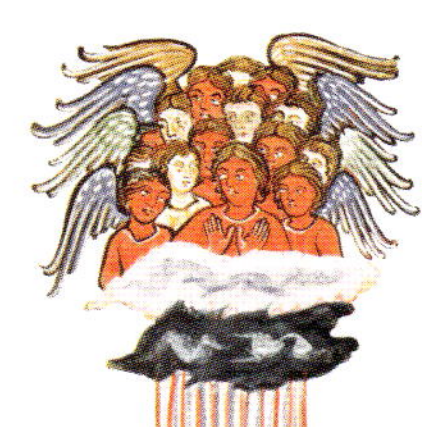

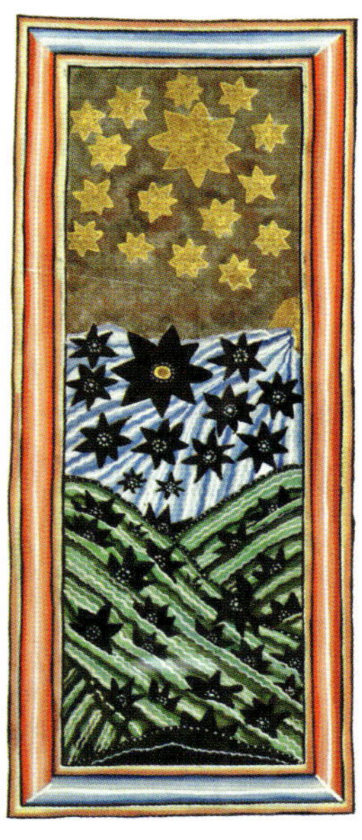

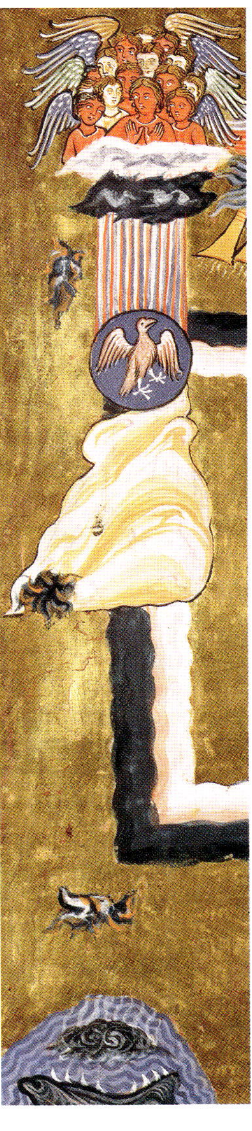

Men of all ages. *The prophets*

And from that stone almost to the southeastern point there appeared as if images of human beings—children and people young and old—like stars through a cloud, uttering a sound to the west like the sea when its waves are stirred up by the wind (III.2,1, 357).

The miniaturist gives the veiled stars, the prophets, a human form. The sound of their voices comes from the south, announcing the coming of the Sun of justice. In *Scivias*, the first prophet is Abraham while the *LDO* begins even earlier, with Adam. Divine Foreknowledge now allows man to understand that everything has existed in him forever, in a return to the contemplation of the original moment of creation in the vision of Divine Foreknowledge. And we read: *For prophecy exists in humankind like the soul in the body* (III.2,2, 360).

Two images. *Before and after the flood*

But next to that eastern edge there stood two other images side-by-side (III.2,2, 357).

The two images mark the time before the coming of Christ. The first, with the head and chest of a leopard, represents the time before the flood, when men behaved as beasts do; its gaze is turned northwards, towards the place of darkness. The second indicates the time after the flood and its gaze is turned towards the west, the place of the new journey, of the edification of man and of fraternity.

The wheel has been placed in the model with its central line corresponding to the base of the mountain, as described in the miniature. In fact, its lower part indicates human time and therefore does not belong to the divine dimension of the building, but remains below it.

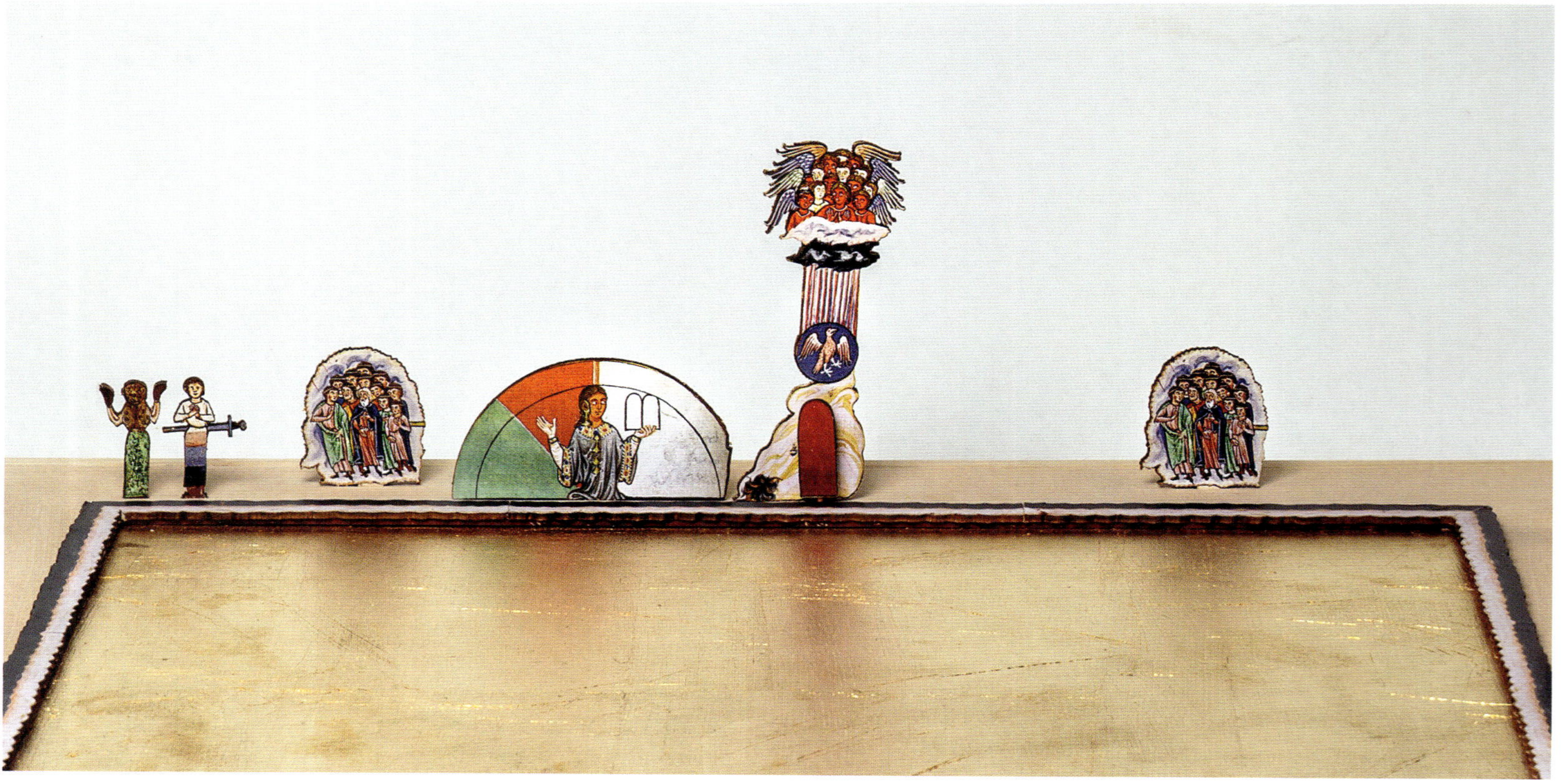

 Rhetoric

South (Visions II and III)

The three virtues. *Believers and saints*

But then I saw as if countless other human images floating in the air like a cloud along the entire southern stretch (III.2,1, 359).

And I also saw three images as if in the middle of the aforementioned southern stretch. […] And before these images appeared the blessed ranks of the saints like a cloud, upon whom they gazed lovingly (III.3,1, 386).

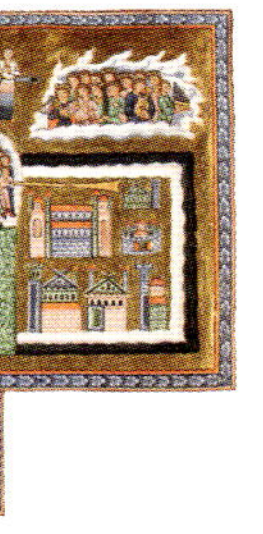

Occupying the entire southern side is the *fountain* of living water with the three images of Divine Love, Humility, and Peace, facing the ranks of saints in a cloud. And this is the side of manifest faith and of the living true construction of the Church. And we read: *For the glory of the highest heaven is achieved through Divine Love and Humility when the minds of the faithful fly like clouds from virtue unto virtue. Then Divine Love and Humility, looking upon them with loving consideration and guidance, enkindle them both vigorously and gently to desire the things of heaven* (III.3,3, 392).

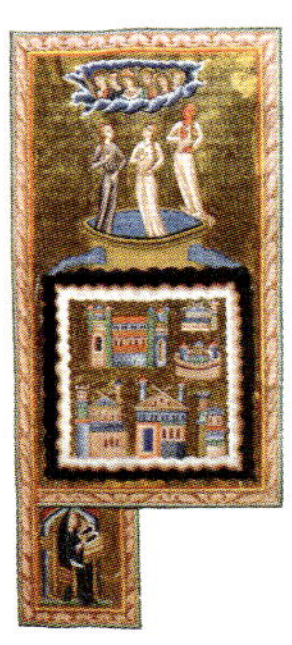

As they admire the fountain of living water, the believers facing the three virtues are led to desire heaven. Virtue by virtue, they are transformed from believers into saints. The description of the vision contains a narrative device underlining the process of transformation leading the faithful/*believers*, guided by the voice of the prophets, to become *saints*. In the second vision, the traveler is guided to observe the eastern side, the side of the prophets, and the voice of the *Lux vivens* invites him to turn his gaze south, where he will see the cloud of believers. After he has reached the south, the voice in the next vision describes only the cloud of saints. The reader therefore finds himself in the south observing only the cloud of believers who have now become saints thanks to the virtues.

There are repeated mentions of the position *to the right of God*, announcing the imminent judgment. In *Scivias*, the two virtues of Humility and Divine Love are on the right hand of Christ, revealed by the purple column in the bottom middle of the edifice, while Peace is situated to the left of the pillar because it also touches those who have not witnessed the revelation. This leads us back to the words in the *LDO*: the fact that *the third [image] stands outside the fountain upon its stone rim. This is because Peace, who dwells in heaven, also defends earthly undertakings that are outside the heavenly realm. For the Son of God, the true cornerstone, brought her forth when he enlightened the whole world with his birth, and when the angels recognized him as God and Man in their song of prai*se (III.3,3, 391).

And this is made possible because *Divine Love adorns the works of God, as a ring is adorned with a precious gem; while Humility has revealed herself openly in the humanity of God's Son, who arose from the undefiled Star of the Sea. […] Thus the Church, adorned and endowed with the virtues described above, was led into the King's bedchamber, as it is written: "The queen stood at your right hand, in clothes of gold surrounded by variety." […]*

For humankind is the work of God's right hand. By him they are clothed and called to the royal wedding that Humility prepared […] so that those who had fallen might rise again through repentance (III.3,3 and 4, 392–393).

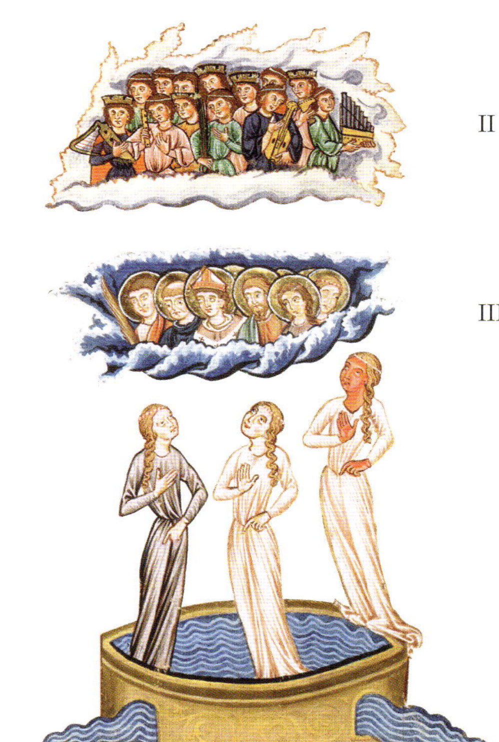

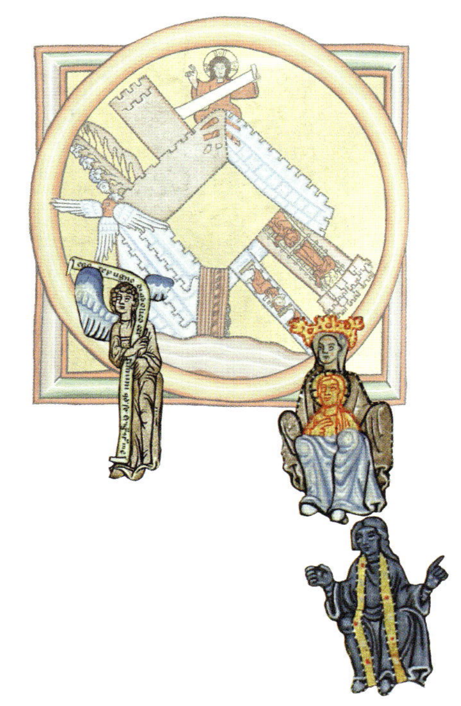

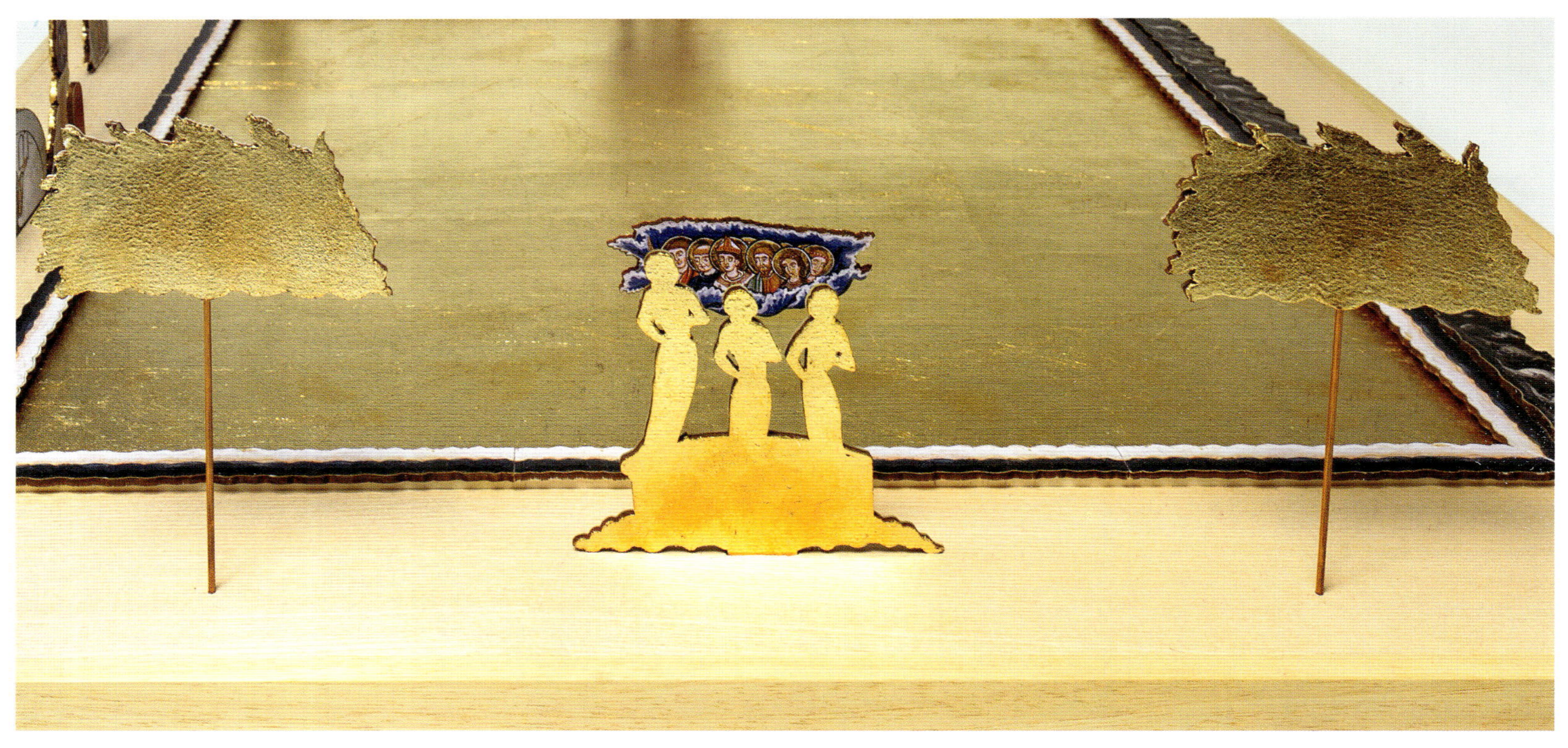

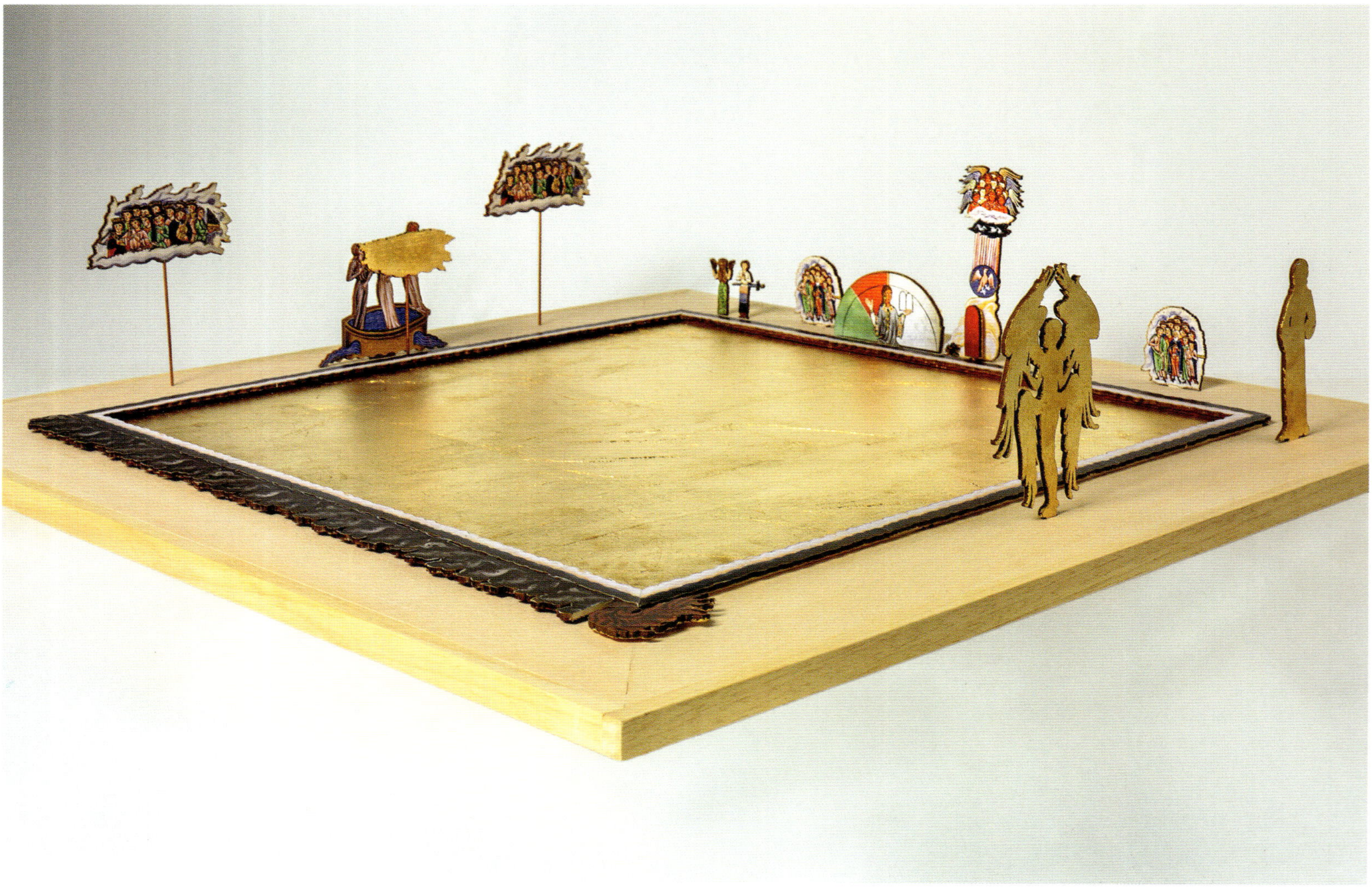

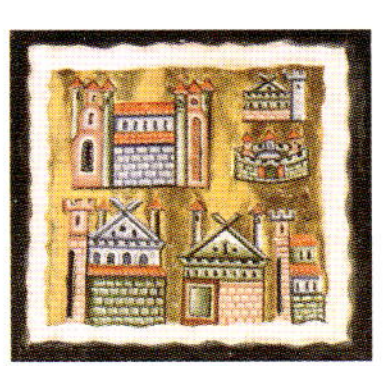

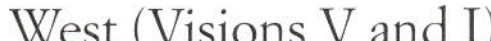

West (Visions V and I)

Darkness

But all along the western stretch, I spied as if the foulest smoking darkness, while near its north-facing corner, the blackest fire roiled forth with sulfur and the densest dark, stretching almost all the way to the middle of the northern part before curving back on itself (III.4,1, 396).

So as the blackness fell to ruin, [the wind's wrath] drove it back, away from the south and over the mountain to the north, into an endless chasm, so that it could never again raise itself up, except sometimes to cast a certain mist upon the earth (III.4,1, 350).

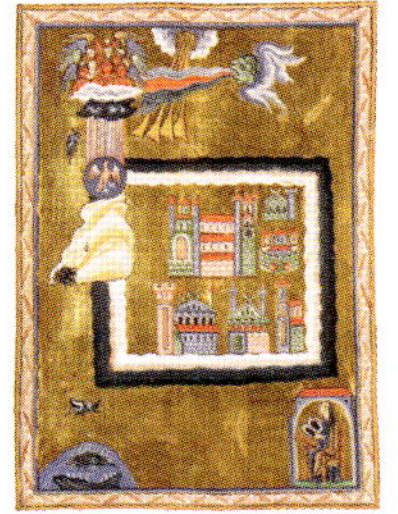

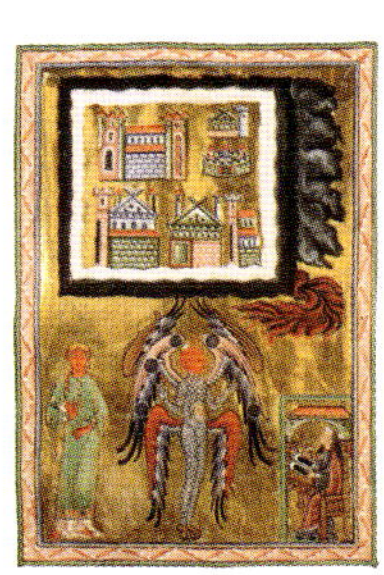

After presenting the winged image of the power of the judgment of God and of Wisdom, located in the northern stretch, vision four describes darkness, which occupies the entire western stretch (see next page). In the same way that narrative anticipation was used earlier as a device to introduce the description of believers transforming into saints, here a postponement makes it possible to delay the vision of evil and darkness until the author has shown that the power of God defeated them through judgment and wisdom.

Evil has been crushed and cast into the corner containing the mouth of hell. This is the corner joining the western and northern sides and where the blackest fire is roiling forth with sulfur and darkness. It is the same place described as containing the mouth of hell in the first vision of the building.

The darkness is not described in itself but as a warning for man: *because there are the places of punishment that hold various kinds of tortures. For when a person tends westward along the downslope of sin, he inflicts upon himself the blindness of infidelity through the iniquity that emits an evil twilight mist. And so, falling into the pains of that darkness, he casts himself into confusion because he ignores his Creator* (III.4,13, 412).

The term "endless" is used repeatedly in this part in order to emphasize the concept of being lost in eternity with no return.

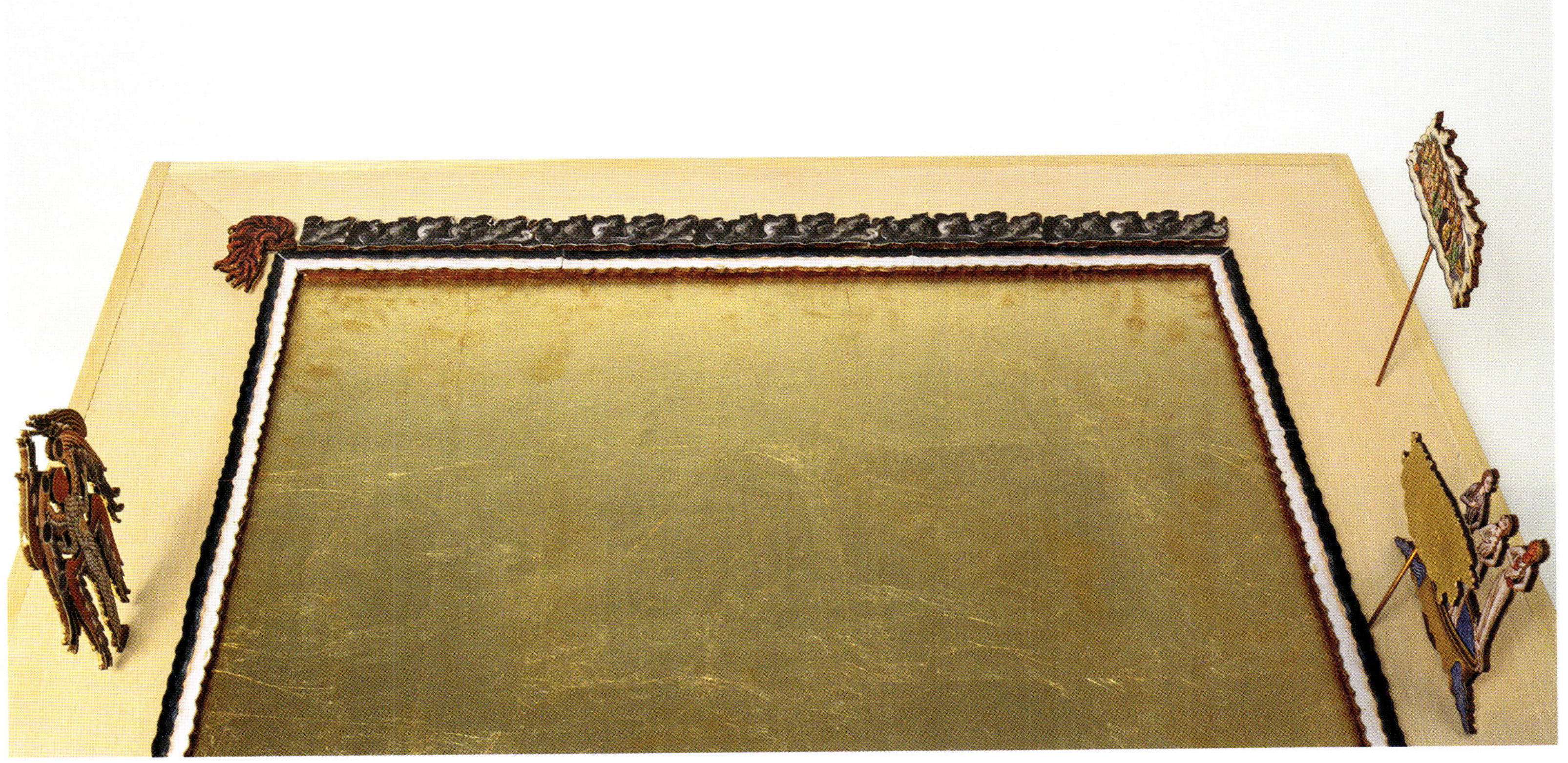

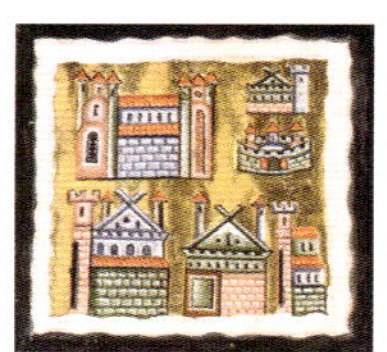

Wisdom and Victory over darkness

Then, near the northeastern facing corner, I saw an image whose face and feet beamed with such brilliance that it turned back my gaze. […]

But as if in the middle of that northern stretch, I saw another image, standing up straight, wondrous in form. At its top, where its head ought to have been, there shone such brilliant radiance that it beat back my gaze (III.4,1, 394).

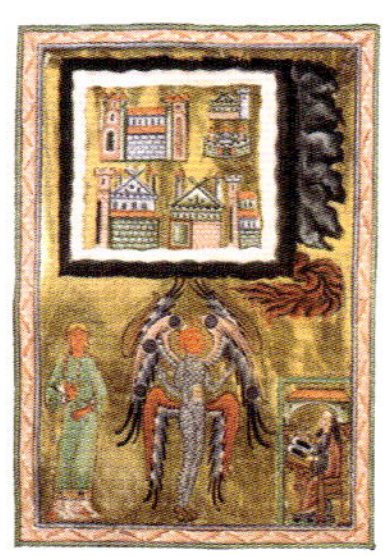

In the northern side are the two images representing *Wisdom* and *God against the might and unjust reckoning of the ancient serpent* (III.4,3, 397). Wisdom is described as having made the firmament using *stars* as *nails*, the *moon* as the *countless sum of the human race*, and the *sun* to signify *divinity*.

Indeed, God founded the firmament with Wisdom and compiled it with the forces of the stars as with nails, as one supports one's house with nails so that it does not fall apart (III.4,14, 413).

So too creation was as Wisdom's vesture, for she caresses her handiwork as one feels one's clothing. […]

God, too, cannot be seen; rather, he is known through creation, as too the human body cannot be seen on account of clothing (III.4,14, 413).

The vision closes with these words: *And so humankind—the enclosure of his wonders—knows him with the eye of faith and embraces him with the kiss of knowledge—him whom they cannot see with fleshly eyes, and according to whom they act. The angel too offers humankind's chosen works to God with a pleasant fragrance, wafting it with goodwill to heaven; and vile works that attend to a path other than God, the angel presents to him for his just judgment* (III.4,14, 415).

In the eastern-facing corner, creation appears in the guise of Wisdom and man is invited to look with the eyes of faith and embrace the knowledge guiding him along the path. Similarly in *Scivias,* Wisdom illuminated the men who undertook to build the Church so that they might turn to the east to contemplate the Son of God and his revelation.

The second winged image, *God against the might and unjust reckoning of the ancient serpent* (III.4,3, 397), recalls the wrath of God in *Scivias*. Both figures stand facing the north, the place of shadows and darkness.

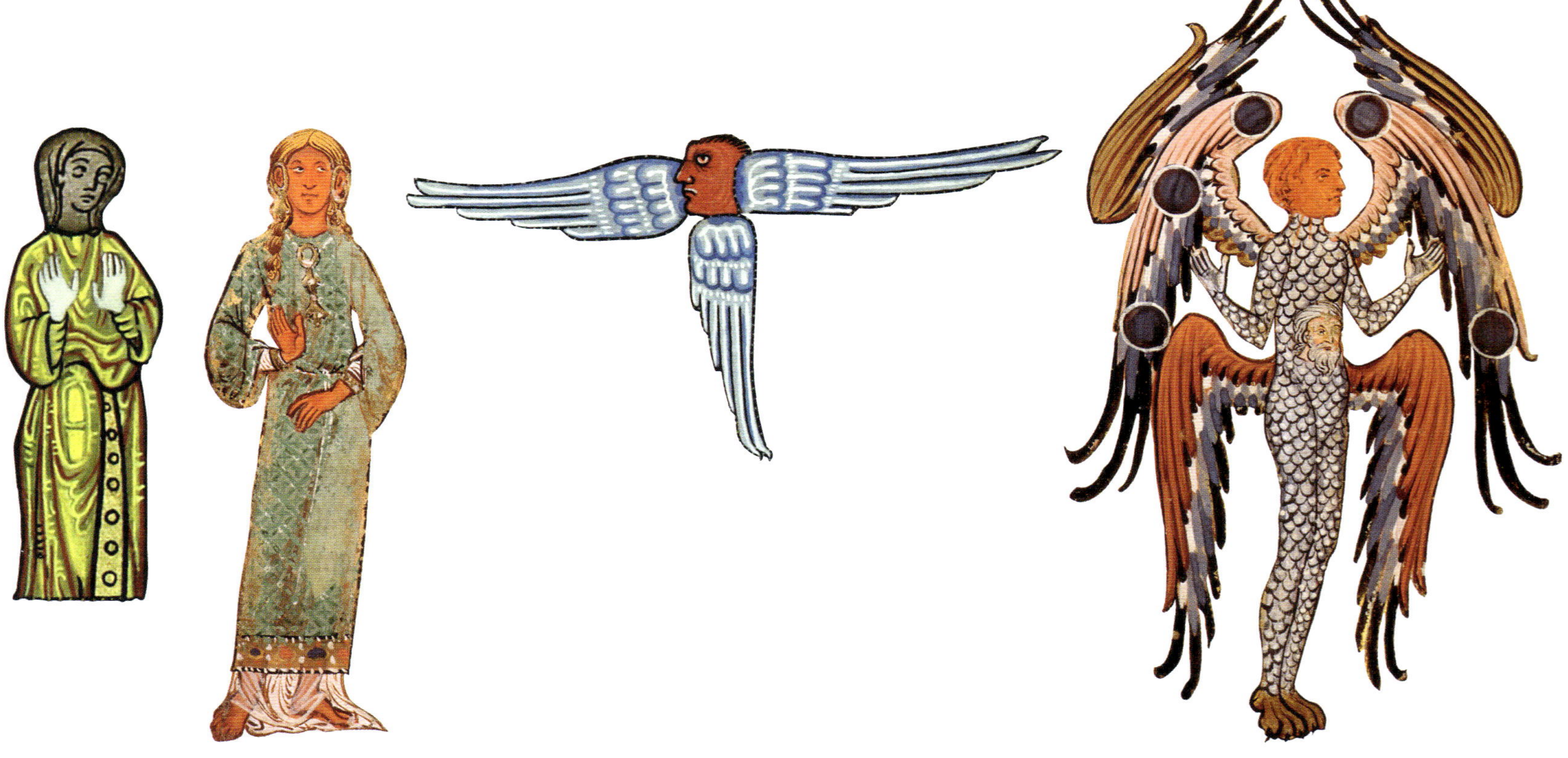

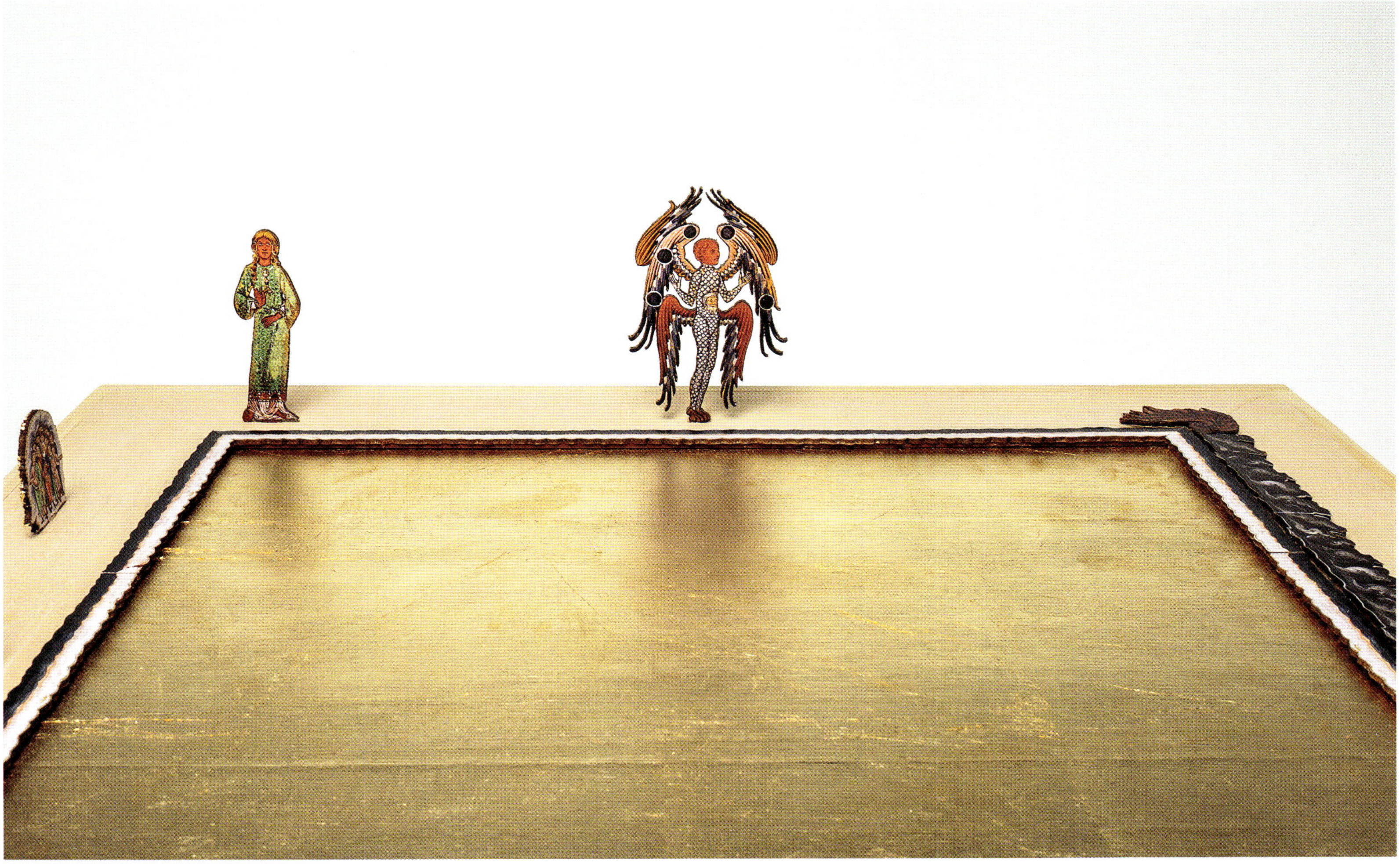

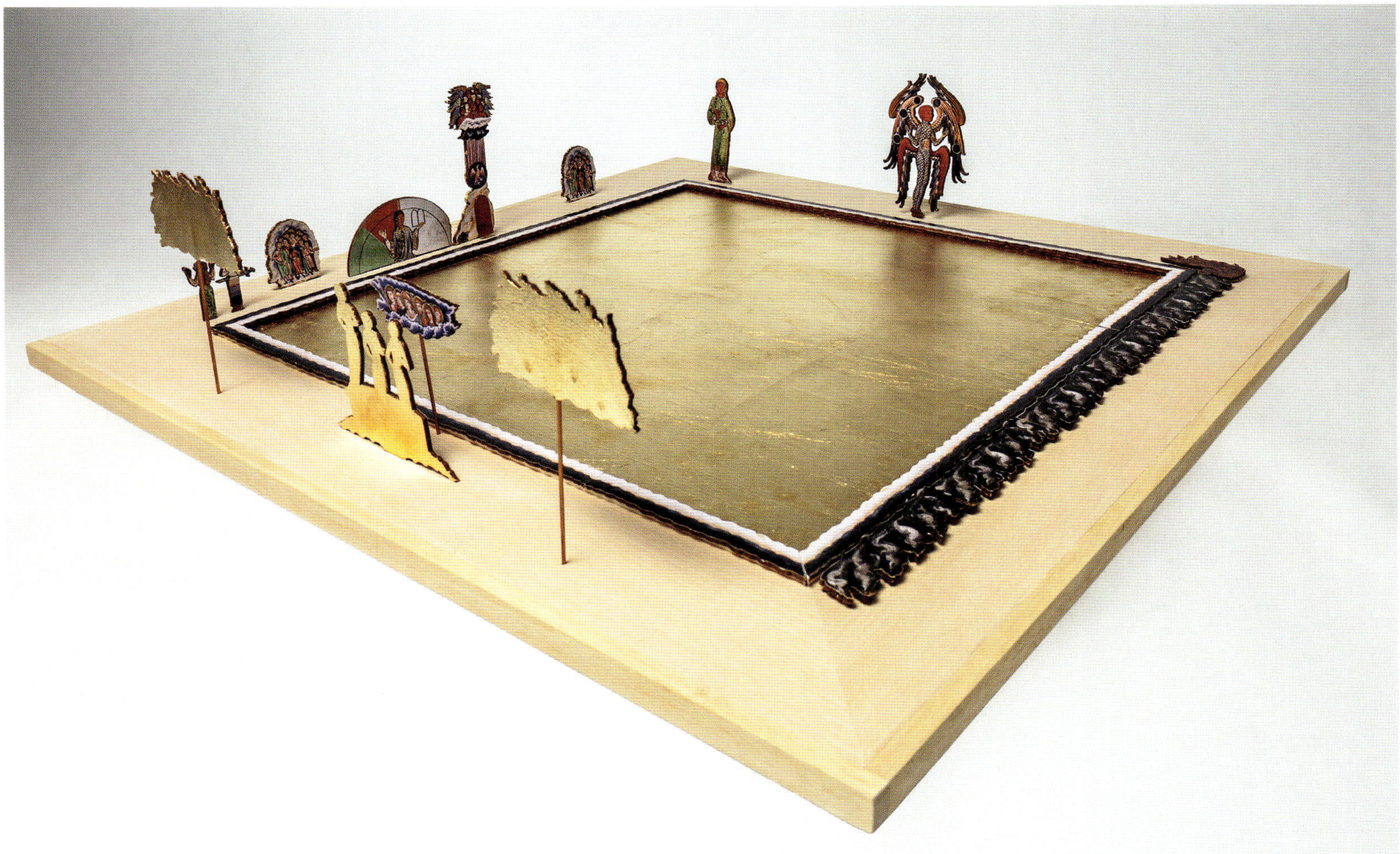

Rhetoric

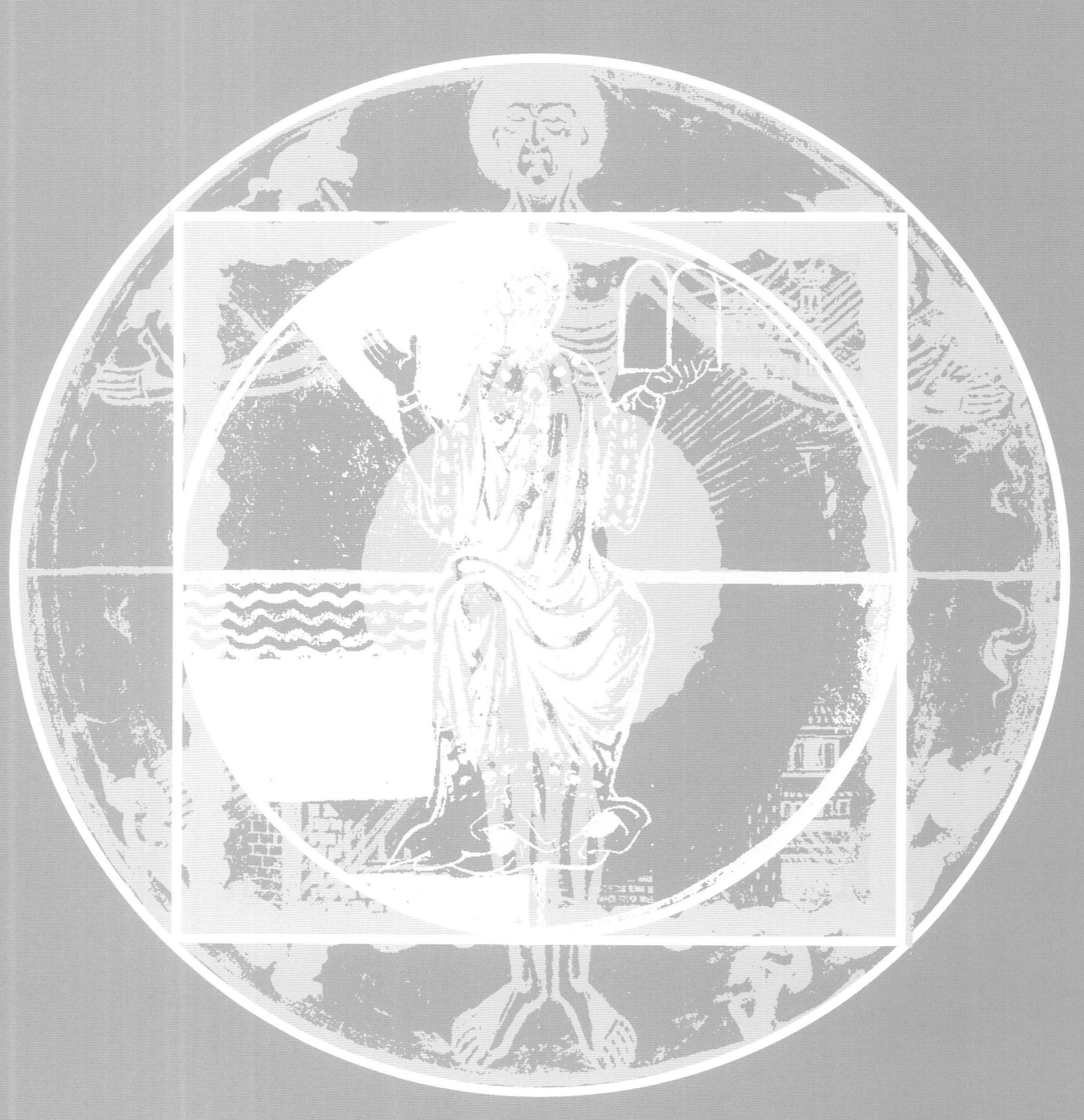

CHAPTER V

Dialectic

In the Heart of God

Dialectic, the last of the arts of the *Trivium*, gathers the *symbol-figures*, their form and their connections into one vast vision, revealing the heart of the message to us. In fact, the constructive architecture of the forms, proportions, and colors, described with great precision in the text of the visions, conceals a series of refined references and connections which, when observed, unfurl the golden threads of the divine order in which everything is harmoniously connected and where everything issues from the heart of God. After expanding outwards from God, taking the most minute and internal forms, the creation returns to Him. Everything is in God before all time and is defined with beautiful precision in the firmament, and in man's body and soul. The minute distinction of these singularities is woven into a golden web that proves them to be part of a single great act of creation. These pages, which seemingly describe the mere mechanics of the architecture of the miniatures, actually reveal the poetic essence of the creative act embraced by the wings of God/Divine Love.

The rich miniatures of the *Liber Divinorum Operum* (*LDO*) are distinguished by their exquisite execution and superb artistic quality. Closely adhering to the text, they convey the complexity of this vision through creative solutions that respect the description without ever compromising on beauty. They offer a sapiential message resembling the robe of silk and light worn by Wisdom. In the pages devoted to the *constructive design of the miniatures*, we can glimpse the unitary project used by the miniaturist to make visible the symbolic architecture through the forms, proportions, relations, and orientations described in the text.

The reconstruction of the images using the colors and forms of *Scivias* together with the use of three-dimensional drawings allows us to explore the work in great depth. The pages devoted to the *constructive syllogism* bring together the indications of measurements and proportions present throughout the work, allowing us to create a unitary design in a single image. The poetry of Divine Love (*Caritas*), who holds the earth and man in his heart and places the spark of divine love in man's heart.

The Constructive Design of the Miniatures

The circle inscribed in the square
From God/Divine Love to Divine Love instilled in man

Let us begin our exploration of the miniatures and their construction by looking at an element that emerged at the end of our studies. The overall work ends with the journey through the building and with the final image of Divine Love by the mountain/God. The miniaturist has drawn the circle of Divine Love and the square of the building, symbolically linking them. The circle of Divine Love is inscribed in the square of the building, divine foreknowledge.

In turn, the circle and square are both inscribed in the circle of thin air in the wheel in which the figure of man is placed. We have thus reached the final element of the long series, which has taken us from the Divine Love in the first miniature to the wheel; in the wheel is man and in man is the circle of Divine Love, thereby revealing the passage from God/Divine Love to the Divine Love of God instilled in man's heart.

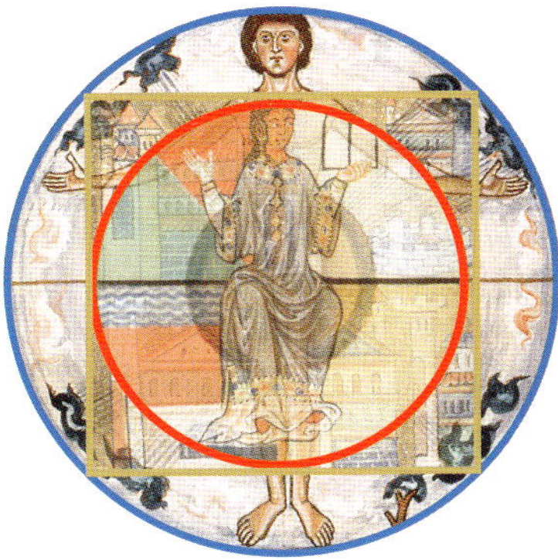

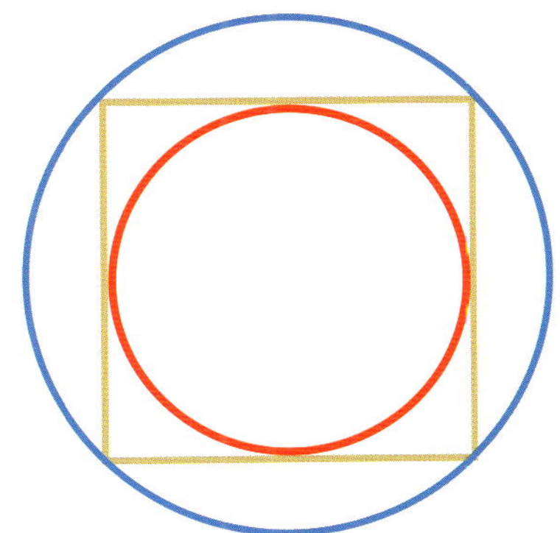

The *form of man*/Divine Love and man:
the division into five parts

The *form of man*/Divine Love has been drawn with
the proportions indicated in the fourth vision, which
describes the proportions of man with respect to the
firmament, divided into five parts: *from the head to the
throat, from the throat to the navel, from the navel to
the place of discharge, from the place of discharge to the
knees, from the knees to the calves.*

The wings
*The strength of Divine Love who supports
creation and man*

The *form of man/Divine Love* is the constructive reference for the entire iconographic cycle. The text provides us with two pieces of information: the lower wings
descend to the knees of the *winged* figure (yellow line);
when the winged figure embraces the wheel that has appeared upon its breast, these same wings extend to the
midpoint of its circumference. This allows us to identify
the center of the circumference. The radius of the wheel
(red line) is the same length as the distance between
the knees and throat of the figure, the outer limit of the
circumference itself.

The *form of man/Divine Love* and the wheel
Entering into the mystery

The wheel appears upon the breast of the figure of
man/Divine Love. The miniaturist redesigns the faces
and feet of the winged figure in order to indicate the
exact location of the wheel. The vision takes us further
into the interior of the wheel, resulting in a zoom effect
achieved by reducing the outer frame while simultane-
ously enlarging the wheel by almost a centimeter in the
final two visions of the first part.

The body of the world/earth/five senses/man
surrounded by the waters
Purification

The miniaturist uses the constructive elements of the
winged figure and wheel in order to build the single
vision in the second part. The wheel and the body of
the world are crossed by the same median axis (yellow).
The square earth in the center has the same dimensions
as the globe inside the wheel (brown). The circumference of the body of the world is the same as that of the
circle of watery air of the wheel, thereby representing
the description of the body of the world surrounded by
waters (blue). The diameter of the body of the world is
smaller than the wheel, giving the impression to have
entered inside it.

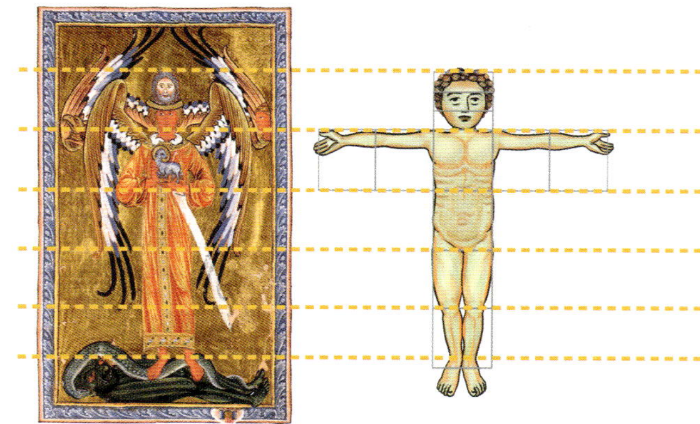

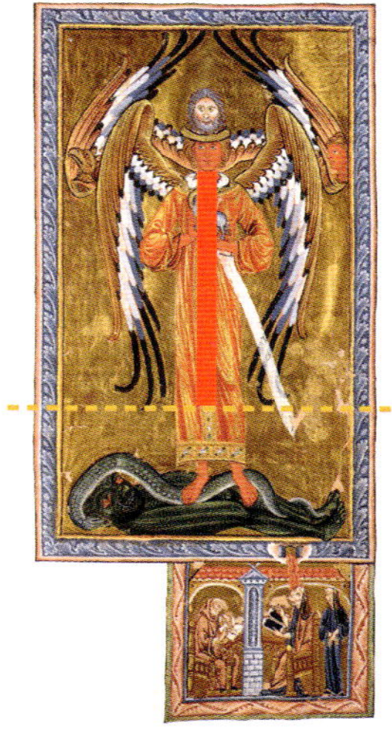
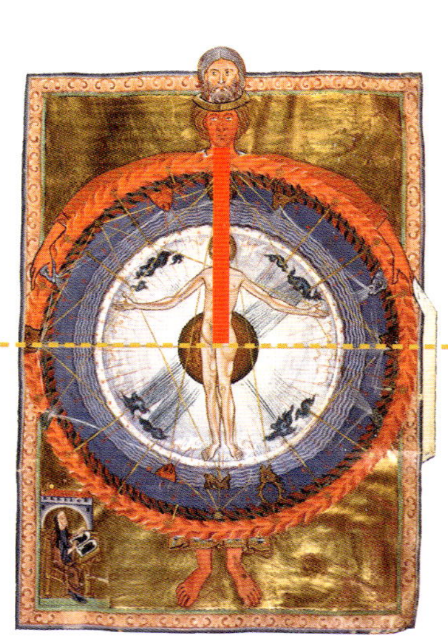

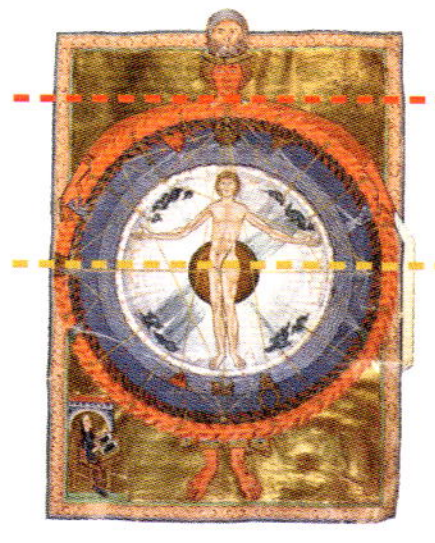
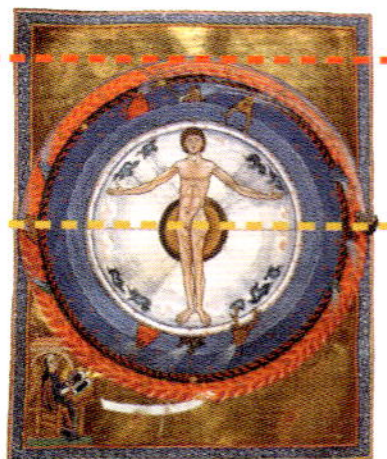
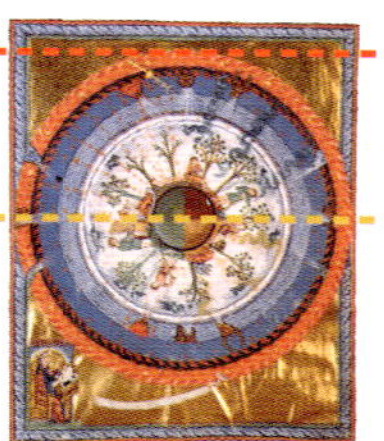

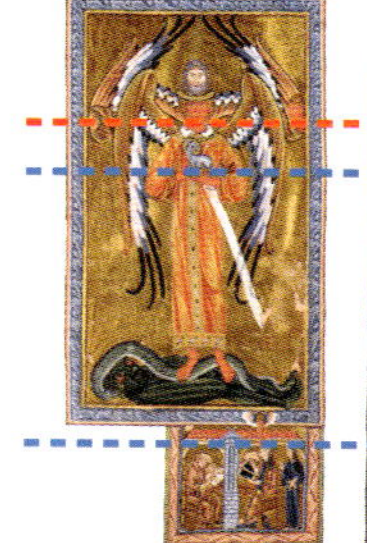
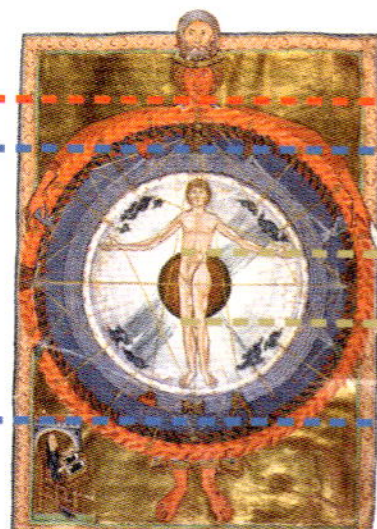
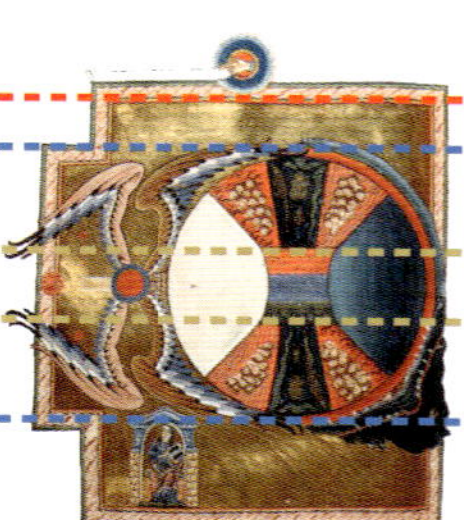

Dialectic

The scroll and the red and sapphire circle
The rising sun and the midday sun

The miniaturist uses two devices to show both the close connection between the two images of the winged figure and of the second vision as well as to visualize them in two positions: one with the wings stretching towards the right of the image and the other with wings raised. The first device causes the frame of the single vision in the second part to jut out towards its right; the presence of this protrusion means that the size of the frame in this point is identical to the frame of Divine Love. As a result, by turning the winged figure towards the right of the image, one fits perfectly into the other, as shown by the superimposed images.

The second device used by the miniaturist involves repeating the red globe surrounded by sapphire (shown by the yellow circle) outside the frame at the top, in the same form as the one present inside the frame. The repetition of the *red/sapphire globe* invites us to rotate the figure by ninety degrees. By causing the globes to coincide virtually, the image will end up with the wings raised in the same position as the figure of Divine Love.

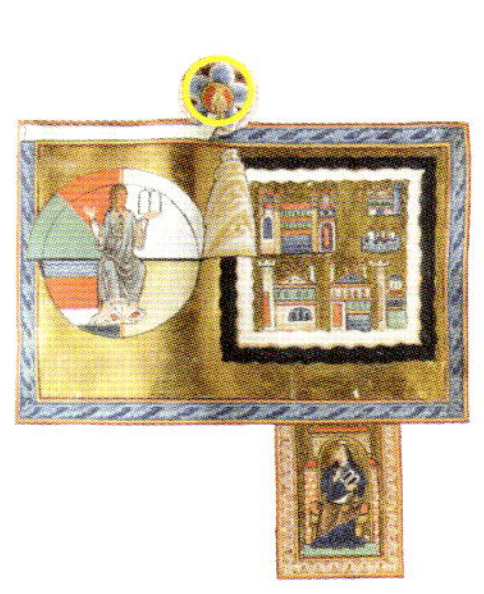 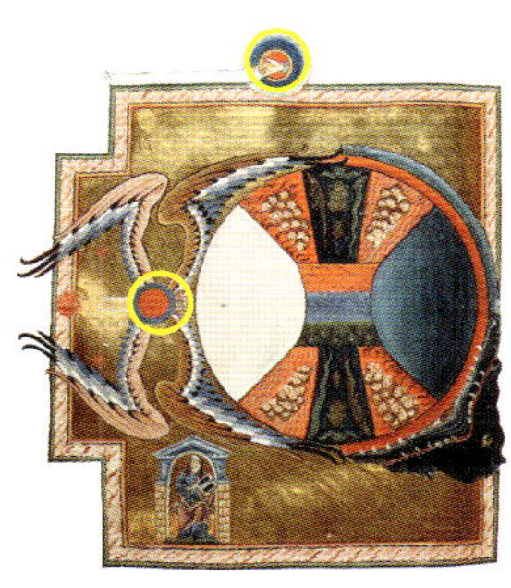 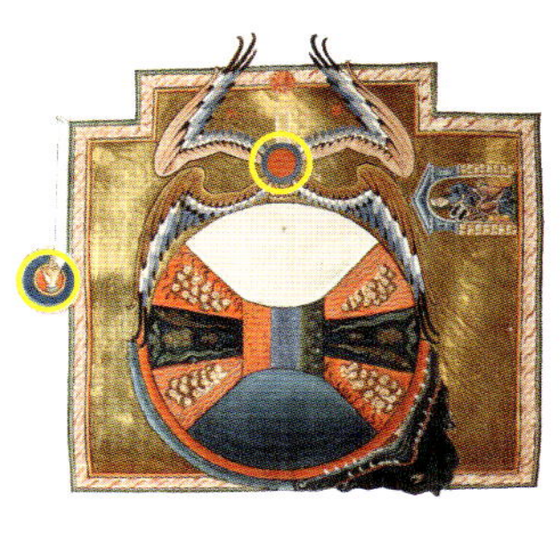 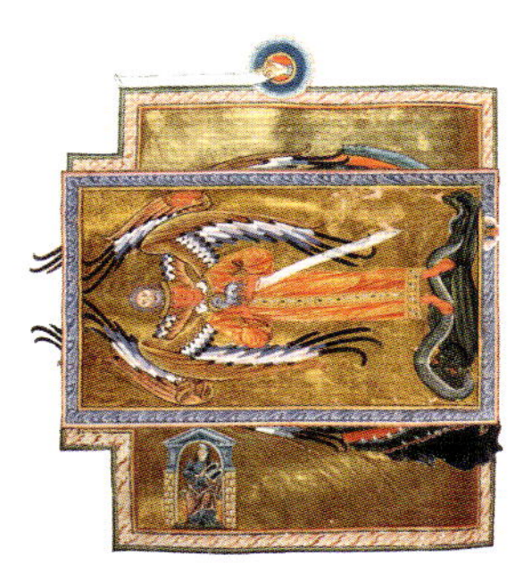 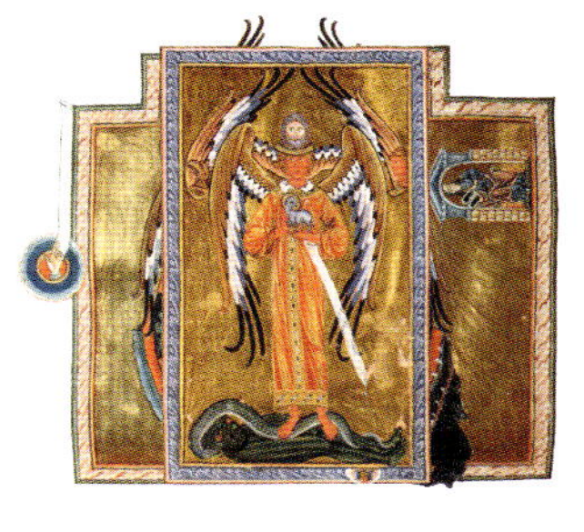

The dark/line of the wheel and the median line
God's will

The median axis (in yellow) is a constructive reference joining the winged figure and the wheel, and also a reference for the construction of the building. The miniaturist places the various elements of the vision on/along this line, showing their position with respect to the cardinal points. Once we have explored the entire work, we can note that the median line is not merely a technical constructive reference but the reflection of a profound symbolic meaning. It passes by the knees of the winged figure, where it symbolizes the strength of Divine Love, which supports creation and man; crosses the wheel/firmament from east to west; and divides the wheel where Divine Love is seated in the final vision, manifesting God's will. The power and will of God's Love are thus the mainstay of the creation and path of man.

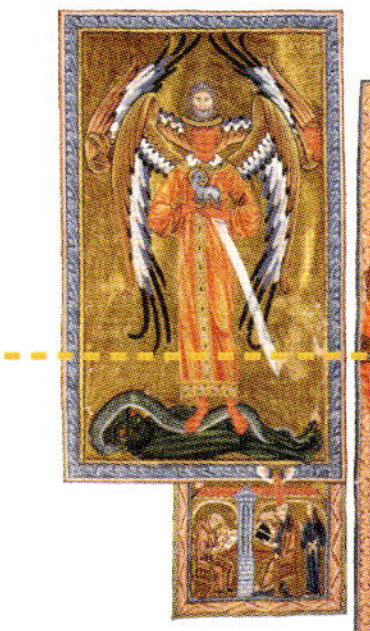 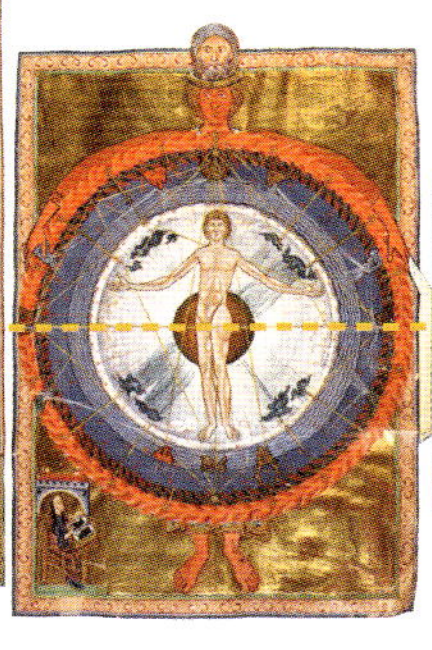 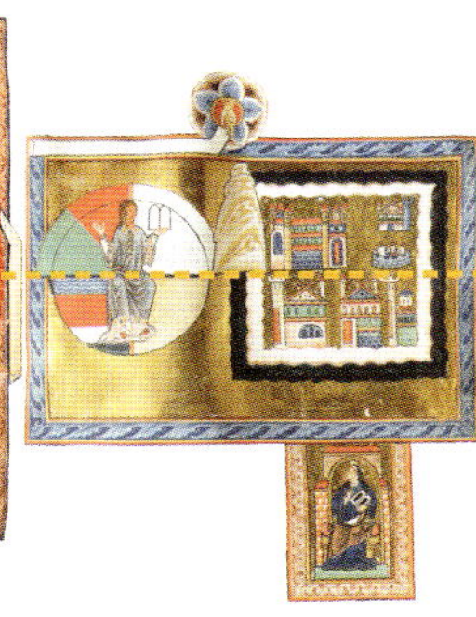 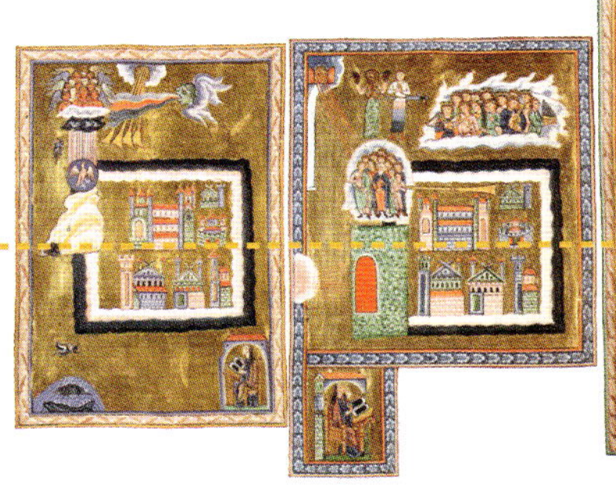 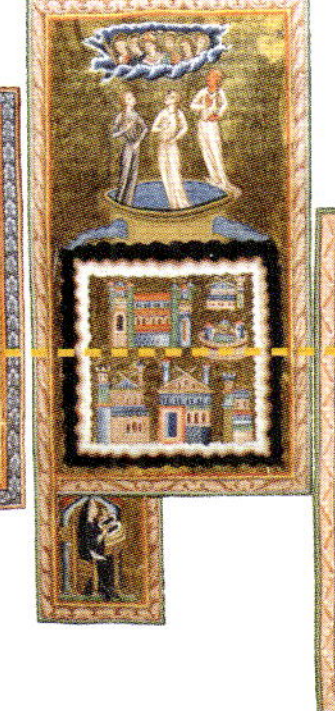 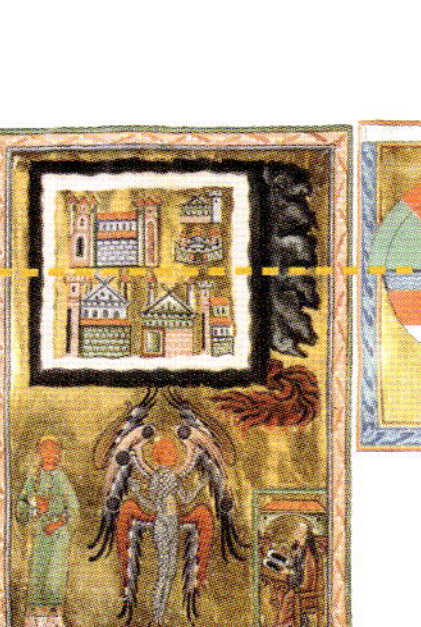 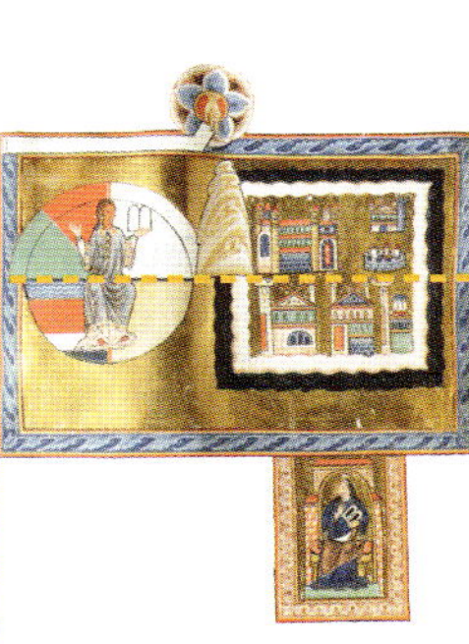

Civitas Dei

The five visions in the third part have the south at the top, with the same orientation as the winged figure of Divine Love. They are constructed around the median axis (yellow line) and the city appears in each one. By placing the four buildings in the first four miniatures (III.1–4) alongside each other, we obtain a single city surrounded by all the figures, to which we can add the fifth vision, superimposing the mountain located next to the wheel and Divine Love with the mountain in the first vision, the alpha and omega of the journey. This overview provides a very clear illustration of a general map of the building, suggesting that this was the preliminary reference drawing used by the miniaturist for the construction of the image of the vision of the building.

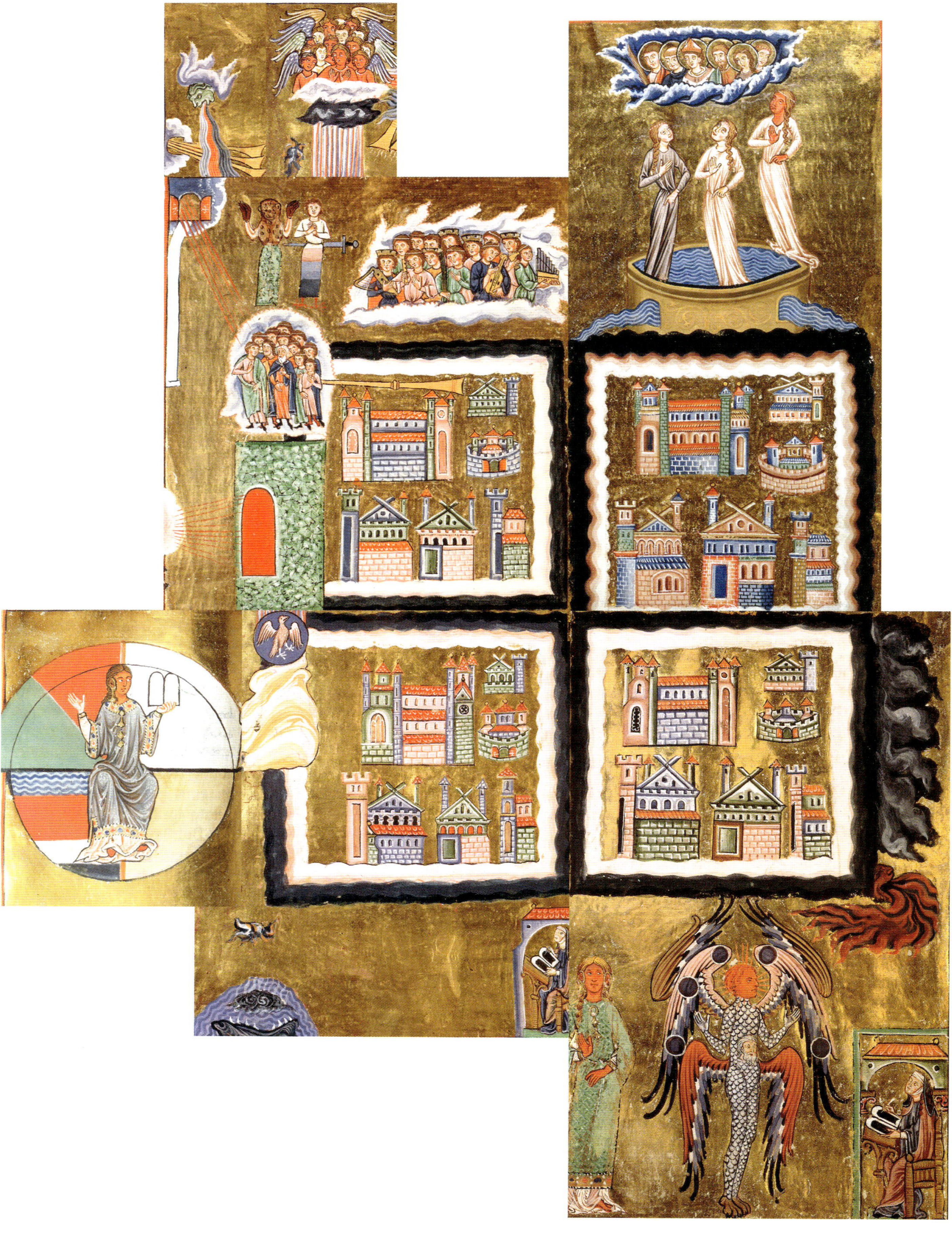

Dialectic

The Constructive Syllogism

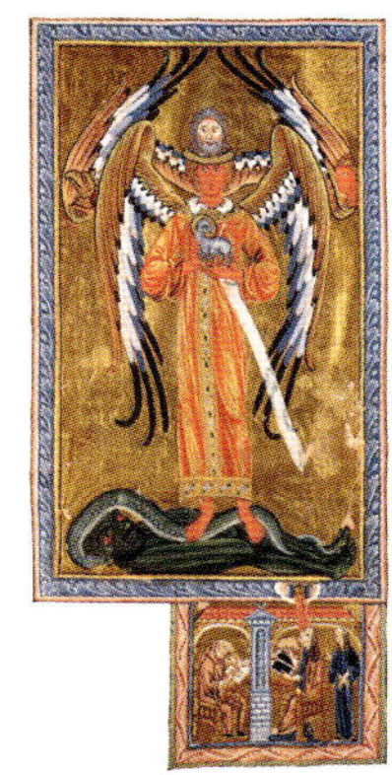

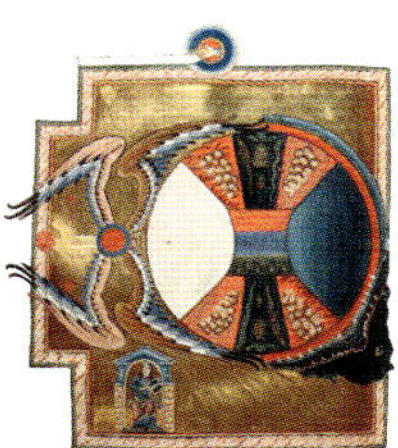

After we have explored the entire work, redesigned every passage, absorbed the harmonious equilibrium of the creation operated by Wisdom and known through divine foreknowledge, in every form and measurement, a unitary scenario unfolds before our gaze. The forms delineate God's love for Man who is created in his image and likeness, and reveal man's path towards salvation. This vision is only accessible once you have completed the entire journey. The measurements and proportions—the relationships between the parts—may seem to be discrete elements but are actually precise signs indicating the path to be followed. In fact, we must embark upon a contemplative reading in order to become aware that we are facing a unitary vision and recognize each piece of information encountered in the text as a clear indication allowing this vision to be reconstructed. The visions demand to be read by going beyond their chronological sequence, connecting each element with other elements belonging to distant visions.

Man made in God's image and likeness

Man is made according to the image and likeness of God and is kept in his heart. This is the extreme synthesis aspired to by the detailed descriptions of the ten visions. Described in a paean of proportions and cross-references, within a sapiential web finely meshing with the fabric of the text, the unitary design is contained in the dimensions of a five by five square. The wheel/firmament is inscribed in this square and contains a cross in which man dwells. The wheel and man are made in the likeness of God and the manifestation of the human figure of Divine Love appears inscribed in the five by five square. In Hildegard's work, the number five is linked to the five senses (the internal division of the body of the world/man, II.1) by means of which man takes in everything reaching him from outside and distinguishes good from evil. During his journey, in fact, man receives the assistance of the 35 virtues, which were given by God and are manifested in the encounter between the seven gifts of the Holy Spirit and the five senses.

We will now examine the passages of the text with the constructive indications followed by an explanation guiding us through the constructive syllogism.

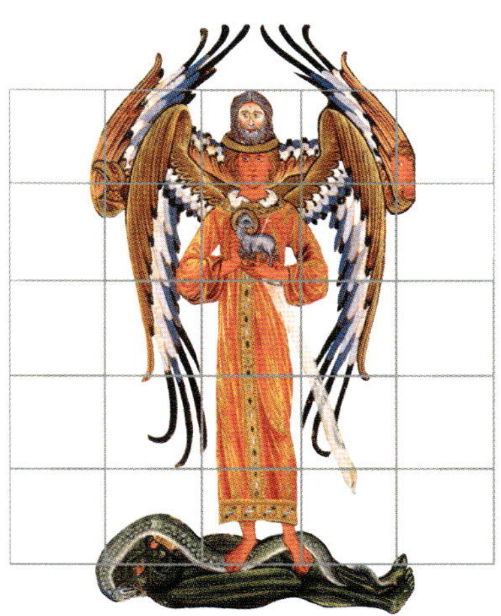

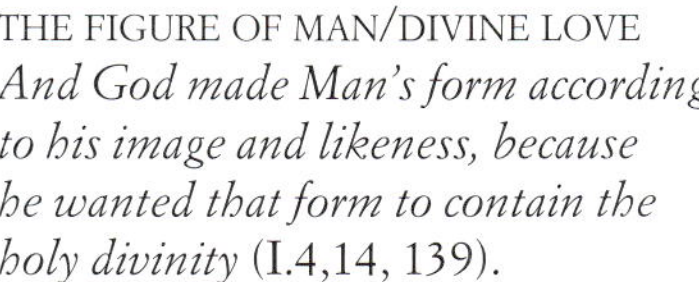

THE FIGURE OF MAN/DIVINE LOVE
And God made Man's form according to his image and likeness, because he wanted that form to contain the holy divinity (I.4,14, 139).

Man is created in the image and likeness of God. Thus the figure of the man in the fourth vision has the same dimensions as the figure of man/Divine Love in the first vision. Both are: divided into 5 parts; the width of their arms equals the height of the figure; they form a 5 by 5 cross inscribed in a 5 by 5 square.

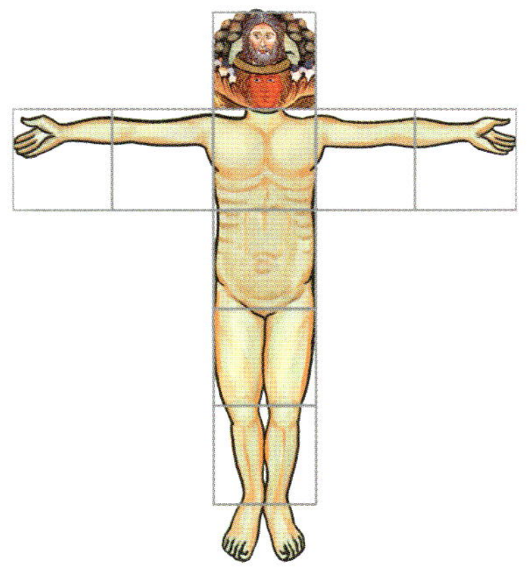

The two faces of Divine Love can therefore be superimposed on the face of the man and occupy the first square on the top of the cross (1/5).
The *circle of golden color* between the two faces coincides with the median line of the square.

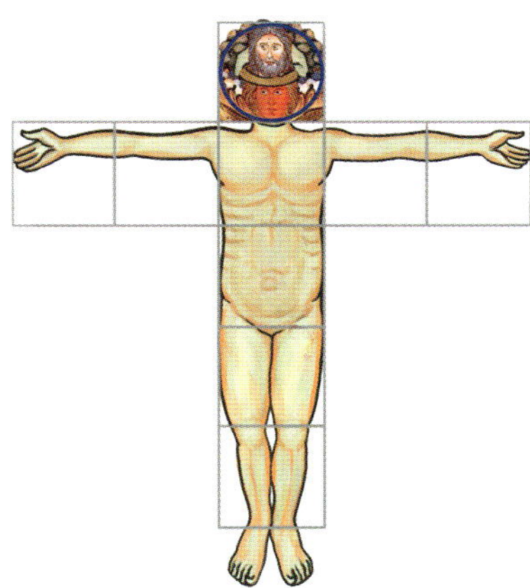

UPPER WINGS
And from each side of the figure's neck a single wing came forth, [both] rising up to join together above the aforementioned circlet (I.1,1, 33).

The upper wings stretch out from the neck of Divine Love, with their tips joining above the two heads.
They form an ideal circle whose diameter corresponds to the measurements of a square of the cross (1/5).

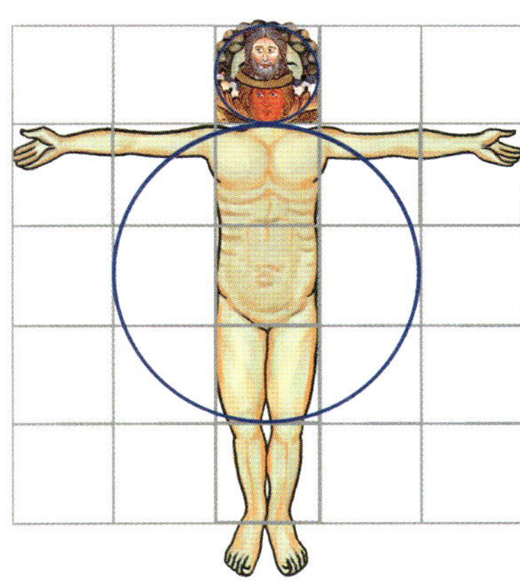

LOWER WINGS
Furthermore, from each shoulder of this image, a single wing stretched forth down to her knees (I.1,1, 33).

The lower wings extend down from the shoulders to the knees.
They form an ideal circle whose diameter corresponds to the measurements of three squares of the cross (3/5).

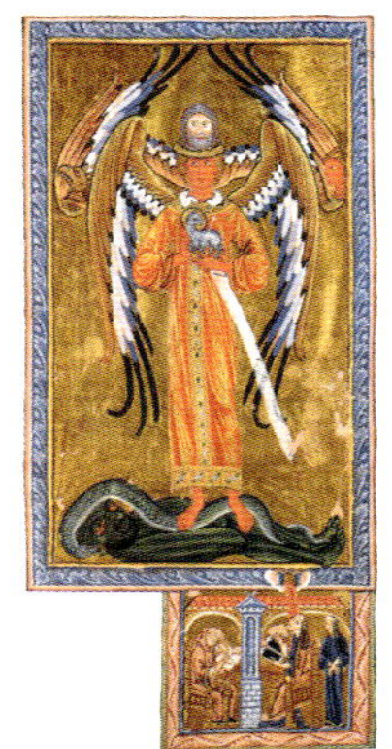
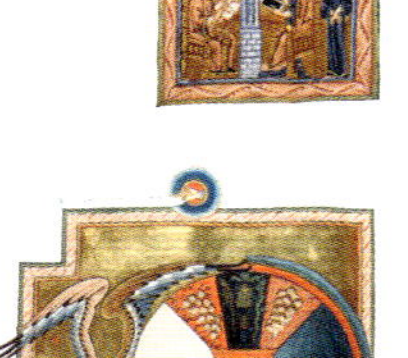

From earth to heaven

In the single vision of the second part, heaven offers Hildegard a comprehensive view of the vast unitary vision. It embraces the entire space, from the *fiery globe* of the Holy Spirit at the top, right down to the infernal chasms surrounding the earthly globe. Once it has left the earth, the voice of *Lux vivens* describes the elements in the upper part: the *building*, the *red/sapphire globe*, Divine Love and justice, the *way*, *virginitas*, the *brightly shining star*, the Son of God, the *fiery globe*, and the Holy Spirit. This space contained by the upper wings is a tripartite space, marked by the same intervals of measurement. This powerful trinitarian image accompanies man on his journey from earth to heaven, on the *way* of *virginitas*, for the recapture of the fiery globe infused in the soul, towards the realization of his own name, written on the white stone given to him by God at the start of his journey.

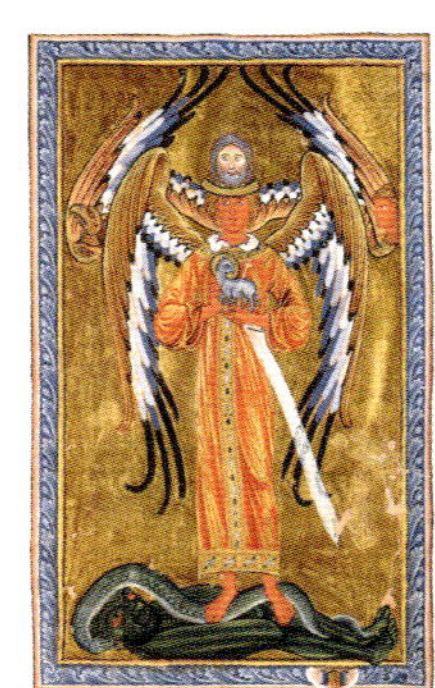
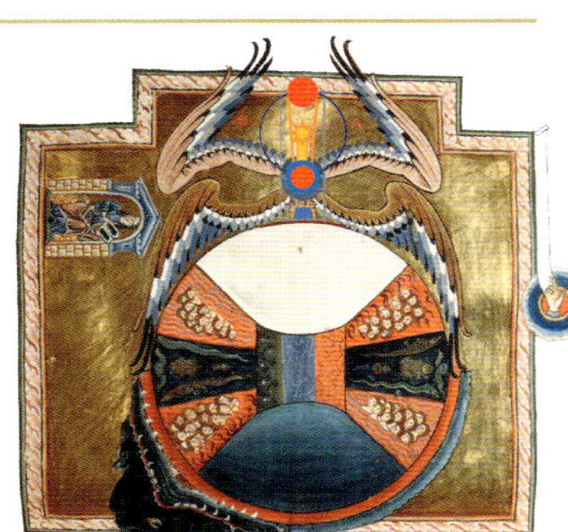

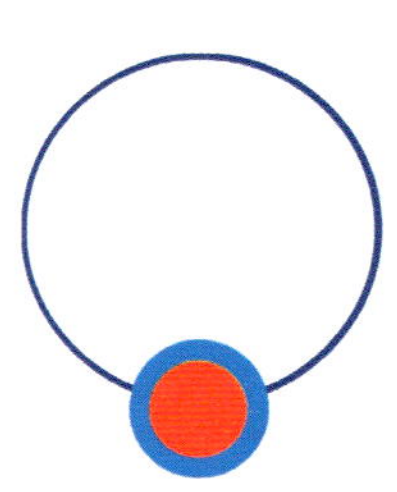
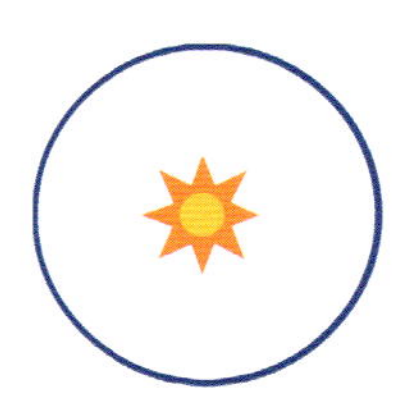
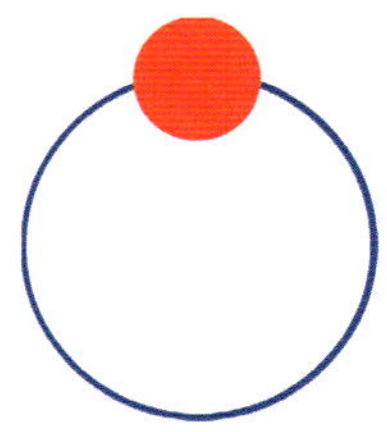
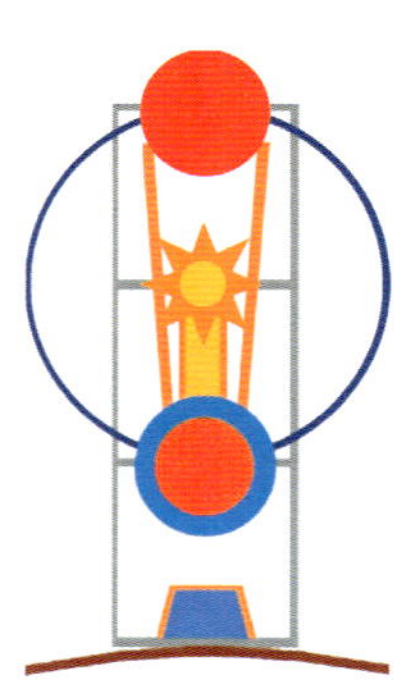

BUILDING	GLOBE	CANDID STAR	FIERY GLOBE	TRINITY
Moreover, from that round between the wings in the east appeared as if an edifice (II.1,1, 266).	*But toward the east and above the aforesaid round of the earth, I saw at a certain height a red globe surrounded by a circle of sapphire color* (II.1,1, 266).	*And from that globe all the way up to the midst of the aforesaid wings there stretched as if an avenue, above which beamed as if a brightly shining star* (II.1,1, 266).	*And then, between those wingtips, as if a fiery globe appeared, casting from itself certain rays* (II.1,1, 267).	*[…] so that the spaces were equal from the top of the earth's round to the red globe, and from that globe to the brightly shining star, and from that star to the fiery globe* (II.1,1, 267).
The Building is located on the circumference of the body of the world.	The *red/sapphire globe*, Divine Love and justice, coincides with the youthful face of the winged figure of Divine Love.	The *star*, the Son of God, coincides with the *circle of golden color* between the two faces of the figure of Divine Love.	The *fiery globe*, Holy Spirit, coincides with the top of the face of the *old man* of the winged figure of Divine Love.	There are three equally sized spaces between the circumference of the *body of the world* and the *red globe*.

The dimensions of the body of the world

We have seen that the upper elements of the single vision of the second part coincide with the two faces and the *circle of golden color* of Divine Love. This superimposition allows us to turn our gaze on what is taking place in the bottom part of the single vision (II.1). An intense image shows how the *building*—manifestation of divine foreknowledge—animated by the *symphonia* of saints, *living stones who praise God*, coincides with the heart and the lamb of God/Divine Love. The holy man following in the same path as the sacrificed lamb, praises God ceaselessly now that, with the awareness of Wisdom, he knows that he is kept in his heart just as God keeps his Son in his breast. The location of the building within the figure of Divine Love near the top edge of the body of the world, together with the measurement of the lower wings that indicate the midpoint of the circumference, allows us to precisely draw the circumference of the world, measuring five squares of the cross (5/5).

The measurements of the body of the world/earth/man, located in the breast of the winged figure, are the same as those of the man. In fact, we read, *the firmament [...] has as great a density [...] as the earth* (I.4,2, 132). The wheel/firmament and the man are *imago Dei*; they are born of Him and are made in His image and with the same measurements. One last element of interest is that the body of the world adds one and a half squares to the figure, resulting in 6 and a half squares, which, when doubled, equal 13, the symbol of YHWE. The symbolic theme of the numbers, of the measurements, and of the forms will be examined in greater depth in *Oltre le immagini* (awaiting publication).

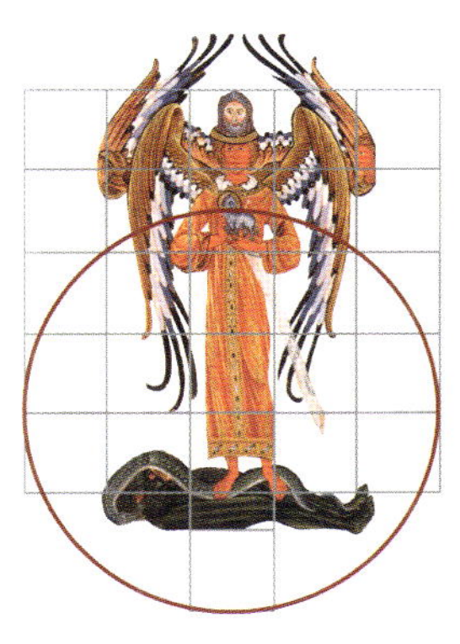
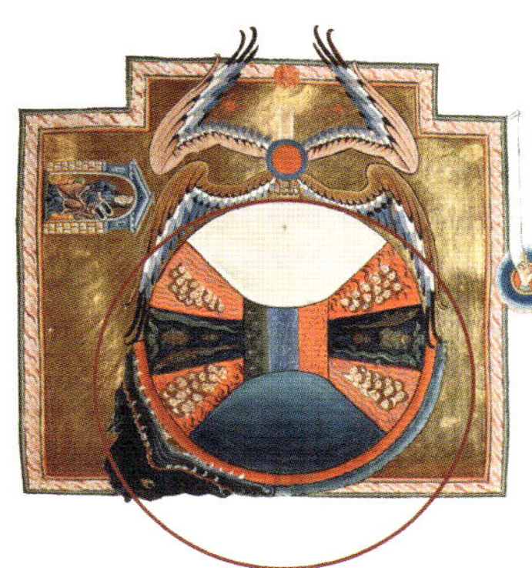

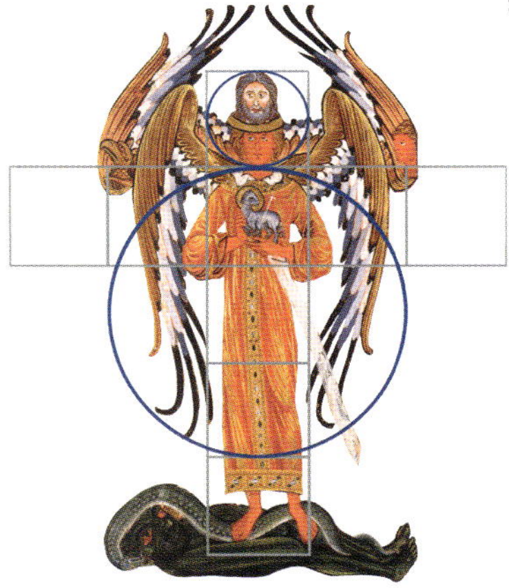
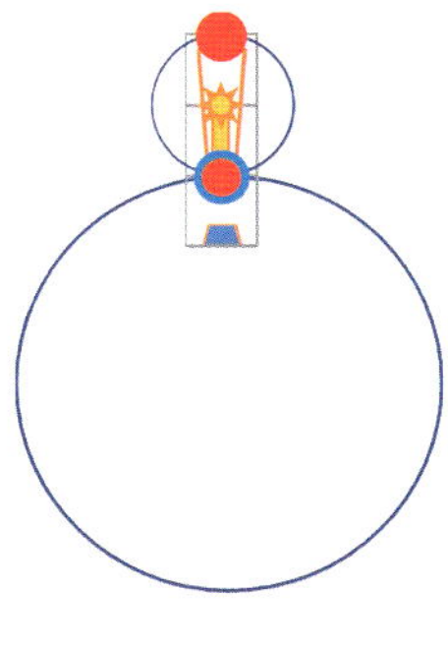
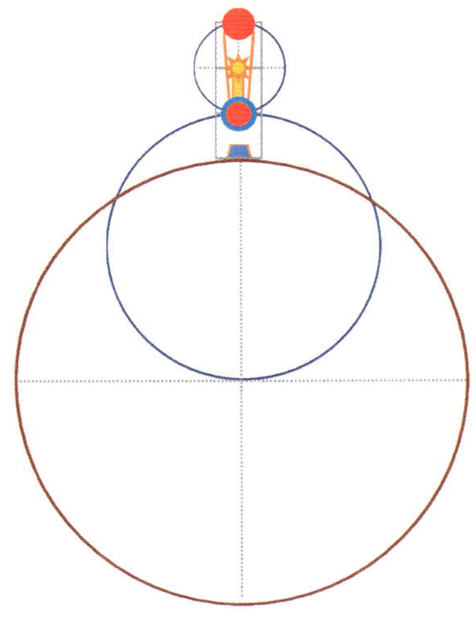
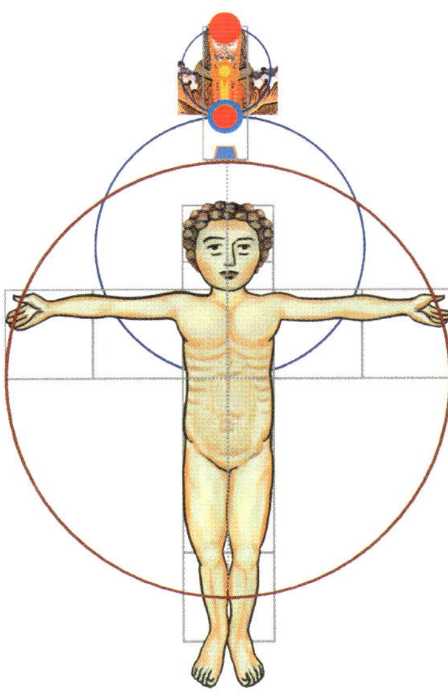

DIVINE LOVE AND SINGLE VISION
The circle of the upper wings is present in both the winged figure of Divine Love and the single vision. It allows us to superimpose the two images and to notice the correspondence between: the *fiery globe*/top of the face of the *old man*; *brightly shining star*/*circle of golden color*; *red*/*sapphire globe*/throat of the figure of the man. This means that the building is located in the middle of the second square, in the heart of Divine Love.

LOWER WINGS
The lower wings are joined to the outline of the upper elements of the single vision.
The two spaces between the two globes coincide with the ideal circle formed by the upper wings, which is equal to one square in the cross. Based on this, we can see that the distance repeated three times from the building to the fiery globe is equal to half a square of the cross.

CIRCUMFERENCE OF THE EARTH
The circumference of the earth/body of the world can be identified thanks to the measurements of the lower wings of the winged figure of Divine Love. We know that the lower wings of Divine Love reach its knees, equivalent to three squares (3/5), and that those same lower wings in the single vision reach the midpoint of the circumference of the earth. This allows us to delineate the circumference of the body of the world, whose radius is equal to the distance between the building and the midpoint of the circumference, or two and half squares of the cross.

DIVINE LOVE, MAN, EARTH
The radius of the body of the world is two and a half squares of the cross. Its diameter is therefore five squares, equal to the height and width of the man made in the likeness of the human figure of God/Divine Love.

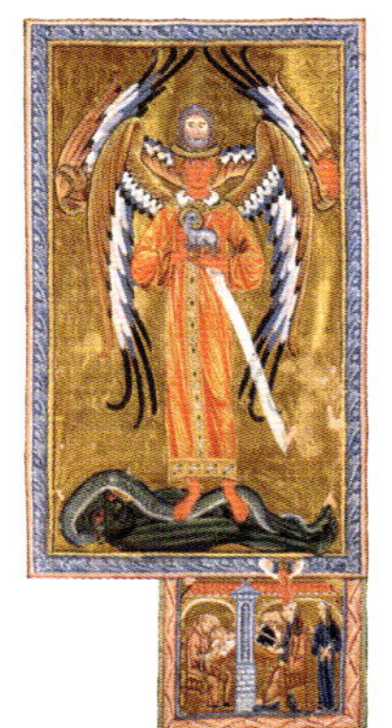

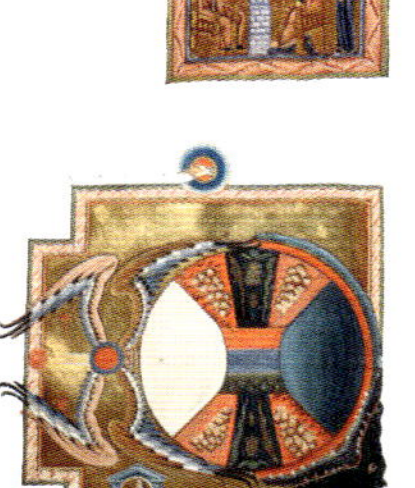

The wheel/firmament/earth, the man, and the figure of man/Divine Love

By carrying out an illuminated reading of the words of *Lux vivens*, we have created a complete reconstruction. The measurements and proportions reveal the golden thread uniting the *form of man/Divine Love* and the wheel/firmament/body of the world: the dimensions reflect the likeness with which God sealed his full love for creation and man, inscribing them within the supreme order, in an equilibrium of forms, numbers, and geometries, harmony and concordance extolled in the symphonic praise of beauty and concord of blessedness.

Threads of light. Supreme harmony

For from the virtue of true Divine Love, in whose knowledge the circumference of the world exists, proceeds her elegant plan of order, shining above all things and containing and constraining all things. By these threads are rightly and distinctly measured the signs of the circles and the signs of the other figures that can be seen within the wheel, as well as the individual signs of the limbs of the human form—that is, of the image that appears within the wheel, as described above and as revealed in all of the foregoing and subsequent words of this vision. Through this vision, the powers of the elements and of the other higher adornments, which look towards the protection and illumination of the world, and all of the fastenings of human limbs—for humankind governs in that world—are gracefully appointed and appropriately fitted together in just measure, as has very often been revealed to you (I.2,46, 103).

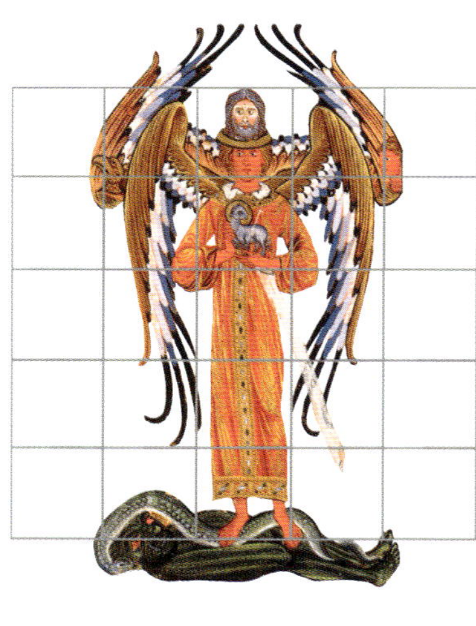

FIRST VISION

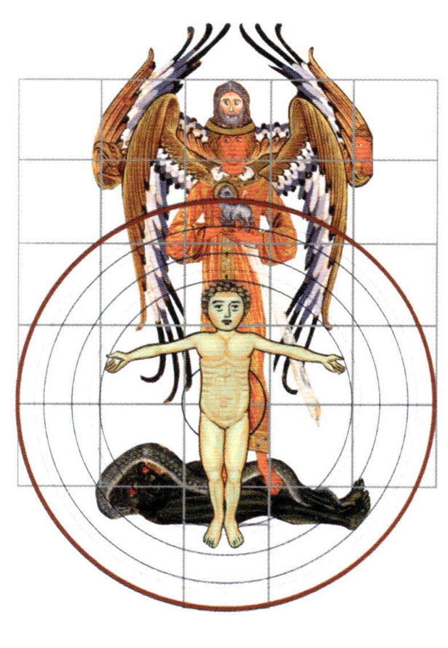

SECOND VISION

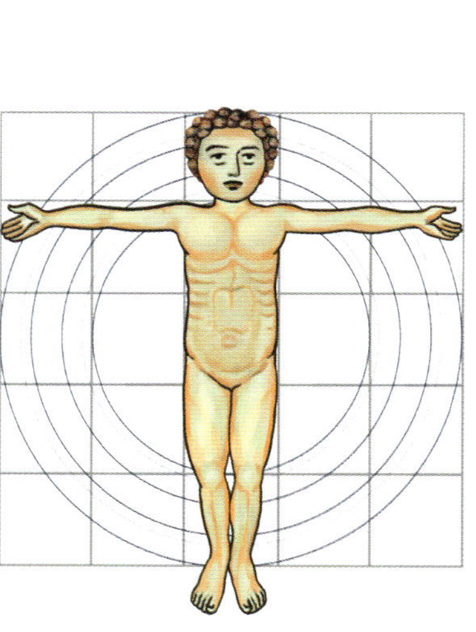

FOURTH VISION

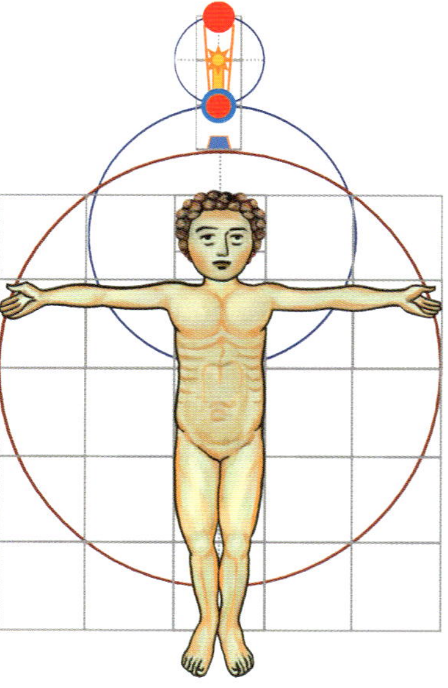

FIFTH VISION

In the heart of God

*For when humankind is perfected in the full number
as God established them, they will arrive at that land
that for earthly humans is called "the land of living,"
and then they will have fellowship with the Lamb
in the heavens. Oh, how great is the joy, that God
deigned to become Man—divine among the angels,
human among humans! So truly one must believe
that he is God and Man. Therefore, too, God
established humankind in his own tunic and in that
full number that never withdraws from them, for
he treated them as a father does his son: he granted
them an inheritance for their care when he made
subject to them the fish and the birds and all living
things that move upon the earth by living without
rationality (II.1,43, 333).*

*In the perfection of good works, God blesses
the seventh day—the person who is a member of his
Son in him. How? That person is to follow the inner
blessing—God's Son, who came forth from God's
heart (II.1,49, 347).*

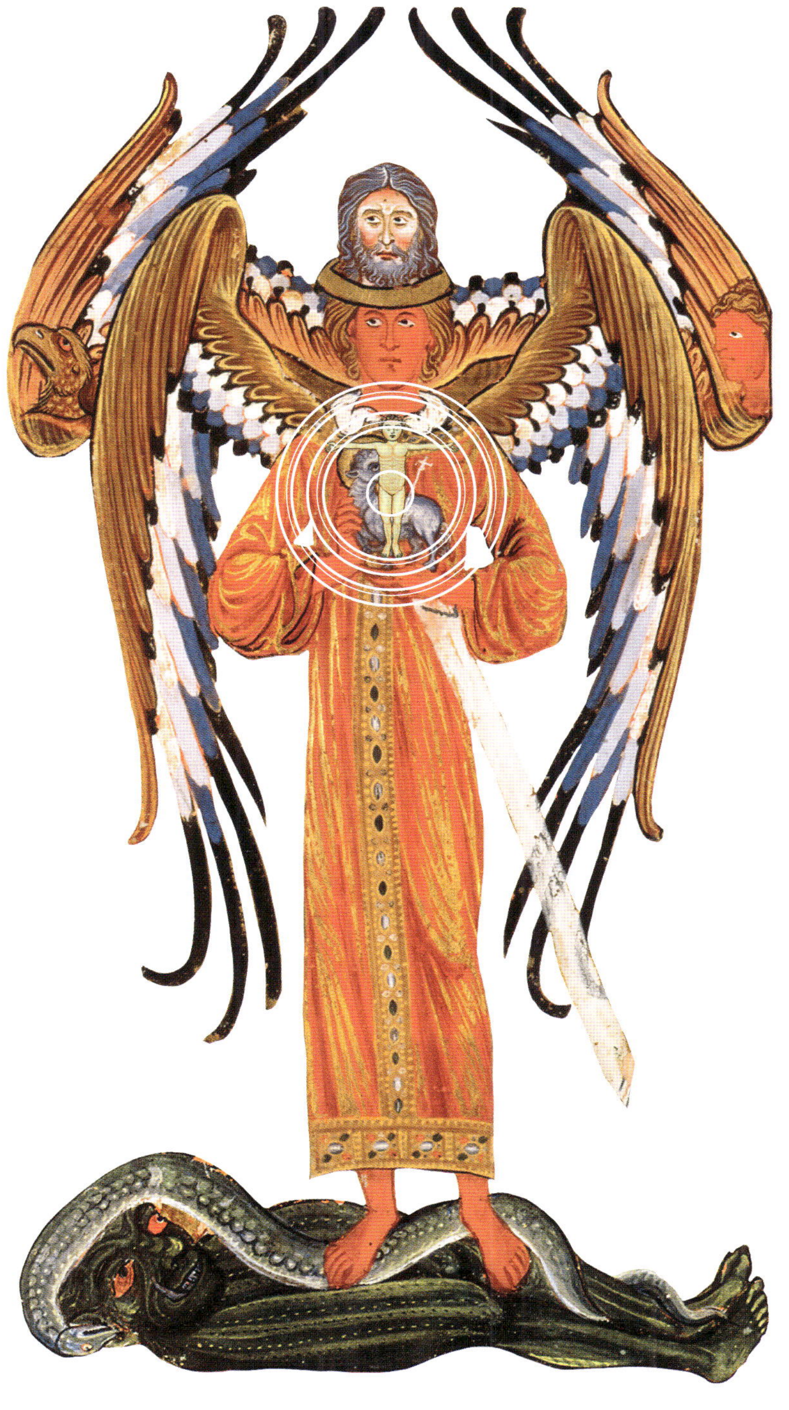

José C. Santos Paz

From Project to Images: The "Berlin Fragment" and the Illustrations of the *Liber Divinorum Operum*

The codex of the *Liber Divinorum Operum* (hereafter *LDO*), *Book of Divine Works*, held in the State Library of Lucca, is one of the most celebrated medieval testimonies of Hildegard von Bingen's work. Although studied by renowned codicologists, art historians, and scholars of Hildegard's work, the lack of evidence means that we do not know where it was produced or how it reached Italy. With respect to the former, the paleographic and artistic analysis suggests that it was produced in the Rhineland, possibly in the Rupertsberg Monastery or in a nearby center, in the first half of the 13th century (probably in the third decade): some authors, including Calderoni Masetti and Dalli Regoli (1973), and Derolez and Dronke (*Hildegardis Bingensis* 1996), believe that it was produced in the context of a propaganda campaign orchestrated by Rupertsberg to promote Hildegard's canonization process, started by Gregory IX in 1227. With regard to its arrival in Italy, the presence of numerous margin notes written in an Italian hand in the 14th century shows that the codex was already in the peninsula by this period. Although our knowledge of the influence that the *LDO*, and, more specifically, the Lucca Codex, may have had upon Dante and upon the creation of art in the city of Lucca—for example in the baptistery of San Frediano or in Piero di Puccio's fresco of the *Theological Cosmography* in the Camposanto in Pisa, studied by Zazzaroni (2009)—is still at the hypothetical stage, this could push the date of its presence in Italy back to the second half of the 13th century. It is possible that the codex reached the peninsula thanks to the Mansi family and in 1762, Giovanni Domenico, bishop of Lucca and descendent of the family, would publish the *LDO editio princeps* based on this very codex (later reprinted in the *Patrologia Latina*). Also the subject of debate are the origin and purpose of the miniatures in the Lucca manuscript: Who created them? What sources and references were used? Were they made under Hildegard's supervision? Various, often contradictory proposals have been put forward in response to such questions, determined on the basis of criteria such as the correspondence of the illustrations to the text or the reuse of existing iconographic models, especially the illuminated codex of *Scivias* which was produced in Rupertsberg when Hildegard was still alive (the lost codex of Wiesbaden, Hochschul- und Landesbibliothek, I, of which a facsimile and black-and-white photographs survive). Both Calderoni Masetti and Dalli Regoli (1973) and Suzuki (1998) believe that the illuminators based themselves exclusively upon Hildegard's text—that is, on the descriptive parts of the visions, and not the interpretations that follow—and that their translation of the words into images was imperfect; moreover, the former deny the existence of an earlier illustrated exemplar of the *LDO*, which could have served as a model, claiming that, for various reasons, in the final years of her life, Hildegard may have renounced the idea of an illuminated edition of her last work. Caviness (1998), on the other hand, not only maintains that Hildegard desired an illustrated edition but that the Lucca miniatures are based on drawings by the author herself, in which single elements taken directly from the *Scivias* illustrations are rearranged in a regular frame.

The specific aim of this essay is to add new material to this debate. While the miniatures in the Lucca Codex may well have been based on the *LDO* text and/or on the miniatures in *Scivias*, I believe there are also reasonable grounds for believing in the existence of detailed written instructions explaining how to draw up the images in the *LDO* and that these instructions came either from Hildegard herself or from her circle of collaborators. I am referring to evidence originating in the as yet under-researched text (for a series of reasons linked to its status as miscellanea, doubts around its authenticity, and so on) dubbed "Berlin fragment" by its editor Schipperges (1956), given that it is contained in a manuscript kept in the Staatsbibliothek Preußischer Kulturbesitz (shelfmark Lat. Qu. 674), in Berlin, in a fascicle (ff. 103–116) missing three pages at the beginning. The "Berlin fragment" (*BFr*), which is the older of the two codicological units currently making up the manuscript, has significant links to the Lucca Codex, in both paleographical (morphology of the writing) and codicological terms (preparation of the page), so much so that Schrader and Führkötter (1956) believes that both originated in the same *scriptorium*, even attributing them to the same hand.

Schipperges (1956) considered the *BFr* to be a unitary text presenting a theory of the elements organized in four parts: the first (deriving from *Cause et Cure*) devoted to water and the other three (on air, earth, and fire, respectively) of various origins but, above all, with links to *Cause et Cure* and *LDO*. Based on this idea, he divided the text into three parts (eliminating the first passage from *Cause et Cure*), numbering them II, III and IV and using Arabic numerals to number the internal divisions marked by paragraph signs in the manuscript. I do not believe in the credibility of the hypothesis of the unitary character of the *BFr* or of its interpretation as a treaty of chapter *de elementis*, accepted also by Hildebrandt and Gloning (*Hildegard von Bingen* 2010–2014). I do, however, share the interpretation of Dronke (2013), who considers this a series of randomly assembled loose notes containing Hildegard's inchoate ideas written down by her collaborator Volmar, in preparation for a later revision (reflected in the fact that many of the notes end with the annotation *quere*: "inquire"). Further evidence of the miscellaneous character of the *BFr* can be found in the thematic variety of the notes, in the fact that many are not linked to either the preceding or succeeding notes, the repetition of various passages in different parts of the compilation (possibly a sign of a dispersed conservation), and the presence of references to original works or to elements of them that are meaningless when taken out of context: for example, fragment III,48 begins, "the fifth of the preceding parts (*priorum*), which is in the middle of all of these," like the *LDO* II.1,5, but there is no indication of what these preceding parts might be or to what they refer; or fragment IV,43, in relation to *Scivias* III.11, refers back to a mountain of which there is no mention in the text: "when the anti-Christ is killed, the mist covers that (*eundem*) mountain." However, I do not share Dronke's suggestion that the entire *BFr* should be placed in the period when Volmar, the Saint Disibod monk, was a collaborator or secretary to Hildegard. In fact, the miscellany not only includes passages referring to works written in this period (*Scivias*, *Cause et Cure* or the *LDO*; in the latter case, Vomar did not participate in the revision and editing), but also others referring to tracts from her final period, like the replies to questions sent by the Cistercian monks from the abbey of Villers-en-Brabant in 1176 (*Solutiones XXXVIII questionum*: fragments IV,18 on the duration of the days of creation, or IV,13 on Christ's activity between his resurrection and his ascension), or the *Explanatio Symboli Athanasiani* (the Trinitarian image also examined in IV,3). It therefore seems reasonable to maintain that the *BFr* is a collection of ideas or notes, most of which later discarded, connected with a stage of the work on non-definitive texts carried out in the Rupertsberg *scriptorium* by Hildegard and/or her collaborators. We cannot exclude that some of the fragments may be connected to teaching or expository activities based on Hildegard's texts, as suggested by Michela Pereira.

Quite a few passages from the *BFr* are connected to the *LDO*. Several are easily recognizable because they repeat this prophetic work verbatim or very closely, as can be seen in the following two examples referring to the upright posture as a characteristic distinguishing humans from animals and to the proportions between parts of the human body: *LDO* III.2,16: *[…] but humans alone stand upright and with upturned gaze look to heaven, while the other animals stoop forward over the earth and are subject to humankind* (383–384). *BFr* III,54: *Humans walk in an upright position because they have received the spirit of the celestial realities from God's secret. But because animals receive the air that causes them to live from the elements, they stoop forward over the earth. LDO* I.4,92: *[…] the measurement from the knees to the ankle is the same as that from the place of discharge or the thigh to the knee. […] Moreover, the measurement from the ankle to the end of the big toe is the same as from the wrist to the tip of the middle finger* (215–216). *BFr* II,43: *Moreover, the distance from the design of the knee to the design of the heel was the same as that between the design of the femur and the design of the knees; and the distance from the design of the heel to the end of the big toe was the same as that from the wrist to the tip of the middle finger.*

The first draws upon a topos encountered in numerous works by classic and medieval authors (including Lactantius and Isidore of Seville) and which can also be read, albeit in a different form, in *Cause et Cure* II,235; unlike the *LDO*, the *BFr* explains this characteristic by referring to the fact that humans receive their spirit from the heavens while animals receive theirs from the elements. Fragment IV,2 of the *BFr* returns to the concept of upright position, this time connecting it to the projection of the six days of creation in man: the first five reflected in the five senses, and the sixth, which refers to the creation of humans in God's image, in the act of walking: "He defined man in the way of walking, saying, let us make man our image and likeness; after which man stood upright gazing upwards and walks in a standing position."

With the exception of some differences in the anatomical terms used, the second fragment expresses exactly the same symmetries between the parts of the body that the *LDO* places in relation to the proportions of the physical world or to moral or spiritual realities (an aspect missing in the *BFr*).

Other notes, also relating to the *LDO,* feature major differences or additions, as in the case of many of the links established between the elements of the *rota* (wheel) of the firmament and parts of the human figure in the middle (see *LDO* I.2), which are linked to health matters and medicinal remedies that do not feature in the *LDO*. In the following pages, I will focus on these parts of the *BFr* dealing with the *rota*, almost all of which belong to the second section. Not only do they reveal what may be provisional stages of the *LDO* editing process but, in my opinion, they also offer signs or even evidence of the existence of instructions for the design of the illustrations.

Disposition of the elements of the *rota*

The disposition of the elements in the *BFr* generally—although not always—coincides with that of the *LDO*. This arrangement is not described in a systematic, organized manner but must be reconstructed on the basis of passages that are distant from each other and, in some cases, by cross-referencing.

Let us begin with the planets: II,26: *The planet Jupiter is at the service of the Sun, which is below the former [Saturn]*. II,28: *The planet Mars, beneath this one [Jupiter], is the servant and charioteer of the Sun*. II,40: *The planet that is the highest, meaning Saturn*. II,48: *Saturn is at the summit of the highest circle. The Sun in the circle of fire. Venus in the ether. The Moon is suspended near the bottom in the ether beneath the wind [beneath Venus?].*

Taking into account passages II,35, 45, and 48, indicating the relative position of the different planets linked to the human figure, we can deduce that the order of these elements coincides with that in the *LDO*: Saturn in the upper circle, Jupiter in the circle of fire, Mars and the Sun in the circle of fire (that is, dark fire), and, lastly, Venus, Mercury, and the Moon in the circle of ether.

No passage in the *BFr* contains a detailed description of the series and proportions of the circles of the *rota*, which are however referred to in order to indicate the position of the planets; sometimes in a concise form as in II,48: "The Sun in the fire (*Sol in igneo*)." This is an indication of the contextual character of various fragments, given that they refer to elements that could not be placed or understood by a reader unfamiliar with the context. Unlike the *LDO*, which identifies the planets through their order and relative position in the circles, here they are also identified by their names. In line with Hildegard's work is the definition of several planets as "servants" of the Sun, albeit using different terms: in the *BFr minister* or the vulgar *reithman* (interpreted by Hildebrandt and Gloning, in *Hildegard von Bingen* 2010–2014, as "charioteer"), while the *LDO* refers to them as *suffragans*, a term probably originating in the Latin translation of the *Liber Pantegni* by Constantine

the African. In the event that this passage was an early draft of the *LDO*, we would be in the presence of an interesting example of the stylistic evolution of the expression of an idea. In these passages, we also encounter an important indication allowing us to link the *BFr* with the image of the *rota* in the Lucca Codex, which refers to the orientation of the Moon with its horns facing downwards; in the *LDO*, however, there is no explicit reference to this orientation.

As far as the stars are concerned, the *BFr*, like the *LDO*, distinguishes between the sixteen fixed stars (called *maiores stelle* or *planete*; *LDO*: *sedecim principales stelle*) and the others (*stelle*).

Both II,38 and II,48 describe the situation of the fixed stars as well as pointing out some of the relationships between them inside the *rota*: in particular, the second stars in each quadrant "tend" towards the underarms of the human figure (when they are in the eastern half) or towards the thighs (when they are in the western half). The two passages coincide in indicating these relationships but differ in the parameters locating the stars: in II,38, they are bounded by the cardinal winds to either side of them (for example, *between the east wind and the south wind*) and in II,48, considering their southern or northern position and taking as reference points the hands and shoulders of the human figure (for example: *the second star of the four to the north beneath the hand* or *the second star of the four to the south towards the left shoulder*).

The other stars in the *LDO* are divided according to where they are situated in the southern region (to the right of the human figure from the point of view of the observer) or in the north (to the figure's left). In the *BFr*, on the other hand, they are located in the eastern or western zone (II,18 and 22). As in Hildegard's work, these stars head towards the clouds opposite (*lingue*). II,39 distinguishes between upper and lower *lingue* (going towards the stomach and thighs of the figure, respectively), while II,51 indicates the position by the right and left side (*latus/femur*) and by the thighs of the same figure.

An important aspect in the descriptions of the *BFr* regarding the *rota*, with respect to the *LDO*, is the relevance of the position of the human figure whose parts serve as references for the location of the other components, especially of the clouds (which are alongside the sides and the thighs of the figure) and of the fixed stars (which are situated in relation to the hands and shoulders). Rather than referring to the cosmos, the object of this type of description seems to be a representation in which the position of the human figure is precisely determined.

The last group of elements belonging to the *rota* is that of the winds. They are referred to in the following parts of the *BFr*: II,31: *The stag to the left*. II,32: *The head of the crab by the calf*. II,33: *The bear wind touches the things to the left*. II,34: *The serpent wind touches the loins*. II,35: *On the left, the wind like a stag*. II,37: *The wind like a lamb is in relation to the navel of the man from both sides. The wind like a serpent is in relation to the loins on one side and on the other. The wind like a crab is in relation to the right calf, the wind like a stag to the left calf*. II,48: *To the right, in the ether, the crab*

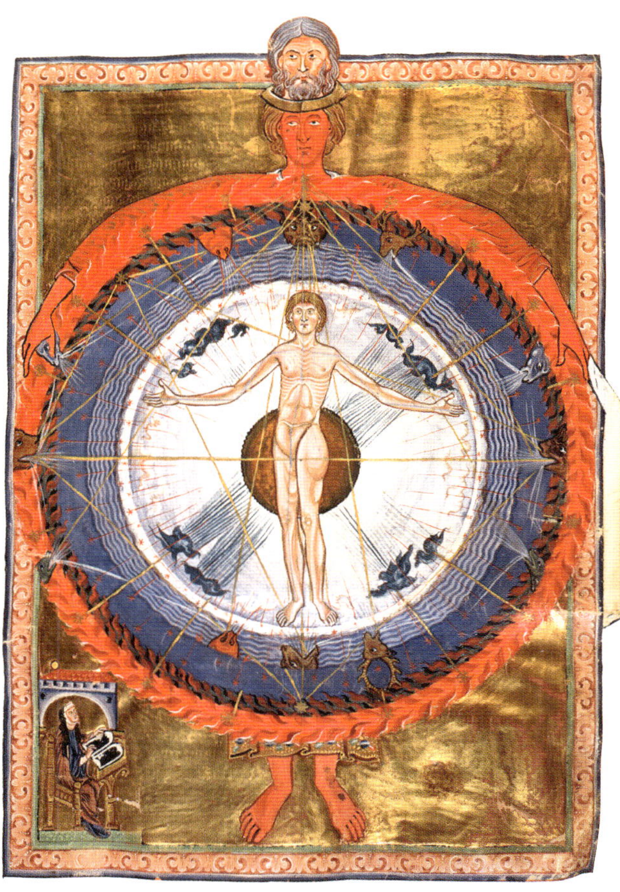

wind, to the left, in the ether, the stag wind. From the crab, a line goes towards the right breast, from the stag, from his mouth, a line towards the left ear […]. The wind like a crab that emerges from the mouth of the leopard, that is, the east wind, sends a line to the right breast. The wind like a stag that emerges from the mouth of the same wind sends a line to the left ear […]. The wind like a crab that emerges from the mouth of the wolf, that is, from the west wind, in the watery air, sends a line to the right calf. The wind like a stag that emerges from the mouth of the same wind sends a line to the left calf. The wind like a lamb that emerges from the mouth of the bear, the north wind, in the ether, sends a line from the left side towards the navel. The wind like a serpent that emerges from the mouth of the same wind, sends a line towards the left loin. The wind like a lamb that emerges from the mouth of the lion, south wind, sends a line from the right part towards the navel. The wind like a serpent that emerges from the mouth of the same wind sends a line towards the right loin.

And again: III,32: *The southern lamb wind.* III,33: *The serpent wind.* III,35: *The serpent wind coming from the bear towards the loins.*

II,48 enumerates all twelve winds in the *rota*. The other passages omit the contextual references permitting the identification of the winds symbolically represented by different animals or to locate them in the *rota*: how can we know, for example, that the *cervus ad sinistram* (II,31) refers to the collateral wind of the east wind located to its left? This clearly shows the non-autonomous nature of these texts which, in order to be understood, require familiarity with the cosmic vision of the *LDO*, to which they add various partial and precise nuances: specifically, the influence of the winds upon parts of the body, and, in connection with this,

medical advice (which I will not include). In my opinion, this type of decontextualized concise allusion—so frequent in the *BFr* and not only in the parts relative to the *rota*—is a sign that some of the passages were provisional or discarded drafts—or in any case, belonging to a phase of the work on the text not intended for readers—whose position in the work was known to the authors of the notes and also to the intended readers of such notes.

Relations between the elements

What distinguishes the passages dealing with the *rota* in the *BFr* is the presence of numerous correspondences between the elements and the human figure, missing from the second vision of the *LDO*. And whereas the *LDO* dwells on the physical and theological-moral interpretation of the relationships between the elements, the *BFr* points out the consequences of such correspondences with the human figure upon health, and also lists medicinal remedies for the pathologies affecting the parts concerned. For example, II,35, 40, and 48 inform us that Saturn moves towards the big toe of the right foot and that, when the air is damp, this relationship leads to gout (for which remedies are proposed); when the air is dry it leads to lameness (indicating remedies for this condition); and that if the air is temperate, men will be healthy and swift. It is possible, although merely conjectural, that this may have been an aspect considered in the initial design of the *LDO* that was later discarded. It is also possible, as Pereira suggests, that the *LDO*'s cosmic vision and/or its figurative representation was used for a teaching or expository activity that took place in the Rupertsberg monastery, linked to medicinal advice, and that this activity was reflected in some passages in the *BFr*.

In the illustration of the Lucca Codex, the majority of the relationships between the elements and the parts of the human body described in the *BFr* are not represented directly or explicitly by means of a yellow line as in other cases. This is not a significant aspect because neither does it represent various relationships mentioned in the *LDO*, like those joining the Sun to the heels or the Moon to the ankles. Moreover, the position of these elements in the *rota* and the direction of the blasts, the rays, and the rain, depending on the case, is consistent with the micro-macrocosmic relationships expressed in the miscellanea: for example, the crab and the stag accompanying the west wind (at the bottom of the page) blow towards the right and left calves; the serpents of the south and north winds (on the sides) blow towards the lumbar region; the crab of the east wind blows towards the right part of the chest and the stag close to this same wind blows towards the left ear, and so on.

I will now comment on some interesting cases in relation to the hypothesis that some passages of the *BFr* may be considered as instructions for the design of the illustration of the Lucca Codex: II,36: *The right horn of the Moon is in relation to the right eyebrow, the left horn with the left brow. The Sun is in relation to the Moon and vice-versa, because Moon is lit by the Sun. The way in which the Sun is in relation to the brain and the Moon with the eyebrows almost forms a scale (*libra*).*

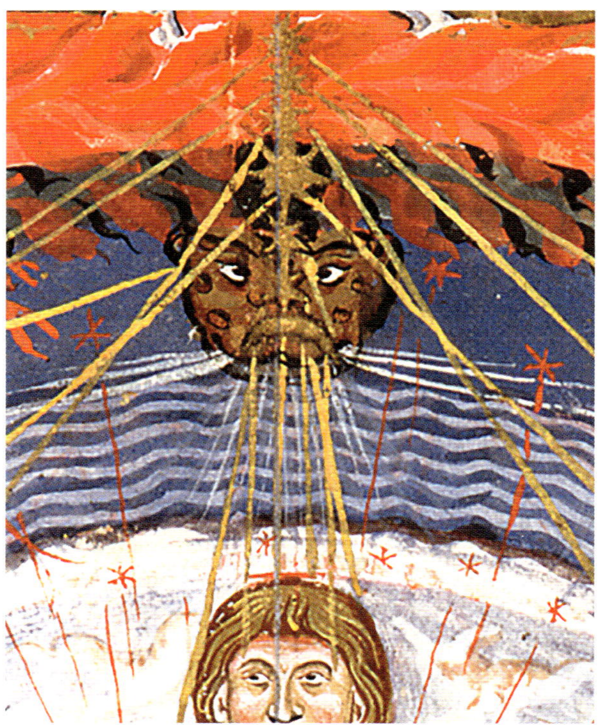

II,48: *A line* (virgula) *descending to the eyebrows from both horns of the Moon [...]. The Sun [sends] a line through the wind towards the* brain *[...]. The Sun in the fire sends a line towards the Moon.*

These passages describe the relationships between the Sun and the Moon, the relationships of the former with the brain and of the latter with the eyebrows, all of which are concordant with the *LDO*. As well as the use of the term *virgula* in II,48, which I will examine later on in this essay, I would like to draw attention to two indications absent from the prophetic work which are directly connected to the Lucca image. The first is *the way in which the Sun is in relation to the brain and the Moon with the eyebrows almost forms a scale*: as can be seen in the figure, the lines of these *planete* and their connections with the human figure form the image of a balance scale (*libra*). The second is the *Sun sends a line* (virgulam) *through the wind* (per ventum) *towards the brain*, where the words *per ventum* make no sense in a cosmographic description but do have meaning in the description of an image like the Lucca miniature where the line going from the Sun towards the man's head crosses the leopard's head representing the east wind.

And again: II,48: *The first star beneath the feet sends a line to the claw of the crab. The second star beneath the feet sends a line to the stag's antler. The second star of the four to the south beneath the hand sends a line to the left thigh* (ad dich). *The second star of the four to the north beneath the hand sends a line to the right thigh. The second star of the four to the south beneath the left shoulder sends a line beneath the left underarm. The second star of the four to the north towards the right shoulder sends a line beneath the right underarm. The other twelve stars head towards the dusky skin.* These indications refer to the two fixed stars situated in the south-west and north-west quadrants. With regard to the sixteen fixed stars, the *LDO* indicates that eight extend their rays into the thin air and the remaining eight into the dark fire. In the *BFr*, however, the second stars in each quadrant go to-

wards the underarms and the thighs of the human figure and the remaining twelve towards the *dusky skin* (that is, the dark fire, indicating it with a term evoking the vision of the cosmic egg in *Scivias*). The text also informs us that the two beneath the feet of the human figure send lines towards the crab's claw and towards the stag's antler without going beyond the bounds of the dusky skin (given that neither is the second star in its quadrant): this indication coincides with the Lucca illustration.

In II,44: *Mars [with] a ray of fire sends the Sun to the right, because he is always close to the Sun as his servant and prevents the Sun from moving northwards. Jupiter sends a ray of fire above the right shoulder, and sends a ray of fire from the left part to prevent the Sun from running towards the north.* This fragment introduces an extremely interesting issue linked to an element of the *rota* not referred to explicitly in the *BFr*, which takes the form of a line going from east to west—according to Hildegard's description—preventing the Sun from entering the malefic region of the north. Calderoni Masetti and Dalli Regoli (1973) have drawn attention to the fact that, in accordance with Hildegard's astronomical orientation, where east is at the top of the image and the north to the right, this line would have been drawn vertically towards the right. However, in the Lucca illustration, it divides the *rota* diametrically and horizontally, leading the two scholars to suppose that the illustrator had opted for a terrestrial orientation, locating the cardinal points differently, with the south on the top and the west to the right. I do not share this belief, also because the heads symbolizing the winds are located in the corresponding cardinal points in accordance with the astronomical or celestial orientation. The mistaken orientation of the horizontal line could be due to confusion with the terrestrial orientation when Hildegard's description was translated into images (see above, page 99) or to the fact that the illustrator was not capable of imagining a solution resolving all aspects of the description: the fact that Hildegard speaks of a line going from the beginning of the east to the end of the west (*from the beginning of the eastern part of the wheel almost [velut] to the end of its western part*) may have caused the illustrator to imagine a diametrical line because if it were vertical it would not have been possible to represent the rays of Jupiter and Mars according to the visionary's indications.

Passage II,44 of the *BFr* postulates the idea of the isolation of the north, attributing it less to the east-west line than to the effect of the rays from Mars and Ju-

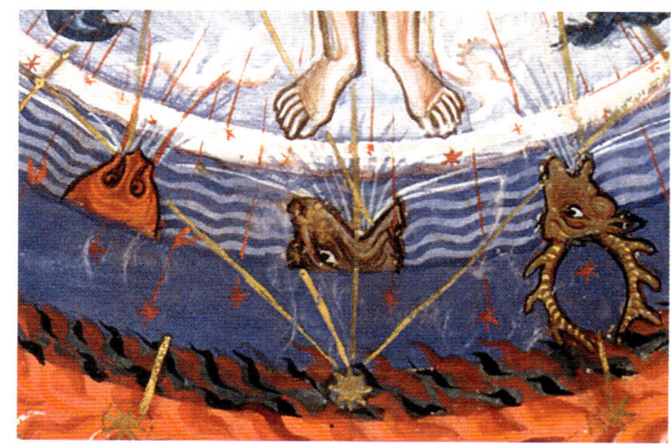

piter, which go towards the right, forcing the Sun to go left and thereby moving it away from the north. I believe that the reference context for the description in terms of "right" and "left" is the image, seen from the perspective of the person looking at the illustration. In general, the *BFr* alternates this perspective with the one normally used in Hildegard's description, which indicates the side where the elements are located (where the blasts emitted by the heads of the winds are also directed) from the point of view of the image; nevertheless, the description of the relationships between the planets in the *LDO* does not use the parameter of left/right but indicates the points of origin and of arrival of the rays emitted.

Proportions of the human figure

The fourth vision in the *LDO* contains a detailed description of a series of symmetries between the physical world, the body and the soul. In several chapters (18, 53, 55, 56, and 92, in particular), these symmetries are expressed in terms of measurements or proportions between parts of the cosmos and parts of the body. The illustrator of the Lucca Codex must have kept some of these proportions in mind when drawing the human figure in the middle of the *rota* in the second vision, where a number of bluish lines crossing the figure seem to reflect precise indications, like the symmetry between the length from shoulder to elbow and from there to the end of the middle finger (see above, page 73). Three passages in the *BFr* describe a system of proportions partly coinciding with the *LDO*, doing so in a more exhaustive manner and without macrocosmic implications. II,43: *Moreover, the distance between the design of the knee to the design of the heel was the same as that between the design of the femur to the design of the knees; and the distance from the design of the heel to the end of the big toe was the same as that from the wrist to the tip of the middle finger.* II,47: *From the hollow of the chest to the beginning of the shoulder and from the wrist to the tip of the middle finger, the measurement is the same.* II, 50: *From the crown of the head to the top of the forehead, from the top of the forehead to the cheeks, from the cheeks to the chin, and from the chin to the hollow at the top of the chest, the measurement is the same. From the top of the chest to the beginning of the division of the ribs, from this point to the navel, and from the navel to the place between the legs where the difference between men and women can be distinguished, the measurement is the same. From the shoulders to the iliac crests and from the iliac crests to the knees, and from the knees to the heels, the measurement is the same. From the shoulder to the elbow and from here to the tip of the thumb, the measurement is the same. From the beginning of the shoulder to the nearby hollow where the neck ends and from here to the hollow at the top of the chest, the measurement is the same. From the crown of the head to the opening in the ear and from here to the start of the shoulder, the measurement is the same.*

Leaving aside a number of terminological peculiarities, there are similarities to the *LDO* in various points (especially in the first note), even though most of the proportions do not coincide. These passages clearly express an anatomical canon although we can notice differences between the first passage and the other two: in the latter, the use of the present tense suggests that these are the general proportions of a human being (as in the fourth vision of the *LDO*), while the first passage refers to a specific image, as shown by the use of the past tense and by the term *signum*, which is systematically used in the second vision of the *LDO* to refer to the representation of various elements of the *rota* (not real elements) and which therefore indicates a figurative approach.

Terminology

The style, or more specifically, the terminological differences between the *BFr* and Hildegard's works is of interest in determining the character of some passages. In general, we can find both terms that are characteristic of Hildegard's lexicon and others that are not. Among the former, we can mention the verb *enucleare*, used to refer to the exegesis of Scripture (in III,48, probably an alternative formulation of *LDO* II.1, 5) or, in the fragments referring to the *rota*, anatomical terms such as *flexura brachii* or *manus iuncture*, verbs such as *firmare* or *perfundere* (in relation to the effect of the stars upon the clouds) or *forceps* and *pes* to describe the claws of the crab representing a collateral wind (the latter is a strange term to apply to a crab, explained analogically by Hildegard: *with two claws as if they were two feet*).

One of the most surprising differences is that the planets are called by their name, unlike in the *LDO*, where their images (*signa*) are identified by their order and relative position with respect to the other planets and to the circles of the firmament (with the exception of the Sun and the Moon): Venus, for example, is indicated as the fifth planet—that is, beginning with Saturn—and as *the closest to Sun from the bottom*. This is an extremely direct and precise way of identifying these elements, in line with the idea of a text seeking referential and denotative clarity above all (possibly a draft version or rough work for a description that was to be reworked in the less "scientific," analogical-figurative style of a prophetic vision). There are also lexical discrepancies, also in reference to the stars and to the anatomical parts of the body: *planeta* for the fixed stars instead of *stelle*, *arcula* (= *artula*) instead of *articulum* to refer to the big toe, *fossula inicii pectoris* (*hollow at the top of the chest*) or *fossula finis colli* (*hollow where the neck ends*) to refer to the part that the *LDO* calls *finis gutturis* (*end of the throat*), etc. Some terms do not belong to Hildegard's lexicon, suggesting that these ideas may have been developed with the contribution of others (possibly her collaborators).

In other passages relative to the *rota* in the *BFr*, we can find terms that are typical of Hildegard's lexicon but not used in the *LDO*: for example, the circle of dark fire (*circulus nigri ignis*) is referred to in II,48 as *tenebrosa pellis*, which recalls the *pellis umbrosa* filled with dark fire (*tenebrosus ignis*) in the oval *instrumentum* in *Scivias* I.3, the first vision of the cosmos in Hildegard's work. The use of *ignea spera* (*sphere of fire*) in the sense of *radius* (of either a star or planet) is extremely rare and can be explained as a peculiar interpretation of passages like *Scivias* I.4, where the infusion of the soul

From Project to Images: The "Berlin Fragment" and the Illustrations of the Liber Divinorum Operum

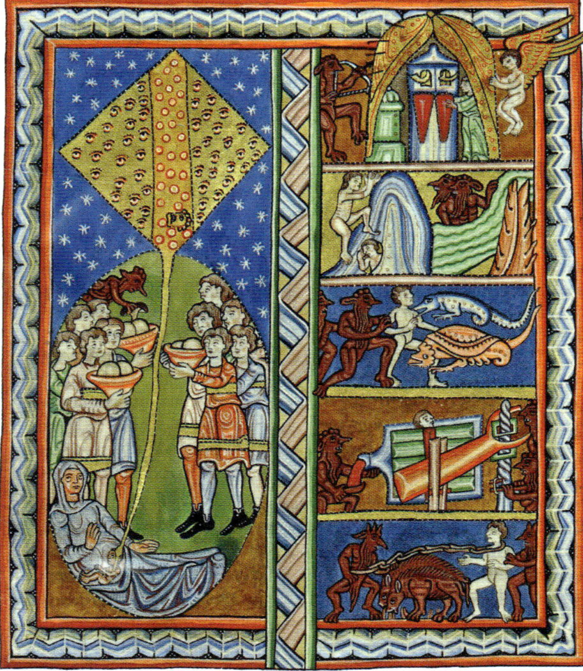

is described as a fiery sphere, which the illustrated manuscript shows descending from the Creator by means of ray to enter the mother's womb.

There are also other differences that may be evidence of a stylistic reworking of the initial expression of an idea: for example, I previous referred to the description of some planets as *ministers* of the Sun in the *BFr*, in contrast with the term *suffragans* (*collateral*) of the *LDO* (I.2,32), which uses the verb *ministrare* (*succoring*) in reference to the assistance given by a planet to the Sun. *Suffraganeus*, a term not commonly used with this meaning, probably derives from the Latin translation of the *Liber Pantegni* and may have been incorporated in the *LDO* during a phase of development of the text that took place after the composition of the passage in the Berlin miscellanea.

A number of frequently used terms in the *BFr* allow us to make comparisons between some of its passages with precise indications for the creation of the illustrations in the *LDO*. I mentioned the cases of *signum* and *ignea spera*, but possibly the most significant example is that of *virgula* (*line*), of which there are numerous examples in the aforementioned passages. The word, which does not belong to the Hildegardian lexicon, is used in the *BFr* to describe the connections between the two components of the *rota*, often accompanied by the verb *mittere*. The term corresponds to several different terms in the *LDO*, depending on the element with which a connection is established: ray or beam (in the case of a planet or star), blast (if produced by a wind), or rain (when coming from the clouds). Unlike these expressions, which refer to natural phenomena, *virgula* refers to the depiction of these realities, that is, to an image.

Conclusions

More than a conclusion, we can only offer a series of hypotheses in response to the questions raised by the data. There is clearly a relationship between numerous passages in the *BFr* and the description of the *rota* or wheel in the second vision of the *LDO*. These passages

do not form an orderly, coherent text but are scattered throughout the miscellanea—in the second section, in particular—and refer to specific aspects. Moreover, many of them require familiarity with the context of Hildegard's vision in order to be interpreted and would otherwise be incomprehensible.

Although the parts of the cosmic vision described in the *BFr* generally concur with the *LDO*, there are a number of significant differences, which I have outlined below:

1. The greater relevance of the human figure, emerging from the fact that its position serves as a reference to locate the other components of the *rota* and that it has new connections with the planets, stars, winds, and clouds (absent from Hildegard's vision), not all of which represented in the Lucca illustration. In the wake of these connections, the text often introduces medicinal indications that are not present in the *LDO* and that could be explained as belonging to an initial approach, later discarded, dealing with the exploration of micro/macrocosmic relations from this perspective, or as evidence of a teaching activity developed in Rupertsberg with regard to Hildegard's vision and/or its figurative representation.

2. Stylistically, the Berlin fragments are distinguished by significant similarities and differences to Hildegard's work, which could indicate a context of multi-authored collaborative writing. Of particular interest are a number of clearly Hildegardian terms and expressions that are not used in the *LDO* but that are present in *Scivias* (*ignea spera* or *tenebrosa pellis*, for example), which may relate to an initial stage of development of certain ideas.

3. The *BFr* contains a number of notes that should not be interpreted from a cosmographic perspective but that are intended to describe an image like that in the Lucca Codex: I refer, for example, to the figure of the scale formed by the connection between the Sun and Moon, to the descriptions in terms of "right" and "left," or to the information regarding the stars beneath the feet of the human figure. Moreover, the term *virgula* (absent from the Hildegardian lexicon) does not refer to a natural phenomenon (like the corresponding terms in the *LDO*: *radius*, *flatus*, *rivulus*), but to the representation of the lines creating the connections.

These observations lead me to consider the *BFr* passages referring to the *rota* partly as outlines that were later reworked or discarded, and partly as instructions intended for the creation of an image or that were eventually used for this purpose. Looking at this from a different angle, we might conclude that these are descriptions of an existing image but the lack of correspondence between some details and the Lucca illustration would appear to contradict these hypotheses. It is clear, however, that this is an extraordinarily interesting document—deserving of further study—of the activity that took place in Rupertsberg in relation to the text and the image of the cosmic vision of the *LDO*.

Bibliography

Hildegard's writings, both in the original and in translation, and the studies cited in the various sections of the volume, are the only texts indicated herein. The Hildegardian bibliography is extensive and somewhat dishomogeneous. For an introduction see Michela Pereira, *Ildegarda di Bingen. Maestra di sapienza nel suo tempo e oggi*, Gabrielli Editori, San Pietro in Cariano (Verona) 2017 (with a large bibliographical section). Also useful are the constantly-updated sites www.hildegard.society.org and www.hildegard-akademie.de.

Works by Hildegard

Hildegardis Bingensis Liber Divinorum Operum, edited by A. Derolez and P. Dronke (Corpus Christianorum – Continuatio Mediaevalis [CCCM], vol. 92), Brepols, Turnhout 1996.

St. Hildegard of Bingen. The Book of the Divine Works, translated by N. M. Campbell, The Catholic University of America Press, Washington D.C. 2018.

Ildegarda di Bingen, Il libro delle opere divine, edited by M. Cristiani and M. Pereira, Mondadori, Milan 2003.

Scivias, edited by A. Carlevaris OSB and A. Führktter OSB (Corpus Christianorum – Continuatio Mediaevalis [CCCM], voll. 43, 43A), Brepols, Turnhout 1978 (anastatic edition 2003).

Liber Vite Meritorum, edited by A. Carlevaris and A. Führkötter (CCCM vol. 90), Brepols, Turnhout 1995.

Symphonia Armonie Celestium Revelationum, edited by B. Newman, in *Hildegardis Bingensis Opera Minora* I, Brepols, Turnhout 2007, 371–477 [3. *O quam mirabilis*, 376].

Hildegardis Bingensis Epistolarium, edited by L. van Acker and M. Klaes-Hachmöller (CCCM voll. 91–91B), Brepols, Turnhout 1991–2006.

The letters of Hildegard of Bingen, vol. II, translated by J. L. Baird and R. K. Ehrman, Oxford University Press, Oxford 1998, 23.

Hildegard von Bingen. Physica. Liber Subtilitatum Diversarum Naturarum Creaturarum, edited by R. Hildebrandt and T. Gloning, 3 voll., De Gruyter, Berlin-Boston 2010–2014.

Beate Hildegardis Cause et Cure, edited by L. Moulinie, Akademie Verlag, Berlin 2003.

Berlin Fragment, in H. Schipperges, *Ein unveröffentlichtes Hildegard-Fragment (Codex Berolin. Lat. Qu. 674)*, in "Sudhoffs Archiv für Geschichte der Medizin," 40/1, 1956, 41–77.

Ms 1942, held in the State Library of Lucca and containing the text and images of the *Liber Divinorum Operum*, is fully available in the digital library at Internet Culturale website.

Works cited

A. R. Calderoni Masetti and G. Dalli Regoli, *Sanctae Hildegardis Revelationes. Manoscritto 1942*, Cassa di Risparmio, Lucca 1973.

N. M. Campbell, *Authorship and the Function of the Chapter Summaries to Hildegard of Bingen's* Liber Divinorum Operum, in "The Journal of Medieval Latin," 27, 2017, 69–106.

M. Caviness, *Hildegard as the Designer of the Illustrations to her Works*, in C. Burnett and P. Dronke (edited by), *Hildegard of Bingen. The Context of her Thought and Art*, The Warburg Institute, London 1998, 29–62.

P. Dronke, *The Four Elements in the Thought of Hildegard of Bingen Cosmology and Poetry.* Cause et cure *and the Berlin Fragment*, in "Studi medievali," LIV/2, 2013, 905–922.

M. Pereira, *Le visioni di Ildegarda di Bingen*, in "Memoria. Rivista di storia delle donne," n. 5, November 1982, 38–39.

G. Rabassó, *L'univers vivent d'Hildegarda de Bingen perspectives filosòfiques*, Diputació de Barcelona-Institut d'Estudis Catalans, Barcelona 2018.

M. Rainini, *"Sanctissimam humanitatem filii Dei negant." Ildegarda e gli eretici fra visione e teologia in Germania nel XII secolo*, in "Rivista di storia del cristianesimo," 16/2, 2019, 333–358.

S. Ritchey, *Rethinking the Twelfth Century Rediscovery of Nature*, in "Journal of Medieval and Early Modern Studies," 39/2, 2009, 225–255.

S. Salvadori, *Hildegard von Bingen. Scivias. A Journey into the Images*, Skira, Milan 2019.

M. Schrader, A. Führkötter, *Die Echtheit des Schrifttums der heiligen Hildegard von Bingen. Quellenkritische Untersuchungen*, Bohlau, Köln 1956.

K. Suzuki, *Bildgewordene Visionen oder Visionserzählungen. Vergleichende Studien über die Visionsdarstellungen in der Rupertsberger "Scivias" – Handschrift und im Luccheser "Liber Divinorum Operum" – Codex der Hildegard von Bingen*, Peter Lang, Frankfurt am Main-Berlin-Bern 1998.

M. Zátony, *"Vidi et intellexi." Die Schriftenhermeneutik in der Visionstrilogie Hildegards von Bingen*, Ascendorff Verlag, Münster 2012.

A. Zazzaroni, *L'uomo al centro della* rota. *Dante e Hildegard di Bingen*, in "Studi e problemi di critica testuale," 78, 2009, 49–80.